THEATRE IN THE EAST

This is a volume in the Books for Libraries collection

DANCE

See last pages of this volume for a complete list of titles.

THEATRE IN THE EAST

FAUBION BOWERS

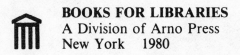

BOOKS FOR LIBRARIES
A Division of Arno Press
New York   1980

Editorial Supervision: Janet Byrne

Reprint Edition 1980 by Books for Libraries, A Division of Arno Press Inc.

Copyright © 1956 by Faubion Bowers

Reprinted by permission of Grove Press, Inc.

Reprinted from a copy in the University of Illinois Library

DANCE
ISBN for complete set: 0-8369-9275-X
See last pages of this volume for titles.

Manufactured in the United States of America

Library of Congress Cataloging in Publication Data

Bowers, Faubion, 1917-
    Theatre in the East.

    Reprint of the 1956 ed. published by the Grove Press,
New York.
    Bibliography: p.
    Includes index.
    1. Dancing--Asia. 2. Theater--Asia. I. Title.
[GV1689.B6 1980]   792'.095   79-7753
ISBN 0-8369-9278-4

THEATRE IN THE EAST

BOOKS by **FAUBION BOWERS**

Japanese Theatre • 1952

Dance in India • 1953

FAUBION
BOWERS

THEATRE IN THE EAST

A Survey
of Asian
Dance and Drama

Grove Press, Inc.

New York

First Evergreen Edition, 1960
Second Printing
Manufactured in the United States of America

Grateful acknowledgment is made to the *New
Yorker, Saturday Review,* and *Holiday* for
permission to use excerpts in this book which
first appeared in articles expressly written for
those magazines. Special acknowledgment is
made to Eliot Elisofon of *Life* and to Ewing
Krainen for their kind and generous permission to
reproduce certain of their photographs.

MANUFACTURED IN THE UNITED STATES OF AMERICA

To K. C. P.

NOTE

In terms of theatre, Asia defines itself clearly as that area which starts with India and extends eastward as far as Indonesia and the Philippine Islands, and northward through China and Japan as far as Siberia.

There is a body of opinion which includes the vast Mohammedan world lying north and west of India in the concept of "Asia," and terms such as "Middle East," "Near East," "Asia Minor," and the like give substance to this idea of a broader area of the East, the Orient, or Asia, even including parts of Africa. As far as dance and drama are concerned, those countries are not, however, what I feel to be characteristically Asian. That area has in common the Mohammedan religion, which on the whole condemns theatre, and must of necessity be omitted from our attention, partly because of the virtual absence of dance and drama there, partly because of the "un-Asian" atmosphere of what little has survived.

When you move into Asia proper, in the sense I use the word, you are suddenly and dramatically in an area of tremendous artistic activity, and even the pockets of Mohammedanism found in the heart of this Asia, such as Indonesia and the South Philippines, teem with dance forms. You can scarcely help being astonished by the widespread, wide-scale popularity of the theatre arts available almost everywhere in all these countries. No other geographical area of the world I know compares in extent or volume at all levels of appreciation. While differences between one Asiatic country and another are enormous, and the arts of each express unique and exclusive qualities, certain aspects and even themes course through them all and unify them on a broad and specific basis—F. B.

TABLE
OF
CONTENTS

5

CAMBODIA........ 165

Historical influences and effects, Palace dancers, royalty and dance, basic exercises, minor dance forms, modern theatre

6

LAOS 183

Types of dances

7

MALAYA......... 187

Influence of English and Chinese, trance dances

8

INDONESIA
Dance 191

Social dances, regional dance forms area by area, court dances and their aesthetics, fighting dances

Drama 217

Folk and traditional forms, plight of modern theatre

Bali 222

Changefulness of Balinese dance forms, description of dances, eroticism and dance, leading dancers of Bali, trance, drama forms, reasons for Balinese dance genius

9

PHILIPPINES
Dance 249

Four types of dances: Spanish, Filipino, aboriginal, Muslim
Drama 264

Folk dramas, operettas, modern theatre, present-day activity

10

CHINA.......... 272

Aesthetic differences with Indian areas, Communist influence, Mei Lan Fang, opera, operatic classifications and techniques

Modern Theatre 293

History and playwrights

CONTENTS

LIST OF ILLUSTRATIONS

(Between pages 54 and 55)

Balasaraswathi
Hashish Smoking Scene
Backstage at the Manipuri Theatre
Kolam Folk Drama
Kandyan Dance
Kolam Scene
The Dancer Tilaka
Gunaya in a Series of Poses
Po Sein and College Sein
A Sword Dance of Upper Burma
Scene from a Likay Drama
A Lakon Dance Drama

(Between pages 150 and 151)

Two Palace Dancers at Angkor
Full Cast of Palace Dancers at Angkor Vat
Folk Dance of Flirtation
Obeisance in Dance
A Dance During the Annual Water Festival
A Demon-Monkey Battle
Menora Dancer in Trance
A Princess of Wayang Orang Dance-Drama
A Heroic Warrior
Combat Scene
War Dance from Sumba Island
Folk Dance of Sumatra
Men's Dance of Flores Island
From the Wayang Orang of Solo
Sumatran Folk Dance
War Dance of Nias Island
War Dance of Nias Island in Full Action
Love Dance of Timor Island
Patriotic Dances—Celebes

(Between pages 246 and 247)

Stock Characters of the Dance-Dramas
Dharmi, Bali's Greatest Dancer
Rehearsing a Gabor Ballet
Two Penchak Performers
Anak Agung Ngurah
Ida Bagus Oka of Blansinga
Scene from *The Love of Lenor Rivera*
A Head-Hunting Dance
Fighting Scene from the Classical Opera of China

x

LIST OF ILLUSTRATIONS

INDIA

The Background and History

In exploring systematically the dances and dramas of Asia, a Westerner and particularly an American finds himself wishing for a somewhat different geography.

If one sets out from, say, New York, one must either pass by way of Europe and the Middle East before arriving in India, the starting point of theatrical Asia, or go via San Francisco and begin one's experiences with Japan, Asia's outermost periphery. In the first instance, by reaching Asia through Europe a certain tempering of point of view takes place simply from exposure to the drama en route. Nothing could prepare one less for Asian forms of drama than the taut realism and naturalism on which the lifelike theatres of Europe focus themselves. And the Middle Eastern countries of Egypt, Arabia, Aden and even Pakistan produce in the theatre-minded traveller a curious sense of dislocation. In those areas, regardless of what other virtues they can boast, there are few if any dramas, and dance for the most part is in such profound disrepute it seems negligible.

If, on the other hand, one begins with Japan and works westward through Asia, one sees theatre from the wrong end of the kaleidoscope. A sort of historical disorder ensues. One finds oneself wondering incorrectly when the Japanese gave the Indian theatre its masks, or if the Indonesians might have introduced sword dancing, say, to China. The confusion would be analogous to that of an American visiting London for the first time and asking how we happened to teach the British their English.

The logical beginning, theatrically, is made in India. India was the source of most theatre in Asia and still remains the immediate origin of some of its most highly evolved and important arts. From there

3

one can orient oneself naturally and with proper perspective for a comprehension of the whole of Asia's variegated and complex fabric of actors and dancers and their craft. From India the miscellaneous fragments and pieces fall into a reasonable pattern of association one with the other. More important, perhaps, is the fact that out of India and from Indian theatre-forms themselves an aesthetic basis applicable to all Asian dance and drama definitely emerges. Even in those instances such as Chinese opera or Japanese theatre, where Asian arts flowered independently, the underlying principles are similar and a subtle relationship binds them. There is a kind of uniformity in motivation, in aim, in style, in execution of dance and drama which connects it all together and makes it "Asian" theatre rather than European, African or anything else. Disappointing as it may initially seem to the foreigner, it is easier for an average Asian seeing a play or ballet of another Asian country for the first time to understand and follow it than it is for a European or an American.

Fortunately this applies only to the beginning. Once the fundamentals are recognized, and a few sample performances witnessed, then Asian theatre becomes as comprehensible and enjoyable to us as Broadway or Drury Lane or even Hollywood has been in the past, and still is, to Asians.

The impact of ancient India on the rest of Asia was, as is well known, one of the most powerful exertions of cultural and religious influence in world history. Several centuries before Christ, a north Indian prince, later known as Gautama Buddha, appeared. The religion which sprang from his holy example and sacred precepts was so vital that it spread as far north as China and Japan and as far east as the farther islands of Indonesia. Its force has not yet diminished because Buddhism remains today as the most widely practiced religion in the world.

Its tremendous extent was partly due to the fact that being reformist and opposed to Hinduism, the religion proper of India, it was after a period gently expelled from its home. Another cogent reason was that it, unlike Hinduism, encouraged converting and proselytizing. Its missionaries and pilgrims consciously set out on their wanderings

4

with the purpose of preaching the truth and propagating the faith. Their success in Asia resembles that of Christianity in the West.

While these pious men were Buddhists by faith, they were Indian by culture, and they carried with them Indian manners and customs. There is, for instance, very little difference between a monk's robe and the modern Indian sari. The language they spoke and the language the devout all over Asia adopted was Prakit or Pali, Buddha's vernacular in India. The scripts they introduced—and much of Asia was illiterate until this advent of Buddhism—and which are still in wide use were Indian. They carried with them dance movements, drama forms, pageantry, musical instruments and a set of aesthetic principles which never would have entrenched themselves along the precise lines they did without this new religion to introduce and sustain them. These aspects of Indian culture, while being of enormous importance to us, were, however, only incidental to the initial religious, and sometimes refugee, impulses of the pilgrims and monks.

Meanwhile for a long period—from a century before the birth of Christ until almost ten centuries later—South India was expanding overseas in another way. Sometimes it was by armed conquest, as in the case of Ceylon where the powerful Tamil kings of South India frequently dispatched their armies, but more often it was the desire for commerce that drove them as individuals to the rich lands and islands of the East. As soon as they began their trade in Malakka, Kambuja, Svarnadipa (land of gold), or what we know today as Malaya, Cambodia, and Indonesia, these Hindu merchants sent for their priests and families. The superiority of the Indian was immediately accepted and India's culture was adopted and imitated by the original inhabitants. They copied the South Indian sculptures, even importing their craftsmen, learned their arts of warfare, borrowed their musical instruments and dances, sometimes without even bothering to adapt or modify them. In many cases the Indians associated themselves with and even married into royal families.

The King of Cambodia, for example, by virtue of this ancient connection, has as one of his names to this day *varman*, originally a royal title for South Indian kings. Even now the court at Cambodia, although thoroughly Buddhist, still maintains a souvenir of this epoch. Three Brahmin priests are permanently attached to the Palace. They wear their long hair knotted at the back according to the custom and over one shoulder crosses the sacred thread of the Hindus. They, while worshiping Hindu gods, officiate at all the most traditional ceremonies.

The combination of the Buddhists and the South Indian expansionists resulted in the civilizing presence of India being keenly felt throughout Asia. This culture reaching out from India and engulfing area after area produced the concept historians refer to as "Greater India," now more narrowly called "Southeast Asia." Never before had India reached such heights of grandeur or fame. The indelible impact of Indian culture was so renowned that it was the "Indies" the West was looking for in the days when Europe began her first voyages of exploration. Whether it was Molukka, the Spice Islands in Indonesia, or merely Malabar, where Thomas the Apostle of Christ first proselytized, the word used was "Indies," and it referred to the whole area, conjuring up a picture of riches, panoply and Asiatic splendor. The name still perseveres—in Indonesia, literally the "islands of the Indies," and as far as Indo-China, the geographical meeting place where India's and China's cultures each stop any further outward movement.

In looking at the past, the present sometimes becomes obscured; in pointing out the dynamism of ancient India I do not imply that the superiorities that once existed over her neighboring countries, particularly in the arts, continued unabated. India abroad represented a supremely instructive element with regard to dance and drama, but over the centuries at home in the very country of their origin, they perceptibly declined. As time passed, India's arts grew more and more fragmentary and piecemeal. Many of them died out altogether.

The great Mohammedan invasions from the 12th to 15th centuries paralyzed most Hindu artistic activity, although, simultaneously, the Muslims were to a great extent being assimilated and absorbed into the ineradicable, if not stronger, Indian culture. The conquering Muslims desecrated Hindu holy places, and today as you visit these deserted or dead temples you will see row after row of statues with the heads chopped off, or empty niches from which the images were wrenched and thrown away. According to the tenets of the Koran, representational arts are disavowed, and dance and drama suffered accordingly, as we will see more precisely later. If art depicted God or

6

was used as part of religious worship, the Muslims regarded it as blasphemy. If it was secular, it was felt to be somehow immoral and a violation of the ethical code. Aside from the abstract arts of architecture and music, and the one important exception, painting, the Muslim domination of India was aesthetically stifling.

The final blow, less tangible but nonetheless real, to the continuity and outward flow of Hindu culture was the arrival around a hundred and fifty years ago of the British in India as a determined colonizing force. One by one educated Indians turned their attention toward Europe, particularly if they hoped to rise in this new world and cope with their foreign rulers. With the removal of this class of intelligent and enlightened people from the scene of indigenous expression, dance and drama fell helplessly into desuetude. Throughout the country a kind of shame in all native arts developed. This was partly fostered by the arrogance of the British of those days, and partly it was due to the Indians themselves, who felt insecure, understandably enough, after having been once powerful and now being confronted with another civilization which brought not a little contempt for everything their way of life offered. Until a few decades ago, when artists and scholars of vision started revivals of various remaining art-forms in several parts of the country, few people in India had interested themselves in the merits of their own dances or dramas. By then the great arts of India's past had been decimated and what remained was to a large extent scarcely more than vestigial. Fortunately, any further decline has been arrested, and now the re-emergence of India and Indian values is being effected with a rapidity that refutes the cliché that the East is "changeless."

All across Asia, however, the evidences of India's past great influence persist. And surprising as it is to the outsider, an Indian as great as Rabindranath Tagore was prepared to recognize the fact that today the finest Indian-based, Indian-inspired dancing in the world is not in India but in Bali, a tiny island off the coast of Java in Indonesia. Equally, even the most amateur explorer can see that the best theatre in Asia is in Japan. Japanese theatre, of course, developed along different lines from India's, but the effect of Indian Buddhism and even Hindu aesthetic principles was vital. Dances such as Bugaku with masks and movements from India are still performed in Japan, although they are forgotten and unknown in India itself. In the oldest dances of No, such as *Okina*, an invocatory ceremony of longevity, phrases of a special Sanskrit are still sung, but they are unused in the country of their provenance.

Perhaps the most vivid carryover, theatrically speaking, of India's artistic influence through the Buddhists is the prevalence of lion dances in Japan or China, either in the form of street performances or in the theatre on a high professional level. The lion is indigenous to India; it was known only through rumor in those countries where it now figures so prominently. Whatever the connections were between India and Japan or China, and irrespective of how they may have been filtered through other countries, the fact remains that the more drama declined in the one place, the more it seemed to rise in the others.

Theatre in India is supposed to have begun with the gods. Brahma himself, the breath of the world, commanded this first dramatic representation. According to the oldest holy books, it appears that in heaven long before the world was created, when good and evil lived side by side, the gods fought and defeated the demons. In celebration of the victory Brahma asked the gods to re-enact the battle among themselves for their own amusement. During the course of the program, the demons became mortified at the recollection and filled the air with their invisible presences to obstruct its progress. Once again a real fight occurred, and once again the demons were beaten—this time with a flagstaff that was near at hand. Brahma then explained that such performances were for the entertainment of all of them, and thus pacified, the demons promised to be amenable. But nevertheless it was decided that in order to protect theatre in the future a sacred pavilion would be provided to shelter the players and the area would be marked and made sacred by a flagstaff. This tradition to a certain extent has endured in villages all over Asia. It is a common practice in many places for the stage to have a roof while the audience sits in the open air on the ground, and nearby a long bamboo pole with a banner designates the area where performances take place.

Brahma later, after the creation of the world was completed and mortals desired to imitate this pleasurable theatre of the gods, confided all his secrets of dramaturgy—dance and drama in all its forms —to a sage called Bharata. This became the massive treatise called

8

Bharata Natya Sastra or Bharata's Canons of Dance and Drama and, although considerably more exhaustive and comprehensive in content, it is roughly analogous to Aristotle's codification of Greek drama. After centuries of oral transmission, the *Sastra* was finally recorded in writing around the fourth or fifth century A.D. In it you find lists of the fullest details of a performance from costume and makeup to the permissible movements of the neck and eyeballs, and from the plot situations and scenes which are disallowed (eating, adultery, and death were not proper for onstage depiction) to the various body positions and postures of dance (one is so acrobatic that to form it a dancer must place her head, face upright, between her legs). Every aspect of stagecraft is prescribed and annotated. No other theatre of ancient times has been so exhaustively documented in a single work.

Dance began with Siva, the creator and the destroyer of the world, and the second (along with Brahma and Vishnu) of the Brahmanical trinity of the Hindus. Siva, like all the deities in Hinduism, has many aspects and attributes, but one of his most important forms is as the King of Dancers or *nataraja*; as such he is worshiped in many parts of India still today. In the beginning of time, Siva once stood with his feet on a demon, and began shaking a little hand drum (exactly like the *tsutsumi* used in Japan, although it has disappeared from most parts of Asia) which he held in one of his four hands. This sounded the world's first rhythm and as he started to move his body in keeping with its beat, the world gradually took shape. During this act of creation, fire appeared in the palm of another of his hands, and he continued to dance until his world was complete and provided at the same time with the means to destroy itself.

This story is rather more than mythology to Hindus. The devout in India regard it as creed or dogma, and believe that at every sunset time on the crest of the Himalayan mountain, Kailasa, Siva repeats this dance for the faithful to see in their mind's eye. As the sun disappears, his dance of creativity asseverates the renewal of the next day's morning light. Siva later, according to Bharata at least, witnessed one of the dramatic representations commissioned by Brahma and found the element of dance lacking. He ordered the angels to emphasize it more, and since that time drama and dance have been inseparably linked. As a result there are no distinctive words in Sanskrit or modern Indian languages for "dance" and "drama" as disparate

9

entities. Drama in the form that we know it in the West existing independently of dance continues to be regarded to this day in many parts of Asia as some sort of aesthetic dichotomy, unfamiliar and disconcerting.

Apart from the world of remote gods and the far distant, legendary origins surrounding India's theatre, two rather more tangible factors began several thousand years ago to govern the structure and themes of the dramatic arts. These were the great and powerful epic poems, the *Ramayana* and the *Mahabharata*. One immediate parallel with the West that springs to mind is the *Iliad* and the *Odyssey*. Like them, the *Ramayana* and the *Mahabharata* are long, rambling adventure stories dealing with gods and mortals, supermen and miraculous animals, and are filled with morality and maxims differentiating between noble and base behavior.

In barest outline the *Ramayana* recites the story of Rama, a king and an heroic man of invincible virtue. His beautiful wife, Sita, a woman, naturally of impeccable rectitude, is kidnapped, while pursuing a golden deer into the forest, by the wicked demon-king of Lanka, or Ceylon as it is known in the West. Rama assembles an army of monkeys led by Hanuman, the white monkey, and after many difficulties lasting ten years finally reaches Lanka and regains his wife. This is, of course, only one (perhaps the most famous) of the several themes within the *Ramayana*. There are other episodes—with Rama's brothers, with his mother, between the monkey-brothers and their enemies, between Ravana and his ogress sister.

The *Mahabharata*, an even more complex and lengthy poem, eight times the bulk of the *Iliad* and *Odyssey* combined, basically tells of the five Pandava brothers opposing their cousins, the five Kaurava brothers, and their vacillating struggle for power over the country. Arjuna, the most beautiful and perfect of all possible men, plays an important if extraneous role in the story, and his moving poetic colloquies with the god Krishna on the righteousness of waging war are renowned as a separate book, the *Bhagavata Gita* or Song of the Devotee.

Summary translations of both the *Ramayana* and the *Mahabharata* are available in several editions; and a knowledge of their contents is essential if the student hopes to follow the thread of not only Indian but most Southeast Asian dance and drama. They make absorbing

10

reading because they are good stories filled with interesting incident, but also they reveal the substance of the mentality of the peoples who have created and perpetuated these myths. Both the *Ramayana* and the *Mahabharata* exceed their merit as literature. They tell almost unconsciously the actual foundings of India, explaining its origins, recording its first history, suggesting even an interpretation of the race's earliest memories. Sociologically, the *Ramayana* probably describes the Aryanization of India which is supposed to have taken place around 5000 B.C. in actual history. The triumphs of Rama over demons and monkeys were the conquest and later absorption of the original inhabitants of the subcontinent by the invading Caucasians from the North. And the *Mahabharata* is the story of intrigue and event within India's earliest ruling houses when the dynasties were connected with planetary worship. Their preeminence in culture, religion, literature, society, and above all else in drama and dance is unique in the world.

The first written and recorded versions of these two epics are now about fifteen hundred years old, but they were recited and acted, sung and chanted, for at least a thousand years prior to this. They are still firmly entrenched in the hearts of the people, and today in any village or city you can for a few rupees call in a professional storyteller who will start his narrative anywhere you ask and continue from memory, of course singing and pantomiming the story until you ask him to stop. Throughout the centuries the *Ramayana* and *Mahabharata* have afforded an inexhaustible supply of incident, anecdote, and plot situation suitable for innumerable drama and dance forms. In areas of Bengal, there are special Jatra or Yatra troupes (something like what our strolling mummers must have been) who will perform these same stories endlessly. The great folk-drama of the north, called the *Ram Lila*, and enacted annually in Delhi, India's capital city, depicts with giant painted-paper figures, like Mardi Gras carnival floats, excerpts from the *Ramayana*. The entire repertoire of the South Indian dance-drama form, Kathakali—where the performers spend all day painting their faces in grotesque, feature-disguising patterns and dance all night scarcely pausing for rest—draws its themes equally from the two sources.

Even today, when poet Vallathol, who rescued the art from near extinction a few years ago and who founded the only remaining

11

Kathakali School in India, writes a new text, he draws upon characters and scenes out of these same religious books. Convention has it that no matter what the originality of the message or the new interpretation of the ancient event may be, it must be said within the framework of the classics. No troupe, and I imagine no reciter either, can perform the whole of either epic—so comprehensive is the potential and so agglutinative have the more recent versions become with the emendations and additions that time and history have grafted on to the originals. For instance, at Vallathol's Kathakali School, if you give them a little advance notice, they could perform their full *Ramayana* and *Mahabharata* programs of all that remains now from the once complete repertoire and give you a different play each night for a month.

To the modern Indian the *Ramayana* and the *Mahabharata* have a significance of considerably more intensity than the words "epic poem," even in their historical and ethnological context, imply. They have, of course, the colorful romance of the *Iliad* and the *Odyssey*, but they also command the allegiance that, say, the Bible does in the West. They hold a deeply religious meaning, and Rama or Arjuna or Krishna are worshiped as gods rather than as humans or mythological characters dramatized from the nation's past. "Rama" is the word Hindus hope to have on their lips when they die. (It was Gandhi's last utterance.) Children are named Sita, Laxman, Bharata, and others, after characters in the two epics in the hope that they will grow to be like them in virtue. They are so named also as religious insurance. Anyone bearing a god's name will be safer, it is assumed, than one with a more mortal one, just as a Catholic is normally given a saint's name.

Passionate attitudes exist toward the *Ramayana* and *Mahabharata* even now. In recent years one theatrical representation, for instance, of the *Ramayana* ended by being a sensational court case. Near Madras in South India, a man named M. R. Radha wrote a new play which he advertised as "The Ramayana." In it he showed a number of the traditional heroes in an unflattering light and introduced a considerable amount of sexual romping. These new twists of the old theme attracted huge audiences, partly out of curiosity and partly because of the scandal the first performance created. However, despite box-office success, the play offended the susceptibilities of a large number of people who quickly assembled outside the theatre to demonstrate against future performances. Before the police could take control a riot between the orthodox and the less religious partisans had taken place. Those who had bought tickets and wanted to see the play lined up against those who did not want anybody to see it. Scores of people including several distinguished local citizens were arrested and charged with unlawful assembly, rioting, being armed with deadly weapons, and the like. While the legal pros and cons were argued back and forth, the public was already certain where the wrong lay. The disparagement of the *Ramayana*, even by a playwright to whom licence is normally given, is the offence, not the lesser crimes perpetrated in connection with that.

Both the *Ramayana* and the *Mahabharata*, despite the sensitivities surrounding them, provide ground for arguments of a more academic nature. In Madras city, the cultural capital of India, the newspapers announce every day at least half a dozen public lectures and discourses devoted to them. At a social party you will often hear educated Indians discussing the meaning of various passages or rationalizing in a novel way on the moot actions found in the texts. There is even respectful comment on the books' fundamental morality. It is often cited that Ravana, although a demon, acted with perfect probity in not taking advantage of Sita after abducting her and whisking her away to his palace. Rama is criticized for being so careless a god as to lose his wife, and then for subjecting her to the ignominy of what amounts to a trial by ordeal to prove her chastity after their long period of separation. The morality of these epics was applicable thousands of years ago and many still operate in vast sections of the country, but time alone subjects it to a more careful scrutiny. For instance, when Rama is wrongly exiled through the conniving of one of his stepmothers, he weeps. The only thing that prevents him from disobeying and curbs his furious desire to be destructive or punitive towards his father's kingdom is simply fear of social calumny (there is a Sanskrit word for this: *lokavadabhayena*). "What will people say if I disobey my father's command?" is roughly the gist of the passage.

While this is comprehensible even in the 20th century, it is somehow an ignoble motivation for a modern hero acceptable to us. The theatrical device of social pressure and arbitrary ethical codes as a determining factor cannot survive, at least in drama, the vast changes

13

history has made in our lives. Even in Japan in the puppet theatre or in the Kabuki plays of Chikamatsu Monzaemon (another instance where fear of society's ill-will often compels the acceptance of evil), the hero is invariably weak and his actions flimsy. Perhaps the most original of new interpretations of either of the epics was Gandhi's exegetical invention that the *Bhagavata Gita* took place within Arjuna's mind and that Krishna exhorted him to fight only the battle within the heart, not in the field. The instigation supplied to drama by these questions rising from changing moralities and critical examination of traditionally accepted precepts can be likened to the intellectual stimulus Ibsen provided the West with in his plays.

The *Ramayana* and *Mahabharata* still hold an unshakable grip on the whole of Greater India, particularly in their dance-dramas. Culturally, just as Homer is familiar in all countries of Europe and America almost as much as he is in Greece, these two epics belong now to a large part of Asia. Throughout all of Southeast Asia, you can still hear these same stories and incidents being recited, and you will see the main episodes being danced everywhere. In Indonesia, the *Mahabharata* may be called the *Brata Yudha* (The Battle of Bharat or India), or in Cambodia the *Ramayana* may be pronounced in an unrecognizable way, but the stories and characters are little changed. In Burma the only surviving troupe of masked dancers still perform episodes from the *Ramayana*. In Thailand, Rama, as he comes dancing into the arena with his high crowned headdress of gold will be called "Buddha" by the crowd of eager spectators and Ravana "giant" or "demon," but it is still from the same *Ramayana*. Or in Laos, Ravana is transmuted into the hero and Rama becomes a subsidiary character. Only at the very end does he get his wife Sita back, and even then she goes home reluctantly and weeping. Again, in Ceylon, Ravana's home according to the *Ramayana*, you will see one popular play-interlude during a demon-exorcizing ceremony titled "The Killing of Rama." Here it seems Rama, when he finally reaches Ceylon in pursuit of his abducted wife, has great difficulty with the Sinhalese language. A merchant mocks him, and thinking he has stolen some cloth, beats him to death. In the end, however, he repents and tries to revive Rama. In high comic fashion he shouts to the dead man, "Your mother-in-law has come; now get up!"—but even that fails to

14

bring him back to life. Finally the gods take pity and Rama is restored. Or in Indonesia, which is the largest Mohammedan country in the world, these Hindu epics still persist in a curiously contradictory way, flouting the newer religion. At the Javanese courts of the Sultan of Jogjakarta, or of the lesser ruler, the Susunan at Solo, the palace dancers moving with slow, sustained gestures against the background of great orchestras of rippling, bell-like instruments, enact precisely as they have for a thousand years the courtship of Arjuna and Sembodro, for example, from the *Mahabharata*, or the battle scenes between the two opposing families of Pandava and Kaurava cousins.

The extent to which the *Ramayana*, particularly, has affected the theatre arts of Southeast Asia is further demonstrated by the fact that the common word to indicate dancing in parts of Malaya, most of Thailand, Cambodia, and Laos, derives from Rama himself and is pronounced variously as *rom, lam* and *ram*, depending on the linguistic facility of the peoples concerned. Echoes of the *Ramayana* are even found in certain Chinese operas. During the recent tour of India by the cultural group of the People's Republic of China, a special scene from one of the classics was performed to the delight of Indians—a good general recruits an army of monkeys to fight on the side of righteousness. This was clearly reminiscent of the *Ramayana*.

While the *Ramayana* and the *Mahabharata* fed the religious demands of the Indians and satisfied most of their instincts for folklore and theatre, as well as simultaneously supplying inspiration and format to their cultural realms overseas, a body of relatively independent dramas grew up in India itself. For a time, for approximately the third century A.D. to the eighth, the first Indian dramas in the sense that we in the West understand the word flourished, and this period is generally known as the Golden Era of Sanskrit Drama. The most celebrated of the great number of playwrights flowering at that time were Kalidasa, Bhasa, and Sudraka, and plays by them, such as *Sakuntala, The Little Toy Cart*, and a few others are even known in translation in the West. The majority of the great Sanskrit dramatists drew their themes at least in part from the *Ramayana* or *Mahabha-*

15

rata, and while their dramas are secular in every meaning of the word, a severe moral and religious overtone was carefully preserved and derived from the older texts.

Sakuntala is a case in point. For it, Kalidasa took his theme from the first part of the *Mahabharata,* and in the course of seven episodic acts tells the story of the love of Sakuntala for the King Dusanta. In rough outline and shorn of its poetry the story is simple. Dusanta while hunting in the forest with his courtiers pursues a stag, shoots him with an arrow, and is reproached by a holy man passing by for his cruelty to living things. He begs forgiveness and is finally pardoned and given a blessing. He sees Sakuntala by accident and falls immediately in love with her. His love is modestly and decorously reciprocated. They are married. Dusanta gives Sakuntala a wedding ring, with the promise that she is soon to follow him to his capital. Because of a strange curse on Sakuntala, the king forgets the incident entirely. The finest scene of the play is the departure of the faithful Sakuntala from her parent's home. There her sorrow on leaving all that is familiar to her, mixed with her anticipated reunion with her husband, is interspersed with words of good advice (vaguely parallel with Polonius' speech to Laertes) from her father on the virtues and propriety a wife must exhibit. Sakuntala reaches the capital, but the king neither recognizes her nor remembers the marriage. Meanwhile she has lost the ring; her last vestige of proof is gone. Shortly afterwards, a son is born to Sakuntala, the ring is discovered by a fisherman who extracts it from a fish he has caught, the memory of the king is restored through the intercession of the gods who have been moved to pity by Sakuntala's plight, and the couple with their child are happily united.

Perhaps an illuminating sidelight on how an Indian scholar differs from the Westerner in his approach to drama can be obtained from Dr. V. Raghavan, the eminent Sanskrit authority, who describes *Sakuntala* of Kalidasa as the presentation of "the ideal of love at first sight getting purified in the fire of separation, and sublimated in the joy of the offspring." While the foreigner is equally moved by the same drama, his reasons, at least as he formulates them, are different.

There were several exceptions to the rule of dominance set by the *Ramayana* and the *Mahabharata.* Some of the masterpieces of the Sanskrit dramatists were entirely original in plot and based on actual events of the times or recent history. Bhasa's best drama, *The Dream of Vasavadatta* or *Svapna-Vasavadatta*, in six acts is an instance of this. The Chief Minister of King Udayana for reasons of political strategy wishes to arrange an alliance through marriage with a powerful neighboring kingdom. He informs the king that his wife, Vasavadatta, has been burned to death during a conflagration in the palace. In reality, he only disguises her and places her in the custody of the new junior queen. Despite his second marriage, the king has various intimations that Vasavadatta is still alive, one of which is the dream-scene from which the title of the play is taken. The crisis between the two kingdoms is weathered; the Chief Minister reveals that Vasavadatta is safe, and she returns to the throne, amicably grateful to all.

The Little Toy Cart by Sudraka, the playwright king, who is remembered more for his dramas than his reign, derives from a popular story of the time and has no direct plot-connection with either of the two great epics. It tells the story of Charudatta, a Brahmin, and clearly the most lovable man of the city, who becomes destitute through his over-generous, charitable practices. He falls desperately in love with a beautiful dancing girl and the play revolves around the vicissitudinous course of their love. Charudatta is for some reason led to the gallows, but the villainy of the accusation against him is discovered in time. As a background and reinforcing plot, the author weaves a story of political intrigue within the realm and vyings for the throne engineered by the rightful king's own brother-in-law.

Nearly all of the work of this Golden Era was in Sanskrit—once the spoken language of ancient India, and, of course, even now that of all the holy books and the great epic poems. Oddly enough, Sanskrit by the time India's first dramatists appeared had already become something of a scholars' language and the preserve of the religious pundits. It had lost touch with the people, pretty much in the same way that Greek and Latin in Europe became dead and were superseded by less inflected, less complicated dialects. In fact, one of Buddha's great reforms was to use the vernacular instead of Sanskrit in his religious teachings. And because of this linguistic closeness between the people and their saints, drama has probably thrived to a greater degree in Buddhist countries—at least until the vernacular in itself became an antiquated language—than it did in Indian or Hinduized areas.

There is an unfortunate historical irony in the fact that India's

17

greatest dramas were, by virtue of the obscurity of their language, destined to be short-lived and, for lack of popular appeal to the less educated masses, forced to disappear from the stages of India. They remained in a sort of hearsay limbo, known only to those professionally concerned. Bhasa illustrates perhaps the extreme of the neglect surrounding Sanskrit drama. Until 1912, when his first manuscripts were discovered, he had been only a name, references to which had been found in other documents. In the nineteenth century the translation of Kalidasa and Sudraka into European languages made Indian classical drama famous among the intelligentsia of the West. Goethe wrote an extravagant eulogy of *Sakuntala*; *The Little Toy Cart* was even performed in a place as far off as New York. This had repercussions in India, and as more and more monographs and theses appeared in the West, the further the subject was explored and reawakened in its home country by scholarly, artistic and even patriotic circles.

Until their recent revival, ancient Sanskrit dramas had long since ceased being general theatre fare for the people. But as narratives and moral forces, their power was somehow consistently present within Indian society. No matter what folk dramas supplanted them, or what new forms evolved, or what dances arrogated pieces of their ideas and themes, or what decline they themselves suffered, their innermost, basic, aesthetic core also remained constant and deep inside the minds and tastes of Indians. The canons of theatrical art which Kalidasa, for example, put into practice and perfected have, with very little modification over the centuries, remained as a kind of invisible law. While India has never again produced so many playwrights of fine calibre as during that brief period, and has not even faithfully maintained recognition of those that were, the artistic principles of their works have been unvarying. Somewhat as we in the West can with reasonable clarity trace our modern theatre successively back to the Greeks, and find that not only its general form but its sense of tragedy and comedy, its concept of the frailty of man and the relentlessness of destiny, its emphasis on characterization of the individual rather than on a stereotype, and even a large part of its morality all still operate and subtend our plays, so does Indian dance and drama of today reflect its own set of ancient tenets and identifying aspects.

Going even further back to the very beginning, we find that the fundamental aesthetic principles propounded by Brahma and Bharata in that felicitous conjunction of god and man have endured, and if in certain fields only thinly, they nevertheless have managed to perpetuate themselves. The actual foundation of Indian theatre and all Asian art affected by it has survived despite vicissitudes for several thousands of years. For the student of theatre nothing proves so abundantly clearly the elaborate development and refinement of India's ancient stagecraft, and, conversely, nothing emphasizes more sadly its later decline.

The formulae evolved at the height of Sanskrit drama (and these in turn were naturally based on still older techniques whose actual examples were never recorded) are still active. Certain broad dramatic principles stemming from this Indian past now are hallmarks of all Asian drama, bringing about a wide difference from other forms in other parts of the world. Broadly speaking, the three root-elements characterizing Asian drama are simply poetry, music and dance. Each of these appears in a balanced fusion, each has adjacent and adjunctive qualities, and each presents certain difficulties for the spectator. But their inextricable and synthetic connection with drama is the premise from which we must approach Asian theatre. From here we build our platform for viewing the entire panorama, and without it we cannot proceed in any effort towards understanding Asian theatre.

Of the three, it may be claimed that the poetic element is the most determining. The poetry of words, to begin with, takes artistic priority over all action and narrative. The staging of drama in Asia is primarily the problem of enacting poetry, and this poetry ranges from the simple representations of epic poems to passages where the playwright toys for as long as he can with chains of assonant words, double meanings, rhetoric, tropes, aposiopesis, and even puns. In Thailand, for instance, actors of Likay, the popular form of drama, interrupt the flow of the play at will with improvisations of rhymed and metrical couplets. Some of the Kabuki plays of seventeenth- and eighteenth-century Japan border on the nonsensical simply because of the fury of their poetic tricks.

Poetry too, being a literary form rather than a medium of slice-of-life modern theatre, leads in a number of instances to a disregard of the unities. Time and place scarcely restrict an Asian playwright when he has an entire language of florid metaphor and simile in which to set his scenes and spread his backdrop. As a result these dramas often have an air of formless, unrestrictive roving about them. Scenes follow uninhibitedly in arbitrary succession, and the poetry easily shifts you in an instant from one place to another. While this is not unfamiliar in Shakespeare and Elizabethan drama, the excess of such poetic licence in many parts of Asia nevertheless surprises us.

The willingness to have a poetic, rather than a logical, action-packed story-play requires a certain patience from the outsider, not only because of language difficulties but also because poetry invites a more static mood. Poetry retards the normal speed of action and forces on an actor surplus time—time to pose, to enlarge and expand a gesture, to draw out a movement, to fill in with "business." In this onstage leisure the artistic purport of a scene blooms. The whole world can be invoked symbolically and the fullest feeling surrounding a phrase embroidered. Poetry provides a springboard for the actor to enrich his action and to entice from the spectator a series of emotions which extend and change the quality of what straight enactment produces. To the Asian, the essence of drama lies here, not within the mere telling of a story alone. Regrettably for us, there is a poverty of plays really adaptable to the Western stage and even synopses in English of many Asian plays border on the pointless while in their original, resplendently poetic form they are often magnificent.

Because of this heavy overlay of poetry, Asian plays require a special device—the storyteller or extraneous performers outside the actors to sing or declaim the most specifically poetic passages. This is partly too a natural extension from the past. Drama everywhere in Asia technically originated out of simple chantings of the holy books and recitals from epic poems. Gradually the narrators began to add gesticulation to their performances and started miming what they said or sang. More and more realism crept in when separate actor-dancers took over the dialogues and delivered their own pertinent lines. But the role of the reciter still continued.

In Sanskrit drama he is called the *sutradhara* or "string holder,"

can follow his words. (He also parrots his gestures in ludicrous fashion to emphasize their difference in station and to make quite clear what is happening.) In China, to cite another instance, after long arias by emperors or generals, a comic interlude in simplest Chinese (or in the local dialect if the Pekinese language of the arias is incomprehensible) will keep the audience abreast of the plot and the story. In the Sanskrit dramas, often it was only these comedians who could make the actual storyteller's meanings clear, the rest of the play being appreciated for aesthetic rather than literal values. Of course, the use of comedy was also for contrast with the sobriety of the main characters and for relief from their dramatic tension. But their function of informing the audience never lessened.

Gradually, as the dramas were enacted again and again, year after year, a kind of familiarity with them arose, and while few could understand the actual words, everybody knew the characters and what their story was. And it was this very familiarity which tided many of the dramas over transitional periods when classics grew even more incomprehensible linguistically, when poetry became even more remote from daily life; fortunately for those interested in preservation of traditions, it was this which finally deterred and delayed the appearance of anything very new in Asian theatres. Asian drama on the whole has remained more traditional and the repertoire more permanent than theatre in the West. The emphasis came to be on how a passage was acted, not on what was being acted. This is almost antithetical to the Western conception of theatre where we want to hear and understand every word of the play. And although the poetic element has determined the form of the play and the style of acting, it suffices in Asia to see how an old, familiar story is being performed and what is being done on the stage rather than to hear what is being said and understand its meaning.

An illustration of this difference in approach became clear to me once when I went to one of the first performances ever staged of a modern play in the contemporary language in Cambodia. Two old ladies who had obviously never seen anything except their traditional dance-plays were sitting behind me. Half way through one of them remarked to her friend with considerable surprise, "It's more interesting if you listen to what they are saying."

Poetry also, I think, was responsible for the religious and moralistic themes of most plays of Southeast Asia at least. All of it in the beginning stemmed from liturgical works and since much of it was supposed to have a divine origin, the gods are nearly always present. No matter what baseness may be described in the poetry, the righteous ultimately win. As a result, there are no tragedies in Indian drama, and, with the notable exceptions of China and Japan, very few elsewhere in the classical theatres of Asia. There is confidence that good has to triumph, and if the gods are in their heaven at all, that is the least they can perform for the mortals on earth. The optimism of Indian drama in particular is most clearly expressed in Bharata's canon that all progression on the stage or development of action in the theatre can only be made, conjunctively or interactively, by five elements: beginning, effort, hope, certainty, and success. No note of pessimism can be sounded here. The theatre to many people of Asia still mindful of its ancient origins is where the gods enact their will, and their will ultimately must be good. Religion often is the only reason for any dramatic representation—temple festivals, holy days, the inducing of the favor of the gods, the expelling of demons—and for a play to have a tragic ending would be as curious as if we perform the Passion Play as far as the Good Friday scene and omitted the Resurrection.

Poetry, itself an abstraction from reality, naturally was inseparable from music, an art even more intangible and removed from the immediate occupations of ordinary everyday life and the subject-matter that preoccupies human beings most urgently. Dance or drama in the form that they took in Asia begged by their natures, obviously, for music to assist their poetry and heighten what otherwise might be verbose or artistically lacking. The place of music in Sanskrit drama is well documented. Chinese traveler-pilgrims of the seventh century describe dramas accompanied by "strings and pipes." One of the musical assemblies mentioned consisted of twelve male and twelve female voices, twenty-six flutes, six large drums and three smaller ones. The earliest commentaries on dramaturgy agree that a production lacks color without music and that every dramatic situation can be enlivened by it. "Instruments are the very bed of a performance," Bharata exclaims in his treatise. One Sanskrit dramatist in talking about the number of songs within his plays justified them because they "delight the hearts of the audience and establish the emotional continuity." Various ancient authorities on drama assigned specific types of melodies and kinds of rhythms for almost every conceivable situation—for entrances and exits, for separations of lovers, for fatigue, for the tranquility that follows anxious thought, for drunkenness, for burnishing a mood already introduced, and even for a type of song that was reserved for covering up a gap or mishap in the production. There is in Asia no exception to the rule that all classical and semi-classical drama must be accompanied by music, and a majority of modern plays as well embrace this ancient aesthetic principle.

From the Western point of view Asian music presents an even greater problem initially than language or poetry. The saying that the appeal of music is universal is certainly inaccurate. Many expatriates in Asia who adopt native dress, master a local dialect, and live happily with the local traditions and customs, cannot listen to the music of the country whose manners they assimilate and whose tastes otherwise they affect with such sincerity. The barrier between countries and peoples musically applies even within Asia itself. In India, for example, the South and the North have irreconcilable musical systems, and audiences who appreciate the one are inclined to feel distress at hearing the other. Music is so intimate a national expression, so collective a reflection of racial and group feeling, so patently a matter of custom and habit, that it of necessity requires the most delicate adjustment and conditioning on the part of the outsider.

Listening habits in the West are basically inimical to hearing Asian music. In the West we expect our emotions to be aroused in a warm and affectionate way, with voluptuous harmonies pouring over us and compelling us to react to mood and meaning within the music. Our ears are attuned to incidental rather than abstract music—a minor key to make us sad, a tremolo if the mood is ominous, a crash of chords if the gates of Heaven are opening, and even a castanet, say, to let us know we are imaginatively in Spain. Of course, there are exceptions to this, and not all music appreciation needs to be so literal. But in contrast with Asia, the pictorial use of sound is the West's most striking quality. And perhaps we do not realize the number of conventions we accept so casually, until we try to listen to Asian music as intelligently as we hear our own.

25

There are, of course, instances where certain drumbeats indicate rain or mountains or snow. There is a passage in one of the Kabuki masterpieces of Japan, *Kumagai's Camp*, where the samisens flutter over a long melismata to indicate the ascending smoke of burning incense. An extreme of this appears in India where special melodies or *ragas* are reputed to produce fire, invoke the night, or even charm snakes. But on the whole Asian music provides no clue, either to us or the Asian himself, except by previously understood conditions and conventions as to what it is trying to do. Happy music can sound more somber than its Western equivalent could possibly permit. Even when you see an audience weeping at a concert, the music will not be sad. Emotions and their moods in the way that we understand them are reserved for other arts, not music. During a tragic moment in a play the accompanying music is designed often only to fill in the silences or in a Japanese phrase "to keep the stage from being empty." Music is thought to intrude if it tries to imitate or duplicate the emotion of an actor and his words. At best it burnishes. At most, it adds only repose or agitation, quiet or exuberance.

Fundamentally, listening to music in Asia is an exercise of the intellect and the emotional experience it induces is abstract and unempathetic. Yehudi Menuhin speaking of Indian music says, "The mathematical exercise becomes an ecstatic kind of astronomy." When you approach Asian music you must wipe from your mind your ears' preconditioning by harmony and the forms you associate with musical structure in the West. You must listen for the infinite melodic variations, the subtle contortions of the basic theme, the gossamer-fine tonal web of clear, thin pitch, and the formality of progressing from the simple to the complex, from the slow to the fast, or for the introspective, thoughtful strumming when the musician plays with after-resonance, vibration, or the contemplative setting of mood.

In principle it works this way. Always there is a steady drone bass or a single tonic which serves as a backdrop to enhance the tonal variation. Over this the melodic differentiations waver like spun thread. Against it sound the intricate rhythmic patterns.

The music in India and Southeast Asia, with the exception of Bali, is nearly always improvisatory, the creation of the performing musician in that moment and almost never the interpretive rendering of another's recorded composition. With the exceptions of Thailand,

Cambodia, Java, and again Bali, no music in Asia is continuously chordal, orchestral, or even contrapuntal, and the harmonic development even here is mostly one of accident and the collision of the several instrumental melodies. While to the Westerner this may appear as a deficiency, to the Asian our vast orchestras and the ubiquitous piano have only deadened our ears to his more exact tunings and more subtle metres. Where one is finely melodic, the other is richly harmonic. Where one depends on drums, and their infinite possibilities of rhythmic intricacy, the other sacrifices this for a broader coordination and variety of timbres. Altogether, the technical and aesthetic differences between Asian and Western music are hard to resolve.

Our responses and appreciation of music naturally rise from the earliest sounds we have ever heard around us and from the fact that our daily life, as it is constituted today, is never without music in the form we now approve. We recognize the evocations of our music as inevitably as we accept our food habits and behavior patterns. The Asian feels the same way about his own music, but because of the long centuries of colonialism and the impact of Western music on Asia, he is better able to accept our music than we are his. If the student of Asian dance and drama is to arrive at full understanding, he must make his greatest effort on music. It must be listened to with the mind without reference to his own conventions. He must try, despite the handicap of inexperience, to catch the microtonic tonal divisions and the elusive pulsating rhythms. At the end, finally, familiarity will allow the unconscious and relaxed attitude which indulges the emotions.

The rewards are great. Emotionally, it is as affecting and inspiring —in different ways and in different areas of aesthetic sensibility—as our own. And certainly Asian music extends our preconceptions of the theory of music into reaches scarcely imagined before by us. Its delights and pleasures, once the fundamentals are grasped, are quite as profoundly gratifying as the more immediately accessible dances and dramas.

With the various attributes and qualities engendered by poetry and music, dance bursts into Asian theatre like fireworks. No matter how full of splendor the drama may be as drama or how beautiful the poetry or music, the spectacle of dance enlivening, interpreting and compounding the aesthetic delight provides the audience, foreign or indigenous, with its most significant area of appreciation. Unlike language and sound, the movement of the body before one's eyes lays few burdens on a spectator. His understanding is less taxed here than in almost any other field of contact between nations.

Of all the components identifying Indian drama and its derivatives, the peculiarly intimate relationship between it and dance is its most salient feature to the student. In the West, the two grew into separate arts. And due in the main, I feel, to the influence of Christianity and the reservations it made regarding any use of the body as an instrument of pleasure, dance as an art became a secondary, almost minor, part of our life. Perhaps because of this drama excelled itself. But in India from the beginning the two have been indispensable adjuncts of one another. Dance approximates in movement the poetic flights of words in ideas. It also fills the stage while the reciter is telling his part of the story. And with the reciter at his side, the actor is free to match with dance the flow of words when simple gestures in mime would seem to be too brief or arid. The Asian stage provides a natural framework for dance in every way. But even this is not enough. Plots are slanted so as to make dance appropriate, and every opportunity is taken to fill the drama with dance sequences. Heroes fall in love with dancing girls. Festivals, which require dancing, are the background to a climactic action. Dancers attached to the courts of kings appear on stage ostensibly to divert the mind of a troubled ruler. Command performances by kings become integral parts of the narrative. A marriage celebration requires a full-scale dance program. A hero dances before going into battle. He dances when he wins. United heroes and heroines dance for sheer joy. And gods dance to exhibit their divinity. After all this, even at the conclusions of plays a character dressed as a god may dance simply as a benediction for the audience. If this preponderance of dance seems undue to the Westerner, it must be remembered that at the time the older dramas were written, it was part of verisimilitude; dance figured prominently, as it still does in daily life and those dramas were scarcely being more than lifelike.

It is a very small step from creating situations in the theatre calling for dancing to letting the dance take over without a specific connection with plot, and finally for dance to become altogether independent of drama. But the majority of dances in Asia even out of their context still retain a strongly dramatic element. Over the centuries of Asian theatrical growth and development, dance came to exceed drama both in frequency and in popularity. Today, throughout a large part of Asia, dance is the only theatrical outlet and the nation's only professional entertainment. With the exception of China, it would be relatively easy to find Asians who had never seen a play, but it may be doubted if there is one who has not seen dance performances all his life, and more than likely, taken part in any number of the non-professional ones.

During the twelfth to seventeenth centuries a shift occurred in the Indian concept of religious worship. What happened was, simply stated, that a cult arose whose founders and adherents had begun to believe that Vishnu in the incarnation of Krishna, the sportive cowherd, was the central and most powerful deity of the pantheon. The themes of the literature, dramas, operas and dances evolving at this time most frequently told the story of Krishna and the milkmaids or *gopis*. Krishna was always in his garden with his cows or playing pranks. The milkmaids were constantly finding him as they went to the well with their large earthenware pots to draw water. All of the milkmaids love Krishna equally, but Krishna, while reciprocating all their love, has his favorite, Radha. The plots centered on these love entanglements in some form or other. Sometimes Krishna and Radha are separated from each other, at other times all of them play together, swinging in swings, sitting in flowery bowers, teasing, laughing, or enjoying their bliss in the garden paradise. Often they become angry with each other, and Radha pouts with jealousy or Krishna prostrates himself with remorse after some infidelity.

Certain new religious techniques accompanied this change in Hinduism. It was thought that the mere repetition of the names of God (and by this time God had accumulated an even greater number of names and reincarnations than in the beginning of Hindu literature) could effect salvation, that the surest, most expeditious way of man to contact God was through organized singing and dancing, and, finally, that the central theme of all religious endeavor should be love.

This latter was the most sweeping of the innovations, and while in the West the idea of God is Love has a certain acceptance, in India the point was more that Love is God. Nothing basically radical or unknown was introduced by all this and much of it was a reiteration of what had been adumbrated since time immemorial. But in sum total the emphasis and approach were sufficiently fresh to make for a semblance at least of a different brand of Hinduism. The widespread acceptance which greeted this mode of worship relinquished none of the hold of the older gods or even of the sanctified books of the *Ramayana* and *Mahabharata,* but it was nevertheless an unprecedented alteration in the religious life of the country. A vast revival of faith swept over the people and the arts of course were profoundly affected since art and religion were inseparable. Music and the singing of hymns were stimulated.

A large and beautiful literature of love appeared—the masterpiece of which remains the *Gita Govinda* (Song of the Cowherd). Its influence was so strong that grammar all over India and its rules of etymology, orthography, phonetics and rhetoric soon incorporated love as a special department with its own syntactical canons of structure. Drama and the underlying principles governing its related arts took a different direction and the new aesthetic theory which ultimately evolved was a peculiarly Hindu one, cut off even from its domains overseas.

In effect, Mohammedanism had forced Hinduism to retreat within itself and the outward forms of worship consequently sank into mystic secrecy. In Bengal, for instance, even these new singing and dancing convocations were often, when discovered, suppressed by the Muslim administrators. The building of temples ceased. And because of the private and interior aspect religion took, art remained well within the country. The days of India's expansion were over. The new theatre and its music did not spread to other parts of Asia. They remained carefully centered in India.

To understand exactly what happened artistically, one must go back once again to another aspect of India's ancient aesthetic theories. The rudiments of India's approach to the performing arts, as laid down in the oldest treatises, concern *rasa* and *bhava.* These words convey so complicated a meaning that even when speaking in English, Indian intellectuals will use the original Sanskrit and, leaving it at that, hope that the thought is communicated. Newspapers refer to the *rasa* of a work, much in the same way that we would talk about its "story" or "gist." An artist will be congratulated on her handling of *bhava*, although the conversation is being conducted entirely in a foreign language.

The concepts of *rasa* and *bhava* are elusive for the Westerner. Roughly put, *rasa* means feeling or flavor and is the permanent mood with which dance or drama concerns itself. There are nine of these: heroism, fear, love, laughter, pathos, wonder, terror, loathesomeness (including its sense of contempt and revulsion), sorrow, and spiritual peace or sublime tranquility. These are the major emotions, with all their attendant psychology, imbedded in the soul of a human being. *Bhava*, on the other hand, consists of the situations and acts which evoke specific responses, and there is a large variety of them. *Bhava* may be either enduring or transitory, a cause or effect, or even an ensuant or excitant. Taking the *rasa* of love, for example, its *bhavas* can be the causal one between a husband and wife or between two strangers. The *bhava* of effect will be that of undying devotion, if it is permanent, or longing, despondency or doubt, if it is transitory. The ensuants can be sidelong glances or coquettish smiles, and the excitants, moonlight, a beach, or a soft, zephyrous breeze. When all these minute *bhavas* are properly portrayed, the *rasa* appears as a kind of telling reaction from within the spectator, and this *rasa* is an overpowering aesthetic delectation which according to the Hindus only true art can arouse in man.

By the intensity of love the new Krishna worship introduced, the *rasas* and *bhavas* became limited, and drama and dance were finally reduced to a few themes and situations. The only *rasa* that Indian art subsequently concerned itself with was love in both its erotic and spiritual forms. The chief *bhavas* left were the various relationships which produced different sorts of love. The *bhavas* rising from these plays and which touch the spectator must depend in the main on five possible relationships between the characters. Drawing upon the Krishna example, we find the following. One of the milkmaids thinks of herself as the servant of Krishna, his mother, his friend, his personal lover, or, finally, the most difficult of recognitions to engender in a spectator, his devotee, and here the point is to show the peace and silence resulting from contemplation of the Lord and the mere

31

sensing of his divine radiance. This is not too strange for the West-erner if he recalls how poetry in the West has virtually become a me-dium for love too and its romantic aspects have for the most part ex-ceeded its epic or heroic capabilities.

But this whole web of flavors and feelings which *rasa* and *bhava* im-ply produces an aesthetic principle which is far removed from anything we are familiar with in the West. Dramatically speaking, a number of obstacles too presented themselves by the new reaffirmation of the connection between theatre and God—assuming again that by drama we mean the visual representation of a story with action, literally and comprehensibly portrayed. The story of Krishna's life and the innu-merable incidents connected with it (he was a naughty child, he was bitten by a snake, he stole butter from the milkmaids as fast as they churned it, he hid their clothes while they were bathing in the river, and the like), and the very real and temporal love that he shares with the milkmaids, are all tangible enough and have some appropriate moments for stage performances in our sense of the word. But when the aim is to induce ecstasy or to demonstrate religious experience, and when love is the means and *shantih* or sublimity is the ultimate *rasa*, drama, and, to a lesser extent, dance are curtailed and become unsubstantial from a Western point of view. When the aesthetic prin-ciples subtending this type of performance are further restricted to love and to possible relationships between lover and beloved or be-tween worshiper and his God, the area of drama in its broadest hu-man sense shrinks. This injures Indian drama and was responsible for its further decline. Such rarifications were too much even for most Indians. It was too difficult except for the saints and the devout either to arrive at intense religious experience or to sustain it once it was reached. The majority of the people looked to those parts where the love was clearly physical, which was comprehensible to them and which they could interpret as being simply the relationship of one human being with another. It was simpler as the centuries passed to transform this new aesthetic into a representation of mortal love rather than let it exist, as it was intended, as a method of spiritual ac-complishment.

By no means am I criticizing the arts produced in India at this time even from the standpoint of international theatre. Nor do I find fault with those illustrations of it which have endured down to the present. This kind of art is simply different from the predilections found in other parts of the world. In its own field and on its own ground, it is a unique and extraordinary theatre. The harmonious unity between man and god in these dramas and dances reveals a happiness and joy that borders on magic and the mystic. Equally powerful is the strange tension the spectator feels when that equilibrium is suspended—when Radha and Krishna are separated or quarrel. And when with the resolution the lovers are reunited and Krishna is forgiven, a tearful, almost hysterical ecstasy of relief floods over even the foreigner. Perhaps these situations are impractical in the theatre as we think of it, but in themselves they are nothing short of miraculous.

From the seventeenth century onwards religion still flourished. Music was still a major form of devotional worship. But drama continued its decline, and the blissfulness of the Krishna impetus remains for us today captured only in excerpts from the dance. (Manipur is a notable exception for reasons explained elsewhere.) Except for itinerant players touring the provinces and performing religious stories of the *Ramayana* and *Mahabharata* on festival days, singing parties devoted to the love of Radha and Krishna, and temple pageants, drama in the form that we know it remained absent from Indian life until about a century and a half ago.

Dance Today

Early in India's history, dance began to dominate the theatre instead of remaining an integral but subservient part of the art as a whole. Consequently, during the dark years of drama's decline in India, disintegration of dance was considerably more gradual. By the turn of this century, many dance forms still remained but there were relatively few dramatic performances to be seen.

A variety of reasons account for this fact. Dance is less complicated to mount as a production. It requires no props. Often it is only a solo with one singer and one drummer as accompaniment. Dance, too, is more direct and personal in its contact with the spectator and therefore more widely practiced by a greater number of people. Drama, on the other hand, needs at least a complement of specialists—a playwright, a troupe of actors and stagehands. Dance and drama both rise from the human being's elementary urges toward make-believe and magic, amusement and recreation, and out of these emerge the complicated, narrative stories we associate with drama.

However, in India, as well as in a good part of Asia, dance absorbed the various disparate dramatic elements as quickly as they appeared and finally overpowered any particular compulsion toward realism, contemporaneity, clear dialogue, or rational portrayal of immediate problems to connect the stage with the people's day-to-day life. These latter aspects of theatre are primary Western conceptions. And while, on the one hand, today we see trends in the West toward the Asian approach to theatre with our new musical comedies, our increasingly unrealistic stylizations, and our warm applause of those visiting Asian dancers who have appeared abroad, we find on the other hand in Asia itself, generally speaking, theatre without dance and without gods and divine beings as the central characters really only beginning after the arrival of the West there. Because of dance, drama movements in Asia were until quite recently often abortive or frustrated.

In India, where there are vast areas of land and huge populations often quite separated from each other geographically and racially, you naturally find a wide variety of cultural habits. In all these communities, whether they are agriculturalists (as, of course, they are) in the majority, or fishermen, or naked head hunters or aboriginal tribes, pockets of whom are still found in every part of India today, you have a people both dependent on themselves for entertainment and infused with an urgency to be in some sort of mystic contact with nature and the elements that determine their lives. Consequently there is no part of India which has not found expression in dance to exhibit and maintain some sort of propitiatory or grateful connection between the people and these forces. Dance anywhere in the world is one of the most primeval manifestations of worship, and its connection with magic, with invocation and appeasement, has been demonstrated now for so many thousands of years in Asia, it almost becomes difficult to discard it as superstition. In India you still find people dancing in the fields before they plant, dancing

34

when the harvest is in, dancing for rain, dancing to stop the rain, dancing to celebrate an especially abundant catch of fish, dancing to drive away sickness and plague, and to prevent famine. Perhaps the extreme example of the prevalence of dance I can cite is a *bhangra* or group dance a gang of masked dacoits (robbers) performed not long ago after they had raided a township in Central India, killing a number of people and looting the area. More pertinently, a group of masked lamas in Kashmir danced recently for "the establishment of world peace."

Despite all this, the path of dance in India was still tortuous. Along with the gradual urbanization of India, resulting from the opening up of the great ports of Bombay, Madras, Calcutta, and others, and the concentration of administrative functions and industries in large cities such as Delhi, Bangalore and Jamshedpur, together with the other changes introduced by colonization and the new kind of civilization from the West, the mood and occasion for dancing lessened. Many of the people who used to dance were sucked out of their isolated villages into towns where they found little excuse for dancing. Their compulsion was lost, and besides they were more busily occupied than they had been in the villages. Perhaps, most important, was the fact that they were no longer responsible for entertaining themselves. They found among the clusters of people in the cities numerous other amusements. There were all the dance substitutes— motion pictures, radios, circuses, theatre houses, books, magazines, public speeches and many groups whose sole profession was to delight, divert the mind, and leave the spectator passive and non-participating. Year by year, folk dances became fewer.

All of these factors have operated in one way and another, to a greater or lesser extent, to the detriment of dance. Still another complication hastened the near-disappearance of dance in India. Somewhere along the years, and it is impossible to pinpoint this moment in history although certainly the Muslims and the British had a hand in it, the exalted perfection of the ancient dance began to warp.

Dance was the art that once dignified Sanskrit dramas. It was the mode of worship that celebrated the gods and sparkled brightly within the sacred, inner shrines of every temple. It was the pastime of kings and queens, or rajas and maharajas, and palace dancers gave glittering performances on every possible occasion.

Little by little this glory started to tarnish, and dance became the province of the degraded castes and the pursuit of prostitutes. Temples dedicated to dancer-queens with their platforms of black marble slabs lay empty and unused. Dance left the hands of men and became a practice of women, who used it often as a means merely to seduce. In the South, *devadasi*, literally servants of gods or girls who are dedicated at infancy to a temple to dance before the idols, turned into women of pleasure, for the priests first, then later for anyone who paid their fee. In a moralistic outburst some years back, the practice of dedicating these girls was forbidden by law, and the law with its clumsy ruthlessness unfortunately banned all their dancing as well. From time to time, even now, groups of enraged citizens when they hear of areas where the law has not yet penetrated distribute pamphlets—the latest one at the time of writing was titled "Devadasi: A Burning Problem in Karnataka (Mysore State)." In the North, the word *nautch* became famous as far as Europe and America as a synonym for a dancing prostitute. In conventional Indian society, if a young man said he was going to see a *nautch*, his horrified family could only feel he was going to a whore. If he did go to a house of ill-fame, it was very likely that the woman would first dance for him as a stimulus.

In the early part of this century in the northeastern State of Manipur, the poet Rabindranath Tagore discovered and extracted from the local religious opera of the region a type of dancing which he imported into his school at Santiniketan. Sadly enough, it was hailed as the only respectable dance left in the whole of India.

Out of this contumely and from among these remnants of dance, a number of Indian intellectuals and artists rescued their dance. Less than a half a century ago, several individuals, working apart from each other and along different lines in separate parts of the country with each pursuing his own special interest, began resuscitating the dances that were in the process of disappearing. Wherever they could find dance, they began protecting and encouraging it. They reconstructed still others from temple sculptures which illustrated dance poses and groupings and even costumes in meticulous detail, and from ancient manuscripts, often relying on the instincts and intuitions with which their national heritage more than generously endowed them.

36

Respectable Brahmin ladies began to dance in public, the first being Rukmini Devi of Kalakshetra in Adyar. Great *devadasi* like Balasaraswathi began to perform on stages before ticket-buying audiences far away from the temples and well within the law. Scholars like Dr. V. Raghavan of the University of Madras made dance a special field of serious study. Pioneers like Uday Shankar performed abroad and attracted a réclame there which added lustre to their names and the art at home. Poets philanthropically gave their fortunes to newly formed academies of dance and gathered together the last remaining teachers to instruct a new generation of performers. Along with all this ferment, political and administrative leaders of good reputation began to grace performances with their presence and write approving, quotable sentiments in the guestbooks and albums of the schools and artists.

From this emerged what we now know as the four schools of Indian dance, Bharata Natyam, Kathakali, both of the South, and Kathak and Manipuri, from the North, all of these being modern designations for ancient forms. At present it now appears that once again dance is clearly delineated and defined, codified and examined, and never before has it cut through regional barriers and geographical distances and become so widely familiar as a whole throughout the entire country.

The achievement of reinstating dance in so short a time was something of a miracle. A complete revival of any nation's dance arts is patently not an easy task, and although all of the Four Schools as we know them today are fragmentary, vestigial, and even have crippling defects and lacunae in many instances (in the same sense that the movements of classical ballet are formalized and restrictive in the range of their expressiveness), a vitality has remained within them. The direct line that runs from them back to ornate sculptures in ruined temples and musty, moldy, faded manuscripts, as well as their relationship with dance forms in other parts of Asia, connects them directly with India's purest antiquity. Despite the growth and decline, the development and regression, the dance in India today testifies to the endurance of a genuine art instinct and demonstrates that the underglow of appreciation never quite died out but smouldered deep within the soul of the nation and its once great past.

In the light of the energetic dance activity of the past few years, to talk about the streams of Indian dance and drama drying up is misleading. So much has remained; so much still is accounted for. The disruption in Indian theatre arts is of course an historical fact, but the amount that still exists and is re-emerging is nothing short of astonishing. Other countries may have more dancing, or more easily procured dances, or even greater arts, but the reminders of the past have always persisted in India. The Indian's unconscious rapport with his great traditions has given a natural continuity. And because of India's geographical vastness nowhere in a single country are there more contrasts, more diversity, more challenging propositions laid before the students of movement and seekers after aesthetic pleasure.

Few will dispute that of the Four Schools, Bharata Natyam (the name is derived from Bharata's canonical treatise on dramaturgy, the *Bharata Natya Sastra*) as it is seen in Madras today where the best teachers and dancers have gravitated, is the most significant in India. Certainly even in its present form it is the most completely preserved and the most anciently documented of any living classic. An entire recital of Bharata Natyam takes around two and a half hours, and the solo dancer, usually a woman (performances by men ceased several centuries ago), presents a series of items designed to display a rich variety of body movements, vertiginous speed in stomping complex rhythms with her feet (made more audible by anklets of tinkling bells), and almost superhuman endurance of strength and stamina.

In the middle of her program she offers a series of Padas. These are songs in Sanskrit, Tamil or other South Indian vernaculars, which are sometimes slow and sentimental, sometimes changeable and abrupt with contrasting expressions of emotions, and always deeply religious and devotional in import. The dancer, either singing the words in unison with her accompanists or forming them silently with her lips, enacts the song in minutest detail with highly exaggerated expressions of the face and clear formations of the fingers and hands, generally referred to as *mudras*, to interpret each word, meaning by meaning, in a special gesture-language.

Padas occupy a special place in the hearts of South Indians whose understanding and feeling for Bharata Natyam is keen. Whereas we in the West are inclined to applaud, say, a brilliant pirouette or the perfect precision of the "dance" part of a classical ballet rather than its thin story, the Indian approaches his art differently. He will watch, appreciatively or critically, the initial portions of the program where the emphasis is on virtuosity, mastery of detailed movements and closeness to the oldest traditions, but he relaxes and settles in when the Padas with their poetic narrative begin. The recital then takes on a private tone, and a kind of intimate relationship develops between the dancer and the spectator. When a genuine artist like the great Balasaraswathi of Madras performs Padas, her forte, she endows the art with a luminosity hard to find among dancers anywhere else in the world.

The secret of the Pada is twofold: one, to convey the meaning of each word, phrase, and sentence with literal gestures and precise facial expressions, and, two, to interpret the sentences of the song over and over again in a variety of completely differing, contrasting ways. For instance, if the sentence is "I worship you, oh my Lord Siva," the dancer literally acts out those words with her hands and face, but then she must improvise further interpretations. "Worship" can be indicated humbly or proudly (as a wife worships a husband), religiously (as a penitent undergoing austerities or praying in the temple) or profanely by coyly flirting with the god as if he were human. Or she can be angry with the god and twist the theme into "Did you think I did not worship you?" Simply put, the gesticulation can describe adoration in any spiritual or temporal manner.

The name of any god in India carries with it an unlimited number of manifestations and forms, all of which lend themselves to interpretive movement. Every god has his attributes, characteristics and symbols. Siva can be the cobra, the bull, the river Ganges, the trident, the moon. He is the creator, destroyer, dancer or warrior. The permutations of any word of a phrase are almost incalculable, and an accomplished dancer exploits them to an extent which exhausts all possible variants.

One of the finest Padas performed by Balasaraswathi is the celebrated *Krishna ni begane* which simply means "Lord Krishna, come to me." There is one line in the song which goes "Thy mother saw all the world reflected in Thy mouth," and here in one of Balasaraswathi's interpretations a climactic moment comes. She shows the god Krishna as a naughty child and calls him to her, but as she looks down into his eyes she is overcome with love—the love of a mother for a son. She cups his face in her hand and leans over to kiss him, but at that moment it suddenly becomes the kiss of a man, and she darts back startled and troubled by the strange shift in the relationship. The god is become a lover. This example shows how far afield from the simple text the acting or expressiveness (*abhinaya* in Sanskrit) can go, but the inventiveness and originality permitted the dancer in Padas is one of the greatest concepts ever advanced in dance.

For the foreigner, Padas at first may seem a little too dense a texture both linguistically and religiously. But if you take with you an expert interpreter who is familiar with and patronizes the dance, the experience of hearing his explanations serves to convey the sensitive beauty of the original. It is possible in this way to sit through a performance enjoying and reacting exactly as any knowledgeable spectator does. The difference is that you are hearing in English what the others are hearing in Sanskrit, Tamil, Telugu or Canarese. But whatever the language, the gesturing is virtually international and the intellectual mechanics of understanding are, of course, universal. As a general principle anywhere in Asia, the foreigner should exercise the greatest discretion in trusting his artistic intuition at first. The initial differences between the arts of Asia and the West are enormous, and until you are fairly well acquainted with the conventions and have a sense of the proper aesthetic approach, you had best rely on an interpreter. I have never heard a seriously unappreciative remark about any of Asia's major dance or drama forms, except from a philistine unsympathetic to his own arts or from an outsider who has wandered into a theatre without a guide to tell him what was being performed. Similarly, I have also heard people dilate ecstatically about a dancer when the explanation has been coherent, and others deplore the same program when they have not been clearly or intelligently informed of what they were seeing.

Of course, the spectacle of dance in Asia is nearly always exciting for the Westerner who is accustomed to more drabness in his theatre. Even a Bharata Natyam recital, which is one of the more restrained and subdued programs in Asia, being a solo and performed in a single costume, is still colorful and impressive simply to look at. The palms of the dancer's hands, the soles of her feet and a large round circle between her eyebrows are stained bright red with temple powder. Her sari, tightly fitted around her body and thighs, will invariably be of gold embroidery and a patterned mixture of clashing, riotous colors. Her jewelry is of special appeal. A dancer can wear as many rings as she likes and on any finger, bracelets, and elbow armlets of gold. In her ears, she wears jewels not only in the lobes but in the upper part of the ear as well. In either nostril she will certainly wear a diamond or ruby, as well as a coruscating pendant hanging from the cartilege separating the nostrils. Down the part in her hair a row of gleaming diamonds will lead to a large oval of gold inlaid with precious stones which hangs over and covers the top of her forehead. In a large circle at the back of her head she wears garlands of flowers —jasmine, marigolds, frangipani or tuberoses—which wind in a chain down the long braid of hair. All these decorations indicate respect to the gods, an ornate display that all the preparations of beauty and devotion have been made before the god is further worshiped through the sacred ritual of dance. To add to the glitter of the stage, the musicians and singers, who are always men, usually have large sparkling diamonds flashing from their pierced earlobes.

After the interlude of Padas, the dancer has rested and recuperated her strength. She then performs a few more items of purely technical and rhythmical dancing. The recital concludes with a Tillana, one of the most exuberant outbursts of sheer dance movements. A Tillana is usually short and explodes on to the stage with swift, lively bends and dips, bursts of smiles, symmetrical leaps back and forth, to the right and left, and concludes in a clatter of cymbals and shouts from the singers, fluttering hands beating the drums, and a shimmering whir of the dancer's anklebells. Tillanas tell no story nor are they even descriptive in a general sense. They are performed to an accompaniment of chanted, meaningless syllables, often without regard for the melody of the music. The dance conveys joyousness and abandonment to that peculiar thrill associated in India with religious ecstasy, the ultimate emotional state of the human being when in attunement with his gods.

Along the West coast of South India, in the Malabar area, you find the home of Kathakali (literally, recited action) dance-dramas, the second of the Four Schools. Because of Kathakali's exotic setting amid lamp-lit, sandy beaches, coconut palms and tree-shaded temple parvis, and because of the impracticability of transferring it to the

41

harsh glare of the stage, only a few sporadic and modified performances have ever been given outside its native home. But even there, performances of it have become rare. The troupe which the Maharaja of Travancore briefly supported before the princely States were merged into the Union of India and had their powers and purses curtailed, has been disbanded. Villages spend their surplus money on other entertainments now, and many of the traditional dancers have been reabsorbed into professions which guarantee them a steadier livelihood.

Today, the only place to see regular Kathakali performances is at the poet Vallathol's school, Kerala Kalamandalam. There it is at its best and under its most ideal conditions. To reach it you must fly to Cochin in the heart of Malabar, then make a three-hour train ride to Shoranur, then either walk or ride in an oxcart (there might be some local official's car at the station which will give you a lift) for a mile further inland across the river to the village of Cheruthuruthi where there is a simple Guest Bungalow next to the school. At your leisure you can see the young dancers practicing throughout the day—the training is rigorous and requires lengthy massages to limber the body so that it can hold the correct positions—and you can order in the evening a full-dress performance for around twenty-five dollars. You can commission specific scenes from the *Ramayana* or *Mahabharata* and even select the type of excerpts you wish to see—love scenes of requited or unrequited love, heroic battles, scenes of cruelty and bloodshed, or the dance sequences which have no story attached to them.

Four aspects may startle the outsider witnessing Kathakali for the first time, and he should be prepared for them. First, all the dancers are men. Young boys take the roles of women with yellow painted faces, false breasts, and a large cloth draped over their head to hide their short hair (short, that is, by Indian standards).

Second, the make-up for characters such as the demons and gods and monkeys is extremely, almost frighteningly, grotesque. On the day of a performance, the make-up artists begin work in the early hours of the morning and continue until late afternoon. They mix the paints (they used to grind lapis lazuli and mix it with mustard oil to produce the special blue) and apply it line by line to the actor-dancer. They slowly and carefully trace design after design of curling, twirling lines of black, white, orange, red and blue over the cheeks and forehead. For demons they stick gobs of putty like huge bulbous warts on the nose and forehead. For other characters, they paste semicircles of scissored paper along the jawbones. Finally the dancer inserts a tiny seed into each eye which immediately inflames the whole eyeball and the bloodshot expression adds to the fearsomeness. At the end of these elaborate preparations, the features of the dancer's face are quite obliterated, and his normal appearance completely disguised.

The third surprise for the foreigner is that the costumes are not only strange but almost monotonously uniform. Nearly all characters of the play wear huge crowns and halos of painted circles, encrusted with shards of sparkling mirrors; all of them wear long-sleeved jackets, on to some of which they sew yards of colored fringe; and all are dressed in huge billowing skirts and underskirts of white cotton cloth. While the performers practice and rehearse in the near-nudity normally appropriate to the tropics which permits seeing the movement of each body muscle, for the actual performance they cover their bodies so heavily with cloth that only the hands and feet are visible.

The fourth unusual aspect for the outsider is the deafening roar of the drums which starts long before the performance opens, continues during it, and does not stop until the morning hours when the play comes to an end. The drummers who pound their instruments incessantly and with all their strength perform in relays. When one exhausts himself, another immediately takes over and continues the raucous tattoo of rhythmic patterns.

Kathakali performances take place around a tall, waist-high, brass lamp stand filled with coconut oil and sputtering, hand-rolled, cotton wicks. The lamp illuminates the performance, a substitute for footlights, and whenever a character has an important moment to dance out, he rushes to the lamp, fans the air around it which makes the guttering wicks flare brightly and light up his weird face of quivering, bloodshot eyes and trembling chin and cheek muscles.

Kathakali is the only dance of India which uses any form of a curtain, but it is handled in its own unique way and at considerable variance from its function in the West. A typical curtain consists of a wide rectangle of tricolored cloth held between the stage and the lamp by two stagehands in ordinary dress (barechested, except for the

43

three Hindu threads over the shoulder and a necklace of balsam beads, and a long draped loin-cloth of white cotton). They stand motionless holding the curtain taut while the dancers perform a series of behind-the-scene dances. When Ravana or Rama are to make an angry entrance, they perform the thrilling and terrifying sequence colloquially known as "peering over the curtain." The character grabs it and pulls it with all his might in and out, thus fanning the lamp until the flames are dangerously high. Then, while still hiding his face, he runs his hands, ornamented with long, curved, silver claws, along the length of the curtain and, stomping loudly, rattles the rows of bells on his legs which encase not only the ankles but the full length of the shin. When the proper tension is built, he finally shows the awesome aspect of his make-up. When the action of the dance proper starts the curtain drops to the floor and one of the men whisks it off to the side until it is required again for another spectacular entrance.

In sharp contrast with Bharata Natyam which is essentially a woman's art, Kathakali is extraordinarily virile. Its actions are bombastic and exaggerated, its pace grandiose with huge leaps and jumps, and even moments when the dancers leap into the air and plunge down on the floor with their legs stretched in a full split. The dancers never speak, except for an occasional shrill cry, and the musicians who stand at the back beating gongs and cymbals sing the poetic stanzas into the ears of the performers describing their actions and exhorting them to greater and more gigantic tasks. Throughout the entire performance, a dancer's hands are active. He forms with *mudras* and gestures each word the singer enunciates. There are specific finger positions and hand movements not only for nouns and adjectives, but special formations which by convention stand for adverbs, conjunctions, and declensions as well. Any competent Kathakali dancer knows about five hundred *mudras* and can, if you improvise a sentence on the spur of the moment, put it instantly, even while you talk, into this sign language of the dance.

The only woman dancer who has ever made a genuine study of Kathakali is the Bharata Natyam dancer, Shanta Rao, who has appeared in New York with signal success. Her femininity within an essentially masculine form gives Kathakali an extraordinarily affecting aesthetic reaction. The original ballets she has composed in

44

Kathakali style are unquestionably the most brilliant contribution to modern Indian dance since Uday Shankar's creations.

Kathak, the third of the Four Schools of Indian dance, belongs to North India. Lucknow in the province of Uttar Pradesh (formerly the United Provinces), maintains the Hindustani School of Music which has a department of this style of dance where the best of the traditions are studied and taught. Jaipur, the important tourist center in Rajastan famous in the West for is enamelware jewelry, its rose-colored palaces, its polo and its affable maharaja, is, artistically speaking, the home of some of the country's finest Kathak artists. There is a friendly rivalry between Lucknow and Jaipur over which has the best dancing. The differences between the two styles are subtle, and for the outsider on the threshold of his dance study, his preference will depend on the personality of the dancer rather than on the intricate difference between specific steps and movements which the local expert finds so engrossing.

The Northern part of India was the first area to be conquered by the invading Mohammedans, and it was from the North that the mighty Moghuls ruled. Near their courts cultural Mohammedanization was most apparent, and Hinduism along with its arts and habits submitted to greater changes there than in the areas further South where vast distances separated the Muslim rulers from their subjects. According to the religious tenets of Mohammedanism—the invasion of India was in the beginning a holy war of conversion—representation of god or the graphic depiction of god or god's work, man, was proscribed in art. The religion of Islam is primarily an austere one. And even today in India the mosques are empty rooms, the sermons advise the faithful on the rigid conduct of their daily lives, and the Muslim when he prays faces an invisible Mecca. Dancing has always been condemned, in theory at least although the practice has been impossible to suppress, throughout the Muslim world not merely because it is often a temptation and corrupting influence in the social life of the people, but because it approximated too closely the worship of god in man's image. This latter has invariably been precisely the point of Hindu dance—to represent god, to imitate him, to copy his celestial movement on earth in front of his pious human devotees.

Thus, while the Hindu arts have been interpretive to the point of

45

voluptuousness, the Muslim ones have been almost antiseptic in their abstraction. Their genius has flourished in the fields of music and mathematics, architecture and decorative embellishment. Kathak is a marriage in dance, workable if not ideal, of these two diametrically opposed religious opinions. The style of North Indian dancing that the Muslims first encountered was sacrilegious and anathema to them. But the dynamics of Hinduism were not quite destructible. Gradually, as the rulers became more and more Hinduized and Indian, the irrepressible place of dance among the people became more acceptable. The result was that Kathak, the old Hindu dance, turned into a mathematical exercise requiring an almost purely intellectual and non-emotional attention.

Kathak as it stands today comprises several hundred rhythmic patterns—some only a few bars long, others of enormous complication lasting for a hundred measures with more than a thousand prescribed beats regulated within them. These rhythms are chanted by a singer sitting near the *tabla* drummer with special syllables, indicating all the stresses, caesurae, slurs, off-beats, and syncopations. This pattern is then copied by the clicks, thumps and thuds of the drums in a simulacrum of the vocal rhythm. Then the dancer taps out the identical meter with her feet, embellishing it with stylized movements of her arms and body. Because of her anklebells, the audience can detect the slightest deviation from the model established for her by the singer and the drummer. The spectator sits in judgment on the dancer almost as if waiting for her to make an error. Because the rhythms are traditional and familiar to any accomplished artist, the singer, dancer and drummer during a performance sometimes plunge simultaneously into the same rhythmic pattern with only the slightest signal or forewarning almost as if by intuition. Artists of the foremost rank, like the Maharaj brothers, will occasionally improvise one rhythm against that of their accompanists. Their triumph comes when they all finish on precisely the right beat at the end of this rhythmic counterpoint.

An audience at a Kathak recital listens rather than looks, and a thoroughgoing critic of the dance prefers to sit with his eyes closed. The bulk of a Kathak program consists of these rhythms, exhibited serially one after the other, and ranging from simple to difficult. The dancer stands in the center of the arena, her flesh quivering as she slaps her feet steadily against the floor (usually of tiles, to increase the resonance) and the allotted metrical pattern increases in celerity and intricacy. The number of body movements a dancer uses in the course of these rhythms is limited. The arms swing in the air picking out of it invisible designs and forming charming configurations of the body and its postures. She spins her body around in a series of turns without leaving the designated spot in the center of the stage. The spectator grows dizzy at the sight, as the dancer looks like a blur of whirls.

After a suitable interval, the program becomes lightly representational with Ghats whose fragments break the focus and intense concentration required of the spectator by the number of successive, complex rhythms. Ghats reveal only the merest suggestions of a specific action—women carrying pots on their heads, a god playing the flute, ladies strolling in the garden—and they are the only Hindu remnants left to this otherwise Mohammedanized dance.

Some Kathak dancers, however, conclude their program informally by sitting down before you and singing *gazals* or short stanzas of poetry. As they sing they improvise vague gestures. Each song concludes with an unexpected play on words or a double meaning, revealed only by the last line which conveys an entirely different meaning from the one anticipated. A Kathak enthusiast once illustrated this convention for me with an impromptu poem. Remembering the court setting of conventional Kathak he recited, "The Queen is uniquely lovely. Her face is round, of a shining beauty. She illumines the darkness of my nights . . ." but at the moment when the poem might be considered lèse-majesté, he added, "She is the queen of the night—the moon." (There was also an interior Indian play on words —typical of the *gazal*—for "queen of the night" is the Hindi name for a sweet-smelling jasmine of romantic associations.)

Gesticulation in Kathak is always understated (as the Padas are always over-played) and there are no *mudras* of any clarity or belonging to an accepted convention. Kathak is an extreme and uttermost attenuation of what obviously once was a literal and expressionist dance form. But this rarification gives it a special flavor unique in India, and a taste for it, once acquired after a recital by artists like

47

Shambo Maharaj, or Brijju, his nephew, or Kumari Roshan, a young newcomer, or the more pyrotechnical, meretricious display of the movie star, Sitara, is hard to lose.

Kathak is a new name for the old *nautch*, that most alluring and most degraded of Indian dance forms. From the foreigner's point of view, the eroticism associated with this form of dancing is somewhat obscure. But the Muslims found it so titillating that women were discouraged from performing it except in the brothels, and young boys in the Court and in public often substituted for them. Scarcely awakened youths were originally introduced in an effort to make the dance sexless. But it was not long before they were imitating the soft feminine movements, tapping out the rhythms, and in the Ghats, enacting subtle, half-indicated love themes, as lecherously as if they were really girls. Even the poetry speaks in places of the lover as a boy, although from the convention you know that actually a woman is meant. To refer directly to love and woman was apparently too arousing.

The predilection for male as well as female dancers endured and Kathak today is the only dance of India which still is traditionally performed by either men or women. With the exceptions of Kathakali folk dances, which are communal affairs and danced by the entire village, and Kathak's sexual ambivalence, dance in India as it has evolved today is preponderantly a pursuit of women. While there is no stigma attached to male dancers—considerably less, one would venture, than in the West—it has now become more usual and acceptable for women to take precedence in the field. I know of no male movie stars, for instance, who dance, yet every actress is called upon sooner or later to perform at least a few steps. There has been for several years a quibbling controversy waged over the propriety of men dancing Bharata Natyam, although every evidence of the past justifies it. This heavy emphasis on women as dancers throughout India is particularly surprising since all dance teachers without exception are men. In most areas, the profession of teaching is hereditary, and generation after generation of fathers have handed their secrets down to their sons. Strangely, some of the greatest dance teachers in India today have never taken a dance step even in class, but continue to produce star pupils among their female dancers.

While the woman dancer may likely never teach, her teacher's sons however will continue the tradition.

The fourth of the Four Schools, Manipuri, derives from the dances found in the princely state of Manipur, now incorporated into the province of Assam, India's northeasternmost province on the border of Burma. Manipur is both a country and a valley. The country, some 7,500 square miles in size, is mostly mountainous (the highest being the lowest of the Himalayan range) and is inhabited by tribes of naked, headhunting aboriginals called collectively Nagas (each of their folk dances is different and engrossing). The valley, only 700 square miles, contains a marvellously civilized and artistic people.

In this valley against the dusty brown hills nearby and the dim blue higher hills of the distance, with a massive dome of sky holding one captive in paradise, live these fair-skinned, Mongolian-looking, gentle and graceful people. Their costumes vary from a loin cloth on casual occasions and in the home to a formal sarong wrapper of striped purple hanging from breasts to knees for the women and a thin, white *dhoti* around the hips and legs of the men.

As one arrives at Imphal, the capital and the site of the maharaja's palace, one is struck at once by the colorful charm of the people, the magnificence of the landscape, and the bracing coolness of the air (the valley is 6,000 feet high). The country is blessed naturally with life's basic necessities and a generous number of its luxuries: rice and vegetables flourish; edible birds and wild game abound; cotton and the silk worm are both indigenous; jungle timber clutters the hill-sides; indigo and tea can be found wild; hashish grows everywhere without supervision; and the orchids are so unusual and profuse that the government forbids their export for fear of undermining the Indian flower market. But of all the attributes of paradise which Manipur has, none is more vital and engaging than its theatrical arts.

For several centuries now Manipur has maintained a prodigiously high standard of art—in music, dance and drama—and the only comparable country I know of for national artistic excellence is Bali in Indonesia. Rabindranath Tagore discovered Manipur sometime in the 1920s and exported to his school the first Manipuri dance teacher ever to leave the country. Manipur became famous overnight, and because of the first teacher's success several other teachers left Manipur to seek their fortunes in Calcutta, in Delhi, the capital, and in Bombay, the commercial capital. The popularity of this new style of dancing was immediate everywhere, and Manipuri dance, in one form or another, is now practiced wherever there is dancing in India. The chief reason for its wide appeal and appreciation is its easy comprehensibility. It is also the least difficult to perform. In general, it has become the amateur's delight.

In Manipur itself, however, the dance now universally known as "Manipuri" is deplored. Whenever, for instance, a newsreel in a theatre shows it being performed before some national dignitary or on some special occasion, the Manipuris titter with exasperation. There is a wide gap between what Indians think Manipuri is and how the Manipuri themselves dance. The costume, for instance, which is always associated with Manipuri dancing is in Manipur itself reserved only for the most sacred performance of their operas. It is the lovely velvety hoopskirt studded with sequins and discs of silver, a tight bodice of bright peasant colors, and a shimmering veil of silver gauze sprayed with mica which hangs over the head and face. The dancer's hair is knotted at the side of the head and circled with a ring of fragrant white flowers.

The short dances on themes which figure in the repertoire of Indian-style Manipuri dancers are usually the created invention of teachers and pupils outside the country and unknown in Manipur. The usual themes for these dances are mood pictures of spring, of going to the temple with flowers to place at the feet of the image of Lord Krishna, the favorite god in the North of India, and his flirtations with the milkmaids, or the dance with flaming trays where the morning sun is greeted with sacred fire. Within the thirty years during which these performances have been seen in India, Manipuri style has managed to establish itself and now it can, despite abuses and the liberties taken with it, be called a genuine school of Indian dance. Its future obviously will grow more and more remote from Manipur, but as each genuine artist adds to it, a profound if eclectic art will eventually develop outside its home area.

The chief attribute of Manipuri dancing, both in Manipur itself and outside the country, is its graceful turning and swaying. The dancer's body continually seems to dissolve and re-arise in flowing, sinuous curves as the gentle hand and arm gestures melt one into the other. Excessively limpid softness was a tremendously new and fresh inspiration for India, whose dance styles had been up to then primarily energetic, electric and explosive. Manipur has given Indian dance as a whole today a sweetness entirely absent from the angular precision of Bharata Natyam, or the vigorousness of Kathakali, or the mathematics of Kathak.

In Manipur itself you find a nation of dancers. In the isolation of the valley, settled originally by religious refugees fleeing from the Mohammedan persecutions of the sixteenth century, you find a form of Hindu worship through dance and music in a remarkably unchanged and unadulterated state. Every village must dance for a month out of every year, for example, otherwise the felicity of the country and its immediate contact with the protective gods is adversely affected. In these dances everyone takes part from tiny children who can scarcely keep in step, to the oldest men, who swagger and improvise new steps to keep the younger ones alert and to prevent themselves from being bored by the years of repetition of the same dances. On special full-moon nights, the young men of the towns roam the streets following the sound of music, and wherever they find it, they join in the dancing even with strangers. During these all-night-long dances they can hold the hands of any unmarried girl allowed on these occasions to stay out until dawn.

The most significant contribution of Manipur to the world of art are its Ras Lilas which have not been performed outside the country and which no non-Manipuri can simulate. These are dance-operas in which specially trained professional artists sing and dance and act to the accompaniment of a large orchestra of conch shells, various stringed instruments, dozens of large, ringing hand cymbals, and drums. The Ras Lila, while being very famous as a legend and as a theme (it is the heavenly dance of the god Krishna amusing himself in the garden of Brindavan with his milkmaids) is a jealously guarded, almost secret art-form. Since travelers to Manipur are extremely rare, it has almost never been seen by non-Manipuris. It is a complex matter for the tourist to find a performance. For centuries there was no contact between Manipur and the outside world, and whenever there was it was unpleasant—neighboring warlike Burmese penetrating the protective cordon of savage Nagas periodically raided the valley (one of Manipur's sub-valleys still belongs to Burma), mercenary traders from Bengal infiltrated and absorbed the economy of the country by their little shops and cornerings of the market. Finally in 1889, when the British were consolidating their colony of India (Manipur was the last to accede), they sent to investigate the country a Political Officer whom the Manipuris promptly assassinated. These events have fostered a reserve and reluctance on the part of the Manipuris to deal with outsiders. Added to this are the exclusive rules and regulations of Manipur's strict Hinduism. They cannot eat with anyone who is a non-Hindu and therefore casteless, all temples are closed to impure foreigners of other faiths, and the Ras Lila, which is their most sacred representation of their most cherished god, is surrounded by a miasma of mystery. If you are lucky enough to be told of a performance, you must stand outside the pavilion erected afresh especially for each performance just beyond where the shadow of the eaves falls.

Ras Lilas are only held during the full moons of March, October and December. To see one, you should arrive in Manipur early, and begin by asking everyone you meet where and when a performance will take place. Once the people see that you are in earnest, someone will probably help you. Your patience will most certainly be rewarded, however, because the Ras Lila of Manipur is one of the most remarkable achievements in Asian art. I know of nothing more musically competent, as spiritually moving, or even vaguely resembling it anywhere in the world. The singers with their lightly powdered faces and flashing, ornamented costumes move through the eight-hour performance with an unequalled vocal ease and brilliance. Their singing, completely different from that found in India, is full of vibratos, trills, catches in the throat, and an ecstatic warmth that the rigid, methodical performances of India lack as far as the unaccustomed Western ear is concerned. The perfect proportion between dancing and arias, choruses and orchestral interludes, produces as finely constructed a composition as any aesthetic law teaches. The overall mood is strange. It focusses on the ecstatic relationship between the worshiper and god. It is supernal, but emotional in a human and physical sense at the same time. The audience weeps volubly from ravishment rather than sorrow, and whether through some

52

sort of mysticism or simply because of art, the effect nevertheless penetrates the foreign auditor and is an overwhelming experience.

The field of folk dancing, aside from whatever decline it may have suffered in the past, still remains a substantial area for research. You need only ask for local dancing wherever you are in India, in the towns and villages and away from the cities, and a performance can be easily arranged. It may be extremely simple and even unexciting, but it will sometimes be beautiful and complex. Dance in some form and of some degree of excellence is always available. You may only see "stick dancing," the one type common to all parts of India, where a group of men or women holding two short sticks dance in a circle while they rhythmically strike the sticks the other dancers are holding, or in places you may find only a motionless, unanimated, slow shuffle, but the dances will always be interesting. The variety and contrasts between neighboring sections of the country is a never-ending surprise. Basically, folk dancing is more amusing to do than to see and participation in it as with our square dancing, for instance, is its chief appeal. But in India these dances number literally in the thousands, and the sum total of this array of movement, foot and hand patterns, costume, and musical accompaniment, is an inexhaustible field of study not only for the anthropologist but especially for the dancer in search of new movements and new areas of exploration for the furtherance of his own art.

The revival of Indian dance at first was a matter for intellectuals and dancers. Soon their success percolated through to official circles and the general public. Where once it was chic for the wealthy society of Bombay or Calcutta to subject their guests after dinner to a program of Western music by a local string quartet, now it has become fashionable to present a dancer. A number of the social leaders in the bigger cities introduce their favorite dance protégés fairly frequently at private parties, and even subsidize their more occasional public performances. All over the country little societies have sprung up to which people contribute a small amount of money monthly, and out of this fund they are able to pay for various dancers from all over the country to appear before them at an evening's performance. It has been extraordinary to watch these groups, such as Noopur in Bombay, and see how in a matter of a few years they have grown from a handful of friends banding together with an amateur interest in dance into big running organizations which pay sizable sums to whatever artists they invite. Another excellent hopeful change in attitude is that whereas formerly these groups considered themselves lucky to present a first-rate artist, now a dancer speaks of performing before them as an honor.

In 1955, for the first time in many, many centuries, dancers in India received national, official recognition of the sort they were once accorded by kings and courts. For the previous three years, the Government of India had instituted what were called the Presidential Awards for which "artists of the year" were summoned to Delhi, feted, and, during an impressive ceremony attended by dignitaries of every kind, were presented with a scroll, gold bracelets and necklaces, shawls and gold-embroidered pieces of cloth. This practice originated with the Government-sponsored Sangeet Nataka Akademi (Academy of music, dance, drama and films—the last three words in English are covered by the Sanskrit word, Nataka) whose aim is to protect the arts and encourage performers in each of these fields. But until 1955 the only recipients were musicians, their art being the most respected and respectable one in India. Branches of the central organization have been formed in each province and each city of any importance with the idea of furthering India's indigenous art-forms after their years of neglect. The Presidential awards are made after consulting confidentially a cross-section of scholars and critics of the country, and the selection of the artist requires virtually unanimous agreement.

The dancers honored in 1955 were Balasaraswathi, the magnificent Bharata Natyam dancer of Madras, and Shamboo Maharaj, the youngest of the three Maharaj brothers whose dancing substantially helped raise Kathak to its present level of brilliance. This occasion, with all its pomp and ceremony, with the highest officers of the government garlanding the artists and making speeches of praise, was to many people far more than the honoring of two deserving artists; it was the crowning achievement in the revival of dance art in India today, and the fullest recognition, at last, of the now established place that dance once again occupies.

INDIA

The great Balasara-
swathi in an interpre-
tive dance gesture

R. V. Leyden

Gerald Eastmure

The hashish smoking scene from Manipur's successful drama *Lownam*

Backstage at the Manipuri theatre

Gerald Eastmure

Ewing Krainin

CEYLON

The king and queen in the Kolam folk drama

Dancers and drummers in Kandyan dance

Two lions in a scene of Kolam

The dancer Tilaka, Kolam's most brilliant and acrobatic performer

Ewing Krainin

Gunaya, the celebrated Kandyan dancer, in a series of decorative and descriptive poses showing the vitality, changefulness and meditative qualities of dance

BURMA   The grand old man of dance, Po Sein, and his partner, College
Sein, in a climactic *pas de deux* of a Zat Pwé

Lionel Landry

A sword dance of Upper Burma among the Shans

THAILAND

A scene from *The Red Bandit*, a Likay popular drama

Siamrath Press

A prince and princess flying through the air in a Lakon
dance drama

Today, it is impossible to consider dance in India without paying more than passing attention to the motion pictures. India's film industry is the third largest in the world, lagging not far behind Hollywood and Japan in bulk of production. In modern Indian life the place of dance is nowhere more clearly indicated. All films must, by a tacit law understood by all the producers, abound in long, elaborate dance sequences. There is one I recall in which fifty glamorous maidens danced on fifty huge tympani drums for the longest time I have ever seen in a movie, and such dances together with their songs are the chief drawing-power of the motion picture industry. If you open any newspaper in India, the advertisements will generally show the leading actress in a dance pose. The number of dances to be seen in a particular movie will be heralded the way one would announce in America the number of star actors. One film led off its première with the phrase, "The Most Stupendous Gevacolour Dance Sequence in Indian Motion Picture History." The movies also buy up much of the best talent of the country and convert it to suit the general level of taste that all motion picture industries everywhere seem inclined to cater to. Several of the best dancers have entered the movies in order to make their livelihood, as performers, advisors or choreographers.

The movies too, unfortunately in India as everywhere else, are something of an enemy to the survival of live-talent entertainment and endanger the art. The average man actually has no need to patronize dance apart from the films. Often he cannot even if he would. The films draw out from the pockets of the vast majority of people, by providing long and full programs cheaply, the little money the family sets aside for amusements. The financial proportion is roughly four to one, that is, one can see four first-grade movies for the price of the cheapest seat at a dance recital by a reputable artist. This is an important factor in a country such as India where wages are low and the standard of living pared down to barest essentials.

The tremendous emphasis dance is given in the movies, while it is an expression of national taste, also carries with it some serious aesthetic problems. Chief of these—there are notable exceptions like Kumari Kamala (Bharata Natyam) or Sitara (Kathak) who are skilled technicians and somewhat uncompromising purists—is the

55

new style of dancing that has evolved. The new style has now become stiff competition especially since much of the Indian instinct for dance is generously satisfied there. "Movie dancing" or "Oriental dancing," with the pejorative connotations of those phrases in English, describe the kind of performance. It draws heavily from the Four Schools but still lies outside any one of them. To explain this we must go into the aesthetics of Indian dance briefly.

Dance, by its nature, is primarily traditional in India, as it is in all Asia. Intrinsically it is not invented or dreamt up by an individual as his own unique personal expression; although the dancer improvises in a thoroughgoing way that has been forgotten in the West, it is improvisation according to classical rules of a controlled character. There is, according to the theory of dance, nothing openly creative about it. An analogy may be made with the function of a pianist performing Beethoven or Chopin; he is not expected to create. Here, as in Indian dance, the artist is concerned with re-creation or interpreting other media than his own (one is a performer, the other a composer) and ones that are removed from him personally by belonging to other times and even other countries. The spectator's pleasure derives from the genius of the interpreter-performer shining through the façade of the already familiar, well-known form.

Dance as it has been reconstructed in India has to a Westerner and Westernized way of thinking a certain number of limitations about it. Many situations or emotions cannot be treated within the orthodox forms. Non-religious subjects or modern, everyday life below the level of the eternal verities, for instance, are expressed with difficulty, notwithstanding a few Padas on Gandhi, his spinning wheel, the Salt March and his martyr's death. The ordinary entertainment seeker, too, finds himself vaguely dissatisfied with rigid adherence to dances of the past as a tradition alone. In Asia this feeling is also a Western contamination spread by Hollywood. He now demands quicker contrasts and more restlessly changing and divergent movements. This, naturally enough, is the outcome of the increase in pace and tempo which seems to characterize our modern world.

There are also technical factors working against classic dances. The more tradition regulates form and formula, the greater the difficulty of perfecting their execution. It is, generally speaking in a practical sense, harder to reproduce perfectly what is accepted as the rule of the past than it is to branch out into one's own new set of regulations. A dancer in India ends up being forced to devote his or her entire life to the mastery of a single form. Dance in this light presents almost insurmountable difficulties. Although there are Four Schools, a dancer normally belongs to only one school. This point needs clarification for the Westerner. From the beginning of the revival, certain dancers and certainly all those who have appeared abroad in Europe or America or before Westernized audiences in the large cities of India have attempted a variety show of all the different schools. This was necessary in order to include sufficient contrasts within their program to appeal to audiences who were neither specialists nor born to a knowledge of indigenous dance.

Some of these attempts were successful. Shanta Rao, for instance, is almost as familiar with Kathakali as she is with Bharata Natyam. Ram Gopal moves almost equally easily between Kathak and Bharata Natyam. Uday Shankar, the most successful of all Indian dancers abroad, offers excerpts from all the schools but his special contribution was that he added an entirely new element to Indian dance, that of Western showmanship. Shankar approximates the Westerner's concept of dance most closely in that he treats it as a creative art, and in fact bases it only opaquely and cloudily on Indian classical movements. His extraordinary genius lies in his magical ability to create atmosphere. The dreamlike air about his dancing which so enchants the spectator is oddly enough totally absent from dance in an Indian sense. His weakness as an Indian dancer is the fact that although he personally places Kathakali as his foremost vehicle, he has never attempted it in public except suggestively and by indirection. He insists that unschooled audiences cannot follow the *mudras*, would be deafened by the drums, and find the costumes and make-ups absurd. Perhaps this idea belongs to the past, to another era, not to today, which seems to be at least so far a decade of reciprocal international art understanding and indulgence of the genuinely exotic.

But aside from this group of artists, many of the other dancers have been failures in their attempts to inject variety and range into their dancing. They neither had the technical ease to cope with the Four Schools, nor the necessary creativity to add to the art. One of these dancers in a certain ballet she performs holds a contest with

herself before the gods dancing all the Four Schools in rapid succession (each more badly danced than the last, in my opinion, and
the gods, according to the ballet, in a dilemma, I surmise, award
each a prize). Another group performs to the accompaniment of
loud-speakers declaiming English. Regardless of how one may condone or deplore the various artists of this kind, the fact is that they
are attempting solutions to the very real problems of classical dance
and how to adjust it to the new conditions in which it finds itself.

The same problems besetting serious artists of the classical dance
also involved the movies. They needed to find a dance which was not
exactly ignorant, because the ticket-buying spectator in India is on
the whole moderately aware of at least one of the Four Schools (the
one belonging to his part of the country) and yet which would satisfy the new demands of modern taste. Undoubtedly they were apprised of the international success abroad of Indian dance and the
compromises its artists made there and even in India. Large numbers
of people enjoying a program generally represent a somewhat lower
standard of appreciation than that required by smaller, more select
audiences. So the problem was easier to solve by the movies than it
was for the artists who sought a blend of styles without losing the
initial quality of each. The movie dancing which resulted now combines aspects of technique and virtuosity of the traditionally trained
dancer, along with the sweet softening of the Manipuri influence,
plus a mélange of movements from every part of the country.

In the beginning of the movie industry this caused horror. To the
traditionalist it seemed a jumble of inexpert violations of all aesthetic principles. Some of the monstrosities that flickered on the
screen made one apprehensive that before the revival of serious dance
could be consummated, the movies would already have corrupted
public taste for it. Fortunately such fears were ungrounded. The two
approaches are still being made independently, each evolving according to its own requirements, each attaining the recognition it deserves. Almost fortuitously, and most happily, movie dancing has improved. While to my taste it still is flaccid and emasculated, lacking
in the clear intensity which must mark great art, it is nevertheless
beginning to produce its own special flavor and most of all it has
created an entirely new dance area. It would not be surprising if this
medley of movement and gesture ultimately turns out to be the

dance of new India. A wildly demonstrative public certainly savors it avidly, and possibly this is the clearest proof that it expresses the mood and feelings of people in contemporary India. Strangely, after the years of cultural silence from India and almost as if in repetition of the expansionist days of the past, today wherever Indian films penetrate—in Malaya, Indonesia, Thailand—traces of its influence are beginning to glimmer faintly in local dance recitals of the cities.

The jeopardy to pure classic dance which this new dance of the movies and which even the international dancers induce is well recognized today. Radical action is being taken in an effort to protect and preserve this ancient heritage, finally and ultimately, against any further encroachment the present or future might bring. The most significant innovation in the world of Indian dance for many centuries occurred in 1955. Balasaraswathi after years of aloofness— partly because of the prestige lent her by her mother, one of the greatest singers India has produced, and her grandmother, an equally great player of the intricate stringed instrument, the vina, and partly because her position as a *devadasi* with her own personal entourage of devoted patrons has kept her outside the tensions and storms that affected the public at large—finally capitulated to the growing pressures on the serious artists of India. She presented herself, barefoot and carelessly dressed in a black sari the border of which was gaudily studded with sequins, at the distinguished Music Academy of Madras. In memorable and humble words she said, "New vogues are sweeping everywhere. I will start teaching for you the true and real dance as far as I know it." And now outside the Academy, an unprecedented sign and one deeply significant in the dance history of India announces:

BALASARASWATHI'S
SCHOOL OF BHARATA NATYA

This marks the first time a great practicing woman artist of India's most correct and aged traditions has placed her services as a teacher before the general public.

Drama Today

The history of drama anywhere in the world shows, broadly speaking, a thematic progression from gods to kings to ordinary men. The material in the beginning usually starts with the exploits and deeds of heavenly beings as its sole concern. As theatre develops and grows more independent of its sacerdotal origins, it treats of events in high places and important happenings in the ruling circles of the country. Finally, to complete the devolution, the common man begins to represent himself on the stage. The masses then derive theatrical enjoyment from seeing themselves and people like themselves depicted in situations which, while they probably never will occur, still might happen to them in real life. In the various countries, this progression usually evinces the changing tastes of the public and the efforts of its theatre people to keep abreast of the times. Normally, as one type of subject-matter supersedes another, the past is forgotten and its plays abandoned. Japan probably is the only country in the world where all these levels of subject-matter are still performed popularly and on an entirely profit-making basis. In the West, however, the last of the three stages of theatrical development, modern theatre, has taken priority over the rest, and Greek dramas, Miracles and Moralities of Europe, and even classical and historical plays of England assume something of a museum atmosphere or are performed almost as oddities or a cultural obligation rather than as expressions of general appeal.

The shift in India away from their theatre of the gods was a long and slow process. There are of course examples of kingly events and even of social satire in the Sanskrit dramas, but the bulk of the dramas and their motivations always dealt with godly events. As soon as drama took a step away from religion, it immediately returned, as we have seen. And while ordinary mortals may have been depicted amid gods, or later, kings, they were always in the guise of comedians, or presented in interludes and sub-plots coincidental to the more important enactions of their splendid superiors who enlighten and edify mortals. Of course, in India where the gods are made in the images of many men (instead of man being made in God's image—the more familiar theological point to us in the West), you feel less limitation in subject-matter. The gods have all the human failings and weaknesses as well as their virtues. But undoubtedly the thick coating of religious sentiment over drama deferred the ultimate growth of a modern theatre by centuries.

The new Indian theatre began around a hundred and fifty years ago, and it is now axiomatic to recognize that it stems directly from the West, and this was true as well of the rest of Asia. Modern theatre as a talking, non-religious, danceless, realistic, action-packed, abbreviated entertainment was for the most part the special preserve of Europe, and it initially received its highest development there. This is certainly one of the best legacies the West left its colonies in the East. Of course, it can be argued that Easterners would have discovered modern theatre by themselves without the tribulations of being colonized. There were innumerable evidences of a non-classical theatre even within the classics, and several theatre forms were "modern" at the time they first appeared. And certainly the adaptations of Western theatre were made according to Asian rules and predicated on Asian aesthetic values. For instance, rarely was the three-act formula of the well-made play used. Themes and techniques of singing and dancing so generously interspersed were of course typical of the individual countries. Perhaps the most striking contrast with the progenitor of the new theatre was that until very recently it remained the province of men. Men played all roles, including those of women, as they had done since the conception of drama. And to this day, despite a number of subsequent innovations, drama as the domain exclusively of men characterizes one facet of Asian theatre.

By the time modern theatre was introduced to India by the British, the hold of Sanskrit over all literature was broken. The local vernaculars had taken a long time to build a literature of poetry and religious documents which, despite their Sanskritized vocabulary, were nevertheless independent and even beautiful in their own right. The growth of modern drama was of necessity a provincial concern. There are around sixty languages, not counting obscure dialects, current in India today, and the most important of these all produced their own dramas without regard for what was being done in the other areas. Today the most important of these linguistic or, as some people call them, regional theatres are in Mahrashtra, Bengal, Madras, Gujerat, and Andrah. In addition, there is the theatre of the Parsis in the Bombay area, who speak Gujerati; also in Bombay a professional,

English language group operates, and there is another separate theatre in Hindi or Hindustani, the most widely understood language of India as a whole. There are still others. Every province of India has some form of theatre, but these eight deserve special recognition and have from the beginning produced the most worthwhile dramas in modern India. While the word regional theatre to the Westerner may sound inconsequential and lacking the broad national impulse so necessary to theatre if it is to survive, it is well to remember that the least of these languages, Gujerati, is spoken by sixteen and a half millions, and the largest, Hindi, is spoken by one hundred and fifty millions. The new theatre used these languages of the people exclusively and was immediately understandable to large areas of the population.

Ironically, the modern theatre and its languages lent itself most happily to politics, propaganda and anti-colonial ideas. With the arrival of the British, a cohesive nationalism began to form in India, and the Indian's subsequent history—the struggle against the British, the iniquity of collaborating with the conquerors, the heroics of those who resisted—took on an immediate, almost compulsive interest for audiences. The modern theatre form and the contemporary subject-matter for it were both provided by the one accident—the advent of foreign rulers—and the potent weapon of theatre was used sometimes subtly, sometimes openly, against the people who had introduced it.

One rather oblique example which illustrates this point is found in the famous Mahrashtrian historical drama, *Bhau Bandki*. The Mahrashtrians, who number twenty-seven millions and who live along the Western coast of India centering in Bombay province, were among the most hostile of the Indian peoples to their conquerors and the most nationalist-minded, and their attitude is reflected in the play. The central character, Anandibai, is a venomous Lady Macbeth-like character whose connivances in actual fact contributed substantially to the successful operations of the British against the Mahrashtrians in the early days of colonial rule.

The story deals with palace intrigue at the court of the Peshwa, the title for Mahrashtrian rulers. The cruel, powerful and ambitious Anandibai is married to Raghoba, Regent to the youthful Peshwa. Since she has received assurances of support from the British if her husband seizes the throne, she arranges the murder of the rightful ruler. Raghoba is proclaimed Peshwa, but Ramshastri, a venerable judge attached to the court, is suspicious, and suggests that Raghoba undergo a religious ceremony of penance. Anandibai fiercely opposes this as she fears that the action might lead the public to suspect the murder. Ramshastri withdraws from the court and protests the succession to the throne. The people grow restive, and Raghoba, to distract them and in the hope of achieving some valorous deed to justify his position as head of the nation, leads an expedition against the Muslim ruler of the neighboring Hyderabad State. The campaign fails. Raghoba, overcome with remorse and failure, places himself at the mercy of the elders of the Peshwa Court. The infant son of the murdered Peshwa is proclaimed the rightful heir, and Anandibai in a final impassioned and bitter speech addressed to the unborn child within her womb vows vengeance against the Peshwas in perpetuity.

Bhau Bandki was written less than a hundred years ago in the rich and florid rhythms of the Mahrashtrian language, and has remained a standard item in the repertoire of all Mahrashtrian troupes, even during the years when it was intermittently censored by the British. It has gained special popularity in recent times, despite its having outlived its once pertinent message, largely because of the brilliant histrionics of Durga Khote, one of India's senior actresses. Less than twenty years ago, Durga Khote was the first woman to appear in women's roles on the Mahrashtrian stage. More significant even was her personal social standing and respectability. She belongs to the Brahmin—the highest—caste and aside from her enormous talent, her presence in such a milieu was revolutionary. It paved the way later for women of all classes to join the theatre without fear of ostracism. Although Durga Khote, now in her fifties, devotes most of her time to appearing in movies, the annual two-week-long Mahrashtrian theatre festival would not be complete without a performance by her, and according to her fans, preferably in *Bhau Bandki*. In 1955 the play won the first prize in the government-sponsored, week-long Drama Festival held in Delhi to which troupes from all parts of India were invited.

Another signal distinction was accorded the Mahrashtrian stage when Bal Gandharva, a seventy-year-old actor and leading light of the Mahrashtrian stage, received the Presidential Award in 1955 as one of the "artists of the year." He was cited especially for his "emotional and expressive acting in feminine roles." This was the first time an actor has ever been honored officially in India. Although Bal Gandharva rarely appears now, he is still spoken of with almost legendary awe for the sweetness of his voice in the songs he always sang in each play, and for the fashions he set with the saris of unusual pattern which he wore on stage.

Bengal boasts the oldest modern theatre in all India. More than any other area, it is indebted to the British for its present excellent theatrical attainment. On the Northeast coast of India, Bengal was the headquarters of the original East India Company, and from this foothold it turned into the first colony of the English. A large concentration of foreigners has always been stationed in Calcutta, the capital, and they exposed the people to foreign ways and habits more thoroughly than anywhere else in India. Amateur theatricals by the British throve from the earliest days, and little acting troupes came all the way out from Europe to entertain the homesick colony of Englishmen there. In 1776 the British opened a permanent playhouse of their own and its first performances were *The Disguise* and *Love is the Doctor*. It is not hard to imagine what these plays must have been like; but the Bengalis were quick to recognize the possibilities of a new kind of entertainment. They immediately adapted it to their needs, and finally the first theatre for Bengalis in the Bengali language was opened in 1795, oddly enough by a Russian.

Theatre houses continued to appear—one of them, the Star Theatre, is still standing and dates back to 1880. The Bengalis translated plays, borrowed plots, and invented a repertoire of their own. Over the years the corps of regular actors grew, and by the beginning of the twentieth century, a first-rate artist, Girish Chandra, a combination actor, stage manager, playwright, and jack-of-all theatre trades, emerged. His name is revered, and his photograph garlanded in theatres and homes, along with those of Tagore, Sri Aurobindo, Ramakrishna, and Swami Vivekanada, the mystics, all Bengalis. Calcutta University, one of the few places where drama is recognized academically, officially designates its professor of theatre as the "Girish Chandra lecturer."

64

Early in this century, another actor, Bhaduri, began to bring distinction to the Bengali stage, and he is now the doyen of Bengal's many actors. He still performs despite his age in a small theatre every Sunday afternoon in Calcutta. Bhaduri is known abroad and thirty years ago he toured Europe and America with a program of episodes from the *Ramayana*. Unfortunately his troupe met with little success. The reason for the failure probably was that theatre in a Western sense was so recent in the minds of Indians that the right proportionate blend between the West and East had not been found. While Indians found Bhaduri exotically Western, the West found him disappointingly un-Oriental and a pale imitation.

At the present time, Ahin Choudry is the most popular figure among Bengal's senior actors. He usually appears at the old and distinguished Adelphi Theatre and attracts a large and devoted following. The splendid bravura of his acting projects to the distant spectator sitting in the gallery and elicits alternate tears and smiles with masterful ease. His chief vehicle, and a perennial favorite with Bengalis, is *Misar Kumar* or Daughter of Egypt. Written in 1918, the play was a thinly veiled protest against British discrimination against Indians on the basis of color. Choudry plays the part of an Uncle Tom sort of character, with thick, black makeup and wearing a gray, salt-and-pepper wig. He has fled the Egyptian capital with his adopted daughter because of the savage persecutions of the Negroes or Kaffirs by the King, Ramases. Known only to the foster-father is the secret that the girl is in reality the daughter of the King by his now abandoned Negro mistress. The two are finally tracked down and wounded in an attack on them by the King and his troops. The climax of the play is a long speech on the injustices of color prejudice, and little by little it becomes apparent that the true identity of the girl is going to be revealed to the King. (At this point the enraptured audiences usually call out "slowly, slowly" to prolong the suspense before the disclosure.) When the King finally realizes with horror that he has harmed a daughter of his own flesh and blood, he relents in his persecution.

Calcutta is the only city of India which has and still consistently maintains professional troupes of actors and theatres for them to appear in. And for this reason the Bengalis have a right to claim the most advanced theatre of India. It is possible almost any weekend to buy a ticket, walk into a theatre, and see a play. One success, *Shyamalee*, has already had at the time of writing more than 300 of these weekend performances and its star, Suchitra Chatterjee, may easily develop into one of Bengal's best actresses. Her role is silent and curiously moving. She plays the part of a slightly half-witted girl who cannot speak. Her father marries her off to a man who discovers her affliction only after the Vedic marriage rites are performed. She wins his love, however, and finally, through her husband's gentleness, she learns to speak.

The growth of the modern theatre, even in Bengal, has by no means effaced the religious content so essential and traditional to the Indian temperament and mentality. More than half the plays which reach the stages of Calcutta today are intrinsically concerned with religion, and a play will be advertised as "a daring devotional" much as we would publicize a comedy as "delightful." One example of this is the sensational success, *The Life of Saint Ram Prasad*. It has been played around 400 times (1955) and its appeal is not yet exhausted. It is of course full of spectacular miracles, and abounds in moral maxims quoted from Ram Prasad who actually was a saint in real life. "The Service of the people is to God alone," "Only through piety can nations be awakened" are samples of the general tone of the play. Other types of plays you can see in Calcutta are called "social" if they deal with ordinary life in modern dress (like *Shyamalee*) or "historical" if they are in costume and concern Kings and Queens (*Daughter of Egypt*, for example). As a general rule the three classifications of "devotional," "social," and "historical" are used throughout Asia. Terms such as comedy, tragedy, musical, opera and the like, except in translations of plays from the West, are rarely used because of their imprecision in describing Asian theatre which mixes emotions and techniques usually kept separate in Europe and America.

Madras, which is both a city and a province, is a very special part of India. The city is the pleasantest in India for the intellectual. Matching the charm of its long curving beach, its clean streets, and its excellent restaurants, where you can get delicious *dossas* and *idlis* (stuffed pancakes and puff balls of cooked rice flour) are its extraordinarily intelligent and approachable people, the Tamils. The University of Madras, which has the highest academic standard in the country, scatters its scholars over the city and this studious atmosphere somehow pervades the air. The ubiquitous Brahmins, the traditional repositories of scholarship and knowledge, with their repetitious caste-names of Iyer and Ayengar, their shaven pates and long hair tied in a knot at the back of the head, are sprinkled throughout the city. In a suburb, Adyar, is the Theosophical Center, which is in India regarded simply as another center of learning. There they teach admirably and ably Sanskrit, dance, and the almost forgotten ancient handicrafts now desperately in need of protection and resuscitation. The stimulus Madras offers reaches every level of the city's inhabitants. A room boy at a hotel can likely as not sing for you a prayer-song in an obscure *raga* (melody or mode) and tap out for you on the table a complicated *tala* or rhythmic pattern. Madras audiences are acknowledged to be the most critical and discerning in India. It is said that even celebrated dancers are so terrified during their débuts that they sometimes stumble or fall.

Theatre is largely controlled by the enterprising T.K.S. brothers, who are probably the wealthiest, most successful theatrical producers in India. They stage plays with periodic frequency ranging in subjects from problems of marriage and domestic life to musical extravaganzas. Madras abounds with playwrights as well: some of them borrow wholesale from the West and write like Shaw or Ibsen; others restate and extoll those values in their traditional life which were temporarily placed in abeyance by the period of colonial rule; a few merely write about their milieu as theatrical people in a realistic way —a character will seduce a dancer who is seeking employment, or a wife will resent her artist-husband for spending so much time in the theatre instead of with the family at home. But, as with Bengal, despite this ferment of varied activity, the invariable box-office success is the play on religion. Here, too, it is manifest that even with the trappings of modern stagecraft, and after the field of contemporary drama has been fully opened, the tastes of the people remain rooted in the past, in that original, ancient connection between worship and theatre.

Recently, the Walltax Theatre, a large, semi-open-air theatre house near the central railway station, produced another in a long line of successful plays, *Kumara Vijayam* (The Son of Siva). In order to accommodate the crowds who pay anywhere from twelve annas (about fifteen cents) to four rupees (eighty cents) for their tickets, it was held over, revived and repeated over a period of months, and it now belongs in the permanent repertoire. The play, like most dramas in India today, is episodic rather than sequential, depicting somewhat desultorily the life of the god Kumara Vijayam who was born on this earth of stars which fell into a lotus flower, who set himself higher than all terrestial kings, who fought and conquered the spirit of evil in the world, and before whom even Brahma, the beginning of the World, had to bow in heaven. The details of the story and its characters are familiar to the Indian brought up close to temples and amid the annual pageantry associated with festivals and religious celebrations.

At the beginning, six gleaming stars slowly descend at the back of the stage and suddenly burst into six celestial maidens. The hero, Kumara Vijayam, appears as an infant with six faces and twelve arms. The women vie for the child and struggle over him. Six pink giant lotuses open their petals and as they spin around magically six little kewpie dolls emerge. In rapid succession an enormous cast appears. They wear huge headdresses of silver and gold encrusted with glowing jewels the size of hen eggs and stand under unfurled umbrellas of brocades and tassels. Some of the gods have blue faces, others elephant heads. Brahma has three identical faces and an extra pair of arms stemming from his shoulders. Leopard-skinned holy men smeared with white ash and with matted long hair appear uttering prophetic words of doom. Enormous thrones caked with gold leaf are shunted on and off the stage at appropriate moments. At intervals temple incense is fanned from the stage to float out over the audience. During battles the hero fights a demon who assumes a series of forms each more terrifying than the last. The stage is blacked out between each new manifestation of the demon and at intervals he is shown laughing which keeps the connection and tells the audience clearly that all these nightmarish figures are all one and the same person. Spears float through the air mysteriously suspended in space, pause, and explode in a burst of gunfire. Of course, in the end, our hero wins and peace reigns among the gods as on earth. *Kumara Vijayam* gives the newly arrived visitor a staggering concentration of spectacle and glitter—as well as an insight into how, in part, the Indian mind sees its gods.

At the center of all the Walltax Theatre activity is the leading actor of South India, a Tamil from Madras named Rajamanickam, but known affectionately among the fifty million Tamils of South India as Nawab (the Anglicized form of this title is "nabob") derived from one of his most popular roles. Rajamanickam started his troupe, the first modern theatre of the Madras area, twenty-three years ago. He took a midnight vow before a wayside Kali Shrine in Tanjore that he would kill himself if he did not become a great actor. Fortunately for Madras theatre his prayer was answered, and his heroic, almost blustering style of acting in the grand manner has won him fantastic popularity. He has built a theatre of his own, with a library, and he even tours as far afield as Bombay and Calcutta to perform before the large Tamil communities there. His troupe, the largest in India, has a hundred and fifty members—all men. According to Rajamanickam, men can play women's roles as well as women can, and besides the theatre offers too many temptations and dangers for the weaker sex. His approach to theatre is deeply religious. Actors must pray before appearing and they must remove their sandals before setting foot on the stage—and all his plays are "devotionals" ranging in theme from an old favorite like *Kumara Vijayam* to the latest success, a sympathetic life of Christ.

The Gujerati theatre, like the Mahrashtrian, centers—in part at least—in Bombay. While its tradition is shorter than either Bengal's or the Mahrashtrian, it still is remarkably active. Gujerati theatre, until less than half a century ago, consisted only of little folk dances and half mimed story narrations of an elementary sort.

Gujerati theatre in a modern sense of the word began largely through the efforts of K. M. Munshi, a Sanskrit scholar and a grand old man of Indian politics who has served his country in a variety of ways ranging from cabinet minister in the post-independent government to his present post as governor of the important province of Uttar Pradesh. Munshi began his sideline of writing plays with a two-fold aim—to restore Gujerati history and culture distorted by the weight of colonialism to the dignity it deserved, and to use the theatre as an instrument of political and social reform. In doing this, he also introduced the element of love in Indian drama in a way that it had not been used before.

Many of his plays deal with the affections and the place of women in the social structure of modern India. One, *Brahmacharya-shrama*, lampoons continence. Another, *The Afflicted Professor*, tells of the relationship between a professor and a pretty, young student, and only strong moral character saves the situation. Still another, and perhaps Munshi's best play, *Kakani Shashi*, is a plea for the emancipation of women from the restrictions old-fashioned Gujerati society placed on them. Many of his plays also used political themes and under the British were banned from the stage. Because of his activity in other fields, Munshi was imprisoned, which gave him time to write still more plays. To summarize Munshi's plays, it must be said that they are always humorous, full of revolt against accepted social conventions or political injustice, and invariably they accord women a free and noble position. As this book is being written, he is writing what will probably be his last play, to be called *Well Done Myself*, in which he himself appears and is teased and tormented by all the characters he has created in his plays and novels and which have become symbols of progressive thought in Gujerati households.

In 1952 an extremely important group, Nat Mandal, was formed in Ahmedabad, a Gujerati stronghold and the second largest city in Bombay Province. This group secured the services of Gujerat's greatest actor, Sundari (the "beautiful one"), who in his youth was famous for his roles as women. Now he is too old to act very much, and in any event the taste for female impersonation has declined. His knowledge of the theatre, particularly its folk forms, stands him in good stead, and as a director he is of immense value to the modern Gujerati stage. His most recent success was the controversial *Meena Gurjari* which played over a hundred performances in Ahmedabad, Baroda, and Bombay, and which for the first time combined the folk elements of Gujerati dance and story-telling with modern theatre.

At the heart of the theatre movement in Ahmedabad is the wealthy Sarabhai family, one of whose members, Bharati, has written a number of plays in both English and Gujerati dealing largely with the problem of the British-influenced Indian shedding the foreign values he has acquired through colonialism and rediscovering his own. The Sarabhais started a school of the theatre a few years back, and they now have their own small and intimate theatre house where almost any play written by almost anyone of their friends can be tried out. Their participation in the Nat Mandal organization assures it of a security and stability which will certainly carry it through this initial experimental period of Gujerati theatre history.

One Indian critic describes the Gujerati theatre as a "story of arrested growth, of a loss of dramatic points even before they were made." Another refers to it as consisting of "jerry-built plays," "awkward adaptations" and even sums it up as "a mass of ham." Adib of the *Times* of India and the most brilliant theatre critic in India has written of Gujerati theatre that it was "an oversize egg. No one knows when it will be hatched . . . maybe the egg is addled." Undoubtedly, these criticisms are harsh, but looking at the problem from another point of vantage, it seems to me that this unsparing concern with the Gujerati stage is possibly a most healthy and hopeful sign. Certainly an enormous amount of worry and artistic fretting in high quarters is taking place and out of it will come the new theatre the Gujeratis want. Any critical judgment at this juncture would be premature. The movement is still exploratory and groping. It is obviously in the hands of experienced and bright intellectuals. Where exactly it will lead during the next few years is problematical, but meanwhile it is growing in popularity and has already begun to reconcile the theatre needs of a large, entertainment-hungry population.

Centering partly in Madras, northwest of it and including part of Hyderabad, is found the state of Andhra, consisting of thirty-three millions whose chief language is Telegu. Their province is one of the poorest in India. The theatre movement here was spearheaded a decade ago by the Andhra Indian People's Theatre Association. There can be little doubt that this was from the beginning a purely Communist movement. Its goals were characteristic of propaganda-inspired artistic efforts. They wanted to utilize folk forms already familiar and aesthetically acceptable to the majority of people—particularly the outdoor dance-dramas (*vidhi natakam*) performed by strolling players who travel from village to village. They attempted to purge them of their religious import, and to imbue them with "messages" such as anti-landlordism, glorification of the peasant, political martyrdom, and the like. The new and revolutionary ideas were expected to take root in the minds of the people while ostensibly they were being entertained by their accustomed amusements. However, with the decline of the Communist impetus in India, and particularly in Andhra where the Communists have met their most disastrous defeats, this type of theatre has suffered. The people are now dependent once again on their old dance-dramas and have returned to them just as they were before.

The Parsis are a small community of scarcely a hundred thousand people centered chiefly in Bombay city. But their prominence in the financial and industrial life of the country is out of all proportion to their actual numbers. So, too, is their immense contribution to the growth of modern theatre in India. Parsis originally were religious refugees from Persia (hence the word *parsi*). They are by religion Zoroastrians or, more colorfully put, fire-worshipers who over a thousand years ago sought asylum in India from the Mohammedan persecutions at home. They adopted Indian dress and manners and even Gujerati, the language for commercial transactions in the area at the time.

From the outset they retained a sense of their Western origins, however, and when the British came they were the first Indians to become "Westernized" in a genuine sense. Naturally they quickly responded to the new kind of theatre the British introduced. Today the visitor to Bombay is more likely to happen upon a performance by the Parsis than by either the Gujeratis or the Mahrashtrians, the largest of the groups composing that cosmopolitan city. Parsi theatre is divided into two kinds: plays in Gujerati, and European or American plays performed in English. (Included as part of their Westernization was an almost bilingual command of the English language.)

Of the two, those in Gujerati are the more popular and the less impressive. These are invariably comedy of different sorts: one, for instance, deals with honeymoon couples getting into the wrong rooms in a hotel; often marital difficulties are presented in which the wife subdues the husband (always a laughable situation in Asia as it is in the West); and frequently the humor borders on slapstick and vaudeville.

Chief among the groups who perform in English in Bombay is Theatre Unit. While it is inaccurate to imply that they are part of the Parsi theatre movement, a number of their actors are Parsis, as are a large portion of their audience and ardent supporters, and certainly their Western connections in a theatrical sense link them more with the Parsis than with any other single community.

Without question, Theatre Unit is the most competent troupe of actors in India, and their productions on occasions rank in quality and polish with the modern theatres of Japan, Europe or America. At the head of Theatre Unit is the gifted young Alkazi, trained at the Royal Academy of Dramatic Art in London and Dartington Hall, and now India's most brilliant actor and director in a rounded, international sense. Theatre Unit has to its credit over the years, almost a decade by 1955, a number of distinguished performances. Their range is wide and they have presented plays as disparate as Sophocles' *Oedipus Rex*, Eliot's *Murder in the Cathedral*, and *The Heiress*. Recently, they have started performing plays in Hindi written by their actor-students. *Oedipus Rex* was rewarded with an Honorable Mention in the National Drama Festival at Delhi (plays in English were not permitted to compete in the main contest).

Some of these productions have been simple Theatre-in-the-Round, and the happy combination of genuine acting talent, a sense of stagecraft, the negligible cost of performing on the second floor in an ordinary office building after hours with the help of volunteers who freely donate their time and energies, have enabled Theatre Unit to build up a financially sound organization despite the restricted appeal of foreign plays in English.

They have recently been able to open a school of theatre, rather like Actor's Studio, in which Europeans and Indians both teach and study. From time to time they organize balls and parties to increase their funds, and a trust has been established which guarantees temporarily at least a measure of regular performances. The steady stream of the best dramas of Europe that they introduce has been a wholesome influence on India's drama as a whole. They import the most suitable plays, stage devices, and techniques. Several members of the staff make relatively frequent visits to Europe or America, and the fresh currents of acting styles that they experience there are healthy stimuli for them. But Theatre Unit is essentially an Indian theatre performed by Indians before Indians. This shows most clearly in the rich acting texture of their performances and their feeling for the near-melodramatic or almost overplayed gesture and extended climax. While this may not be exactly in vogue in the West at present, it has however dynamics which make theatre more theatrical and its effects more affecting. The warmth of Theatre Unit's style would easily be as welcome in the West as our theatre is to them.

Of all the purely indigenous theatre movements in India today, the most expert and the most consistently professional in the fullest sense of the word is Prithvi Theatre named after the star actor Prithviraj; it plays in Hindi or Hindustani. Unfortunately, this group performs only rarely, perhaps three or four times a year, but it is invariably an event of the first order and a success always artistically and sometimes financially. Prithviraj began his career as a movie actor, and as such was one of the pioneers in elevating the general level of the Indian motion picture. As a young man, he was a popular matinee idol, and in his sixties he still commands an intensely admiring following. He appears usually as a father, as a sober and wise judge, or as a kindly and gentle elder, with a special feeling for tragedy.

The secondary star of Prithvi Theatre is Prithviraj's own son, Raj Kapoor. He in turn is the idol of millions of movie-struck, cinema-going Indians, both for his good looks and his playing of love scenes. While he shares his father's acting gifts, his special field is comedy. Raj Kapoor's sparkling sense of the ridiculous makes him one of the most endearing, lighthearted actors performing anywhere today. For their infrequent stage performances, which they first began in 1945, father and son combine talents, and sometimes one acts while the other directs.

Because of the linguistic advantage of being in Hindi, the national language of India, and now a compulsory subject in all schools regardless of the particular vernacular of the province, they touch the masses of India in a way that few plays either in India's past or present ever have. Their plays, always specially written for them, are literate and comprehensible, and they handle problems of nationwide concern. Prithviraj's greatest success, *Pathan*, which has been revived several times since its first appearance a decade ago, is a case in point. It tells the story of the lifelong devotion between a Muslim and a Hindu in a small village in the far North. Their friendship is interrupted by the partitioning of India at the time of Independence when the predominantly Mohammedan North was established as the theocratic state, Pakistan. In the final climax, the Muslim sacrifices his own son to appease the bloodthirsty rioters and to protect his friend. Somehow through those two characters—simple, old men who know only the ancient codes of their ancestors—Prithviraj manages to epitomize the whole tragedy that was shaking India at the time. When the play first appeared tension between Hindus and Muslims had broken out into violence, and the colossal transfer of population—Hindus to India, Muslims to Pakistan, eight million in all—was marred by rioting and atrocities. *Pathan* served as a quieting note of sanity in that time of disturbance when confusion and rumor dominated, when fears and uprootings, reprisals and suspicions were the torment of the day. The social need for *Pathan* has now disappeared, the problems between India and Pakistan have lessened into a sort of postwar wariness, but its quality as a play persists.

Prithviraj has gone on to other plays, each tackling some pressing concern of the people at the moment. The latest at the time of writing was called *Money*, and Prithviraj's dual role of poor man—rich man was one of the strongest diatribes against greed and corruption to appear in modern theatre. Each theme of Prithvi Theatres is deeply Indian, handled in a characteristically Indian way. Perhaps the genius of the group lies in its subtle balance between national theatre and international art. And this has not appeared in India since the Sanskrit dramas.

The effectiveness of Prithviraj's theatre is due not a little to its staging, the main characteristic of which is its successful adaptation of movie techniques. Modern Indian theatre has virtually grown up simultaneously with the movie industry, and Prithviraj of course developed primarily as a movie actor. His competence as a legitimate actor, like that of his son and Durga Khote among others, is almost a chance circumstance. Prithviraj inescapably must treat the stage almost like a film. There are numerous set changes, dance sequences, incidental music, changes of atmosphere, and the restrictions of the three-act one-set play are submerged as far as is commensurate with the limitations the stage imposes. The extravaganzas of color and movement, and particularly the mood projections through processions and literal, graphic, onstage depiction of events (there is little "I hear fighting in the streets" while the heroine looks out a window and informs the audience of what is happening) gives the movie-nurtured audience everything they want from the camera, plus the gratuity of seeing their favorite actors in person.

Prithviraj faces this relationship between theatre and the movies realistically. If the unrestricted freedom and variety of motion pictures are a threat to the legitimate stage, then the best of that technique must be transferred to the stage. As for the cheapness of the movie over the heavy expenses incurred by a regular stage performance, Prithviraj makes every feasible economy he can. He gives his performances only in the mornings (when theatre rentals are lowest), in the largest theatres possible, such as the Opera House in Bombay, so that a greater number of cheap seats can be sold. Since his productions are intrinsically a family affair between father and son who can if necessary contribute their labor without remuneration, the price of admission is kept at a bare minimum.

One other problem which challenges India's modern theatre is how to establish a taste for live acting before the lights and shadows of the movies have vitiated its appeal. Prithviraj has gone far towards solving the question, simply by continuing to present plays; one a year is his average. At one time the Prithvi Theatres, despite their success, were in such dire straits that during intermission Prithviraj and his son dressed in plain clothes and carrying a beggar's bowl canvassed the lobby and aisles for contributions. If in a few years Bombay, as it very likely will, becomes something of a Broadway where people from the provinces come into the town just to see the theatre, the credit will be to a great extent Prithviraj's. The threat the movies pose will then be over and the stage freed once and for all.

One of the more active groups in India, but one which stands apart from regional theatre in something of the same way as Prithvi Theatre or Alkazi's Theatre Unit is the Indian National Theatre. Originally encouraged by the distinguished Socialist leader Kamaladevi Chattopadhyaya, a group of young and enthusiastic amateurs assembled their talents several years ago to present shows all over India in theatres, in mill areas, and among the farmers, on any subject and of any type that struck their fancy. They appeared first in the cities, and with the profits, whenever there were any, hired a truck which also served as a stage to transport their performances into the provinces, where the people at large could see them.

Because of language difficulties, lack of playwrights, and the dearth of trained actors, they started by performing dramatic ballets, not as classical or erudite as the traditional dances of the Four Schools, and yet not as alien and removed as the drama-style imported from the West. In a way, their performances were pantomimes in which a story is graphically enacted with a minimum of words. The themes they chose were usually on a national level and their message, without being either Communist or pro-government propaganda, dealt with the questions of the day in a cooperative and helpful way.

One of their chief successes did however assist the Government in its "Grow More Food" campaign. The ballet described the work on the soil, the wickedness of the rice profiteers in the cities, the tragedy of famine and the helpless agony of the people affected by it, and finally the renewed efforts to "grow more food." Another successful ballet of theirs was *Discovery of India*; it showed in panorama the march of India and its people through their early history down to Gandhi and Independence. Other performances by the Indian National Theatre have been dance-drama playlets on popular themes of the past—the gifted singer Mirabai who enchants even the Moghul court with her Hindu devotional songs and who finally becomes a saint, or the Ras Lila re-enactment of happenings in the heavens and the celestial dances of the Gods.

Indian National Theatre now has branches in every major city all over the country. They draw upon all the talent they can find, tour when they can, and always present themes which are of real interest to the people. In encouraging national unity, as well as furthering theatre in India by excellent, well-thought-out programs, they have been eminently successful.

77

There are in India also a few isolated pockets of theatre, developing independently of regular theatre movements and achieving in lonely splendor precisely what the groups elsewhere are striving after. Manipur is perhaps the best example of this. There, the intensely sensitive and drama-conscious people have evolved a practicing, active theatre all their own. It derived at first from British and American movies, which were occasionally shown in the capital, Imphal, and the rumors of Calcutta's thriving theatre travelers brought with them. But because of the special theatrical genius of the Manipuris, it has achieved something its prototypes might well envy. Manipur's population numbers only about half a million, but the country manages to support and maintain more than seven modern theatre troupes, not including the thirty or so old-fashioned troupes of the strolling mummer type called *lilas*, and the several opera troupes described earlier in the section on Indian dance. It would not be surprising if this were the highest proportion of live-talent theatre per capita in the world.

Of acting troupes, all of whom reside permanently in Imphal, Rupmahal Theatre, Inc., is the best and most prosperous. A large, square, brick building, bigger even than the maharaja's palace, and constructed at the considerable cost for Manipur of a lakh and a half of rupees (about $35,000) stands in the center of town where the State Highway and the Market Road cross and proclaims the importance of theatre. This building translates the meaning of the troupe's name, Rupmahal, literally "beautiful palace," into actuality according to the Manipuris. But for the outsider it is rather less grand. It seats about 350 people on rusty iron chairs. The first five rows, the most expensive seats, are covered with drab Army blankets. In addition to having a number of permanent sets and a relatively complete wardrobe (the costumes are resplendent with the gold, silver and hand-spun or woven materials), the troupe sustains a regular staff of fifty people, each working full-time on a fixed, if modest, salary. The wage scale when computed in dollars seems infinitesimal, but the Manipuri, born in a paradise where a pair of sandals from Calcutta is considered an extravagance, finds it ample. Leading stars, for instance, like the first class actresses Tondon and Tambal, or the *jeune premier* Nabakumar, receive the equivalent of around fifty dollars a month. Electricians (there is one power plant in the whole country and Rupmahal Theatre is its only customer as far as I could ascertain) and lower grade stage hands average around ten dollars a month. Ushers, ticket-takers, tea carriers, curtain-time bell ringers, and the like get even less, but everyone manages to live comfortably, and most of the staff supports wives, children, mothers, or aged fathers.

Rupmahal Theatre is guided almost exclusively by its director and secretary, Nilmoni Singh. Nilmoni Singh has carefully selected for his Rupmahal Theatre a collection of all-round actors and actresses. In Manipur, imitative talent (Indians sometimes refer to them as the "Japanese of India") is at no premium. According to them, almost anyone can act in a sense. But in true Indian fashion the artists must also sing and dance. Altogether Rupmahal is a curious conglomeration of gifted and charming people. Each too is something of a story in himself. Given the perspective of time and distance, their stories should one day make interesting and original plays.

The most glamorous of the Manipuri actresses, Tondon, is an instance of this. Her charms once jeopardized the troupe and the future of theatre in Manipur. Tondon's life in part sounds like an old-fashioned fairy tale and in part it tells an important chapter in the growth of theatre in this region of India. Modern theatre in Manipur rose at a time of political unrest and general economic dislocation. The war brought foreigners into the country, the Japanese pushed as far as Imphal in their war in Asia, India gained independence from Britain, the country was divided, and the princely states including Manipur merged into the Indian Union. News of all this reached Manipur and foisted an awareness onto a people who had formerly lived in virtual isolation. A sense of social conscience developed and found expression in the theatre. In Manipur, the stage soon became a sounding board and spoke out with courage and emphasis against the feudal Maharaja and the ineffectuality of his government. The criticisms expressed in their various plays were sometimes direct, sometimes through historical parallels, but their barbs were clear and began to reach the ears of the Maharaja himself. His advisors persuaded him that perhaps a royal command performance would flatter the troupe into silence. But Rupmahal Theatre, despite its exalted patronage, continued as before—never flagrantly enough for lèse-majesté, never pointedly enough for a libel suit, and never revolutionary enough to be Communist and punishable for that reason. The Maharaja, as the story goes, at his first experience with modern theatre had been particularly interested in the beautiful star, Tondon. And, as gossip has it, he determined to please himself and finish Rupmahal by depriving the troupe of its chief attraction.

His method was to kidnap her. The State Police surrounded the theatre and when Tondon left by the stage door, she was whisked away into one of the court cars and sped down the road into the Maharaja's private confines. His avowed intention was to marry her, making her his seventh wife. The Manipuris claimed to be outraged by this combination of strategem and immorality. Their chief complaint, however, was that they were deprived of their stage idol. Powerless to revolt openly, they registered their point through mockery. As the Maharaja moved through his official functions, giggles, leers, and taunts greeted him, quietly but persistently. As he drove through the streets, catcalls of "So Your Highness is marrying an actress!" and other more abusive shouts were hurled by anonymous, unidentifiable bystanders. Finally, at the end of two months, to prevent the matter from becoming a further issue, Tondon was returned. She resumed her career with an enormously increased following, and still today she is good-humoredly called "The Two-Month Maharani."

Modern theatre in Manipur, as elsewhere in India and Asia, implies the two types of plays, social and historical. The plot situations of both are similar. Poor men marry rich and beautiful girls; rich men are cruel to the poor; and the heroes abound in pride while women exhibit undying devotion. Most of Rupmahal's plays turned out by its staff of six writers are like this. Any play has a guarantee to run three or four nights at a minimum. A hit means a play that has ten or more performances. Revivals are included in this figure because the run of a play is not necessarily on consecutive nights. One of the most recent popular successes, and one which already has been revived a sufficient number of times to rate as a perennial, is *Lownam* (The Disbelieved). The story in outline is simple. A poor but honorable boy called Nobo finally marries a poor and beautiful girl called Mani. Before this match is consummated, many obstacles arise. She is led away to marry the local tax collector, she is forbidden to see Nobo ever again, she is held captive in a far-off house, and other general tribulations beset her. Nobo out of loneliness and despair begins to doubt her love. He takes up hashish smoking to ease his sorrow and to forget. Mani finally finds him, but he is still uncertain of her. Later, during the marriage celebrations she accidentally stabs the tax collector. A trial scene uncovers the truth of the situation and her innocence. Mani is exonerated and Nobo, now certain of her love, joyfully marries her.

Each playwright in Manipur has his own special approach. One is an ardent member of the Indian Congress and writes plays based on his own life to propound the history and theories of the party. Another feels that since drama is a waste of human time, actors while acting should be employed in useful pursuits such as basket weaving, sewing, pounding rice, making sandals, etc. Gitchandra Singh, to cite still another, has the unique distinction in Manipur of having read Ibsen and Shaw, and sees the theatre in terms of problems and protest. He limits himself, however, to a single theme, the place of women in society, and to a single approach, the comic.

On the whole, historical plays are the most popular in Manipur. The all-time favorite of Manipur is the historical romance *Khamba and Thoibi*, based on an actual event that took place more than 500 years ago. In it, two lovers, a poor fisherman and a beautiful princess, finally marry after even greater trials than those which beset Mani and Nobo. When it is performed on the stage, it takes four nights, as each section of the exciting and pathetic lives of the lovers requires a full evening.

The Manipuri Theatre, the Indian National Theatre, Prithvi Theatre, and especially Theatre Unit demonstrate perhaps more clearly than the other theatre groups of India a curious phenomenon which is very rapidly taking place in India. The amateur is turning into a professional. Nothing, say fifteen years ago, could have been more amateur than the enthusiastic founders of the new modern theatre movements. The personnel had no experience, they had no expert or experienced models to follow, and unlike America where for generations we have had a body of professional, regularly employed artists, craftsmen and businessmen to absorb the yearly crop of new talents entering the theatre, they had no cadre of trained people. Even the old-fashioned artists like Bal Gandharva of the Mahrashtrian stage and Sundari of Gujerat were surrounded by a milieu so ignorant as to impair their standing and reputation. Everything anyone did was improvised, experimental, temporary and exploratory.

Somehow the new groups have weathered these turbulent beginnings and already the pioneers are teaching the new adherents. From the days when K. M. Munshi had to train his classmates to act in his own plays, it is a long step to Alkazi's school, or the Bharatiya Natya Sangh (Theatre Centre, India), an affiliate of UNESCO, with a dozen branches all over the country and 200 member theatre troupes, and its own academy of drama study in Bombay. The ferment of dramatic activity while still amateur in many respects is extraordinary. When the Sangeet Nataka Akademi announced its drama festival, 741 scripts were submitted and twenty-one were actually staged in Delhi with full sets, costumes and lighting and original casts. By now there are directors who know what they want and how to create it, there are designers who can produce precisely what they want without a surprise or disappointment when they see it mounted on the actual stage, and there are actors now who have made so many errors, have happened upon so many delightful accidents, discovered so many elements of pleasurable theatre, that a firm competence has spread over the group. Flair for the theatre has been converted into a genuine knowledge. When one looks at a performance today, it is hard to remember the early beginnings when one felt embarrassed for the actors and made excuses for the production. And this happy phenomenon of improvement and advancement is spreading all over India.

The history of drama in India has been a troubled one. From great heights it sank low. The present is trying to repay its debt to its own traditions. With the tremendous revival of Sanskrit studies all over India today and the return to ancient values which modern India has begun to feel so keenly since Independence from the British, that great past period of Hindu drama is belatedly coming into its own. *Sakuntala* in Sanskrit opened the Drama Festival and others of the masterpieces have been adapted for the movies, and there is a wide movement today to elevate Kalidasa to the posthumous status of a national hero, with a monument erected in his honor, his birthday a national holiday. Already the newspapers not infrequently editorialize on the pros and cons of this intellectual flurry over the golden age of Indian drama and the establishment of a National Theatre in his name. But this is not all.

The colonial era too had its importance, and the seeds of new drama it sowed have also taken root in India's fertile aesthetic soil. The movies emerged in the West long after the necessity for live theatre was already known and recognized. But in India the two were like uneasy, distantly related, stepchildren growing up together under the same roof. Finally the turning point has been reached. Theatre is established. The amateur is becoming professional. The next stage is already upon us: the professional is producing new professionals. Within the next ten years or so, barring a complete collapse of the foundations so far established or a reversal of every trend of the present, we shall know the final form Indian drama is to take this century. It will, of course, be something along the lines of Western drama in stage effects, in intellectual content, in formal outline. But it will also be inevitably Indian in mood and effect, in gestures and thought processes, and it will continue the long link with the past with a magnificent sense of dance and music and color. And it will be good theatre. Of this no one has a doubt.

CEYLON
Dance

Ceylon, a small island around 25,000 square miles in area and with a population that numbers about the same as New York City's, hangs like a pendant just off the southernmost tip of India. Because of its jewel-like shape, Ceylon is affectionately referred to as the "Pearl of the Indian Ocean," and this sobriquet does indeed suggest some of the qualities which make the island one of the most appealing tourist spots in the world today. It has a pleasant range of climate. The cool central mountains complement the warm luxuriant seashore. The thousands of beaches along the coast are thick with palms and fruit trees, a typical tropical landscape.

Its history has not been quite so idyllic. Ceylon has the somewhat dubious distinction in her relations with the West of having been three times a colony—first under the Portuguese, then the Dutch, lastly the British.

The West was not alone in exerting pressure on Ceylon. The massive civilization of India to the North was also a determining, but not destroying, factor. The Indianization of Ceylon, indelibly recorded in the *Ramayana*, began first when Rama with his armies pursued Ravana to Ceylon or Lanka as it is called by the Sinhalese. (The Sinhalese are the indigenous and original inhabitants of Ceylon who comprise a majority of the population. A large number of Indians, Muslims and Burghers of Dutch descent are Ceylonese without being Sinhalese, the true native of Ceylon.) It was continued by the converting Buddhists who arrived in successive waves from a few centuries before Christ until a few centuries after. In fact, the great Buddhist King of India, Asoka, sent his own son, Mahinda, to Ceylon as the first apostle of this new religion. Still later, warlike Tamil kings from South India arrived, desecrating the Buddhist centers in a

84

vain effort to establish Hindu rule and religion over the country.

Culturally, Ceylon is an extension of India, and its civilization is derivative in most essentials. The people look Indian, their costume is similar, their food and manners approximate, and their music (despite efforts of the xenophobes to reconstruct their now forgotten Sinhalese tunes) is deeply indebted to India. Today, sections of the population are so heavily and purely Indian that it constitutes a genuine problem for the government who wishes to keep Ceylon for the Sinhalese. Most of the Indians in Ceylon today are Tamils from the Madras area. They were first imported by the British for indentured labor on the tea estates because the local Sinhalese were too easy-going. They of course retain their customs and because of their numbers exert a not inconsiderable influence on local thought, manners and politics. But with all these pressures from the outside, Ceylon still has managed to remain unmistakably individual—in temperament, in the special gentle charm of the people, and in their manifold arts of dance and drama. It has, in fact, retained a surprising degree of cultural consistency and steadfastness.

Devil-dancing and its attendant exorcistic ritual, more than any other expression, show the hardiness of the original Ceylon. Its concept and execution are indigenous and in their particular local forms are unknown in India or anywhere else for that matter. In this way as a still surviving, actively practiced art, it represents one of the oldest and strongest traditions of Ceylon's earliest inhabitants.

Ceylon today, as it has been for two millennia now, is Buddhist. Its special Buddhism is of the *hinayana* or Lesser Vehicle sort which is more rigid and austere than the brighter manifestations of the *mahayana* or Greater Vehicle as practiced in China and Japan. Buddhism in theory discourages devils, especially in the orthodoxy of the Lesser Vehicle. One of the principal tenets of the Lord Buddha was that man is superior to gods and demons since he, because of Buddhism, is in control of his destiny and can, by accruing merit from good deeds, determine his ascension up the spiritual ladder. But by the time Buddhism reached Ceylon, there was already living there a people with their own convictions who believed in a regular hierarchy of personified forces of evil. This was their explanation for illness and the visitation of sorrows which beset the world. According to the original Sinhalese, these had to be placated and dealt with in special ritualistic ways. They would not exchange their devils for the cool reasoning of the superior religion; so the two have lived together, side by side, in an easy, unimpinging symbiosis.

Almost every pure Sinhalese is a Buddhist and a devout one, but in the back of his mind ineradicably exist his pre-Buddhist, atavistic fears and superstitions. Their clearest expression is devil-dancing, still as popular now, apparently, as it has always been throughout history. Devil-dancing is performed whenever a person is sick or insane, when a woman is pregnant, whenever misfortune seems to have hounded a family or household, or when good luck generally is needed. Women seem more subject to the need of exorcism than men for some reason, and the older they grow the more often they seem to want a devil-dance. In some instances, one is told, some of these women find themselves feeling ill simply so they may have a chance to dance with some of the young and handsome professional devil-dancers.

The dancers themselves belong to a special class, one of the lower castes, and earn their living exclusively by these performances. The locale for a devil-dance is usually outside the house of the afflicted person along the road or in the garden, if the person is rich enough to have grounds, and under moonlight and coconut trees and against a background of flaming torches for added illumination. The action takes place before specially erected shrines and in front of a temporary dais on which the sick person lies.

The greatest of the devil-dancers in Ceylon today is Henegamaya, an old man around seventy-five years of age. He lives in a village two miles from Galle, along the southern tip of Ceylon, and there his sons and grandsons assist in his performances. His youngest grandson of twelve is rapidly becoming a sought-after star with his sense of showmanship, his vertiginous leaps and whirls which defy gravity and the generally accepted sense of balance which limits the human body. For a hundred rupees (around twenty-five dollars) the family will perform the flashiest parts of devil-dancing, without the long ceremonies and without an actual patient on hand. But even such a tourist performance as this is sacred and must be done before the proper shrine. The fullest impact of the devil-dance is felt in the genuine setting and only there, with the ailing person before your eyes and the villagers crowding around in wide-eyed wonderment, does one savor its greatest excitement. All devil-dances properly presented must start in the evening and continue all night until dawn when the final purification is made and the patient supposedly cured. This is something of a strain on the foreigner accustomed to seeing his theatre after an early dinner and then going home before midnight. But it is worth keeping awake for the experience of spending the night at a devil-dance. And since the Sinhalese are almost inordinately polite, you will be given the most comfortable chair in a place of honor, and you will certainly be offered a bed to sleep on if you want to nap.

An enormous amount of ritual accompanies a full-scale production, and a number of books in German and English on demonology and witchcraft in Ceylon have gone into elaborate detail recording and explaining the significance and the ethnological meanings behind these curious and, to us, weird practices. Perhaps the most useful book for the student or visitor to Ceylon who wishes to go deeply into this subject as well as into the whole of Ceylon's theatre arts is Dr. E. R. Sarathchandra's brilliant and authoritative *The Sinhalese Folk Play*, published two years ago by the University of Ceylon at Peredeniya.

Roughly described, a performance obeys the following outline. The details of each devil-dance vary from troupe to troupe, but the general idea and underlying principles are always similar. It begins with a prodigious number of preparations. Quantities of pale yellow, new palm-leaves must be collected and skillfully woven into varying patterns. The main shrine, off to one end of the dance area, has walls of braided and plaited stalks and stems. Around it stand chest-high ledges of smaller shrines woven and cut into designs of leaves and flowers. From the improvised ceiling of matted palm fronds hang slivers of soft pliant leaves which tremble in the breeze and quiver wildly as the dancers plunge into the shrine and crash against its sides. Everywhere sprays of areca palm flowers, which look like etiolated sheafs of unripened grain, dangle from the sides of the walls and ceiling. The number of small, miscellaneous properties essential to a program is considerable—baskets of palms with exact replicas of flowers woven into them (one of these must be held over the afflicted person's head whenever she becomes possessed and rising from her sick bed insists on dancing), long switches of shredded strings of palm bunched together to hang like hair down the backs of the dancers and over their shoulders, and a large number of items made from the soft inner core of a banana stalk and carved to look like hand mirrors, combs, necklaces, bracelets, spinning wheels and carding implements. There is also a long slender arrow which plays an important part like a magic wand in controlling the demons and exhorting them to confess themselves despite their invisibility. Its tip is twisted and tied in a filagree of curlicues. In a pile off to one corner lies a stack of what looks like giant cigars. These are torches of rolled dried leaves to be lit and stuck between the lattices of the shrine. As they burn away, they are replaced from the stockpile. From time to time, the dancers seize them, perform a fire dance, and throw them away. From within the house at intervals a tray of burning charcoal is brought. This relights torches extinguished by the wind generated from the whirling dancers, or it ignites the pieces of sweet, fragrant temple incense thrown on it, or, most frequently, during recesses after each exhausting bit of dancing, dancers and audience use it to light their cigarettes.

The palm-leaf shrines are dedicated to a devil or demon by name, and the chief exorcist-dancer impersonates Vesamuni, the king of all demons, and the only one who can control them if during the performance they become obstreperous. The number of demons who cause illness is legion, and they range from simply being wicked forces inhabiting certain trees or stones or rivers to those who cause particular ailments like bilious attacks, discharges of blood, blindness, dumbness, lameness and colds (the last come from the demon in the wind).

Then there is a whole category of mysterious phenomena which pertain to the evil eye, the evil mouth, or evil thoughts. The symptoms are swoons, insanity, fits of hysteria, or generally odd behavior, and listed among the causes are "complaining after good luck" and "expressions of envy." Since a devil-dance refers to a specific person suffering a clear and evident malady, not all the devils need be represented at one time. Four or five shrines usually suffice to cover most emergencies. The idea is that through propitiation, the demon is attracted to the area, made to enter the afflicted person's body, and then threatened, cajoled, teased, tortured or begged and bribed with offerings until he promises to leave.

The dance is the main lure, and the dancers, all of whom are men, are dressed suggestively like women to augment their appeal. They cover their heads tightly with a red cloth from which switches of palm leaves hang down like a woman's long hair. Over their chests they wear an abbreviated cloth to indicate a breast covering, and a long skirt covers their legs and hides the enormous anklebells which fit at the calf of the leg and jangle raucously as the dancers move. This strange note of femininity may indicate, according to some authorities, that the dance was originally a fertility rite, or again it may stem merely from the fact that the majority of patients are women and as such the dance in this form is more applicable to their sex and ailments. After the demons reveal themselves, the dancers reappear as men without their breast covers and artificial palm-leaf hair. Throughout the performance bare-chested male drummers with their long hair tied in a simple knot at the back in the old-fashioned Sinhalese style sit or stand at one end of the arena near a chorus of singers.

The actual dancing comes sporadically in spurts and during passages of other theatrical or ritualistic action which will be described in the section on drama in Ceylon. The most impressive dancing comes when fire is introduced into the exorcism. It begins with a long white strip of cloth being thrown over the roof of the shrine. Then the leading dancer seizes a handful of gunpowder with his right hand and tosses it over a tray of charcoal which he holds in his left hand. It ignites in the air and streams over the cloth as the area is plunged into a blinding flash of trailing flame followed by dense black smoke. Then, holding burning torches in each hand, the dancers begin to whirl in a series of brilliantly executed turns and spins until the flames form a continuous circle around their blurred figures. Pieces of the flaming torch sprinkle the spectators who press around the dance arena, and a special attendant rushes everywhere after them, stamping out the sparks and ashes that fly from the dancers' centripetal propulsion. Then they nervously prance around the arena, jerkily marching in rhythm to the deafening roar of the drums and pausing momentarily to make a quick, hiccuping gesture of the torso. They stop to wash their faces and necks in a sort of fire bath with the flames from the torches. They hold the torches in front of them and increase the tempo of their pacing around and around the area until the breeze pushes the flames against their bodies. Then they put the torches under their chest-cloths and they flicker balefully, licking the flesh and shining transparently through the white cotton. Miraculously neither skin nor the cloth burns.

The dance steps themselves are simple—arms outstretched, waving softly to the music, the feet clanking out the rhythms proposed by the lead drummer. The pyrotechnics begin with the whirls and spins as the dancer circles the area, sometimes keeping his face directed at the shrine, sometimes leaping in the air as he turns and throws his body in small circles so rapidly that the torso keeps parallel to the ground as if by levitation. Occasionally the dancer stops stock-still, plants his feet firmly on the ground to swing his torso dizzyingly until his streamers of coconut hair swirl around him in a wide arc.

At about four o'clock in the morning, the devil-dancers put on masks and represent the demons in all their most terrible aspects. According to the demons impersonated, the masks vary; some are snake heads, others have a wooden corpse hanging from between their fangs of carved wood, and still others have faces of solid black, green or red. Their costumes vary from uniforms of crisp, rasping straw to skirts and collars of huge green leaves sewn together with bark. They rush around the circle in a parade, singing out their identities. The demon concerned explains his reason for having afflicted the sick person. Finally, exorcism is completed and the demons leave. The sleepy patient, now restored (although the main devil-dancer usually succeeds only in striking a bargain—the demon promises to disappear for a specific period of time and may return), goes to bed as the sun rises.

Devil-dancing is not confined to the Sinhalese alone. It is also practiced among the few remaining aboriginals, the Veddahs, who are primitive, unassimilated, almost prehistoric inhabitants of Ceylon. Their devil-dancing is elaborate as a ceremony, although less so as a dance, with many offerings of shoe-flowers, margosa leaves, plantains, young coconuts and burning slivers of camphor. The dancers and spectators often become overpowered by the smoke and incense and falling into a trance themselves dance until they collapse quivering into the arms of their friends. The devil-dance of the Veddahs is primarily directed towards driving epidemics of disease into the sea. They believe that most of their sicknesses were brought by the white man in his sailing ships many years ago. And to this day

90

their word for both smallpox and plague, for instance, is *kapal-pay* or "ship demon."

While devil-dancing, because of its exoticism and lurid, mystical overtones, attracts the tourist seeking a special thrill on a tropical island paradise, the dances of Kandy, or Kandyan dances as they are commonly referred to, are more important artistically. Even more exacting and considerably more refined or polished than all the island's other dances, they alone can be regarded as a complete art-form of a recognizably international, aesthetic standing. Unlike devil-dancing (as explained later in the section on Ceylon drama) there is no ritual connected with them, nor are they ancillary to a play or story. They are straight dances in a true sense of the word, and because of this intellectual accessibility and their remarkable qualities, they have well merited their recognition beyond the borders of Ceylon. Within the country, the government is making every effort to encourage and protect Kandyan dance. Part of this is national pride in line with the measures to Sinhalize Ceylon, and part is simply reaction against colonialism so widespread in Asia today. Kandyan dance is now a compulsory subject in all the larger schools, and where dance teachers formerly were lucky if they could assemble a single class, some of them now can count their pupils in the thousands.

The government's active and energetic Tourist Bureau is so eager for outsiders to experience the joys of Kandyan dance that they arrange for special troupes to board the ships that stop briefly at Colombo en route to other parts of Asia, Australia or Europe. There, on the deck, sandwiched in between snake charmers and special licensed merchants selling sapphires, opals, zircons and tourmalines, the dancers and drummers exhibit a sample of their art for passengers who cannot disembark and see the dances in their proper setting. But Kandyan dancing rightfully belongs in Kandy, the cool, pleasant hill-station a couple of hours out of Colombo, and where the tooth of the Lord Buddha, the most sacred relic in the Buddhist world, lies enshrined in the celebrated Temple of the Tooth.

Kandyan dance in contrast with devil-dancing is not indigenous, although in its present form it is now a Sinhalese accomplishment.

Originally, nearly 2000 years ago it came from South India and was introduced by Indian scholars and missionaries and later encouraged by the conquerors who followed in their wake. Basically, the dance was what we know today in India as Kathakali. As such it was naturally a part of Hindu religious life. Many of the songs which the Kandyan dancers still sing even now (the drummers are the dance's only accompaniment and all singing is the responsibility of the dancer as it once was in India) describe Rama and his joy on refinding Sita in Ceylon, or the miraculous powers of Ganesa, the dancing, elephant-headed son of Siva, and many other aspects of Hindu mythology. But Ceylon differed from its parent country in that it was Buddhist and scarcely inclined to propagate a new, foreign faith so soon after its conversion to Buddhism. Over the years adjustments and permutations occurred making Kathakali more suitable to Sinhalese taste and to the mentality that geographical and religious differences foster. In this way the dance style became an extension, and a most valuable one, of Indian dance.

Fortunately, at a time when the art might have perished or degenerated into a forgotten form, as often happens when dance outlives its immediacy or historical justification, a new era began in Ceylon and dance was swept along with it. Beginning in the sixteenth century, the rule of the Kandyan kings established itself, and while other parts of the island were buffeted by vying powers from the outside world, Kandy remained stable and the Kandyan kings the most powerful series of monarchs the island had ever known. They lived in almost uninterrupted isolation until the nineteenth century when the British absorbed their last vestiges of control and assumed the functions they had hitherto guarded for themselves. During this long period Kandyan dance was under royal patronage and turned into a kingly amusement for the entertainment of the court and for the public on special occasions of temporal celebrations. Dancers were given grants of land, and their descendants perpetuated the art much in the same way that fiefs transmit their loyalties and labors over the generations within a feudality.

Divested of the necessity for the religious and mythological themes of India, many new dances were composed. These included scenes of court life, paeans extolling the king, and even more secular aspects of daily life and comic events all of which lightened the original

Hindu flavor. Some of the dances were about elephants, some imitated swooping hawks, and one dance, the "Stick dance," is performed with the dancers erect and rigid as if they were sticks.

While the new themes introduced were rarely Buddhist—the Lesser Vehicle never forbade dance but still provided little opportunity for it—Kandyan dance nevertheless found its way at this time into the country's most important Buddhist ceremony, the showing of Buddha's tooth annually in August during the great *perahera* or procession, which remains even today Ceylon's most gala festival. For this, along with trains of elephants and howdahs, rows of saffron-robed *bikkhus* or monks, palanquins of objects from the temple, and the umbrellas and paraphernalia characteristics of Oriental pomp, all moving in slow progress before the monstrance of the tooth, scores of drummers and dancers also participate in the parade. They pause at intervals along the route and perform fragments of their dances before the throngs who line the streets of the city. Kandyan dance has become so integrated with this all-important festival that it is now hard to think of the annual showing of the tooth without associating it with dance. Since the word *perahera* (parade or procession) is a Portuguese word, it is also a tempting thought to date this and its inclusion of the dance at the end of the sixteenth century when the Portuguese arrived in Ceylon.

The connection with Buddhism was curious for several reasons. Firstly, because the dance derived from an alien religion, and, secondly, because it was latterly concerned with kings instead of with gods. But once the sympathy between the two was established, it later served an unforeseen purpose. By the time of the decline of the Kandyan kings, when they were no longer able to support the dancers or maintain their palaces, the temples took over willingly and naturally. Since the nineteenth century, the temples of Ceylon have assisted the art, providing it with their courtyards as a place to perform in, their holy days and celebrations as the occasion for it, and even contributing money and perquisites to the artists for their subsistence. Recent times show that somehow despite the long years and the changing turbulence of history the connection between dance and religion was never really broken, and at a time of peril the two have worked well together for the mutual benefit of each. The inclusion of dance as part of temple services created an aura of attractiveness around the religion that the people needed to counterbalance the austerity otherwise of Lesser Vehicle Buddhism.

The costume for the Kandyan dance traditionally followed since the era of the Kandyan kings (with only slight variants) is one of the most spectacular to be found anywhere in Asia. It consists almost entirely of beaten silver. The hat-like headdress of silver starts from a high cone sticking straight up in the air, and levels out into a wide brim which shadows the face just above the eyebrows. From this tiny silver paillettes like the heart-shaped leaves of the peepul tree (the sacred tree under which the Lord Buddha first attained spiritual enlightenment) dangle, and when the dancer moves they glisten like raindrops in the sunlight. Huge mango-shaped cups of silver studded with large square-cut blue sapphires hang from the hat like earrings to frame the ears. Plaques of silver fit over each shoulder as epaulettes and extend down to the biceps. On each wrist the dancer wears matching bracelets of silver moulded like bowknots and studded again with blue sapphires. A triangle of silver, ornamented with three bulbous half-circles, points downward from the meshed chain of mail that serves as a belt at the waist. The dancers are normally bare-chested except for a cobweb of milk-white strips of beads dotted with circles of faded brown and yellow elephant tusk-tips which look like slices of agates. Each dancer wears on his feet a narrow silver tube filled with grains of silver to rattle like bells and bent to circle around the instep under the ankle. This is tied with string around the great toe. The only cloth used in the costume is the long white skirt around the loins, the razor-sharp pleated flounces at the hips, and a long strip of red, blue and white braided cotton ending with a tassel which hangs from the peak of the headdress and reaches well below the hips. The drummers who stand close to the dancers as they accompany them are naked except for a long, close-fitting skirt of white cotton and a matching half-turban showing the top of their wavy, black hair. The drums are unornamented, strung around the neck, and played with both hands which beat each side either separately or together. One end of the drum is made from monkey skin, the other from deer hide. The wood may either be coconut, jak, or other local woods for which I know no name in English.

Kandyan dance, like Kathakali, is virile, energetic, almost violent, and performed exclusively by men. You immediately recognize its

94

origins in India from the postures and gesticulations. The dancer's knees are always splayed, spread to form a diamond shape from the crotch to the joining heels on the ground with the buttocks drawn slightly back. The torso weaves back and forth while the arms are held out at shoulder level and bent at the elbow. The hands and fingers design further patterns in the air. The dance is performed barefoot.

There are some significant differences, however, between Kandyan dance and its Indian counterpart. Today, the *mudras* or hand gestures are almost completely lost in Ceylon—partly because the language they signified originally was a foreign one with a different syntax and connotations, and partly because dance there leaned more toward the ornamental than toward the specific and literal as in India. What *mudras* remain in Kandyan dance are only vaguely suggestive. They represent, for instance, the walk of an elephant, or can indicate fright or laughter, but the dance code of conveying meaning through conventional hand positions and formations has dissipated itself. The basic hand characteristics of Kandyan dance, such as the fingers curled backward with the thumb tucked in at the palm, or, again, the forefinger bent and fastened with the thumb which lies over it, are now without any particular significance. When a Kandyan dancer tells you that in his dance he can communicate anything, he is referring to an emotion or idea which he believes is conveyable as a mood or an atmosphere. He cannot however recite a sentence exactly and precisely as a Bharata Natya or Kathakali dancer can.

Certain elements, however, of the dance described in the ancient treatises of India are preserved in Kandyan dance while they have disappeared from India proper. Most notable of these are the whirls known in Sanskrit as *brahmari*. The Kandyan dancer makes a speciality of spinning around, pivoting on one foot or throwing himself in the air in a complete circle, *tour jeté* and the like. Another form of this is the turning of the torso around and around until the tasseled string attached to the headdress swirls around the dancer. Still other movements now characteristic of Kandyan dance may never have been specifically Indian. One is the shoulder shudder, where the body of the dancer is immobile but his two shoulders flutter up and down in a series of involuntary reflexes. Another is the strange movement the dancer makes when he rolls his eyes upwards until only the whites are showing and shakes his head from side to side on the stem of the neck until it looks as if he has a dozen faces. At other times, the dancer will look behind him first to the left, then to the right, and as he increases the speed of this movement, the effect is that the dancer's head is revolving on his shoulders. In addition to these somewhat sensational aspects of Kandyan dance and its high degree of acrobatic virtuoso skill, there are the quieter, more sober chains of movement in which the dance progresses simply through the three speeds, slow, moderate and fast, as it does in India, and where the performer acts out passages of homage to the gods or kings, or where there are interludes of abstract or pure dance, and ponderous passages where he sings and enacts a short descriptive story.

The training of a Kandyan dancer is rigorous and lasts for six years. The pupil starts first by stamping the simpler rhythms with his feet. When a certain number of the metrical patterns is mastered in perfect time, he adds a few simple arm and hand gestures. Then he begins learning a repertoire. These are traditional pieces which follow special songs and their prescribed movements. After this, the dancer has learned all the basic elements there are to know. If he is talented, he can then add his own embellishments to the gestures and add syncopations to the already established rhythms. If he has genius, he is permitted a number of liberties but he must keep within certain regulations and the aesthetic framework. He must retain the proper posture, execute all the more famous of the traditional movements in their exact place and understand perfectly the subtle meanings of the songs he sings before he can elaborate on them. The onus on the creative Kandyan dancer is heavy. He is re-enacting age-old traditions for new audiences. On him falls the burden of clarification and interpretation before people not born when the Kandyan kings were at their height, and who now require more exhilaration in their dance than the culture which Ceylon fostered and developed originally provided. This creative latitude given the Kandyan dancer is fraught with the possibility of solecisms. Not all of the ones today are entirely successful.

The greatest of living Kandyan dancers is Gunaya, pronounced Gunia. There is little doubt that he is Ceylon's flashiest showpiece. He is, for instance, the only dancer I know of whose picture has been used on a postage stamp. His photograph also appears on no less than a dozen pamphlets issued by various tourist bureaux dedicated to convincing foreigners that they should come to Ceylon. Calendars, posters and advertisements bearing his likeness in color or in black and white can be seen anywhere from humble shops along village roads to swank airline offices in the capital, Colombo. The government is fully cognizant of his importance, not only as a cultural attraction and a tourist asset but as a significant part of Ceylon's renascent nationalism and Sinhalization. He is the foremost instructor at the recently organized National Academy of Dance supported by the government. When a very important ship comes into Colombo's harbor briefly, Gunaya himself is dispatched, along with a few other dancers and drummers, to give one of the famous shipboard performances. And he is, I believe, the only Kandyan dancer of importance ever to have appeared abroad. He has toured India with enormous success; thirty years ago he visited Germany as part of the Carl Hagenbeck Circus where he was billed along with "The Wild Man of Borneo" as "The Devil-Dancer from Ceylon."

Gunaya's preeminent position in Ceylon's world of dance may suggest to the foreigner that he is a professional artist with all the trappings of temperament and authority we associate with our more complicated performers of the West. No picture could be more misleading. Gunaya, now in his fifties, remains exactly as he started, a simple villager, smiling, amiable, modest and unaware of the prerogatives to which similar attainment entitles other artists in other countries. He lives in a small and modest hut a few miles out of the town of Kandy, and to reach him you must drive along bumpy, rocky roads, following narrow tracks out into the side of a ravine running along the twisting curves made by the river below. At a point, you stop the car and begin a downward trek of several hundred yards before you reach his house. But if you send advance word through a servant or errand boy, Gunaya will be patiently waiting at the top of the hill to spare you the climb down and back.

Gunaya generally speaks only when spoken to and only answers questions rather than initiate a subject of conversation. He is extraordinarily articulate about technical aspects of the dance, and can explain what he does and how he does it with an acumen that belongs more properly to the academician. If you pose him less specialized questions you are apt to receive rather less satisfactory answers than you might hope for, and the grave simplicity of his approach to art shows itself here more than in his forthright exposition of dance detail. I once asked him what made him become a dancer, to which he replied with a note of surprise, "My father was a dancer; it is in my blood." And again when I asked him why he continued to dance, he answered, "When I dance I feel happy," and then fumbling a bit, he rephrased his answer, "I dance to feel happy." Somehow in these two simple answers the aesthetic of Gunaya emerges. Dance is a conscious skill, but his approach to it is as instinctive and inexplicable as the fine motions of an animal, and his motivation in the art is as innocent as the human's most basic impulse, that of pleasure.

Without question, the two outstanding dancers of Ceylon today are Gunaya for Kandyan dancing and Henagamaya for the lesser art of devil-dancing. Both men are distinguished artists. Both are old— Gunaya says he has ten more years to dance, then he will just teach —and each has a mellow command of his special medium so great as to discourage the younger, more boisterous and athletic dancers who emulate them. When you see either of these two artists, you are not only seeing the best in this exuberant island, but you are witnessing as well an insight through dance into the workings of the gentle and delightful people of Ceylon.

The dances of Ceylon are not confined, however, to these two highly evolved forms alone. There are numerous miscellaneous, almost fragmentary, forms which occasionally appear on holidays or festivals. As you drive along the roads, your car may be stopped to let a procession pass. There will always be a set of white-turbaned, bare-chested drummers prancing in double file, who at intervals dance a series of backward and forward steps, and pivoting side movements. Or outside your window at a hotel or house you will hear from time to time the faint beats of a tiny, miniature hand drum. There, for a few annas, two boys dressed in blue silk and with white-painted, lip-sticked faces will perform a little dance of embrace. In rhythmic posturing they will throw their arms around each other, at the waist, over the shoulders, then one hand at the waist while the other arm flies over the shoulder, the movements alternating in rapid succession as the speed increases. When they are tired, they stop and walk along to an-

98

other likely house where they will repeat the same dance until they have collected enough money to warrant their day's effort. The meaning and origins of these bits and pieces of what once were more extended, fuller expressions are now lost in the long, forgetful heritage of the Sinhalese nation.

Although nearly all dancing is the private sphere of men in Ceylon, two dances are performed by women. One is a simple dance of welcome, which consists of the girls dressed in colorful blouses and skirts, with rows of beads around their necks and their hair tied in a high knot on the top of their heads, bowing and bending in a series of stylized obeisances. This dance is performed for distinguished visitors arriving in the country, or in honor of local dignitaries who take up their abode in a new area. Another dance for women is the "Pot Dance," where a group of ladies, swaying gracefully, toss lightly into the air earthenware pots of a kind used daily to fetch water from the community well, and catch them as they turn slowly around, first one way, then the other. Among the Muslims in the South, and there is a sizable minority of them, there are fierce sword and stick dances of mock combat. It is claimed that during these performances, if the fighters are not carefully watched, they may injure each other seriously. But all the ones that I have seen were safe, exciting, and more artful than angry.

The Ceylonese are rightfully proud of their dances, not only for their intrinsic qualities or their variety and degree of excellence, but for their prevalence. The people of Ceylon love their dances and admire their artists, and many of them see their country as one whose primary charm is its dance. One patriotic acquaintance of mine, in trying to make very clear to me that Ceylon is a country of dance, pointed out that every day at five o'clock at the Zoological Gardens just outside Colombo even the elephants dance. And this too is true.

Drama

Ceylon, despite its abundance of dance, is not without drama forms. In fact, devil-dancing as it is presented in a full performance contains a number of sections which are entirely theatrical in intent and character. In between bouts of dancing and periods of actual ritual procedure, little skits of comedy are always enacted. It is here that *The Killing of Rama* referred to in the section on India's epic poems appears. Many of them pertain to marriage, its trials and tribulations, and some, because of their connection with rituals of the past now lost in obscurity, seem almost meaningless and incoherent.

Each devil-dance troupe has its own repertoire of playlets which can be inserted at will in a performance. These not only vary from troupe to troupe but from year to year, and the creativity and originality needed to keep the people's interest expresses itself here. Although a few playlets are traditional and handed down from generation to generation, many are invented as soon as the old ones become boring or stale. Sometimes the dancers interrupt the show and improvise a series of jokes on any theme they choose. Unfortunately because of the language barrier, some of these interludes are of less immediate appeal to the foreign spectator than the passages of dance which are more exciting visually and need no interpreting. But for the student of drama, they are fascinating, and if you have a guide who is not squeamish about translating their licentiousness you will also find them extremely amusing.

Some of them are nothing more than passages of pure mime and afford the spectator no difficulty in understanding them. One episode in the most interesting of the devil-dances occurs when the lead dancer, dressed as a woman, begins a long solo performance. A tray with all the implements of a woman's toilet, each made of banana stalks and palm leaves, is brought into the center of the arena. The actor imitates all the actions of a woman's life, her walk, her mannerisms and her vanity. She bathes with water literally, then washes her hair of shredded palm leaves, combs it, rubs it with oil, and ties it up in a knot on the top of her head and pierces it with a large hair-pin. She preens before the hollow mirror. Then she spins and weaves, and finally, taking a little puppet from the basket, she washes it, suckles it, changes its clothes and carries it around the arena, making it click its wooden hands together in a begging gesture to collect extra cents from the spectators. Then she sings a lullaby and rocks the doll to sleep. The mime in these instances is always of an astonishingly high quality. Without benefit of make-up or lighting and with only the patent artificialities of the false accoutrements of hair and toilet articles, the actor perfectly impersonates a woman. The audience cheers with appreciation and never tires of seeing these graphic enactments of the life of woman by a member of the opposite sex.

Originally, this interlude was connected with the legend of the Barren Queens, part of the vast folklore of Ceylon. It told the story of seven marvellous queens who through the efficacy of the devil-dance and its faithful mirroring of woman's life through sympathetic magic were ultimately able to conceive. Whatever the ethnological significance may be, the interlude stands like the others as a brilliant bit of acting and a respite from the taxing acrobatics of the dance and the opiate ritual and the religious mysteries of the evening.

For the foreigner the passages of mime afford a particularly interesting glimpse into not only Ceylon's dance and drama, but into that of all Asia as he will later discover. We in the West associate mime primarily with the clown, and it is nearly always used to make us laugh at some sort of hilarious behavior. Whenever it is treated in a serious way, it is pathos rather than tragedy which emerges. In Asia, however, mime has neither ludicrous nor pathetic connotations although it is occasionally handled in either way. It is accepted primarily as a legitimate theatrical device. While one may laugh or weep, the laughter does not come from the slapstick nor the tears from the helpless, sentimental enactments of the Chaplin or Marceau convention. The mimes of Asia have humanity and individual personality, and the Asian can see himself in their actions as richly and clearly delineated as we see ourselves in, say, the characters of a modern play. The mime's trick of making us see what is not there, of feeling what is happening without witnessing the actual causations is somehow more real in Asia, and the special, circus, off-beat taste it evokes in the West is entirely absent.

Ceylon also has a number of theatrical forms on the order of folk plays which are as much dramas as they are dances. Several of these have survived among the people and without becoming classical are still available away from the larger cities in the villages of the island. These are Kolam, Sokari, Nadagam, and the Pasu. And the merits of these are not to be minimized despite their present state of decline and now attenuated, vague contact with only restricted sections of the people. Of these the most important is Kolam, a masked dance-drama, which is to be found exclusively in the village of Ambalangoda about sixty miles from Colombo along the Galle road. There, two troupes, one belonging to Gunadasa, the other to Ariyapala, still perform occasionally, and for around a hundred and fifty rupees will present a special, abbreviated performance for the interested tourist. Both troupes are equally good as artists, although Gunadasa's leading actor-dancer, Tilaka, a young fisherman in his teens (the performers earn their living between the rare performances by fishing) is a spectacular attraction for his gymnastic ability, his fluid grace in combining the sport of tumbling with the art of dancing, and his range of roles as diverse as fierce and heroic demons or cringing, unsavory jackals.

Of the four drama forms or folk plays Ceylon has, Kolam is of the greatest antiquity, although in its present form it is obvious that a number of modern innovations have been made and some of its traditional aspects have disappeared. The word Kolam derives from Tamil and means "costume," "guise," or "representation." According to the introductory story which is usually sung at the beginning of each performance, Kolam was used to amuse a pregnant queen whose particular craving took the form of being pleased by this particular masked performance unknown in her own country. There is little doubt that the form originated in India. However, while the art with its enormous masks of carved and painted wood throve in Ceylon, similar masked dances have entirely disappeared from the Tamil areas, and most of India. Kolam masks are of extreme delicacy, and they are, I think, probably the finest examples of wood carving still being executed for the theatre in the modern world. Since the life of a mask used in actual performances is normally around fifty years, and the masters of the troupes hold their position by virtue of their carving skill as well as acting ability, the art has been perpetuated. They range from small surface masks for simple commoners, which cover only the immediate area of the face, to huge hollowed-out tree trunks which fit over the whole head for the King and Queen. These latter combine the smooth painted face of the character with a headdress pierced with holes and filigrees of flowers and birds, crowned with petalled domes and knobs.

The masks for royal characters are so heavy and tall that the actor has to steady them with a wooden sword held tight within one of the perforations at the crown. Even then, the actor totters into the area guided by an attendant who sees that the way is clear for him since he himself cannot bend down to see where he is going without running the risk, were the mask to topple, of breaking his neck. After a few minutes of standing stationary and delivering a few brief lines, the King and Queen are led back to the dressing area, exhausted and sweating. Because Kolam masks are unsuited for talking through, and it is extremely difficult to hear the actors when they speak, the drama originally must have been entirely in pantomime.

The structure of Kolam is easy to grasp. To the accompaniment of drummers and musicians who sing out the story in short melodious phrases, the masked characters make their appearance in steady succession one after the other. Each, except the King and Queen who scarcely move, perform an introductory dance. Then they leave and reappear only when the course of the play requires their presence again. All characters are stock stereotypes, and additions to the cast are made only when the master of the troupe decides to create a new mask to suit a new play.

In the two remaining troupes of Ambalangoda, the characters of each are identical and their introductory dances follow the same general outlines. First appears an aged peasant woman looking for her drunken husband. This is followed by a set of two policemen. Then comes a quartet of soldiers fresh back from war. Their masks are puffy distortions of the human face with gashes of red painted scars to show the agony of their wounds. These are followed by a Dutch couple, greatly caricatured in a souvenir of the days of Dutch rule, a laundryman and his wife, a pompous village chieftain, and finally the King and Queen together with their mustached Prime Minister. A second series of introductory appearances and dances of mythological personages then occurs. These are demons and gods of various sorts, with large brilliantly painted, flamboyant and sometimes terrifying masks: the Naga or snake demon with dozens of hooded cobras stemming from his head like hair and huge white teeth and a scarlet tongue sticking out; the Garuda bird with feathers and an enormous beak; and a series of further demons climaxed by Maru Raksasa, the most malevolent and awe-inspiring of all, from whose bloody fangs hangs the carved, limp body of a child. A miscellany follows them: lions and jackals and various gods and goddesses. Some of these look like Egyptian figures with sphinx-like claws and shrouded faces, or *kinnaras*, half-man half-bird creatures with simple, plain faces of pink or yellow, and body frames of wings and bulging chests. The play proper finally begins. Its theme varies, but often the play is an episode from the life of Buddha or his disciples.

One of the most famous plays in Kolam repertoire is the story of two *kinnaras* who are living happily in the forest dancing, singing, and playing musical instruments. The King of Benaras (India) who is hunting sees them and is struck by the beauty of the female. He kills her mate and begins to woo her, but she is obdurate and only grieves. He promises her wealth and position but these fail to move her from her bereavement. The King becomes angry and just as he starts to kill her, Buddha appears, saves her, and as a boon restores her mate to life as well. The play ends with Buddha's homily on conjugal fidelity.

Another extremely popular play is the story of a prince who goes to Taxila (formerly India, now Pakistan) to study and so excels as a scholar that his master gives him his daughter in marriage. On their way home they encounter a hunter who falls in love with the young wife. The prince and the hunter fight, and at one point when the prince's sword falls out of his hands, the wife picks it up and becoming enamoured of her husband's opponent, hands it to the hunter who thereupon kills the prince. The hunter then asks the wife to hand over her jewelry which she does, and then he abandons her, saying that if she could be so foolish with one husband, she would surely be the same with him. Buddha appears in the form of a jackal and there ensues the enactment of a pertinent fable which comments on the play proper. A greedy jackal, performed by the masked actor bouncing stiffly and at full-length along the ground in a series of pushups, is carrying a chunk of meat in his mouth. He swims across the river, and seeing a fish, opens his mouth to catch it. A hawk sweeps down at this moment and seizes the meat, leaving the jackal without either his meat or the fish.

Sokari is, roughly described, the same as Kolam, although on a much more fragmentary scale. It is found in the hills of Ceylon, especially those of the Kandy and Badulla areas. These stories nearly all concern a beautiful wife called Sokari and her infidelities. Sometimes she thinks her husband is dead and accepts the physical advances of her servant. Sometimes she sends for a doctor to attend her ailing husband. He falsely pronounces her husband dead and succeeds in seducing her. In nearly all these plays, the concluding scene or finale is a curious one of mat weaving, in which the revived or reconciled husband and wife work together to make the mat on which they are to sleep that night. According to Dr. E. R. Sarathchandra, the symbolism of the mat weaving is one of "amity, reconciliation or union," the ultimate reconciliation of husband and wife.

Nadagam (again a Tamil word and a derivative from the Sanskrit for dance-drama) is an entirely recent theatre form, having been introduced around the beginning of the nineteenth century. It consists in the main of a series of songs with only the thinnest thread of a story to link them. Sometimes they are based on Christianity, sometimes on Western fairy tales, and occasionally on themes of Buddha's life in India. Nadagam is only rarely performed now and remains in the life of the people largely in its songs which are still somewhat popular, and in the tunes and airs that still accompany the infrequent puppet plays of the villages of Ceylon.

Pasu is the Sinhalization of what we know in the West as the Passion Play. It is performed at Easter time in Negombo, a town on the coast north of Colombo where the densest Catholic population of the island is found. The characters of Christ, Mary, Joseph and the rest are represented by statues carried around the stage area and placed in appropriate positions during the action. The events themselves are described sometimes by a narrator and sometimes by a chorus singing four-part harmony in hymn style. The Pasu, despite its innocuous subject matter, has met with a surprising number of upsets during its life in Ceylon. Some years back it was the custom on the day before the performance for the village boys to blacken their faces and assume the form of certain devils who ran through the streets heralding the arrival of Lucifer. Lucifer then appeared and questioned them. The boys would respond by revealing all the scandals of the village and the various family secrets which were not widely known to the public. Because of this, the Pasu was eventually banned.

Again, not long ago, it was decided to dispense with the statues and to have human beings portray the characters, with the parts of Veronica and Mary and the like performed by actual women. This met with immediate Church disapproval, and the Archbishop of

Colombo proscribed these live performances on the grounds that the appearance of women in theatricals was "contrary to the traditions of the country," and therefore, it was assumed, of questionable morality.

Theatre as theatre is not a part of the best of Ceylon's traditions. Dance, however, is very much one of the country's most impressive attractions. As in every Asian country, there is an inseparability between dance and drama, and it is difficult to think of, say, devil-dancing without its acted or mimed interludes. In the same way, it is difficult to disassociate Kolam plays from their brilliant introductory and explanatory dances. Ceylon theatrically is a wonderfully rewarding country. There is a superabundance of dance activity. There is a remarkable standard of dazzling, pyrotechnical body movements. There is as well a genuine core of serious and meritorious artistic achievement which courses through every production no matter how simple its setting. Fortunately for us these arts of Ceylon are available to the outsider without difficulty and require only minimal arrangements which any Tourist Bureau can undertake for an enterprising visitor.

For some reason, perhaps because of the very preponderance of separate and distinct dances, Ceylon lacks a modern theatre or a purely dramatic art. In the past, beginning with the end of the nineteenth century and continuing through the early part of the twentieth, various attempts at creating a modern theatre were made. One of the more successful but brief ventures was begun by a Parsi whose troupe in Colombo popularized modern, Westernized Indian music. Another group had a success with an adaptation of *Romeo and Juliet*. But these attempts melted into oblivion. Until a few years ago there was also a group of actors in Colombo who performed a few social plays, mostly translations from the West, and some historical plays dealing with the exploits of ancient Sinhalese kings, those of Anuradhapura, the capital for centuries before the birth of Christ, of Polonnaruwa, the short-lived but architecturally productive period of the thirteenth and fourteenth centuries, and, of course, of the more recent Kandyan period. But even this troupe was forced to close, and the historical plays that are now performed—as part of the Sinhalization of Ceylon—appear only occasionally at high-school or college graduation ceremonies, or as an excuse to solicit funds for the building of further extensions to schools already in existence.

Theatre as a modern or independent form in Ceylon is too inchoate at present to merit more than cursory attention, and what little there is, even with its generous admixtures of music and dance, is either in bad taste or a poor imitation of theatre elsewhere. It is quite possible that Ceylon may never have a genuine, flourishing modern drama outside occasional amateur productions in its schools and universities. For the present and probably for many centuries to come, dance and the more dramatic folk plays seem to suffice and afford all the aesthetic outlet the nation requires. Certainly this is enough to elicit no complaints from the visitor.

BURMA

Burma is a startlingly charming, friendly and devoutly Buddhist country in the heart of Southeast Asia. It is bordered by India on one side, Siam on another, and with China on a third, the Burmese frontier is two thousand miles long.

It is the only colonized area of Asia whose theatrical arts have from the beginning been unstintingly admired by the conquering Westerner. Even the John Murray *Handbook for Travellers in India, Burma and Ceylon,* that biased, ultra-British guide first published in 1859 and successively revised through something like sixteen editions down to the present, makes its only mention of dance or drama in connection with Burma. "The traveller should make a point before leaving Burma of seeing something of the *Pwé,* the national amusement of the people," it says, and adds in consonance with its general patronizing tone "the majority of the audience stay the whole night, but an hour or two of the performance will satisfy. . . ."

Burma also has the distinction of being the only ex-colony to have produced a book about its own theatre, written in English in 1937 by a Burman, and published abroad. This excellent little manual by Dr. Maung Htin Aung is called *Burmese Drama* and the Oxford University Press wisely reprinted it in 1947.

Moreover, Burma, with the possible exception of Japan, is the only country of Asia where the foreign colony of diplomats and traders, usually so aloof from local arts, have nearly all witnessed a local theatrical performance and responded to its pleasures without the condescension and indulgence which until recently have characterized many of their attitudes.

The reason for so much kindliness towards Burma lies, I think, in the overwhelming pleasantness of its people. They are enthusiastic and outgoing, even to strangers, and it is hard for the dourest of foreigners to resist Burmese appeal. The happy acceptance of Burma and Burmese life which the country elicits from the visitors applies not merely to its amusements, but to its politics as well. Somehow even when the Burmese are being most controversial in an international sphere, their national character, through the mysterious alchemy of charm, transforms their actions into something sweetly reasonable and acceptable. A possibly significant sidelight is that some years back Burma's Prime Minister U Nu himself translated Dale Carnegie's *How to Win Friends and Influence People*. The book became a best-seller in Rangoon.

The outgoing warmth that the Burmese people bring to bear on every aspect of their life, regardless of whether it is religion, politics, or the simple, social graces, spills over into their theatre. A delicious sense of humor affects even their most sober moments. In Burmese masked plays, Ravana, the villain of the *Ramayana*, for example, is treated as a comic, and however wicked he may be according to the plot, the actor must turn him into a delightful, laughable, even harmless character. In the spirit dances, where the *nats* or thirty-seven ancient and animistic spirits of Burma have endured despite the influx of Buddhism (something along the lines of devil-dancing in Ceylon), much of the performance is comic. When the women are possessed by the spirits, their actions are often humorous—one *nat* is a drunkard and offers the spectators whiskey, another is a child who plays pranks on the other members of the cast, another is a vain and silly woman.

Even in war Burmese good nature asserts itself. Burma in the middle of the eighteenth century after her victorious war of conquest against Siam and the sacking of the Siamese capital brought back as captives whole troupes of actors and dancers. Their punishment was to dance at the courts of the Burmese kings. Burma also, except for the hill tribes and fierce peoples of Upper Burma, is the only country of Asia lacking fighting dances and the elaborate, stylized sword dances of mock combat which appear elsewhere in Asia almost with supererogation.

Part of the contagion the outsider feels about Burmese theatricals also comes from the popularity showered on them by every class of person within the country. There is a *pwé* of some kind or other each full moon night everywhere in city and village. Every festival, and Burma is a country of festivals in a very literal sense, means a theatrical performance at some place near by. To accommodate the crowds who flock to see the newest play, or their old favorite dancers, even the downtown section of the modern city of Rangoon mushrooms overnight with a number of thatched roof huts fenced off by woven palm-leaf fences in every park and clearing. Some of the larger ones hold a thousand spectators who sit crosslegged on the ground on tattered reed mats or off to one side in low-slung canvas beach chairs and watch the actors on their temporary stages of bamboo. At all these performances, a special reserved area is roped off for the shaven-headed, bare-shouldered, yellow-robed Buddhist priests who cluster together watching the spectacle with as much secular enjoyment as the most profane of the audience. And among the audience you will find government officials, scholars from the universities, and foreign guests brought by their Westernized Burmese friends. During the lulls between full moons, you may easily be entertained after dinner at a friend's house with a private showing of a dance performance or one of the rarer, informal puppet shows by a master just arrived in the capital from Mandalay up North. When a new play is successful, the avid Burmese public wants not only to see it but to read it, and one play I know of sold something better than twenty thousand copies within a few weeks of its first edition. This, even in a country where literacy is a problem and where money is not abundant, betters the reading public of most Broadway or West End plays.

Aside from the ancient folk plays which tell, and have told for centuries now, the life of Buddha or the dance-drama forms borrowed from neighboring India and Indianized Siam, the first real drama dates from the end of the eighteenth century. Although Burma's theatrical history in this respect is fairly recent, there has always been a special regard and notable respect for theatre throughout the country. In the ninth century, when a portion of Upper Burma was ruled by China, the Burmese ambassadors presenting themselves at the Peking Court sang songs and danced alphabet dances in which they formed in gesture and posture the felicitous ideographs for greeting and homage. Again, in the eleventh century, when one of the mightiest of all Burmese kings went on a marauding expedition as far west as India itself, he set up at intervals carved stone figures of Burmese musicians and dancers as symbols of his successful conquest. When his grandson repeated the exploit and raided India once again, these stone statues are reputed to have come to life and rendered the soldiers homesick with their melodies and movements.

At the beginning of the nineteenth century Burma became the first country in the world to create a Ministry of Theatre. Its aims were various: to exercise some sort of control over the widespread and sometime unruly theatricals; to ensure that performances respected both the sanctity of the Buddhist religion and depicted the courts of Burmese kings with propriety and decorum; and possibly, too, to stimulate the theatre, particularly the puppet theatre, along lines agreeable to the State and to keep it in political accord with the policies of the King. (In actual practice this worked in another way. The puppeteers conscious of their new patronage used their art to air grievances and spoke out through their puppets with a boldness that actors never dared.)

By the beginning of the twentieth century, Burma had developed the "star" system in her theatre, and three actors attained such fame that they were worshiped the length and breadth of the country. These were Aungbala, whose funeral was an occasion for riotous behavior and mass expression of emotion; Sein Kadon, who dazzled audiences with his special costume of hundreds of tiny electric light bulbs that flickered on and off at dramatic moments in his plays; and the greatest of them all, U Po Sein, who continued to dance and act until his death in 1950. U Po Sein's eccentricity, if it can be called that, expressed itself in that he never appeared on stage without two real-life, British ex-soldiers, each carrying a rifle, standing prominently near him. But he also was concerned with lifting the position of the actor to one of fullest respect and consequently devoted himself to good works and to a display of exemplary moral character—qualities rather lacking in the actors of the past. His gifts to charity were unbounded and his fund-raising performances for the Red Cross during the First World War finally resulted in his being awarded special recognition and a title from the government. Through him the taste of the people was elevated and the highest quarters acknowledged his art—a feat even the Ministry of Theatre had been unable to achieve. At present his son, Kenneth, is carrying on the tradition in his own way. To the delight of Burmese audiences, and to the annoyance of his foreign admirers, he inserts bits of Ray Bolger-type tap routines and "boomps-a-daisy" in the middle of a *pwé*.

A loose connection between theatre and the government has continued to the present time, and many officials and members of influential families have tried their hand at playwriting, and sometimes have even acted on the stage themselves. Prime Minister U Nu, very much the hero of his people and one of the most reasoning and seasoned politicians the country has ever produced, has expressed himself on the stage as a playwright on a number of occasions. In his youth he wrote well-conceived, charming little plays about subjects as diverse as marriage problems and their equitable solution (one is about incompatibility from a Freudian point of view) and religion. His latest play, a success as much for its distinguished authorship as for its content, is called *The People Win Through* and describes the failure of Communism as a means of government in Burma. During U Nu's recent tour of America, the Pasadena Playhouse entertained him with a performance in English of a translation of the play.

The relationship of politics and the stage is a traditional one in Burma. The masterpiece *Wizaya* by U Pon Nya, Burma's most distinguished dramatist who was born at the beginning of the nineteenth century, is a case in point. It appeared at a time when there was a jockeying for power in the country and an erring froward prince, after assuring his followers that he had had a change of heart, wanted to usurp the throne. To disguise the contemporaneous content of his theme, U Pon Nya set the play in Ceylon, and drawing on various themes from Buddhist stories already dear to the hearts of the people, he described how the glory of Ceylon resulted from just such a reformed leader. The play was immensely popular as a play, which fact contributed substantially to the opinion at the time that the prince might succeed in taking over the country. But his revolution failed, and both the prince and the playwright were killed for their participation in the attempted coup.

The word *pwé*, which covers all varieties of theatrical entertainment in Burma, means something that is "shown" and is exactly the equivalent of our word "show." At present there are around six different types of current *pwés*. These exist all over Burma, but are now most concentrated in the port city of Rangoon, where you find the largest population and the most money to be spent on luxury and amusement. The most important is the *Zat Pwé*. *Zat* comes from the ancient Indian word *Jataka*, which refers to the enormous body of stories and legends concerning the life of the Buddha.

Because Buddhism figures so vitally in Burmese life, it is necessary to digress a little. *Jataka* stories are normally confined to Buddha's youth. After his enlightenment, he is considered so holy that any representation, either in temple carvings or on the stage, is offensively sacrilegious. At the great stupas of Sanchi in Central India, for example, where some of the finest Buddhist carving in the world is to be found, the oddly shaped gateways and lattice fences of stone, while showing his disciples with remarkable verisimilitude, represent Buddha simply by blank spaces in the air or vacant chairs and empty daises. Similarly, in Burma no actor ever performs the role of Buddha, and the form of Buddhism is so strict there that even a lesser Buddha or monk is handled with circumspection. However in the Burmese transcriptions of the *Ramayana*, although Rama is treated as a "future" Buddha, the details of his life are freely and secularly represented.

To return to *Zat Pwé*, the word now means colloquially any performance of the "classical" theatre by a troupe of actors who, as the story progresses and the narrative permits, indulge in long passages of dance sequences. By "classical" theatre is meant a theatre of ancient origin, subject to formal rules of structure, confined to an almost procedural dramatic sequence, and suitable only for historical themes and their stylized portrayals. However, within this "classical" framework, sufficient latitude is allowed to keep the artist creative and even to permit certain innovations, but not enough to make him "modern" or contemporaneous in feeling or style to the point of transgressing this aesthetic barrier.

Usually a *Zat Pwé* starts around nine in the evening and continues until four in the morning. The plays, which are often newly composed for each run of a performance, are always set in one of the classical periods of Burmese history. They deal with kings and queens, deceitful courtiers and scheming, plotting prime ministers. There are questions of succession to the throne, flights by night into woodland hideouts, concealed identities and finally happy marriages and restorations to the throne. The structure of the plays generally calls for alternating scenes of comedy and scenes of pathos, the over-all theme

113

being the progress of the happiness of the leading characters into separation and hardship. The ending, however, is always a reunion and gladness prevails. At intervals, each character sings a song to emphasize the mood of the action which has just taken place. The costuming is gorgeous and exotic, with the kings and nobles robed in orange or peach satins studded with brilliants, crowned in cone-shaped head-dresses of gold, and carrying flashing, gleaming swords of silver.

Well after midnight, around two or three in the morning, the main dance scene begins. This part is called *Huit-Pa-Thwa*, a sort of *pas-de-deux*, in which the two foremost stars of the troupe dance their most brilliant routines. It is here that the audience sits up and takes notice, and while many innovations have been made in the *Zat Pwés* since their inception, this section has stood inviolate. The excuse in the plot for the *pas-de-deux* may be a festival at the court, a marriage feast, or an irrelevant interlude with no bearing on the plot. After it, the play resumes and leads towards its denouement. Throughout the evening, a full orchestra of Burmese instruments plays constantly—to announce the scene as one of gladness or sorrow, to lay its setting in the court or in a forest, to indicate the tone of prowess or dalliance, and to subtend the over-all mood. It accompanies each dance in a pulsating, vibrant, explosive symphony of sounds.

The full *Zat Pwé* orchestra called *saing* consists of about a dozen different instruments, and is the largest assembly of musicians used in Burma. It has ornately carved teakwood xylophones whose keys, made from a specially resonant bamboo which grows only near river banks, are struck with chamois-skin mallets that look like tack hammers. It may have several large drums shaped like enormous stemmed goblets which stand erect on the ground or which are suspended by a thong around the player's shoulder and played sidewise at the hip. There are ivory horns from which dangle silver funnels loosely fitted over the bell to augment the sound. There are various other percussion instruments—small, foot-long tubes of bamboo split like the straws of a broom which crack and snap as the player jerkily shakes them, and one man plays a set of square-shaped castanets in his left hand while he clanks two tiny thimble-size cymbals in his right.

The two chief instruments of the *saing* orchestra are extremely ornate and as pleasing to look at as to hear. One is a circle of twenty-one small graded drums ranging in sound from low to shrilly high. Each is tuned by placing a glob of moist rice paste in the center of the hide-covering to keep it taut. The tuning takes an hour, lasts only for overnight and must be repeated each time the drums are used. The pitch corresponds fairly closely to our own. The scale is septatonic, but *fa* and *ti* are much sharper and flatter, respectively, than in our well-tempered scale. The tuning varies according to whether the music is modern or classic, but each has sufficient similarities to our music so as not to sound altogether alien or unpleasant even on first hearing. The drums are encased in a sort of circular picket fence of gold-painted slats studded with bits of sparkling, reflecting mirrors. The performer sits at the center of the circle on a small stool and swirls around while he plays the rippling arpeggi of ascending and descending melodies on these drums. Above him stands a large, red, frosted glass light, something like an old-fashioned street lamp, attached to a wooden stand carved in the shape of a bird, and this illuminates the whole orchestra. The other of the special instruments is the pole from which hang two large gongs of heavy metal. The frame is shaped like a mythological beast, actually five animals in one—the horns of the stag issuing from the head, the hooves of the horse curled up over the gongs which hang from the center, the wings of the eagle along the body, the long thin body of the snake, and the tail of a fish. Altogether the instrument looks like a slender dragon. From its mouth at one end dangles a Christmas-tree decoration bulb of glossy red; in its curling tail is stuck a large chunk of ruby-colored glass. The deep, reverberating resonance of the gongs punctuates the main pulses of the music and determines the basic tuning of the orchestra.

The sound that this conglomeration of strange and beautiful instruments makes is without question one of the most satisfying in the Orient. For immediacy of appeal, at least to foreign ears, Burmese music ranks second in Asia only to Indonesian music. With this latter, it too shares the orchestral concept of music, which has become so indispensable a part of our musical thinking. The simultaneous playing of several different instruments gives music a texture and sensuous complexity which is now almost an essential prerequisite to our enjoyment, and the ensuing concord and consonances of several notes being struck or sounded at the same time, harmony in other words, is manifestly one of Burmese music's most satisfying charms. To the Asian in general, orchestral music may sometimes be akin to a jumble or confusion and an impediment to the transparent lucidity he likes to give his unadulterated melodies and rhythms; but for most Burmese only the thick fabric of orchestra sound can match the richness of his theatre arts. Sometimes the music accompanying a *Zat Pwé* sounds like bubbling water, sometimes remotely like a jam session of American jazz, with the several drums pounding out deafening meters and syncopes, one clashing with the other; often the music will begin with a synchronized burst like a packet of firecrackers suddenly going off, and then it will subside into languid tenderness only to break again into still more joyous, uncontrollably happy throbs of contrasting and conflicting timbres and resonances.

Nearly all dancing in Burma is based on or derived from the classical *Zat Pwé*, and it is invariably energetic and designed to excite, agitate and stimulate. Men and women always dance together, although there are some women who like to dance as men, and vice versa. The costume for each is lavish, generously sprinkled with spangles and diamantes sewn in patterns of dragons or birds. The colors are bright or pastel according to the dancer's whim, with the men wearing the gayer, louder hues. Women often wear a shade of peach color, which I find somehow characteristic of and peculiar to the country. Both men and women wear the *longyi*, a skirt-like sarong, which hangs from the waist to the floor, fastened with a belt of silver or studded rhinestones. Women attach an extra hem of white silk to their skirts, which trails on the ground, hides the feet and makes walking movements difficult and invisible. Each wears a blouse—the man's being loose fitting like a Chinese pyjama top, and the woman's being usually of a transparent material and tightly moulded to the figure. Around the smooth cylinder of hair pinned high on the crown of the head, the woman wears flowers. The man also wears flowers in the thin silk cloth of pink or yellow tightly fitted over his head and tied in a wide spray, rakishly flaring off to one side. In his earlobes he wears diamonds. Each carries a folding fan, and its opening and closing are integral, decorative motions of the dance.

The principle of Burmese dancing works in the following way. The dancer sings a short phrase. Its words determine the rhythm, as Burmese is a carefully regulated tonal language which abounds in precise long and short sounds. To extend the length of one of the words, for the sake of a melody, for example, would automatically alter the meaning. The drums repeat the rhythm. Then, as the full orchestra repeats the same passage of melody and rhythm, the dancer springs into dance. At the end of several of these phrases which altogether form a poem, and in which the whole procedure of song, drums, dance, full orchestra is repeated each time, a particular dance is completed. A sample dance fragment is: "From the palace rooms / The lady is waiting for the King / Now, up to dawn / He has not come." The concluding flourish is: "She loves him to the end of the world." Songs sometimes praise the sights of the countryside, the mysteries of the jungle, or the sanctity of a holy city. The themes, only as long as they are romantic or poetic, are unrestricted in their content.

The dancing itself is among the most virtuosic to be found in Asia. The dancers leap into the air with arms twisting and curling. Then down again in a series of deep knee bends, and sometimes from this squatting position they perform a series of Russian pliés. They whirl around on one foot with the leg extended. Sometimes the woman kicks her train back with a violent gesture and throws her hands backwards and forwards as if fighting the air. The performers smile throughout the dance and occasionally they break out laughing at their own good-natured exuberance. Both in the dance and in the drama parts of a *Zat Pwé* the actors laugh almost as much as the audience, and instead of being distracting for the Burmese, they find theatre more enjoyable if it is clear that the performers are having a good time too. Sometimes as a finishing movement of a dance, the woman will spring with lightning speed and land supine into her partner's outstretched arms. Because of the explosive nature of Burmese movement in dance, it is performed sporadically in short, sudden outbursts of energy. Although a dance program (out of its context within a *Zat Pwé*) normally lasts for about two hours, only about two-thirds of this time is actual dance. The pauses between phrases, the interval afforded by the singing of the phrase, and the drums' repetition of the rhythm give the dancers ample time to rest and recuperate from their exertions.

The basic starting posture for Burmese dancing is close to a crouch. The knees are spread as far apart as the *longyi* allows, buttocks thrust back and the pelvis retracted until the dancer hovers just above the

117

floor. The heels of the feet are held together with the feet splayed outwards in a wide "V." The elbows, with the hands at the hips and fingers pointing towards the audience, are thrust backwards and held close to the body so that they look like featherless, folded wings. The uplifted face looks high towards the ceiling. While actually moving, the thumb and forefinger of the hand which does not hold the fan, forms an "X" with the other fingers extended stiffly. At the end of a passage, the arms drop limply against the sides of the body, but the face remains upturned.

The dance which normally begins all performances is one of greeting and obeisance. During it the dancer bows with his fingertips placed together in front of his face, the fan balancing between the "V" of the two thumbs. The fingers flick in time with the music while the triangle formed by the thumbs remains. The hands separate and each twists and weaves in alternate wavering circles. The dancer undulates in a series of curving motions from his crouching position until he stands upright. There are many gestures. One is like a casual face-washing in which the hands pass before the face effortlessly and gracefully. Another is the concluding movement where, after a sudden leap, the dancer runs towards his spectators, pauses, claps his hands three times and crosses his wrists, with the relaxed hands pointing downwards.

It takes about six months for an average eight-year-old child (the usual starting age for a boy or girl) to learn this dance of greeting and to master the ten basic steps it contains. The study begins with the feet. He practices the rhythms by lifting his feet as if marking time. This is followed by the walk, and finally he adds the hand gestures and the more advanced turns. As dancers practice, they sing a mnemonic song which follows the tune of the music. The words are simple: "This is the first step; this is the second step, etc. . . . This is the changing of the hands, this is the turning of the head, this is the turning of the shoulder, etc." It is a curious sight to see a classroom full of slightly built young children, quiet almost to the point of listlessness, suddenly come to life with eyes flashing and little voices shrilly chanting as they jump and gyrate to the restless, demanding dance steps of Burma.

The emotional range of Burmese dancing is limited. Sorrow can only be represented inadequately. The Burmese say that you cannot

118

dance if you are really sad personally, and grief, simulated or real, affords no chance for dancing. There are, however, song passages where princesses are supposed to weep, or where the words go something like this: "My dear wife, our love is short-lived." Here the dance is more measured, the music is slower than ordinarily, the drums boom leisurely, and the dancer moves with a touch of restraint which is otherwise uncharacteristic of Burmese dance. But these are like interludes of quiet which only set off more dramatically the next passages of dance. As for love or the expression of lovemaking, the closest approximation is the final leap into the lover's arms at the end of a particularly lively flash of movement.

To a certain extent the stylized artificiality of the dance and its conventions is due to the influence of the puppets. Many passages are borrowed imitations of the stiff, jerky walk of the puppets, and certainly the almost excessively frequent soaring springs into the air belong more logically to a stringed marionette that can be held in the air indefinitely than to a human body.

To summarize, dance in Burma is dynamics of poses. Our dance for the most part is meaningful motion or the expressive interpretation of music's sounds. Burmese dancing, however, is a series of gesticulations, specified and determined by the aesthetic pleasure the sight of them gives. They are emotional only in that they capture the single mood of exaltation. The graphic or pictorial elements associated with interpretive dance are absent. Happily, no burden of understanding is placed on the spectator. The only thing required of him is an appreciation of virtuosity and technical brilliance.

Anyein Pwé is an abbreviated form of the *Zat Pwé*. Its cast consists of four people—two dancers and two clowns. The comic element, fully in keeping with the national character of Burma, has, naturally enough, wide scope in all Burmese theatricals. Throughout a *Zat Pwé*, regardless of its story, courses the thread of comedians who appear at intervals, dressed indigenously and in a ludicrous make-up of white eyebrows and cheeks, blots of rouge and black lines around the eyes. They crack jokes aimlessly, often unrelated to the plot, and amuse the audience with slapstick antics. *Anyein Pwé* simply extracts this favorite element, combines it with the dance interludes, and condenses them into a short evening's entertainment.

Yein Pwé is a combined dance and drama form based on religious themes, usually of allegorical significance. It is lengthy, involved, and embraces a vast cast whose actors often are amateurs. So elaborate in fact are the preparations for it that it is only performed on the most holy of festival days and before the highest ranking officials and dignitaries. In effect it is scarcely more than a pageant.

Yousshim Bwé or *Yokthe Pwé*, both terms are common, refers to the puppet or marionette shows for which Burma is famous. It is recognized that *Zat Pwé* and their derivatives of today owe a considerable debt to the puppets for many of their specific movements, actions and stylizations. During the late eighteenth and early nineteenth centuries, puppets had a tremendous vogue, and for this reason they received special attention from the Ministry of Theatre. But proving no more amenable to State jurisdiction and interference than live actors, they fell into decline. Inevitably, live actors displaced them. At present, there is only one living descendant of the once many lines of puppeteers. He lives quietly in Mandalay giving occasional performances and infrequently comes to Rangoon, the capital, where his services may be hired for an evening's exhibition. He infuses an astonishingly lifelike magic into his two- and three-foot high dolls, and the single singer and small-size orchestra which accompany his dolls cast a salon air of intimacy over a performance rather like a chamber music concert. Being divorced from popular support for so many years now, the puppets have had one advantage. The aged master has been able to concentrate on the perfection of his own idea of the art without the hindrance of appealing to a public whose tastes may not always be of the highest order.

Another type of *pwé* Burma offers is the *Nat Pwé* or spirit dance. These can be arranged for around thirty dollars, and they last for a few hours from late evening until after midnight. They can be performed only on astrologically auspicious days (there are a number of these every month), but most frequently spirit dances are held during the Burmese New Year celebrations during the time of the April full moon (the equivalent of our Easter). Although entirely different in style, they still bear several striking resemblances to the devil-dancing of Ceylon. They concern themselves with spirits most of which were recognized by the earliest inhabitants of the country before the advent of Buddhism, and they are in essence exorcistic rituals and may or may not, depending on the occasion and the mood of the medium, turn into trance-dances of possession.

Unlike Ceylon, however, the spirit dance of Burma is also used as a means of divination. At a certain moment in the performance, a candle is lit and the medium bites into the tallow; then you ask any question you like and the answer the tallow reveals is supposed to be correct. Most of the questions the Burmese ask concern love ("Which girl shall I marry?" The answer is often equivocal—"The one who writes a letter to you within the week"), but gambling, almost a national habit with the Burmese, also occupies the attention of a spirit dance audience ("Which horse shall I bet on tomorrow?" One answer I once heard was, "Not the one you have in mind, but the other one").

A spirit dance, like its counterpart in Ceylon, requires a number of appurtenances and a number of performers. A large altar of bamboo and palm leaves is constructed at one end of the area where the dance is held and is stacked high with headdresses (there is one for each of the thirty-seven spirits infesting Burma), young coconuts, bananas, offerings of flowers and betel nut, pieces of cloth, eggs, apples and bottles of liquor (the last despite Buddhism's prohibition of alcohol). The orchestra assembles at the opposite end of the area, while the mediums, usually several aged women and a couple of equally old men, arrange the altar, fuss about the area or sit smoking cigars and chatting with the spectators who begin to gather around as soon as they hear the tuning up of the drums.

The actual performance begins when the leader of the orchestra, the man who plays the circle of rippling drums, calls out *"nat pwé! nat pwé!"* Then follows a musical preamble. The dancers remove their plain white uniforms, the mark of the professional medium, and dress in the gayer and gaudier colors of the spirits. Throughout the performance there are several costume changes in rapid succession since all thirty-seven spirits must be appeased in the course of an evening's performance by the mediums' impersonation of them. Some changes are scarcely more than the putting on of a different headdress or sticking sprigs of scented grass behind the ears, others consist of draping a piece of striped cloth around the waist, while still others require a complete change of outer and inner garments. Each

121

preliminary to the dance must be accompanied by ritual and deferential homage to the spirits supposed to be inhabiting the altar. The mediums clasp their hands high above their heads and pray amid lighted incense. Holy water is doused on them by their attendants.

When the dance starts the performers begin to hop about, shuffle, and wave their hands in the air. Sometimes, if they are seized by one of the spirits they stand riveted to a single spot and quiver. Each spirit is personified in a specified order. One is a child. The medium who assumes this role begins to run about the arena, and stopping in front of one of the spectators asks in a high squeaking voice, "Isn't my scarf pretty? Do you like it?" or says, "I am the daughter of a king. That is why I dance so delicately." She takes some eggs from the altar and balances them so that they stand up in the flat palm of her hand. If they start to topple, she blows on them and they stand erect again. She then passes them out to various members of the audience as a gift from the spirit. Then she sings a song to herself, "This child is fond of hard-boiled eggs. She likes bananas too. And plain, boiled rice. That's because the spirits are *all* vegetarian." Another of the spirits is the embodiment of generosity. She grabs pieces of cloth from the altar and ripping them in half tosses them to members of the audience or, more frequently, among the players in the orchestra. (At the end of the performance these gifts to the orchestra are divided among all the participants in the spirit dance.) Sometimes a male medium dons a woman's dress as a special form of flattery to one of the female spirits. From time to time, as the various dancers turn and spin, with one hand extended out in front and the other hand flung backward, they work themselves into a trance. If the possession begins to get out of control, or the dancers begin to stagger or stumble, an attendant quickly sprinkles them with holy water, and makes them breathe the smoke of incense to bring them back to normal.

These spirit dances, according to the Burmese, were also an element of democracy in the old days during the sometimes tyrannical rule of the kings. If a medium in a trance fell upon some member of the audience and attributed godlike qualities to him, even the king was forced to respect him and listen to his advice.

One section of the spirit dance which is particularly moving and which contains elements of sequential drama as well as dance is called *Ton Byon* and re-enacts the martyrdom of two young boys. The story goes that a thousand or so years ago one of the Burmese kings was preparing to attack China, and in order to ensure the success of his venture, he decreed that an enormous pagoda be constructed. Every male member of the country was required to contribute one brick towards this gigantic edifice. There was at the time a certain well-known family whose members consisted of a Burmese mother, an Indian father, and two beautiful sons. In accordance with the King's command, the two sons were despatched with their bricks to make their contribution. But en route they became engrossed in playing games and forgot their mission. They were crucified for this negligence. The Burmese were so moved by this event that they deified the boys and made them *nats* or spirits.

The dance shows first the affectionate devotion between the mother and her sons, then the children at play, and finally their farewell as they are led off to their crucifixion. Wearing a gold-spangled, fuchsia-colored cloth over her head, the mother blesses her sons and gives them each a peacock feather. Then she feeds them their last meal. Finally, the boys take some sprigs of ferns in their hands and while paying homage to their mother walk tremblingly and fearfully to their doom. This section of the spirit dance is extremely moving for the Burmese, and they regard it as sacrosanct. Recently, a film company made a dramatization of the story, but while the cameras recorded it inside the studio, a full-scale spirit dance was performed outside in the open—to make sure no offense was taken by the secular telling of the story.

After all the thirty-seven spirits have appeared and been represented in dance and mime, the grand finale consists of a ritual for collecting additional money. The mediums bring on an earthenware pot shaped like a cock covered with gold leaf. They pass it around while various members of the audience place coins and bills in it. Then the medium waves it in the air as the orchestra plays energetically, and pretends to throw it away. The cock is then shown again to the audience but the money has disappeared. (It has a false bottom, I surmise.) This process is repeated until sufficient money to satisfy the spirits is collected. The spirit dance ends, until the next New Year season or another need for questioning or propitiating Burma's oldest, most deep-rooted religious forces arises.

123

The most recent form of *pwé* to develop in Burma is the *Pya Zat* or modern play. Usually these are comedies (there are no real tragedies even in the classical theatre) and if you go to the Win Win Theatre in Rangoon, the only regular legitimate playhouse in the country playing every night of the year, you will very likely happen on a *Pya Zat*. Modern plays received a special stimulus during the occupation of Burma by the Japanese. Movies, except Japanese ones, were forbidden and there were no imports from Europe or America. The irrepressible Burmese began writing their own equivalents and performing them in as contemporary and realistic a style as their natures allowed. Since the War, their popularity has not yet diminished, although it is obvious from the attendance that they cannot supplant the warm and affectionate place the historical plays and classical theatre hold in the hearts of the public. Perhaps the most interesting aspect of the modern plays for the foreigner is the acting talent and ability they reveal. Despite the classical traditions and the song-dance-drama-puppet mélange Burmese theatre involves, a special instinct for theatre—a native sense of acting in a Western sense —clearly exists in Burma, and more obviously so, in my opinion, than in the West. This seems curious to us, the outsiders, to whom modern theatre is an actual heritage and almost a birthright. The answer probably lies in the fact that no Burmese can escape his theatre, and sheer exposure to *pwés* from childhood, with all the rigid complexity of their classical tenets, equips an actor in Burma and grounds him in the technique of movement in a way the actor lacks it in the West.

Burma divides itself geographically and ethnologically into the Lower and Upper areas. The *pwés* belong to Lower Burma or the fertile plains of the South. Upper Burma is composed of hilly, even mountainous country, and is inhabited by a variety of loosely related races known variously as Shans, Chins, Kachins and Nagas. Of these perhaps the most important are the Shans who live in the Shan States, where some of the most beautiful scenery in the world as well as some of its most engaging peoples can be found.

The Shans are more Chinese or Mongolian in appearance than the typical Burman of the plains, and their dances and customs differ accordingly from their more Indianized kinsmen. No drama exists in the area at all, and while dance is not as evolved as it is in Mandalay or Rangoon, and its instruments are exceedingly simple—consisting only of drums, gongs, and cymbals—there is nevertheless a special excitement about a performance in this area.

Shan dancing is, of course, best seen during a festival or at harvest time when whole villages participate in the one vast celebration. But it is also possible to see in Taunggyi, the capital of the Shan States, an excellent introductory and representative view of the area's several dance arts. These will be performed by students or teachers or local residents who simply make a hobby of their dances. The Shan Literary Society, under the enterprising direction of Dr. Banyan, is interested in preserving and encouraging all the folk arts of the Shans and can be prevailed upon to arrange a special performance for the visitor. Of the several dance enthusiasts living in Taunggyi, Thein Maung, a handsome young man in his early thirties, easily qualifies as the most able and competent. All dancers in Upper Burma are amateurs, since there are no professional arts in the sense that we know, but Thein Maung's talent sets him well apart from the others and indicates the potentialities of the dance there, were it to be taken from its natural setting and encouraged along creative and professional lines.

Roughly classified, the dances of Upper Burma fall into three groups: the processional, those imitative of animals, and the fighting displays. Processional dances are simple, elementary troupings and traipsings of boys and girls of the villages. They walk about single file, forming circles and arcs, and sing as they gesticulate with their hands and arms. Usually the thumb and forefinger curls to form a circle (like the advertisement for Ballantine's beer), and as the dulcet drums and gongs softly resound in the chill night air, the dancers spin out their unenergetic and graceful patterns.

Animal dances are more complex. These are usually presented in full costume imitative of the animal to be reproduced in dance—a flying horse, bird, yak, or the half-bird, half-human *kinnara*. The dancer mimics the animal with precise and exact verisimilitude. If it is supposed to be a bird he hops on one foot, pecks at invisible food, cocks his head, juts his neck out, preens, pivots amorously in a circle, and utters imitative cries and squawks. In the hands of Thein

125

Maung, for example, such a dance becomes more than an amusing human approximation of a zoological phenomenon. It has composition and a logical flow of emotion. He chains the movements together in graceful connected succession, and you can even follow his embryonic story. The animal is hungry, he looks for food, finds it. Then he seeks out a mate, flirts and shows off. But the season is wrong. He exits in a flurry of frustration and ruffled anger. To enact the story if he chooses to give it one, he moves in a circle filling the dance arena with his remarkable imitative motions. The dance is a representation but by skill and artistry he is able to make it an improved and sensible depiction. The scope for humor and even vulgarity is clear. The dancer can mock the animal, exploit its stupidities, make its antics grotesque, ungainly or awkward. To the Burmese there is something humorous anyway in a human bedecking himself like an animal and going through the motions of a lesser creature. Or he can exhibit its serenity and fill you with envy at its placid calm and majesty.

Animal dances occupy a place of special interest for students and a digression at this point is necessary. They are invariably found in mountainous areas away from the cities and particularly among isolated aboriginals, pockets of whom are found in almost every country of Asia. Some scholars assert as a theory that the animal is the source of all dance, that primitive man in watching the animals around him first began to dance by imitating their dance-like movements. There is, of course, an intimate connection between animal life and mankind in jungle areas. And from watching animals to worshiping them is apparently an easy sociological step. The introduction of religion gives these dances of animal imitation a further propulsion. In areas where a particular beast occupies a good deal of attention—either because it is a menace (like the tiger) or the source of good (like the vulture who disposes of refuse) or even when man's livelihood depends on it in some special way (like the cow or buffalo)—the animal dance takes on still greater motivation. So you find lion dances in Africa, or tiger dances in India, or bear dances among the Ainus in Northern Japan (they drink the blood and live off the meat), or even pony dances in Sumba in Indonesia (an island where the sole export is the special breed of tiny horses). Such dances serve two contrasting purposes: either to placate the evil spirit within it that drives it to harass the human being or to thank the gods for the benevolence the animal brings into the community's life. But even in the most highly developed dance forms of Asia, in their most sophisticated theatre houses, the animal remains.

Whatever the deeper explanation may be, they appear sometimes because the plot or story refers to them and require their special attributes, like the monkeys in the *Ramayana*. But sometimes, and I think this is the most pertinent aspect of animal dances, they merely add a note of special aesthetic delight to the theatre. The stage is not complete enough with only the human to fill it. While the concept of animals in the theatre may appear childlike to many Westerners, they do awaken a particular response in us, and it is a pleasurable one. Whether this is atavistic or primitive or is in our natures seems to be beside the point. If the swan part of *Swan Lake*, for instance, is silly, or the bear in *Petrushka* ludicrous, we, the spectators, are nonetheless richer for them. And some different and legitimate response inside us is awakened. The cult of realism and naturalism or actuality seems one-sided to the Asian if it disregards the aesthetic fundamental that the impersonation of an animal induces.

The *Lai Ka* (literally fight-dance, but sometimes translated as Defense-Offense) of the Shan States is its most systematized dance. Basically, it is a kind of training or rehearsal for actual combat. Its principle, like a palindrome of logic, is: if you can dance, you can fight; if you can fight, automatically you can dance. Fighting dances or *Lai Ka* are performed exclusively by men, almost nude except for an exiguous pair of shorts. This nudity is not only for freedom of movement or to show off the dancer's muscles, but to display as far as modesty permits his dark blue tattoos of floral designs which extend solidly around the body from waist to just above the knees. In fact, at one performance of Shan dancing in Taunggyi, one of the young dancers came forward to apologize to the audience for his lack of tattoos. He had not yet acquired enough money to have the proper tattooing done, he said. Although this custom is gradually dying out, the majority of Shan men still vaunt their tattoos as a symbol of virility and fortitude. Certainly the process of covering the man's entire pelvic region with tattoos is painful and even opium, which is socially acceptable in that part of the world, is only partially anaesthetic.

127

The basic beginning fighting dance is called the Free Hand. It begins with the fists held thumbs-up at the chest. Then the empty-handed performer flails the air, restlessly pacing back and forth, pivoting and reversing suddenly, punching and striking blows at imaginary, invisible enemies. The dancer twists around and sinks crosslegged to the ground only to spring up, as if unwinding his legs, and recommences his watchful, alert probing of the air. At all times the dance matches the rhythm and speed of the music which change from time to time according to indications from either the drummer or the dancer himself.

The second of the fighting dances is the Sword Dance. Here the dancer swirls two sharp and gleaming swords about his body, at whirlwind speed over the head, near the neck and around the knees. There is real danger in this dance. If the performer miscalculates or his timing falters he would slice off an ear or gash his knee. The unsure beginner practices with his swords well away from the body. As he grows more expert, he brings the swords closer and closer in towards him. A master dancer will in the heat of the dance keep the swords continuously grazing his body until they seem to be slithering and sliding over him.

The third fighting dance is the Fire Dance, where the ends of a long wand are wrapped in thick cotton wads, then dipped in kerosene, and set aflame. The dancer twirls it in his hands like a drum major, passing it through his legs, over his head and bringing it closer and closer to the body until the sparks sprinkle over him. Finally, he tosses it in the air and catches it, still spinning like a Catherine Wheel, in one hand. The dance is made even more complicated when a pair of dancers, each with two flaming wands in their hands, perform a mock fight, ducking and avoiding the feints and sallies of their partner, and skipping to each side to escape the burning thrusts of their lively opponents.

Burma's unrestrained responsiveness to dance arts in the North and its abandoned pleasure in the theatrical *pwés* of the South, are impressive to anyone coming from the reserved-seat, hushed auditorium atmosphere of much of Western theatre. Few countries have as much gaiety in their theatre and few offer as many genuine dance and drama delights within so small a geographical area. There have, of course, always been periods of rise and decline in Burma's theatrical world, but we are fortunate today to find Burma at one of its heights with scores of good actors, dancers and musicians. The new government, as in other parts of Asia, riding on this wave of enthusiasm, is encouraging a further waxing of the country's arts. In 1953 the Union of Burma Cultural Department (with almost as much power as a Ministry) created a Department of Fine Arts and Music at Mandalay, the old cultural capital of the country and seat of some of the most famous kingdoms. They select students from all over Burma for study there and pay them around ten dollars a month simply to learn dance and music. For their regular studies, the pupils attend a free night school. Crowded together in a single two-story building, they learn everything from playing the silken strings of a Burmese harp shaped like a swan and so faint you can scarcely hear it, to the most complicated and advanced dance steps Burma has yet invented. At present the Department has around a hundred students and the number is increasing. What effect such a large annual outflow of qualified and competently trained performers will have is hard to assess. One thing is certain: Burma's popular arts of the theatre will continue and grow and spread, and it will take more than wars or bombs or a troubled uncertain future to destroy the happy arts of this happy people.

THAILAND

Whatever else may be said about Thailand, or Siam as it used to be called, it must be stated at the outset that it is aesthetically mature as a country. Aside from splendid dance and acting ability among its people and its professional rather than folk or amateur level of production, the pleasantness, availability, and the intensely protective sense which surrounds the dance and drama arts there make it one of the most satisfying areas of Asia theatrically speaking. This does not mean that you cannot find points for objection and criticism if you look hard enough. Nothing is very old in Thailand and nothing is overwhelmingly great—Japan has better theatre, Indonesia finer dancing, and India is more original—but Thailand nevertheless spreads before the visitor and student an impressive array of theatrical attainment, particularly in Bangkok, the capital city. Added to this is a peculiarly Siamese enchantment prevalent everywhere which affects even the most cursory of tourists and makes foreign residents fall gently and inextricably in love with the country.

The first things you are told about Thailand, and certainly these impress you almost immediately on arrival, are that the country is small, that it is rich, and that it never was a colony. This fortuitous conjuncture of circumstances produces an openhearted, happy, uncomplicated people, and no matter what faults you may later find or think you find with them, such as the Thais being superficial, derivative, even opportunist, if you like, there always remains a radiance about every contact with them and every display of themselves they choose to make.

The convenience and smooth mechanics of theatre-going in Bangkok, while this doubtless is a mundane consideration, is perhaps its most endearing quality. Programs are announced everywhere from

English language papers to hotel lobbies. Tickets can be bought at box offices or on street corners or at hotel desks. Synopses of performances are printed in English. A small body of intelligent, explanatory literature on dance and drama has recently grown up and can be bought at any bookstore. Most guide books devote more than a third of their pages to dance alone. And the Thais are so proud of their dance and drama that if an article on the subject appears abroad, it is sure to be pirated and reprinted in the local newspapers as a testimony of Thai greatness. Most of all, the friendly Siamese will take pains to accompany you to the theatre, to interpret for you, and to encourage you to think that their arts are wonderful. This eases the way for the outsider, and its effect not only on your disposition but on your appreciation goes far in helping you along the sometimes tortuous and devious path of understanding Asia.

Bangkok is a sprawling city, a compound of many elements. The people with their brown complexion, stocky stature and Mongolian look are unmistakably Asian, but it is a mixed race of several types. They are not as Malay as most Southeast Asians nor as Chinese-looking as the purer Chinese. Visually, the city also shows even more importation, adaptation, and amalgamation. Bangkok abounds in Chinese statues amid its gaudy Indian-style *wats* or temples. Its *stupas* are covered with bits of foreign-made crockery and glass. And even the costumes of the classical dances are indebted to far-off Portugal for their velvets and shiny metallic discs. Nearly everyone on the street wears Western clothes of some style or other, and the foreigner draped in Thaibok scarves and foulards is apt to be on the surface more Siamese than the native. Expensive, new, American cars glide up and down the show street, Rajdamnern Avenue, in front of its row of fine modern buildings, almost colliding with the rusty, worn-out pedicabs and rickshas that the majority of Bangkok's population can afford.

Thailand is a country of change. One of Bangkok's great avenues was built expressly for an international exposition. For the SEATO conference, fountains were flown by air from Germany, and overnight the city blossomed with spraying water tinted by colored lights. Political changes are easily made, too, as the complete about-face from a Japanese alliance and declaration of war on America to the present American-backed government has shown. Artistically, Thailand also changes. In 1949, when I first visited Bangkok, there was an active modern theatre movement in de luxe auditoriums of gold and crimson with sculptured prosceniums of elephant-headed gods. Today these theatres show only movies and the modern theatre movement is finished. All this flexibility in race, culture, politics and art is not, strangely, a sign of weakness or vacillation. It is rather, to my way of thinking at least, an example of Siamese genius. The feeling for change and willingness for it within the people makes them, and I am speaking primarily now of their arts, lively, vigorous, and even virile. It is perhaps this enterprise and lack of rigidity which makes Thailand a most thoroughly comprehensible country to the American or European—and much more so than any other country of Asia.

The power inherent within the nation has not only made itself felt in the past through both political and cultural domination of neighboring states but even today Thailand is culturally one of the soundest countries. Theatre fashions start in Bangkok, and within a year they are felt in Cambodia, in Laos, in Vietnam, in Malaya, in Indonesia, and even Burma. A startling example of this is Rambong, a Thai invention and contribution to modern dance, still as popular in neighboring countries as it is in Thailand itself, an almost inescapable activity of any dance-hall in Southeast Asia. Rambong, roughly described, is a somewhat sexless version of ballroom dancing performed in open-air pavilions at night by dance-hall girls and men who buy tickets to dance with them. In Rambong the couple weaves around the dance floor, waving arms and hands in circular patterns and shuffling feet, but their bodies never touch. The woman leads, setting the direction and course of the movement, and the man follows, although it is he who selects the partner. Meanwhile a Western-style band plays the jazzy, stepped-up rhythm of the Rambong, which never varies regardless of the tune. In most Southeast Asian dance halls now, there comes a Rambong time, and the floor fills with swaying and aloofly separated pairs gracefully forming Siamese dance gestures. The fad will probably soon reach the Philippines too. Some Filipinos recently visiting Vietnam were entranced by the dance and have launched it, first among Manila society, and there is every likelihood it will spread.

If in the past Thailand borrowed her dance arts from India and nearer neighbors, she has in recent years repaid to some extent that

132

international debt through Rambong, and there are reasons for its immense popularity. Rambong meets a social need. It is easy and anyone can do it. It replaces the antiquated folk dances which, because of their simplicity, have begun to pall on modern Asians. It is an excuse for men and women to be together openly. It fills the vacuum in entertainment created by the general decline of classical dancing. Perhaps most of all, it answers the requirement of Westernization which inevitably rises from the pressures and effects of Europe and America. Yet it does not offend the innate sense of modesty and sexual segregation which forms so definite a characteristic of respectable Asians and their social mores. While the songs of Rambong may be moony and the dance rudimentary, it still is an absorbing way to spend an evening, either watching or participating. To draw a comparison, it may be said that Rambong is to Southeast Asia pretty much what the jitterbug was to America, both being excellent and delightful dances not only as popular pastimes but for their value within the total framework of the world's endless search for new movements and body configurations. The Thais deserve credit for this new pleasure.

Dance-Dramas

When you say the word "dance" to a Thai, two things spring simultaneously to his mind, Khon and Lakon, and both of these belong to what is more clearly expressed as "Classical Dance and Drama."

Khon is sometimes described as "masked play" or "masked pantomime" and this conveys a general idea of it if you add to the Western connotation of these words generous portions of dance and music and song. Khon is the oldest theatrical form still seen in Thailand, and it is filled with reminders of its ancient connections with India. Although India's Kathakali as it is presented today is not as old or unchanged as Khon, the relation between the two is obvious. Khon uses masks, while Kathakali, which once used them, now substitutes mask-like make-ups. The actors are mute, and all dialogue is sung by a set of side-singers who sit with the accompanying instruments of

133

the orchestra. Both contain gesture language (*mudras*) which interprets the action and substitutes for actual speech. Both are performed exclusively by men. Both arts were until recently patronized by royalty and the princely courts.

The texts of Khon are highly Sanskritized but an outsider with the slightest knowledge of Siamese pronunciation and who knows only a scanty amount of Sanskrit can follow the gist of the story. All Khon themes are translated from the *Ramayana*, called in Siamese *Rama Kian* (or "The Fame of Rama"), despite the fact that Thailand for centuries now has been intensely Buddhist. The reconciliation between the Hindu religious epic and the Buddhist faith has been adroitly effected in Thailand. The Thai, in the first place, see the *Ramayana* as a simple story, something like a fairy tale, and part of their non-religious traditions. In this connection it is worthy of note that the religious aspects of the *Ramayana* are neglected in the theatre and the episodes most frequently performed are the abduction of Sita (or Sida in Siamese), the animal battles, and the intrigues involving Ravana, called *Thosakan* (from the Sanskrit for "ten-necked"). In contrast with the deification of Rama which is its Indian summation, the general moral the Thais derive from the *Ramayana* is, to quote an ancient poet-commentator, that "Even the lower animals [Hanuman, his monkey army and a cortege of bears] help a person who is in the right; and even a brother [Hanuman and his brother are on opposing sides in the battle against Ravana] abandons one who is in the wrong."

Khon essentially is a nobleman's art. It was confined exclusively to the palace, with only infrequent open-air performances for the people until 1932. At that time the first of Thailand's several famous *coups d'état* took place, and the King was deprived of his power, the country was turned into a constitutional monarchy, and a number of recessions in court extravagance were made which in turn affected Khon. Thai kings up to then had always found special pleasure in the arts.

Rama I (1736-1809), the first of the present dynasty, drove out the Burmese who had occupied Thailand, and established his new capital at Bangkok in 1782, but in the midst of all this he found time to compose the first modern version in Siamese of the *Ramayana*. His son, Rama II (1767-1834), wrote a number of plays, some of which are still occasionally revived, including a version of *Krai Thong*, the popular story of a commoner who wins the hand of a millionaire's daughter by killing the crocodile king who has abducted her and carried her away to his underwater lair. The long reign of Rama VI, who lived from 1880 until 1925, is sometimes referred to as a Golden Age for theatricals. During this period the King wrote a large number of plays of various types, some even in English and French which by then had become compulsory subjects for Asian monarchs, and patronized Khon on a grand and lavish scale. He was responsible for what came to be known as *Khon Bandasakti*, or Noble Khon, and all male members of the Royal Family learned it and even danced in public. Of course, these occasions were special as a part of good works or public welfare, and were always for charity. And while this Noble Khon shocked the conservative element of the people, it was a response to the gradual democratization that was infiltrating everywhere. It showed that the nobles were human after all, and that they delighted in pleasures applicable to the whole country. In addition to their own performances, many members of the Royal entourage maintained private troupes (ostensibly they practiced the art in order to judge it more astutely) at their mansions for their own personal entertainment, and partly, too, for a display of their greatness. Today, only one prince of the blood I know of, the enthusiastic Prince Bhanu-Phan Yukala of Bangkok, can still afford to maintain his own staff of dancers. The King has none.

This custom of public performance of Khon by nobles still continues today, although the Royal Khon troupes are formally disbanded. It may happen that when you are in Bangkok, a Khon performance of this sort will be announced. One was arranged in 1954 for the purpose of collecting funds to build a new wing in one of the local hospitals. It was, as the publicity read, "under the gracious patronage of His Majesty the King." The cast was composed of "gentlemen of His Majesty's household who had been trained in classical dancing in the days of His Late Majesty Rama VI." The venue was the large open-air stage and grounds at Suan Ambara near the Marble Throne Hall. There, under the stars of a soft Bangkok night, with the King sitting alone on a brocaded divan, with the Queen sitting a respectful distance behind him and the rest of the audience spread out like a fan still further behind her, the performance began.

135

The excerpt from the *Ramayana* chosen was one of the more ambitious passages, one requiring the largest cast of characters in all Khon, "Hanuman's Violation of Maiyarab's Defense." The scene tells the story of Hanuman's elevation by Rama's brother to the rank of general of the army and his mission of rescuing Rama from the nether world where he lies under a magic spell cast at Ravana's behest. The stage which was especially constructed for this performance was unusually high so that people in the streets outside the gates and walls could see even from a distance. The platform stood between two tall trees, and huge flood lamps on either side beamed down over the area like bright moonlight. On a lower platform to the right an assembly of twenty musicians and singers sat crosslegged. Before them lay the rarely used, intricately carved musical instruments of the Royal Household, each varnished a deep mahogany color and inlaid with mother-of-pearl.

The performance began with an orchestral introduction by the Piphat band of clattering xylophones, strident, stertorous horns of rosewood, drums which sounded like the nervous, restless flapping of wings, and clappers. The dozen or so dancers emerged in costumes glittering with paillettes and silver studs. Their long-sleeved blouses of velvet and moiré, so tight-fitting that the dancer must be sewn into them at each performance, clashed flamboyantly with the colors of the shot-silk, knee-length trousers which were elegantly draped and tucked through the legs to fasten at the back into a silver belt. On their shoulders glinted silver epaulettes which curved upwards like eaves of a pagoda roof. The round face of Rama's brother was powdered chalk white with only a thin line of red to delineate his lips. On his head he wore a gold-spired crown from which tassels of red hibiscus and white frangipani dangled at his temples. The other characters wore masks which fitted closely over their entire heads. Each was painted a different color—orange, green, black, and various pastel shades. The dead white mask of Hanuman, the "white monkey," matched his costume of silver lamé and set him apart from the others.

As the plot began to unfold, the singers in the orchestra in conventional Khon style sang out each character's name, saying "Lakshmana [Rama's brother] announces . . ." or "Hanuman speaks . . ." so that the audience could recognize each character as

136

he began to move. Then changing the tone of their voices, they chanted the separate speeches of each personage on the stage in short-breathed, sing-song but mellifluous fragments. The actor approximated the meaning of each phrase with gestures and movements, first slowly, and then repeated in a quicker tempo. While one actor performs his given set of actions, the others remain, as they do in Kathakali, immobile. (This convention does not apply entirely in battle or love scenes.)

The segments of orchestral music consisted, as is true in all Siamese theatricals, of special interludes somewhat like incidental music. These are interpretive and explanatory, not because they express the feeling of the drama in an exact or imitative way, but because the time and rhythm have been arbitrarily accepted by convention as appropriate to the occasion. These passages are rigidly fixed and any theatre lover must be familiar with them. They stand for particular situations and emotions such as exits and entrances, tears, battles, and the like. Three of them are considered sacred even today: the music indicating a scene of copulation (the actual action on the stage shows only a caress or a stroke of the hand); that which accompanies a magical act or the recitation of a secret mantra; and there is one other, a special composition played when leading dancers assemble for a name-giving ceremony or to award an accomplished performer with a higher stage name. On hearing these, savants among the audience or those trained in the discipline of the dance immediately salute by bringing their hands together and placing them, thumbs at the nose, before their face in a gesture of homage and respect to the sacrosanct art of music.

At this point, the music which is particularly delightful should be briefly explained further. Siamese music uses the diatonic scale as we do, but its tuning is different. The octave is divided into seven equidistant whole tones. The pitch is pure, not tempered like ours, and at first sounds slightly out-of-tune and bland, since there are no tensions or pulls between the evenly separated notes. The fourth and seventh tones of the scale are generally avoided which gives the sound a hollowness and quiescent emptiness. To accentuate this the music is played almost without dynamics—it is always moderately loud—and once a piece begins there are few accellerandi or ritards.

The pyrotechnics of the Khon play I am describing begin when

Hanuman is alone on the stage and, after many characteristic acts like rolling on the ground, scratching himself for lice, and monkeylike frolicking over the stage, sets out on his hazardous journey to the nether world. In an attempt to block him en route, a magician creates several obstructions. First, an enormous elephant of gray cloth, with two men to act as the fore and hind feet, walks out from underneath the stage and romps around the grass before the audience. Hanuman grapples with him and kills him barehanded. Then there is an explosion of gunpowder and the rocky crag off to one side is filled with flames made by off-stage attendants rapidly fanning bright red strips of silk. Hanuman heroically lifts a huge papier maché boulder and throws it over the fire to smother it. Then follows a horde of enormous paper mosquitos, the size of crows, slowly pulled along wire suspended across the top of the stage between the two trees. They attack Hanuman, but he fights some of them off and crushes the others with his hands. Finally Hanuman reaches a lotus pond which miraculously appears on stage. There he finds a young guardian at the gates of Hell who is half-fish, half-monkey. Hanuman recognizes him as his own son, the product of an early indiscretion with a mermaid, but in order to prove his identity to the boy, he performs the great "miracle of Hanuman," that of emitting the moon and the stars by a single yawn. The sacred magic music sounds. Suddenly the moon and stars appear, bright and shining in the air. Finally, Hanuman divines that the quickest route to Rama in the nether world is down the stem of a lotus, and the Khon is concluded as he leaps head first off the stage into the petals of a giant lotus in front.

As the finale, a *corps de ballet* of high officials of the Royal Household, all of them aged men, appeared in full costume but without masks. The entire orchestra of musicians sang and played a farewell salutation. Following their words in the special language of the dance, the dancers, in flowing, stately motions, thanked the audience for their charity, praised the King for his benevolence, and wished His Majesty and us a long life and one of graciousness. The King rose and faced the audience who also stood up; everyone remained motionless while the Thai national anthem was played tremulously by the xylophones and drums. A black, open-top convertible drove up to the stage, the King climbed into the back seat and left. A black, closed sedan followed for the Queen. The audience wandered around for a while, inspecting the ornate instruments, bowing to musicians and dancers who still lingered and looking at the mechanical contrivances which had produced the stage effects; finally they started home, only to find the gates still crowded with the citizens of Bangkok who could not afford the exorbitant admission price but wanted to hear the music, to peek at the performance, and possibly, too, to stare at the more distinguished of the spectators.

Royal Khon is performed infrequently nowadays, and it grows increasingly rare with each year. One or two troupes of ordinary dancers without palace connections are in Bangkok and have for some years now eked out a livelihood practicing the art on a professional level and appearing before anyone, including tourists, who calls them. The Thais used to put on a performance of Khon when there was a marriage that they wished to make specially festive. But the sons of the now aged performers, the inheritors of the tradition, have found it alarmingly difficult to earn their living by art and are turning to more lucrative, reliable occupations. One reason for the decline is, of course, the absence of royal support. And, besides, Khon has lost the cachet and chic that high society once gave it. Another cause is that Lakon, the second of Thailand's classical dance-drama forms, because it allows women to dance in it, has superseded Khon in popularity among the general public.

Lakon means "theatre" generally, and the correct designation for what one thinks of as Lakon should be Lakon Ram or "theatre dances." Within this generic classification, however, a number of specific words describe the various types of Lakon in Thailand: Lakon Nai for the pure dance performed until recently exclusively within the Palace by the King's special harem; Lakon Nok for the dance troupes outside the palace who emphasize the story part of the dance plays; and Lakon Duk Damban for dance-plays which require scenery. But these subsidiary classifications are now more technical than actual and the Lakon we see most frequently is a medley of all of them, or extracts of their dance portions. When the modern theatre began some years ago, the only word the Thais could find for this new form was also simply "Lakon." But in the Siamese language there is no confusion, because the context, the theatre or place of performance, the names of the artists and so forth, tell you what type of Lakon is meant automatically.

Roughly defined, Lakon today as the word is currently used is predominantly a dance-drama performed by women, who act male roles as well, with or without scenery, either against a plot or story-background with literal gesticulation or consisting of meaningless abstract movements, and with music and certain conventions that stem from the older, more austere prototype, Khon. This connection becomes even clearer from the older pronunciation of the word Lakon as La-Khon. Unlike Khon, Lakon stories are not exclusively from the *Ramayana*. They may be from Siamese legends (like Krai Thong), or Hindu-inspired legends, or even from that source of plots called the Panji cycle which came to Thailand from Indonesia. This Lakon, with Bangkok as its main center, certainly is the nation's most boastful bid as it appears today for artistic excellence on an international level.

The history of Lakon has been troubled and complicated. It began with the Siamese conquest of the neighboring and artistically more developed Kingdom of Cambodia a couple of hundred years ago. A troupe of Cambodian palace dancers were kidnapped bodily and brought to the Thai capital along with the Emerald Buddha and several other cultural treasures. Lakon immediately delighted the King both for its art and for the additions to his seraglio it gave. Gradually the dance underwent some changes which rendered it more Siamese in character and imitators of the King's dancers sprang up in other parts of the country. With the later democratization of Thailand, Lakon troupes of the court were disbanded, and a few of these performers became teachers. During World War II, along with pressures of various other kinds from the Japanese, Lakon was looked upon as frivolous and inconsonant with the dignity of a Westernized, progressive Asia. The then prime minister, Phibun Songgram, who, as I write, again holds the office, and whose theatrical tastes are, according to rumor, limited to the music halls of France, remained indifferent to its fate and Lakon was allowed to disappear from Siamese life.

However, in the midst of these difficult days, some scholars and members of the princely class, foreseeing a tragic fate for Thailand's

Lakon, banded together to agitate for the creation of a Department of Fine Arts as a full-fledged subsidiary of the Chulalongkorn University of Bangkok, the largest university in the country and subsidized by the government. Such an organization, they felt, could salvage what remained of the dance, and at the same time protect the art as royal patronage had once done. They finally succeeded, and the government agreed, somewhat reluctantly, to its establishment on a modest scale. The subjects taught were dance in all its phases, painting, sculpture and music. Western music too was introduced into the curriculum, and the school orchestra—called the State Orchestra—gave concerts of Weber and Von Suppé and Wagner from time to time. However, artistic training could not be elected in place of the general academic education offered by the University's other departments. Its pupils, and some of them are artists, are therefore actually college students. Even after the establishment of the Department, for a long time controversy raged over it and there was no basic agreement on its true function. Many feared that its connection with the government would turn it into a pawn of the politicians. Others felt that any substitute for royal patronage could only lead to a lack of elegance. Some felt the Department's scope should be broadened to include drama in its fullest sense, and modern or Western-style acting should be introduced. Others wanted to see it limited only to Siamese classic arts. Some regarded it as a money-making proposition that must depend on the public for support by giving performances. But however much attitudes toward the Department of Fine Arts varied, a few of its organizers persevered along their own lines and its aims and goals took shape. The fate of Lakon, in particular, has remained entirely in its hands and the decay of all Siamese classical dance and drama has been arrested, and a return to their former popularity clearly resulted.

Today, the Department of Fine Arts is contained in a large compound of several whitewashed, moulding and lichened buildings not far from the Royal Palace. The largest, a long, barn-like rectangle is known as the Silpakorn Theatre where public performances of full-length, three-hour-long stage shows of Lakon dancing, Khon dramas, and usually a pleasing mixture of all their elements including scenery and costume changes, music and dialogue, are given by the Department's students. Outside the theatre stands an ancient stone carving

141

of Ganesa, the Hindu patron-God of theatre, and inside, amid ticket windows, posters and more statuary of ancient gods, are huge cartouches of perforated buffalo hide. These represent characters from the *Ramayana* and *Mahabharata* used in the shadow-plays, once popular but now rapidly dying out, being performed only in remote villages. There is little trace of Buddhism here. The dancers worship Vairavana, another of the Hindu gods of dance, and pray before the Indian-derived masks of Khon.

The hall seats almost a thousand people, but it is packed to over-flowing for both the matinee and evening performances held regularly throughout the year on Fridays, Saturdays and Sundays. This theatre now earns more than any other single entertainment house in Thailand, including American movies. The last dance-drama they produced earned a net profit of a million and a half ticals (about 30,000 dollars) in seven months of its thrice-weekly run, and this was achieved with tickets selling at the top price of a dollar and a half. The fantastic success of the Silpakorn Theatre is due almost exclusively to the untiring efforts of a single person, a former *première ballerina* of Lakon at the court, and now an old woman. Around her she has collected a staff of former palace dancers, court dancing masters, and savants from various parts of Thailand. She rules her organization with something that amounts to eccentricity, a quality rare in Thailand. She frequently perches her spectacles on the end of her nose fiercely, thumps her heavy black cane, and loses her temper in fits of rage. But in her milder moments, she organizes, directs, and arranges each show with a skill that has made them so important a part of Bangkok life and Thai culture. Despite her tyrannies, she has another side to her character which is unstinting in its kindness and appreciation of genuinely talented pupils. She supports a number of them privately out of her own slender resources, until they are able to earn their living professionally by appearing at the Silpakorn regularly, or teaching at the Department of Fine Arts itself, or establishing themselves as private teachers in other cities of Thailand. The salaries at the Silpakorn Theatre may be low according to American standards—around 3500 ticals or $50 a month—but there are increments which augment this considerably, including shared profits from the more successful performances.

Aside from the popular success the Department has achieved and its resuscitation of the classical arts, one of its most valuable functions has been to offer a haven to artists and teachers of Thailand. It rescues folk and country dances which, as Thailand's villages change more and more under Western influence, run the risk of disappearance. This is done by bringing the greatest teachers or practitioners to the school and incorporating their knowledge into the repertoire of classic dances as far as a given story permits. The Department even provides livelihood for artists whom time and modernization have to an extent by-passed. Most notable of these is Kunwad. He was in 1955 sixty-five years old and is the school's senior teacher. Originally he was attached to the Royal household as a teacher and performer of Khon, and specialized primarily in female roles. He initiates all the Department's artist pupils into the greater profundities of their art. He formally places and adjusts the headdresses of the leading stars of the Silpakorn Theatre before they make their entrances; and he instructs both men and women in their craft. As in most of Asia, the best teachers are male, and while it is all right in Thailand to study in the beginning with a woman, the first dance step in public must be taken with a male teacher amid candles, flowers and appropriate offerings that reaffirm the sacredness of dance and the supremacy of man in the arts. His back-stage position contrasts strangely with his actual appearances before the public at the Silpakorn Theatre. He participates in each production but all the spectator sees of him usually is the person of a very old man comically dressed as a woman, performing the daring or silly actions, such as jumping into water and doing somersaults, required of a ludicrous duenna or female attendant. Unfortunately, the artistry of Kunwad in his serious roles has ceased to meet the fancy of Bangkok audiences who attend this Lakon and who are on the whole educated and somewhat Westernized. The Thais are already beginning to adopt in part a Western attitude towards female impersonators. Although Kunwad remains the doyen of classical dance, his livelihood now depends entirely on the Department—as a teacher and comic.

Lakon is one of the most extraordinary visual experiences. The performers move with slow undulations like an underwater ballet. Their movements sinuously flow from one into the other until the dance seems to be functioning in an altogether different dimension of time and space as we conceive them in dance. There is a surrealism about the motion—at times very slow, at times speeded up—which disassociates it from usual stage action. There is an odd, unfamiliar use of the body for the Westerner accustomed to ballet or even the convolutions of the Martha Graham style of making the body exteriorize inner complexity. The fingers flex until the hand arches back like curling petals of a tiger lily. The arms break and bend at the elbow double-jointedly. The torso tilts to one side giving the body an on-the-bias look and forming an irregular line of angles from the head, which is erect, to the hips which are thrust slightly back, through to the splayed knees, and down to the toes which are turned up like points on a Turkish slipper.

The movements, while clearly modelled on those of India, are softer, somehow more cushioned, as if they belonged to gentler gods and less impassioned heavenly beings. The most characteristic, perhaps, of these is technically called the *hom chang wa* (literally, mark rhythm). It is a delicate, upward bounce of the chest, a sort of silent catching of the breath or hiccough which punctuates the rhythm and keeps the body active in a static moment. The effect is to lighten the dancer and make her appear almost suspended off the ground. To this are added long periods when one foot is held in the air, and the continually outstretched arms heighten the feeling that the artist is flying or floating just above the ground and a separating mist hovers between her feet and the floor.

The gesture language is common to Khon and all the Lakon derivatives. In Khon it was necessary because of the masks which compelled the dancers to show their moods and feelings through hand movements. In Lakon, the dancers' faces are so thickly covered with white powder that they are mask-like, and throughout the dance not a single facial muscle moves. It would be undignified in their godlike roles to grimace, and besides it would muss their fine, fragile make-up. Hand gestures in all Asian dance originally stemmed from India, where, as *mudras*, their intricacy has taken on something of the aspect of a code that only initiates can follow. In Thailand, these are attenuated and mollified to the point of being merest suggestions rather than explicit systematic indications. Many factors have determined the modifying course of these gestures. Partly it is a matter of temperament. The Thai is not as explosive or intellectual

144

or intense as the Indian in general is, and he asks greater placidity and relaxation from his arts. Of course, too, the long centuries that have intervened since the original Indian teachers first brought the gestures have added vagueness and transformed them into something more intrinsically Siamese. And probably the distance between these teachers and their homeland, where their masters remained, contributed from the beginning to a forgetfulness or disappearance of much that they themselves once knew.

Roughly classified, there are three categories of gestures and these are common to all Siamese dancing: those that express general emotions such as love, hate, anger, joy, sorrow; those that endow ordinary movements with grace or ennoble them like standing, walking, sitting, and making an obeisance; and those that indicate intentions such as refusal, calling, acceptance. Many of these are thoroughly comprehensible at first sight, even to the outsider—the wiping of tears (always with the left hand), the pointing of one finger and simultaneously stamping the foot to show anger, the crossed arms slowly patting the chest to depict bereavement or agitation, or the two forefingers drawn along the mouth to form the shape of a smile for laughter. Others are not, but their range is fairly limited. The pattern of the plots and their concomitant emotions are repetitious in all Thai dancing, and any average foreigner after being helped along by an interpreter for one or two programs can follow them adequately without further trouble. The intermittent spurts of music also assist the audience by informing it of the major climaxes of mood and situation, but since the ear is less alert than the eye, these conventions require rather more conditioning.

All productions at the Silpakorn Theatre are along the same basic lines. Perhaps a detailed description of their greatest success of recent times, *Manohra*, is the best means of explaining how the Lakon works in actual practice. *Manohra* is advertised as "a dance-drama in six scenes—specially rearranged," and its summary informs us that it is a story of the half-bird, half-woman *kinnaras* who live in their celestial abode high in the Himalayas. The curtain opens, revealing a bathing scene, set against a backdrop of blue sky and snow-covered mountain peaks, reminiscent rather of ice-cream parlor decorations. Furry white rabbits, the size of a child's toy, dart across the stage, and against the sky tiny *kinnaras* made of paper and covered with flossy, Christmas-tree snow flit across the proscenium. A *corps de ballet* of seven live *kinnaras* with their attendants appear in the usual Lakon costume of pale-green, pleated skirts and a red flap of velvet which hangs behind them from the shoulders like a half-train. To this are added paper wings to show they are *kinnaras*. After dancing briefly, they remove their wings and part of their clothes and reveal themselves in modest bathing suits. They step into an imaginary pond and begin to play in invisible water. A gauze veil of blue stretched across the stage and circled by a row of pink-paper lotuses represents cool mountain water. Kunwad, the female impersonator, plunges into a trough of actual water and splashes around the stage amid the shrieks and gleeful gestures of the ballet. A hunter appears and the chorus stops singing. He speaks his lines himself, and informs us that he will capture the most beautiful of the *kinnaras*, Manohra, and present her to his king. He takes her wings so she cannot fly away and lassos her with a long snake for lack of a rope. Manohra pleads with him to free her (the orchestra plays *od* or "crying" music), but he forces her to follow him (the orchestra plays *cherd* or "exit" music in quick time).

The next scene shows Manohra sitting on a dais in the center of the stage. She has been married to the crown prince of the kingdom, Prince Sudhon, and although she has come to love him truly, she still bemoans the misadventure at the bathing pool. Sitting alone with her knees tucked under her, she matches the chorus' melancholy words with the gesticulation of her hands—she misses the cold air of the mountains, she thinks some deed in a past life must have brought this upon her, and she shows us that despite her love for her husband, it is difficult to live among human beings. She crosses her arms and as her hands pat her chest slowly she expresses sorrow. A *corps de ballet* of eight handmaidens, wearing narrow tiaras instead of the high, tapered, golden crowns of the chief Lakon dancers, enter and announce that they will dance to dispel her gloom. They perform what is called *Rabam* or a dance of no meaning, and designed merely to show the suppleness of the dancer's body. They flex and flick their curling fingers, they shake their shoulders, and pose on one foot with their toes arched. They circle the stage in slow controlled steps, gliding and slithering, rising and sinking effortlessly.

Prince Sudhon, played by one of the taller Lakon girls, enters by one of the side doors of the auditorium (what corresponds in our theatres to a fire exit). He is dressed in a black blouse, sparkling with diamants, and silver shoulder decorations. His russet and gold brocade trousers—derived from the Indian *dhoti*—have a gathering of pleats in front, fit tightly around the knees and flare stiffly out from around the thighs. He mounts the stage and joins Manohra on the dais. He crosses one leg under him, letting the other extend down and rest on the floor, the conventional sitting posture for men. The copulatory or love music is played, and the learned among the audience do the *wai* gesture of placing their hands before their faces. After this love-making, he explains in gesture that he must leave her and go to war as the kingdom has been attacked. He adds, "I am certain of victory; so I shall be back soon." She replies that she will be lonely, "I was taken from my family and I thought I would die then, but I met you, and now . . ." She rests her knee on his lap and leans on his chest. The copulatory music is played again, the lights go out, and instantly dawn comes. The Prince rebukes her for weeping, saying that it is a bad omen to cry at the moment of separation. She answers, "I will wait for your return for ever and ever."

There follows an Army scene in the orchestra pit with the soldiers entering and leaving by the fire exits and marching in procession around this area and the space immediately in front of the curtain on the stage proper. The ancient Siamese battle cry, rather like a bloodcurdling version of Tarzan's jungle call, sounds three times. Two flag-bearers enter, followed by four young boys each of whom represents a regiment. They carry spears and shields, bows and arrows. The cavalry appears (four more boys) with leather, shadow-play horses clipped to their hips. A ballet group of a dozen men perform a mock battle. Prince Sudhon enters in full regalia—umbrellas, standards and guidons, sword bearers, and helmeted body guards. His Army salutes him. He mounts the howdah of a gaily caparisoned elephant of papier maché (played by two men) and rides off through the audience.

The next scene takes place in the palace grounds. Some servants (comedians who speak in ordinary Siamese) are sweeping the court-yard and gossiping. They explain how a wicked Brahmin priest, a sort of Merlin attached to the Court, has taken advantage of the Prince's absence and persuaded the aged King to sacrifice a bird-

147

woman on the pretext that this will keep him from dying on a certain ill-fated day. The priest is, of course, plotting to place his own favorite on the throne. The servants have constructed a pyre on which Manohra is to be burned alive. The King, played by a young girl, enters, followed by the Queen. The evil priest appears dressed in a white, monk-like robe, and wearing a high-pointed turban. The King regrets the sacrifice of Manohra. The Queen speaks up, in gesture, on her behalf. A group of court attendants pass by, see the King, and fall on their knees and slowly cross the stage bobbing up and down like rippling waves. The Queen resumes her pleas, "The people love Manohra. She is the best possible daughter-in-law. Think of your son, her husband, fighting a war for us." She threatens the King, "If you persist in this, I shall kill myself too." The priest says that there is nothing to be sentimental about: "After all Manohra is an animal, not a human." Actors dressed like sacrificial animals—a water buffalo, a cow, a goat—are led on stage. They bleat and cavort before the throne. An official of the court joins in interceding on Manohra's behalf. The King mournfully replies, "Our priest knows the sacred books. He must be obeyed." Word, spread by the gossiping sweepers, has reached the people, and a crowd gathers at a respectful distance from the throne. "Save Manohra," they cry humbly. The priest silences them by saying that the alternative, according to astrological laws, would be for all of them to substitute for her and die in her stead. They are silenced. The King vacillates. The Queen badgers him, according to the custom of all Lakon plays where women are invariably stronger and more noble than their husbands. She openly shows her contempt of him for being an old man fearful of his own death and, to add to the enormity of his cowardice, for sacrificing a young, lovable maiden. Manohra appears to make a request, "May I live until my husband returns?" This is refused. Then she asks if she can dance one last dance before leaving the world. This is granted, and the King sends for her wings which until now have been carefully locked away. She bids the King and Queen farewell. They sorrowfully embrace her. Manohra weeps (there is no tear music for this as Manohra is only pretending). The Queen urges her to dance "most beautifully, so that the very gods will praise you." Manohra begins a *sutee* or "suicide by fire" dance (derived from India, obviously, in that it is a re-enactment of Sati, the wife of Siva, who im-

148

molated herself on his funeral pyre, but as a dance it reached Thailand from Indonesia in one of the Panji dramas). The sacrificial fire is started by the wicked priest. Manohra leaps onto the flames—pieces of cloth blown by a fan to which realistic smoke and sparks are added. She soars—hoisted by a rope—to the top of the proscenium where she assumes the most famous of the *apsaras* or celestial dancer poses with the legs drawn up so that the dancer seems to be resting on her knees and with her arms stretched out in front of her. She is then drawn slowly across the top of the stage and disappears to return at last to her home in the Himalayas.

The next scene shows the hazardous pursuit by Prince Sudhon. He is resolved to find his wife. He crosses a jungle, battles with a tiger and later a python. Finally, he encounters a holy man undergoing austerities in the Himalayas who tells him how to get to the *kinnara* palace.

The last scene shows the *kinnara* King and Queen and six of their daughters, each identical with the other, sitting on a long dais placed diagonally across the stage. Manohra is outside the palace purifying herself of the contamination of having lived among mortals. The Prince enters and the King is greatly impressed that he could find their abode. The daughters are filled with wonderment at the Prince's handsomeness. The King, aware of Manohra's attachment to her husband, proposes a test. If Prince Sudhon recognizes Manohra among her identical sisters, he may take her back with him. Manohra quietly enters and joins her sisters in a dance. The Prince recognizes her long before the dance is concluded, but he waits to the end to speak to her. All rejoice at their happy reunion. Moving gently together, bending their elbows, flexing their hands in the gesture of delight, and stepping with bent knees gracefully, the two lovers zigzag across the stage and make their happy exit.

Dance

As *Manohra* shows, Lakon at the Silpakorn Theatre is a mixed drama form composed of many elements and drawn from a varying number of sources. Chief of these is dancing, and Lakon in the narrow sense of dance alone is the most classic meaning of the word. Most people who study Lakon or Khon in Thailand today study only the dance portions of it, and only the students and artists of the Department of Fine Arts ever appear in the modified, even modernized, Lakon programs of the Silpakorn Theatre. If you use the word Lakon in its narrower sense you find that it has a specific repertoire of its own numbering around fifty separate pieces which embrace remnants from the most ancient dances of Thailand, the purely dance sections both of Khon and of the several kinds of Lakon in the broad sense. This repertoire is performed independently as dances and a recital is composed of selections from them. Among the most interesting group within this over-all classification are the dances of warfare or strategy.

To explain them let us go back a little. Classical theatre of Siam is referred to in intellectual circles as *Sangit*, the Sanskrit word which means "playing of musical instruments, singing and dancing." Music lies at the root of the latter two arts and is indispensable to the performance. But the Siamese interpret the provenance of their orchestra in an original way. According to them music came from the hunter beating on sticks of wood in order to rouse game (these are the drums and clappers of the orchestra), twanging his bow string to release the arrow (this inspired all stringed instruments), and blowing his horn to announce the quarry and killing, and to call other hunters. This emphasis on the hunt—killing, and warfare by extension, and by still further extension, strategy—figures prominently in Siamese dancing.

The *Ramayana's* powerful influence on theatre arts is also responsible for numerous dances concerned with the military arts. Looked at in one way, the *Ramayana* is little more than a battle epic deeply concerned with struggle, defeat and victory. Another factor which helps explain the connection between combat and dance was the war-ridden nature of the periods which accompanied the origins and growth of each dance form in Thailand. While Thailand was busy defending itself from the Burmese or attacking Cambodia, Laos and her other neighbors, dance was always associated with the battles.

Before engaging in war, a propitiatory dance sufficed as a prayer to the gods. Dances of mock engagements or rehearsals of an

Eliot Elisofon

CAMBODIA

Two palace dancers performing a promenade in the ruins of Bayon at Angkor

The full cast of palace dancers with princes, princesses, demons and monkeys at Angkor Vat

Eliot Elisofon

LAOS

A folk dance of flirtation

The obeisance in dance

A dance during the annual water festival

A demon-monkey battle by the palace dancers

Peter Anderson, Straits Times

MALAYA   A male Menora dancer in trance performing as a woman

INDONESIA

A princess of Wayang Orang dance-drama

A heroic warrior

A combat scene between a noble lady and her enemy

A war dance from Sumba Island

A folk dance of Sumatra

Foto Kempen

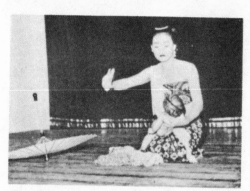

Foto Kempen

The men's dance of Flores Island

A mother with her child from the Wayang Orang of Solo

Sumatran folk dance

War dance of Nias Island

Foto Kempen

Foto Kempen

War dance of Nias Island in full action

Love dance of Timor
Island

Patriotic folk dances
around the flag—
from Celebes

actual battle scene were used as calisthenics are by modern soldiers. One of the ancient classics enjoins persons who are trained well in battle to display their skill so "that one may enjoy the sight." The result has been that a large number of dances today still involve rapiers, krisses, lances, long and short swords, sticks and shields of silver, of wood or buffalo hide, each weapon requiring a different style of performance. As much as combat is retained in dance, the converse has also remained true, at least in the field of sports. Siamese boxing, for example, in which you fight with your feet as well as your hands, requires by law that each boxer dance a few preliminary steps as a prayer before a bout, and music accompanies the whole match.

The occasions for combat in dance are various. The gods often battle among themselves. Hanuman fights Ravana, Ravana is beheaded and his ten heads are dissevered, generals are captured and armies of monkeys cross rivers and scale mountains amid fighting. Of a more complicated nature than two or more people engaged in combat are the dances in which opponents practice their martial art as a means of stratagem. In these the story content grows complex and may or may not show actual fighting. In one example, the "Dance of the Killing of Hiranya Kasipu by Norasing," the problem posed is that Hiranya, a demon, cannot be killed by god, man, animal, or weapons, nor during the day or night, nor within the confines of living quarters or out in the open. With this tremendous invulnerability on his side, Hiranya has made a nuisance of himself among the gods. Pra Naray (Vishnu the Preserver) assumes the form of Norasing (Narasimha), a creature with a lion's head and human body whose fingernails are as "corrosive as acid." Norasing, as he is neither god nor beast nor human, and as fingernails are not considered a weapon, attacks and kills Hiranya at the gate, which is neither in nor out of the house, and at twilight which is neither day nor night. In this way heaven is rid of the demon.

Another of the strategy dances also concerns Pra Naray. Nontuk, a half-god, has always been teased by the other gods and goddesses, so he gets his fingertip turned into a diamond whose deadly rays kill anyone towards whom he points it. He kills many of the gods and goddesses and heaven is in distress. Pra Naray the Preserver assumes the form of a beautiful girl and asks Nontuk to dance the "Alpha-

151

bet Dance" with him. He inserts the gesture of the "Snake Coiling on its Tail," in which the dancer must touch his two fingertips together, and Nontuk taken unawares turns his deadly finger on himself and dies. One variant of this dance represents Nontuk as Thosakan (Ravana) who enters into a contest with Pra Naray. Instead of actually fighting they agree that they will challenge each other in dance. The better dancer will be the victor, and they dance the "Alphabet Dance" together.

Related to the strategy dances but more abstract in character and more purely Lakon in its limited meaning than these dances are the ones where disguise plays an important part. The stories of both Khon and Lakon are full of people assuming other forms in order to deceive their opponents. One of Hanuman's enemies, for instance, takes the shape of an atom and hides in the foam of the sea to escape from his relentless pursuit, and in other instances gods become women, women become crocodiles, and monkeys become men. Some of these are transformations in which the disguise is a beautiful one and an evil character represents himself as noble and upright— such as Ravana (Thosakan) who makes himself handsome before visiting Sita with the intention of seducing her, or when a niece of Ravana disguises herself as Sita and pretends to be dead in order to discourage Rama from continuing his search. These occasions all call for a special dance, still popular both in Khon and Lakon, which is known as *Chui-Chai*. The dance is a kind of preening or showing off to indicate vanity and satisfaction with newly acquired beauty. The character admires himself, voluptuously calls attention to his costume, and points out the various aspects of his physical charms. According to the teachers if the role is that of a man, the performer must "strut as an amorous bantam," and if it is that of a woman, she must "coquette and mince like a love-eager maiden." This particular dance is an extremely effective one to look at, but at the same time so difficult to perform properly with the right suggestion of inner ugliness and outer grace that only the best trained of the experts dare attempt it in public.

The portions of pure Lakon, divorced of all drama elements, derive from two basic root dances, called "Dancing to the Fast and Slow" and the *Maebot* or "Alphabet Dance." "Dancing to the Fast and Slow" dates from the time that Ayutaya was the capital of ancient Siam (1350-1767). Since then all students begin with this dance and practice it for at least a year before they can be permitted to enlarge their repertoire. It is said in the old books that once this dance is mastered, the student will look "elegant in all social intercourse," and this is one reason why dancing from the beginning was included among the essential accomplishments of young ladies of social rank.

The "Alphabet Dance," which is the second item all dancers must study, is a connected collection of all the primary gestures and motions of Siamese dance. The steps succeed one another delicately linked like the flowers of a garland. Neither of these items is merely a practice piece for the student. Both must be performed publicly from time to time as a sort of recurring examination to reaffirm a dancer's excellence and to remind the audience of her mastery of the fundamentals. Both dances are prerequisites to the histrionic Lakon of stories and themes. Originally the "Alphabet Dance" consisted of sixty-four "letters" or movements; but Rama I abbreviated the list to nineteen, and this is all that remains today of what must once have been a much fuller, more highly developed and varied vocabulary of dance. The nineteen fragments of the dance are named descriptively and the performers execute their corresponding motions while the side-singers of the orchestra sing out the words in rapid succession. They are:

> Salute to the Gods (the obeisance movement of the hand
>   placed together in front of the face with which all dances
>   begin in Thailand)
> Preliminary Movement
> Prohm (Brahma) with the Four Faces
> Tucking in the Garland's Tassels
> Stag Walking in the Forest
> Swan in Flight
> *Kinnara* Walking around the Cave
> Putting the Lady to Sleep
> Bee's Caress
> The Cockatoo
> The Little Hill as High as the Shoulder
> Mekala Playing with her Precious Jewel
> The Peacock Dances
> Wind Swaying the Plantain Leaf
> Transformation
> Wedded Love

153

Changing the Posture
Fish Playing in the Ocean
Pra Naray (Vishnu) Hurling his Discus

These "letters" in dance have become so mutated and stylized over the centuries that some of them as we now see them are unrecognizable as anything more than abstract motion. The fanciful names attached to them seem to be a teacher's reference for identifying the posturing rather than an actual description of specifically meaningful sentiments. Animals, however, in every instance are indicated fairly graphically by clear finger positions of the hands to show realistically their wings, horns, or mannerisms. Even these movements, although closely related to the Indian *mudras*, are at considerable variance with the originals. Specific meaning or literalness has virtually disappeared from Siamese dancing. Most of the dance remains in the abstract, as decorative grace and charm and delight in sheer body movement without the pictorial associations one would normally connect with dance based on a drama form. One well-known item, the "Dance Before the Elephant," where Hanuman's monkeys pretend to be gods and dance like them, illustrates this clearly. The words of the song are simply:

> They float in pairs through the air, dancing in different ways: stretching their arms gliding gracefully to the left and right, falling into line, gazing into each other's eyes, circling around, grasping, marking time together, stamping their feet cleverly, turning around, passing through intervening spaces, circling and barring each other. (I have paraphrased here P. S. Sastri's translation from Dhanit Yupho's excellent book on Siamese dancing, *Classical Siamese Theatre*.)

A large number of the other dances involve dancing with objects other than weapons and the instruments of warfare—fans, long pieces of silk cloth, candles, flowers, flower pots, peacock feathers, long fingernails of silver, and even lighted lanterns. In this group comes the most ancient of all Siamese dances, known today only in a vestigial form called *Praleng*. *Praleng* is a preliminary piece to introduce formal performances of both Khon and dramatic Lakon, and is danced by two persons wearing simple masks and holding peacock feathers in their hands. No singing accompanies this dance, only the orchestra plays a relentless chattering and clicking on its bamboo

154

xylophones. It is said that the dance reveals how supernatural beings comport themselves—the nearest approximation of the gods mortals can make—and therefore it begins a performance in order to invoke and please the gods and thereby to ward off evil. Rama IV (1804-1868) at one point substituted gold and silver flowers for the peacock feathers which he felt had become vulgar by their popularity with the people and among professional dancers outside the palace. He was aware of the danger of tampering with the sacredness of the traditional dance and apologizes to the audience in one short verse of the song which he added to the dance—"Spectators may object to this innovation as it breaks with tradition, but is it not indeed an auspicious sight?"

Other dances with objects or those in the purely dance parts of Lakon have their origins abroad and although they are now integral parts of the Thai repertoire, they still retain certain foreign aspects. The "Fan Dance," for instance, is Chinese dating from the time of Rama II, who once commanded the Chinese and Mohammedan communities of Bangkok to participate along with the Thais in an enormous dance festival. The Chinese used fans (the popularity of this was increased during the Japanese wartime period, and the fans used in this dance today are all Japanese ones) while the contribution of the Muslims was apparently "breast beating" and a special tune, both of which still remain as characteristic features of the "Dava Dung Dance." The artistic adaptability of the Thais is also shown in the *Farang Ram Tao* or "European Dance" which originated with the early Portuguese traders who came to Thailand in the seventeenth century. It differs from the purer Siamese dances in that hand movements are not used, hands are held at the hip in the style of certain Western folk dances, and the feet move as in a clog dance or a jig. This creates an interesting effect for the foreigner. Since Siamese dancing is always performed barefoot and the pace is much slower than in Western folk dancing, the feet pat the floor almost silently in a reposeful slow-motion.

Drama

The excellence of classical dance-drama and dance forms is only part of Thailand's theatrical maturity. There is also a thriving popular theatre called Likay with drama completely predominating over dance, which attests to a genuine response to realism and a fine interest in the sustained unfolding of a story which may or may not have been told before. Likay is better known to the majority of Thais than even their traditional Khon and Lakon, which seem a little formal or forbidding to the average man. The converse, however, is true with regard to foreigners. I know of no traveler to Bangkok who has not witnessed and enjoyed a program at the Silpakorn Theatre. Unfortunately for Likay, very few have explored this theatre.

Likay is in every sense of the word a people's entertainment, with no less than twenty theatre houses distributed all over the city of Bangkok. Every night from eight to midnight persons from all classes, ricksha coolies, white-collar workers, and even those among Bangkok society who are genuinely keen on theatre, pack these Likay houses. If no single troupe or theatre appears as financially impressive as the Silpakorn Theatre, it is because competition is keen. There are hundreds of Likay troupes who perform nightly the year round, and the price of tickets is absurdly low—the best seat costs around thirty-five ticals or ten cents. Likay has never played to an empty house. A failure is unheard of; a play is either more or less successful. If an all-star cast is assembled for any special occasion, it is impossible to get tickets. You must resign yourself to standing at the back or down along the aisles. No temple fair or national holiday is complete without a special Likay performance—often out in the open air—with the actors performing on temporarily erected stages of rickety, shaking boards, against flimsy painted backdrops. Likay occupies an almost exaggerated position in the life of the average Thai, and its importance to him is disproportionate with regard to what in other countries are more serious concerns than theatre. Perhaps this starts in childhood, because children are admitted free and they can even stand on the stage off to one side behind the orchestra or in the wings, and as long as they stay out of the way, they can even peer at the action from the stage entrance doorways.

Curiously enough, Likay, a thoroughly secular drama form, has a special connection with ordinations when a Thai boy or man becomes a priest, and it is compulsory for every male to spend at least a short period of his life as a monk. If the family can afford it, a special Likay performance will be provided free for the neighbors or any passers-by who happens to be in the vicinity. For marriages, which are if less sacred at least more permanent spiritual obligations, only Khon is appropriate among the theatre forms of Thailand.

Likay is recent by Asian standards. It began a little more than a hundred years ago, and its origin is attributed to the Muslim community of Bangkok—the Malay traders and *mullah* priests who came to proselytize. The word "likay" derives from *dikay ichai*, the Siamese equivalent of "praise to Allah," and became current when the Thais first noticed the strange musical chants which the followers of Islam sang during their annual period of penance. The Thais somehow created a drama out of this, and invented their own stories, but the connection of these plays today with their Mohammedan origin remains only in the prayer song, vaguely along the lines of the original tune, which is sung at the beginning of each performance.

Like most plays in Asia, Likay is episodic and consists of short, active scenes which follow one another in rapid succession. And like nearly all Southeast Asian plays, they are comedies with many humorous moments, always ending with the triumph of right. In order to foster the habit-forming aspect of Likay, the custom in recent years has been to continue the same story night after night, chained together rather like old-fashioned movie serials. This leads to a certain discursiveness and over-intricacy of plot, but the Likay writer tries to spin a story out as long as possible. This is the diametrical opposite of the Western playwright who tries to condense all he has to say into a compact two and a half hours of a single evening. Some Likay plays last for a week or even more if they are successful, and many are revived again and again either in identical versions or as sequels and continuations.

In actual performance Likay incorporates a number of elements from Khon and Lakon and is a continuation of Siamese classics. The Piphat Band sits at the side of the stage (without singers, however, because the actors do all the talking and singing necessary), and accompanies all main moments of action. The actors do some

157

dancing, especially the kings and queens who are standard role-types of every Likay and who are dressed rather like Lakon dancers. They perform prescribed movements and steps for all entrances and exits. As they enter, they follow an imaginary line on the stage—like a large question mark, if you actually drew it—then step over an imaginary threshold before they sit down and commence their dialogue from the dais in the center of the stage. There are other conventions. All actors must kneel and bow to the audience when they first enter the stage; the counterpart of this in Khon and Lakon is the dance of obeisance where the ensemble performs a long preambular salute before beginning the story. All the movements of the dance portions are what the foreigner thinks of as characteristically Siamese. One essential difference is in the torso bounce or the "catching of the breath" rhythmic punctuation. In Lakon this is upward as if the dancer is lifting himself; in Likay the motion is downward to make it heavier and more emphatic.

Like Khon, all the actors are men. However, nowadays a few women do appear on the stage in female roles despite the fact that more often, in order to meet the changing tastes of Bangkok's general public, a number of these male actors impersonating women simply wear modern dresses to make them appear more realistic. The role of *jeune premier* is always played by the handsomest young man of the troupe. In ordinary conversation if you say a certain man is a likay, you mean he is extremely good-looking. But the Likay actor who plays these roles is always rather weak and effeminate, and his make-up of solid white and thick lipstick, his silken costume and diamond earrings accentuates this.

The predilection for feminine-looking men is on the whole common to all Asia and carries with it no sexual overtones of the sort the Westerner might expect. In Japan, the *iro-otoko* of Kabuki, a beautiful man of attraction, is often played by men who normally take only women's roles. His part on the stage is usually hapless and pathetic and his only consolation in this life lies in his appeal to women and his sexual prowess. In China, it is the young scholar who is so happily attractive and so unhappily treated in life. And everywhere in Asia, even in the movies, the most beautiful man has to the Western eye a slightly feminine flavor about him. This point makes one of the sharpest contrasts in theatre taste between Asia and the West. We go in for the virile-looking, muscular man of the Lancaster or Brando type. In Asia, however, where homosexuality is more rare and fear of it virtually unknown, in consequence, the cult of the masculine as an aesthetic end in itself becomes psychologically less important. The rather gentle, effete male is physically greatly desired by the opposite sex, both on stage and off. The men who play these roles are, it is necessary to say, almost invariably well-adjusted sexually. They marry as a matter of course, although their portrayals on stage which give them such advantages with women in private life, often make them the despair of their wives. The Asian explanations for this fact vary, but there seems to be general agreement that the greatest beauty in the theatre is offered by the woman, the greatest villainy is typified in a kind of crude masculinity, and for creating a good, handsome man, you must depend more on the feminine than the male. And in Asia where, for the most part, sexual differentiations are less marked—in stature, in amount of hair, and the like—and where theatre has so long a tradition of role interchangeability and fluidity, the good and the beautiful, lying as they do between extreme beauty and villainy, naturally tend to a less sexually defined art and a more androgenous, even epicene, aesthetic delineation of character on the stage.

The chief difference between Likay and Khon or Lakon is that Likay is literally and realistically acted and follows a precise if wandering development of plot. There are no gods or superhuman characters in Likay, and although kings and queens are central causative agents, the main roles represent ordinary human beings, often in a lowly social position. The actors speak their lines in modern every-day Siamese. There is also a preponderance of songs. At intervals, whenever the situation requires or permits, the actor will sing a song into a microphone near at hand which either emphasizes his emotions, explains the action which has just taken place, or foretells what will be presented in the succeeding scene. Except for minor speeches both Likay declamation and song follow strict rules. The phrases must be poetic, according to elaborate laws of rhyme and meter, and they must be improvised on the spur of the moment. These verses are ephemeral and evanescent. The plays are never performed quite the same way twice, and since there are no manuscripts or tape recorders, it is quite impossible to build up a rigid, traditional, transmittible repertoire of dramas. The actors and playwright agree upon the theme, set themselves a cast of characters, a time-length, an outline of the succession of scenes and their high points, select the tunes for the songs, and the rest depends on the inspiration of the moment.

The majority of Likay themes in the past dealt with stories of the Burmese wars, that troubled period of history when Thailand constantly lost to the Burmese and was forced to allow them not only to sack Thai capitals, but to seize the dancers and musicians and export them to Mandalay and Rangoon as part of the spoils of war. In 1955, the Prime Minister of Burma, U Nu, in a journey of apology and atonement for Burma's past sins toward Thailand, planted a peepul tree (Lord Buddha's meditation tree) on the site of the ruins of Thailand's last capital, and as a result of this effort to create good relations between the two countries, the Thailand government has issued an ordinance to all Likay troupes abolishing all plays dealing with the Burmese wars. This, of course, is a blow to the theatre, as it always is when governments interfere with artists; but to supplant this loss of thematic material, Likay troupes are now being encouraged to put on anti-Communist plays.

Likay lends itself admirably to this, not only because its kings and queens are always heroic, if subsidiary, nor merely that being a people's theatre on a somewhat unsophisticated level it is therefore deeply Buddhist in mood and sympathy, but because banditry and treachery to the throne (or government) generally provide the pivot around which the action of the plots spins. These intrigues, uprisings, revolts, and martyrizations of the innocent have always had ample scope within the energetic stories of Likay, and it is a simple matter to adjust these to refer to Communists. According to the latest rules, the villain must wear red, attempt to overthrow the ruling power, set out to destroy religion, and owe his allegiance somewhere abroad. This latter must not, however, be Burma. But Likay has always been a popular theatre and because of its intimacy with the people it has expressed more the wishes of the common man than those of the government. Because of the improvisatory character of the plays censorship is a difficult matter to enforce. At present the Likay troupes are cooperating with the government, since Communism is an unpopular political theory with the Thais and unacceptable to the Thai conscience, at least as of today. But how compliant Likay would be were it to cease pleasing its audiences is problematical.

This recent interference—more in the nature of a request to cooperate with the government in its foreign and internal attitudes—is in one way a sign of recognition of Likay. The last time the government stepped in was more unflattering. It happened when Thailand was under Japanese influence. The Foreign Minister at the time, feeling that Likay was a vulgar and suspect art, forbade the use of the word "Likay" and substituted the Sanskritized-Siamese word *nata dundri* meaning dance and music. At the same time, because bare feet were considered unseemly for a nation fighting against the West, they compelled the actors to wear long white lisle stockings. This is the only reform from those days which has remained. One may be sure that any new changes made in Likay will have to suit the public fancy if they are to continue longer than the tenure of the government that enforces them. Likay is certain to be around for a long, long time, and it will certainly change according to its audience's desires rather than the government's.

One of the biggest Likay successes has been *The Red Silk Bandit*, and it has run serially for several weeks. It is a long and involved collection of fragmentary scenes in which a variety of disconnected incidents are gradually brought into focus. The King appears in a certain village (there are no stage settings in Likay except for a single backdrop, which has the name of the troupe embroidered on it, a dais and some chairs brought on by the actors as required), and we learn that his capital is being besieged. A villain in a red shirt and red short trousers and wearing earrings and a wrist watch informs us that he and the Prime Minister are traitors to the throne. The Queen, who has remained in the capital, learns that the King has married a girl in the village and that she is the sister of the wicked Prime Minister. A young man enters and sings about how he lives in a temple for lack of other shelter and at night has only a thin cloth to cover himself. He explains that he does not even know his own father. A comedian and the Prime Minister discuss the Red Silk Bandit and measures to form an army to combat him.

The Queen (number one) is now seen in a forest awaiting rescue. The Queen's daughter who is with her in the forest assumes the disguise of a man and forages for food in a Robin Hood manner for her mother. A small boy dressed in green with a purple veil over him representing a bird rushes on the stage and dies. He has been killed by an arrow. The young man (the one who doesn't know his father, but by this time we already suspect he is a prince) and a clown jump on the bird and with imaginary props pretend to cook it and eat it. The Queen's daughter, who has shot the bird, enters and is furious since the bird was intended for her mother's supper. She rebukes the two, and learns that they are joining an army to fight against the King. She slaps the young prince, and he vows he will make her his wife. The plot continues to thicken. It finally transpires that the Red Silk Bandit is a woman, that the wicked Prime Minister is killed and his sister, the Queen (number two), is disposed of. The King returns to his capital, and the boy marries the girl despite the complication of their being brother and sister.

Summarized like this, the play does not make much sense, but in action, oddly enough, there is considerable suspense and interest. In any case, the charm of Likay is far less in its stories than in its actors and the skill with which they dance and improvise their poetry and sing their periodic songs. It is unfair to look at it exclusively from the story point of view, and a synopsis can only mislead one as to the extent of its value. Some of the actors are accomplished, subtle, and convey a real sense of theatre to the spectators. Likay, as can only be expected from any theatre that caters to the poorest classes of the country, has about it certain crudities, but these, weighed against the cheerful exuberance and high standard of acting, seem minor. With guidance or even kindly support from the government, and the introduction of certain technical improvements in stagecraft that would emerge were the actors exposed to other theatres of wider, more international scope, Likay would soon appeal to many more people than, as it does at present, to the Thais alone.

For a short period immediately after the War and lasting until a year or so ago, a modern theatre called Lakon, for lack of a better word, was popular. At this time, Thailand had no movie industry of its own and was dependent entirely on importations—Western, Indian or Chinese films. Perhaps this lack of contemporary theatrical expression—even Likay is old in the eyes of the progressive younger groups—was the inspiration for the new Lakon. Its plays were all exceedingly fanciful and colorful and somewhat on the lines of what we mean by musical comedy in a turn-of-the-century sense. Nearly all the stories were unrealistic and romantic and dealt with kings and queens; these were usually killed by wicked enemies, and their deaths are avenged by loyal and devoted brothers. But Lakon was up-to-date in its techniques, fast-moving and essentially modern in style of costume and make-up. The music was purely Western, with song after song crooned in vaudeville-like succession, while an orchestra of saxophones (the present King of Thailand's favorite instrument), pianos and violins played sentimental parodies of American popular hits. There was no dancing except for excerpts from the Rambong.

Out of the large number of Lakons written and acted during this period, one serious playwright of genuine merit emerged, Kumut Chandruang. Kumut originally came from a theatrical family, and his father headed a classical Lakon troupe. But he had also gone to school in America, where he is known for his book *Boyhood in Siam* written some years ago. His experience and contact with modern theatre there equipped him well and gave him an insight into theatrical techniques unique in Thailand at the time. These advantages automatically assured him a natural place in the theatre. His particular likes ran along the lines of Eugene O'Neill, who still remains his favorite playwright, but he was unable to avoid the pressure of the Siamese public.

His attempts at this new Lakon were like the others—grand, flamboyant, extravaganzas. But he did try to widen the scope in so far as popular opinion allowed. His first real success six years ago was an adaptation of *Death Takes a Holiday*, which he named "Death in Disguise," and for a wild, sensationally dazzling second act, he inserted a scene from Dante's *Inferno*. He followed this with an adaptation in fairy-tale style of F. W. Bain's *Livery of Eive*, which he transposed to fit Siva and his consort, Uma, and in it he developed mildly the theme that beauty was a danger to itself as much as to others. His last attempt, and this signalled the end of this new Lakon all over the country, was *Macbeth the Traitor*, taken from Shakespeare of course, but laid in a completely Siamese setting. During this moment of modern theatre, the first new note in Thailand's drama since Likay, playwrights made a good deal of money. Almost any Lakon earned for the writer more than twice what an author of a best-selling book could expect, and it seemed as if something of lasting interest had been started. At one point, a serious, genuinely modern play was put on, *Thunderstorm*, a tragedy of incest and murder written by Ts'ao Yu, China's most distinguished modern playwright. But this led to nothing.

Today there is no modern theatre of any kind. Kumut Chandruang is prospecting for diamonds in the Siamese jungles of the interior. His actors and actresses have either gone into the movies or taken jobs far from any connection with the theatre. One or two have returned to teaching classical Lakon. But the absence of a modern theatre strikes the foreigner more woefully than it does the Thai. If you ask a Thai what happened to his modern theatre, he is apt to ignore the question by countering with another: what happened to Western classics? To most Asians, the failure of a modern theatre is no more reprehensible than neglect of a traditional one.

There is no reason why another attempt at modern theatre in Thailand should not be made. The Thais are patently a theatre-loving people, and restlessly so. When a modern theatre appears for good, the theatrical maturity of Thailand will be complete. And with it, the plots of even the older theatres will change and probably come to be as skillful and as significant as the high standard of acting and dancing is at present.

5

CAMBODIA

The tiny Kingdom of Cambodia, little larger than Connecticut and with a population about the same as Iowa's, used to be part of French Indo-China. It is now independent as a result of the Geneva Conference (1955), and today the only Frenchmen remaining there are the High Commissioner, a handful of rubber planters and pepper growers (Cambodia produces the finest pepper in the world and the most expensive), and a cadre of instructors at the Ecole Militaire in Pnom-Penh, the capital of the country.

Of all the colonies (with the possible exception of Louisiana) that France has ever lost or is in the process of losing, none has caused more pangs of sentimental heartache among educated Frenchmen. The French ruled it, or rather "protected" was the gentle word they preferred to use, for less than a century, but the position the country held within the French Empire was something like that of Bali to Holland—one of affectionate, even indulgent, regard. In common with Bali, Cambodia has a number of charming exoticisms both in its countryside and its people.

Like most of Southeast Asia, Cambodia alternates wild, primeval jungle with rich squares of paddy cultivation. Cambodia is so fertile in fact that many areas yield four crops a year. The people live high off the ground in wooden frame houses built on stilts. For a period each year, the rivers flood and the Cambodians go about in little rowboats of hollowed-out tree trunks. When the waters recede, and they do this with clock-like regularity, the people are provided with the rest of their food—fish. But fishing is neither an effort nor a sport. During the dry season they merely dig a series of holes around their houses which trap the fish as the floods recede and keep them fresh and handy. When the supply is exhausted, the next year's rise in the waters brings in another catch.

165

The people racially are called Khmers, the sturdy and well-built remnants of an ancient civilization, with a sultry, voluptuous look about them that one associates with the Malays whose blood also suffuses most Cambodians. On the whole they are handsomer than their Siamese or Vietnamese neighbors. The men wear longish hair, while the women crop theirs in a cross between the boyish bob of the Twenties and a crew cut. Women "refresh" their faces with daubs of rice-paste which make them look as if they were going into battle with full war paint. Men tattoo their chests; the decorations range from pictures of temples pinpricked over the whole chest, to little phalli, with the Buddhist Wheel of Karma as a scrotum, over the solar plexus. Nearly everyone in the villages has a large, blurry circle of blue between their eyebrows, like an Indian caste mark. This is a lifelong discoloration caused by applying an eye-glass cup of burning cotton to the child's forehead to protect him from the evil eye.

France's intoxication with Cambodia stemmed from rather more important aspects of the country—primarily the magnificent collection of ruins known as Angkor, where something like six hundred buildings, elaborately sculptured and powerfully constructed, stand in the jungle clearings of Siemreap. Secondly, the marvellous troupe of dancers belonging to His Majesty the King of Cambodia at the Royal Khmer Palace in Pnom-Penh provide a comparable living treasure. In both of these France had a hand, and whatever her colonial follies may have been, her expert and sensitive artistic acumen redounds to her credit. The French discovered the ruins, where they had for centuries lain overgrown by the thick jungle, protected them by establishing an archeological department, reconstructed many of the buildings out of scattered piles of crumbling stones; and it was French scholarship that revealed the story of this fantastic period in Khmer history. It was also through a tactful and subtle post, that of *Conseiller Artistique* (Cultural Adviser) to the Throne, that interest in Cambodian dance was first stimulated and the extraordinary purity of the performances has been preserved for us to the present day.

From the French, the world has learned the history of the Khmers magnificently recorded in the details of the construction of the great buildings of the Angkor environs, and these in turn have provided a commentary on the extravagant place dance held at the time. The eminence of dance, at least within the palace and within the people's hearts, still holds today. These palace dancers, despite being deeply influenced by Thailand and, as it were, restored by the Thais to the country of their origin, still provide the only clear link of modern Cambodia with its antiquities and its once-forgotten magnificence.

Khmer civilization, of which today's Cambodians are direct lineal descendants, reached its first importance in the eighth century, which time also marks the first inscription referring to dancing so far discovered in the area. Before this, there had been invasions from India and Indianized Java, and the conquerors mingled with the conquered until they were completely absorbed by them. In exchange for the joys of victory and tribute, the foreigners gave dance and religion. Their incursions, actually more cultural than military, brought not only priests but women dancers. Some were prostitutes, others of noble birth, but both performed at sacred and secular ceremonies to induce favorable attitudes from the gods. By the beginning of the great Angkorean period, which lasted from about the ninth century to the twelfth, these dancers had already become identified in the Cambodian mind with the Hindu *apsaras* or celestial dancers, who propitiate the gods with gifts, with their bodies, and with their art. Representations of them figure on every column, bas relief, and chiseled stone in all the ruins, either in attitudes of devotion and offering or dancing. Mortal *apsaras* were also attached to all the major temples. Ta Prohm, one of the larger temples, had, according to an inscription, no fewer than six hundred dancers belonging to it permanently.

The Khmers in turn grew aggressive and at one time controlled most of Indo-China, Thailand, and even received tribute from the Malay Peninsula and Sumatra. Several bas reliefs of Angkor show graphically the slave labor extracted from these conquered peoples and used to build the great stone edifices of Cambodia. During this period they accomplished some of the most extraordinarily beautiful architecture in world history. In an outburst of Brahmanical, and later Buddhist, fervor, a series of Khmer kings deified themselves in temples and tombs. Some of the buildings were constructed with such speed that portions were left incomplete or in places even marred by hasty workmanship. The massive central temple of Angkor Vat is known to have been completed in thirty years, a third of the time Europeans required on the average for their Gothic cathedrals. Originally in Cambodia, under Hindu influence, god and king were worshiped phallically, and each temple tower enshrined a diamond-studded golden lingam.

Buddhism succeeded Hinduism and the marks where the lingams have been removed and Buddhas substituted are still in evidence. The god-king came to be worshiped as an incarnation of the Lord Buddha. The atmospheric and strange temple of the twelfth century known as Bayon is a case in point. It comprises fifty towers of four identical faces each, half-smiling in the cryptically tranquil, Buddhist way. They represent not only Lokesavara, or the Compassionate Buddha, but King Jayavarman VII himself. From Bayon, the center of the kingdom, the two-hundred faces of this god-king look out over all his provinces in the four directions of the world. By the thirteenth century, the Khmer people were drained of their energy, wealth and will by the prolonged centuries of frenzied construction. Slabs of sandstone and laterite were carried by hand from great distances, the circulation of gold and precious stones was choked to a standstill by the vast accumulations in the shrines, and thousands of artisans, artists, and slaves gave their lives in frantic carving and chiseling. The last of the constructor-kings Jayavarman VII accelerated the collapse of the empire. He built so many of these sacred edifices that he is presumed to have been Cambodia's mysterious "leper king" vainly hoping the gods would reward his dedicated works by giving him relief from his ailment.

For a while afterwards, a few minor buildings were made, but the greatness of Cambodia was at an end. In this weakened condition, the Khmers could no longer resist the Siamese who in the fifteenth century completely absorbed the country. They abducted Cambodian dancers, ravaged the temples of their riches, and left the Khmers crushed. Their enfeebled state prevailed until circa 1860 when France through the influence of her ambitious missionaries wrested Cambodia's former territories from the Siamese, and set a king upon the throne where he once again held court and resumed patronizing the dances. There then began the curious process of reviving a country which had barely escaped obliteration. There were a few dangerous moments subsequently. In 1941 the Japanese gave a large part of Cambodia, including Angkor, back to Thailand in exchange for cooperation in the war, but these provinces were returned again in 1946 through the Franco-Siamese agreement in Washington.

From the beginning of France's control over Cambodia, news of the marvellous dancing there along with the news of numerous other discoveries filtered back to Paris. In 1908 the palace dancers and orchestra were sent to perform a short series of programs for the Colonial Exposition and Paris intellectuals who flocked to the performances waxed ecstatic. Auguste Rodin, the arbiter of aesthetic matters for much of Europe at the time, sounded the tone of the general reaction. In his enthusiasm he wrote, "These Cambodians have shown us all that antiquity can contain . . . Their classics are as great as ours . . . It is impossible to see human nature brought to a higher state of perfection . . . We have only them and the Greeks . . . They have found postures which I had not dreamed of, movements which were unknown to us even in ancient times . . ."

From then a succession of studies by foreigners commenced. Artists spent months at the palace in Pnom-Penh sketching the dancers in action and in repose. Others prevailed on the palace teachers to train them in the actual dances, and they introduced Cambodian dance styles in London and New York. Altogether the French published nearly a dozen books on Cambodian dance, all now unfortunately out of print. Much of the material concerns itself with matters which are not, strictly speaking, of direct bearing on the art of the dance. One of the writers spends time describing *"les douloureuses céremonies"* at Angkor when the dancers on reaching nubility broke their hymens on a phallus of gem-encrusted stone. Another laboriously describes the life of confinement the dancers lead within the palace walls and dwells on the king's prerogative of choosing from among them for his pleasure. Still another deplores the unhappy fact that when, in the nineteen-twenties, someone wanted to arrange an exposition tracing Khmer culture from the Angkorean period to the present day, he was unable to find in all of Cambodia girls who would dance *"presque nues"* or even pose with bare breasts and transparent skirts in imitation of the celestial dancers on the stones of the ruins. Because of this, almost out of pique, he refused to accept the palace dancers as the bridge between Cambodia's past and present, despite the evidence that technically the extraordinary articulation of the fingers and hands, the hyperextension of the elbow, and the stories of the dances today, can be recognized in and checked against the miles of sculpturing on the walls of Angkor.

In contradicting his conclusions, it would be foolish to imply that dance in Cambodia has remained immutable for a thousand years. The forces from the outside world, Thailand and France in particular, found an easy prey in the exhausted Khmer race. Certainly the greater national vitality which the Thais have displayed in more recent history has had far-reaching effects on dance. In fact, Cambodian dance today differs very little from Thailand's Lakon. The principle of movement is basically identical (this is really Cambodian) and the costumes are almost the same (these are purely Siamese). Today it is a painstaking chore to weed out and separate the conventions and mannerisms which are Siamese from the native ones. Much of this must even be guesswork.

Contributing to Thailand's advantage over Cambodia has been the fairly stable period of kingly rule which followed the seizure of Cambodian dance. Meanwhile Cambodia's line of rulers was, to say the least, tortuous. To begin with, the tradition in Cambodia was to elect a king in times of misrule or doubt as to correct succession (in theory the greatest man of the land was always chosen), and often he was disinclined to promote dance. After the sack of Cambodia the Cambodian throne remained vacant, the kingship idle, and whatever dancers remained near any members of the royal family were there by merest chance and without any substantial subsidy. Regardless of this precarious existence, as the dance situation in Asia now stands, out of all the troupes maintained at the many courts of Asia today, I think unquestionably that the most brilliant, one rating among the world's finest ensembles of dancers, is the one at the Royal Khmer Palace.

At this point, the connection between kings and the dancers should be explained, because in Asia it is of considerable importance. In India, for instance, Kathakali in its present form was invented by a raja, and the best Bharata Natyam until recently was seen at the court of the Maharaja of Baroda far from its home in the South. The relationship of Kandyan dance and Kandyan kings, and of Burmese theatre and the Mandalay court, and the difficulties Thailand faced when the two were separated, have already been cited. The extraordinary preponderance of classic ballets in Asia today, as we shall see even more positively later, is to a great extent due to their protection by royalty. And this makes a sharp contrast between the East and the West where royal patronage has declined into scarcely more than occasional command performances. Perhaps the one picture the average Westerner has of Asiatic dancing—that of an Oriental potentate sitting on cushions watching his palace troupe—is not too far from actuality. For as far back as written records can be found, emperors and maharajas, kings and rajas, sultans and chieftains have all maintained private dancers, and the dances they performed, according to all available descriptions, are remarkably similar to the ones we still see today despite the vagaries of the past. It has been a firm tradition for centuries that court artists and their descendants must be fully supported. Many of them have been granted court ranks and special privileges, some even pensioned for life after they have ceased to be contributing members of the court entourage. The marvellous continuity with the past, the steadily maintained degree of perfection, and, of course, the tremendous bulk of dance which all this has meant is a tribute to the Asian mechanism of art preservation. What the museum is to the West for objects, in a way the court in Asia has been to living, transient and ephemeral arts.

In Cambodia, the relationship between a king and his dancers has been particularly happy—and the French have been helpful in this— and I know of no other ballet group that performs with more magical appeal than the Royal Khmer Palace Dancers. Perhaps the surroundings contribute to the spectators' enchantment. It is a convention that the King's greatest courtesy towards State guests and foreign dignitaries is to give a banquet after which a party, accompanied by retainers carrying lamps and umbrellas to emphasize the King's exalted position, adjourns to another large pavillion within the grounds to watch a private performance by the Palace dancers. The Royal Family's personal interest is so great in the troupe that although a small quota of additional after-dinner invitations are issued to non-official visitors or to persons particularly interested, even these require the King's or the Queen-Mother's direct approval. If you have the opportunity of attending one of these regal evenings, you cannot help being impressed. You sit on antique chairs covered with moiré and embroidered in silver threads. Butlers bring you whiskeys and sodas. You whisper admiring remarks. His Majesty graciously nods or points out some flaw. Meanwhile the fluttering arpeggi of limpid-sounding, dulcet, bamboo xylophones scatter up and down off-key (to Western ears) scales. A gentle, tropical wind blows through the open pavillion, and the trailing trains and scarves of the dancers wafted in the air match the undulating, effortless motions of the fragile and moon-faced dancers.

When the full troupe of Palace dancers in all their regalia and within their splendid surroundings begin to dance, they seem to be the quintessence of Oriental glamor. On each hand they wear diamonds, rubies and emeralds set in rings of gold; their bracelets, armbands, anklets, and *colliers* match. Draped in cloth-of-gold, soft velvets, and iridescent shot silks—the colors of dragonfly wings—and wearing tiaras of beaten goldleaf, they communicate a magic of other centuries, of other countries, and a panoply almost forgotten in the drabness of much of one's usual life.

Formerly, the girls who composed this ballet came from the poorer strata of the Cambodian people. If a family saw that their daughter was turning into a beauty, they offered her to the Palace as an act of religious devotion. In those days, the King was still the *devaraja* or god-king; in Western terms this corresponds to an ultimate degree of "divine right." If he approved of the girl, the family was given a sum of money, the royal blessing, and the girl was taught dancing. In time she became a concubine of the king. Today the practice has been modified. Many of the dancers are hereditary to the Court, aptitude now takes precedence over beauty, and many of them marry outside. (There are fifty of these dancers at present, although an ordinary performance employs only twenty-five at a time.) But in principle the life of a Palace dancer has changed little. She spends most of her time within the Palace compound.

The postures and movements, which impressed Rodin so deeply, are achieved only after long, gruelling practice. Immediately on arrival at the Palace, the young dancer begins her training under *krus* (from the Indian word *guru*) or teachers who are older women and no longer dance themselves. The lessons run every day except Sundays from eight to eleven, lunch is taken at eleven-thirty, and class resumes at three and continues until five. The Asian body by and large has greater flexibility of muscle and softer bone structure than is usually found in the West. Perhaps this is due to diet—meat and milk are rarer commodities even among the rich—or it might be psychological—the Asian is less tense, I think, on the whole than the European or American—or perhaps it is only racial. But whatever the explanation, the fact seems to be self-evident.

Starting with this asset, Cambodian dancers undergo further molding of the body before it can assume at will the shape of Angkor's ancient sculptures. The pupils start with exercises of the hand. Grasping the fingers of one hand the dancer slowly presses them backwards as far as they will go. After a few weeks, the fingers of each hand can be bent back until they touch the outside surface of the wrist. This same exercise is also repeated with each finger separately. If the pupil is too diligent, she may break the tendons and the fingers grow somewhat gnarled.

Another exercise is to place the two palms of the hand together and raise the elbows until the hands form right angles at the wrists. The end result of all this is that during a dance the fingers arch backwards gracefully and the hand hinges in a sharp, abrupt right angle on the wrist. In effect it is the antithesis of the limp, dangling hand of ballet.

Next comes the elbow, which must be as articulated as the hand. As a training exercise, the dancer sits on a stool and puts her arm on her legs. The back of the elbow lies precisely on top of the knee cap. Then she crosses her other leg over the arm near the wrist. She presses gently with the weight of the crossed leg until the elbow flexes. She increases the pressure until eventually the elbow begins to break outward as easily as it folds inward. Another exercise for the elbow is first to lock the fingers together palm downwards, then placing the elbow joints between the legs to squeeze the knees against them until the insides of the elbows touch. But during a dance the serpentine hyperextension undulates smoothly as if the arm is being thrown out of joint rhythmically.

The legs also have their special exercises. One of these consists of sitting crosslegged with each foot on the opposite knee, in yogic fashion, and then rolling forward face down on the floor without altering the position of the legs. The lower part of the body soon

173

becomes stretched or malleable to the point that if you are standing with your arms hanging down at the side, the knees can be spread apart to touch the palm of the hand.

All of these preliminary exercises make the basic posture of Cambodian dance natural and easy—that is, hips held back firmly, knees spread widely apart, feet turned outward, toes up, the angle of the hand on the wrist asymmetrically balanced by the sharp break in the elbow. From this stance all positions and movements of the dance develop and flow, and to it they must return.

After these exercises, which altogether require around a year of practice, the trainee is ready to begin learning actual dances. To teach her, the *kru* pinches her shoulders tightly from behind and maneuvers her through the various routines, kicking her feet to indicate the footsteps and prodding her with the knee to impress the degree and depth of the bends. The movements become engraved upon the dancer's mind and body for life. A talented girl can master the mechanical portions of several dances in two years, but her age determines her position in public performances. No matter how clever she is, the young dancer must play minor roles of handmaidens and attendants until she is older. Eventually the size of the mature girl determines her role type. If she is large she plays men's parts; if she is small, she takes those of women. Two men attached to the palace troupe play all demon, comic, and animal roles.

Although life at court in Cambodia may seem unconventional to a Westerner, the palace dancers are surrounded by a number of moral restrictions. For instance, it is impossible for a man to interview a dancer without a *kru* being present. The girls are never allowed to travel unaccompanied. An unauthorized or unapproved affair would be a criminal offense. And morality and high-mindedness are inculcated, according to the *krus*, from the time the girls arrive at the palace. A dancer, if she is to be great, is judged on three things: her physical beauty, the exquisiteness of her gestures, and the rectitude of her private life. The sacred element of dance has never really been lost in Cambodia, and it is assumed that evil or grossness in the dancer's heart would reflect in the art. The code of behavior may be quite different from ours in the West, but according to its own rules, this conviction is probably quite true.

By thirty at the latest the dancer's career is over. She then either becomes a teacher herself, a singer or time-beater in the orchestra, or a servant in the palace household. In rare instances, an exceptionally great artist such as Nom Soy Sanhvaum, the leading *kru* of the Palace today and the most spectacular dancer of recent times, may occasionally appear in an interlude during a regular performance. But this is always announced specially—the audience is told almost apologetically that she is already fifty-four years old—and she wears an ordinary court costume with a royal sash over her shoulder, crossing her torso; she dances passages of abstract, improvised movements without a specific theme.

Nearly all Cambodian dance tells a story which is graphically depicted both by the action and hand movements. As in Thailand, gestures can be either specific or general. The commonest and most basic of the hand gestures is made by stretching out the thumb and index fingers while the other three fingers curl backwards. In general, this is a gesture of offering. Specifically, it is used to pick flowers, to indicate oneself, to indicate a smile if drawn across the mouth, and if drawn across the eyes, to indicate tears. It also serves as a graceful transition gesture, that is, any other gesture may be begun or completed or even interrupted by this basic one without affecting the meaning. Joy or contentment is expressed by crossing the hands, fingers together, and patting the chest gently. Anger is shown by rubbing the back of the ear; desire or greed by rubbing the palms of the hands together in a circular motion. When both hands are raised palm upward, the gesture refers to the crown; the reverse, both palms downward, signifies the clothing. Many other gestures, such as looking off into the distance, or pointing out an enemy, although always stylized, are easily recognized by their similarity to our own concept of expressiveness.

The most frequent dance movement is the *sampieh* or salute of respect (the Indian *namaskar*). It occurs at the beginning and end as well as at intervals during any dance. It is executed by touching the knees, lifting the hands until they are at breast level, then placing the palms together with the fingers curved back, thumbs out, and raising them to forehead. The religious nature of the dance decrees a formal *sampieh* as a sign of respect to the protecting god of the dance. In addition, the sheltering of dance by the court has created an elaborate protocol of *sampiehs*. These appear often without relation to the story but as marks of respect to the sovereign and his guests for whom the girls are dancing. In the dance stories themselves there are always elaborate relationships of prince to king, daughter to father, pupil to teacher, and man to god, and the *sampieh* figures prominently to comply with the rules of deference.

The walk is highly formalized, executed with knees bent and toes out while the hands, holding the basic position of extended thumb and forefinger, sway forward and back. The length of the footstep is determined by the length of the foot, the heel of one foot is placed at the toe of the other, alternately until the required distance is covered. Most charming of all the *corps de ballet* scenes are the "promenades" or walks of the princess with her ladies-in-waiting. The group symbolically strolls in the palace garden admiring the flowers or walks through a forest or bathes in a court pool.

From the promenades developed the pure ballet movements where dancers dance in an unending series of graceful gestures executed in unison. In these, for the effect of flying through the air, which occurs frequently due to the supernatural beings and gods who invariably figure in the stories, the dancer stands on one foot and raises the other leg backwards, bending it at the knee, until both thigh and leg form parallel lines to the ground. In this posture the back of the heel touches the buttocks, the toes are curled out and the foot points downward. Much is made of standing on one foot over long periods of time while executing elaborate hand gestures and often turning around slowly without quivering or losing balance. Many passages of the dance are performed while kneeling or sitting. The rhythm is marked by a sharp lift of the torso (the bounce or the catching of the breath in Siamese dancing). The torso rises on the beat, and during the succeeding beats it sinks imperceptibly to a level from which it once again can be lifted. There is no downward movement in Cambodian dancing, and the dancers rarely move in a straight line. The direction is always oblique or up and away from the earth towards God.

The plots of the dances are exceedingly simple, and after witnessing a few performances, the clichés and conventions become self-evident. The majority are based on scenes from the *Ramayana* or on Hindu-influenced traditional literature or Buddhist classics. In Cambodia, the favorite scenes seem to be Ravana's stealing of the

176

beautiful Sita from Rama, the fights that ensue and the assistance of the monkeys, and the Mekhala series which explain mythologically the origin of thunder and lightning.

Indispensable to most plots is the role of the sage, also called *kru*. Enormous respect for the sage is maintained at all times, and this tradition of respect is still apparent from the regard Cambodians offer their modern-day Buddhist priests who are also believed to have supernatural qualities. In the stories, the sage usually entrusts some sacred object—a sword, an arrow, or talisman—to a favorite pupil, and after a tearful parting the youth accomplishes some miracle or feat of extraordinary daring.

The Cambodian orchestra is essentially the same as in Thailand, although there is greater refinement in the instrumental performing. The music sounds like drops of water falling in elusive rhythmic irregularity, while the winding melodic line of the horn, through which the player breathes both in and out so that the sound never stops until the end of the music, floats and hovers hesitantly over the music's substance. I have often thought that if summery clouds had sound, it would be like Cambodian music.

A chorus of aged women, *krus* in the sense of dance teachers, sit on the ground near the orchestra. They lean on one arm usually and watch the performance with hawk-like intensity. The lead singer, during pauses in the orchestral music, sings out a line which gives a fragment of the story in poetry. The others take it up repeating the tune and words in perfect unison while the dancers enact the meaning. The sound of their voices is thin and melancholy, and seems to reflect the sadness of their lives—they who once were favored dancers, now old and ugly, empty in heart, watching the young girls rising to the brief glory they once knew and inevitably destined for the loneliness that now haunts them. Among the chorus is also the time-beater who marks the rhythm by clicking two small sticks together. Her rhythm is separate from the drums of the orchestra, and serves to carry the beat in silent passages where the dancers sometimes dance without accompaniment.

The influence of Thailand is most clearly felt in the costumes and crown. For all practical purposes the Cambodians have copied the Thais in these. However, jewelry is an exception. While Siamese dancers use imitation stones and tawdry tinsel, every item worn by

177

the Cambodian palace dancers is genuine. They wear gold and silver anklets and bracelets. Their rings and necklaces are studded with precious stones of every kind. The wardrobe room is actually a museum contained within the palace grounds holding the stage paraphernalia when the dancers are not performing. Some of the many jewels which the French governments have presented to the various kings of Cambodia over the years have found their way to the dancers. One dancer's crown shows an enormous Napoleonic "N" of glittering diamonds. The crowns for male roles are of beaten rose gold, ornately decorated with precious stones, and rise to a height of fourteen inches culminating in a thin point. They weigh about five pounds each. Their weight precludes any violent movement of the head. The activity of the hands with their concomitant meanings removes the need for facial expression, as in Thailand, and the spectator is content with the mask-like, expressionless immobility of the head and face.

Despite the efforts of the Artistic Adviser to the Throne during the time of the French, a number of innovations crept in and now that Cambodia is independent, these experiments will undoubtedly increase. For a while the dancers performed on thick Persian carpets, garishly woven with rosebud patterns, and for a year or so in the past the dancers wore white stockings. On one occasion they danced with little American flags of paper as a special courtesy to a distinguished American visitor. At the last program I saw at the Palace, we were regaled with a new item, "Les Papillons," with a daughter of the King as lead dancer. About a dozen members of the Palace troupe fluttered on the stage with their legs and thighs bare. They wore imported ballet shoes and silken, spangled pieces of cloth to represent wings extended from their wrists to their shoulders. Their heads were covered with velvet bathing caps from which projected long antennae. They queued up like a formation of chorus girls and performed a promenade sequence. The absurd incongruity of their classical gestures in this new routine filched from European vaudeville was a discouraging sight. But the episodes from the *Ramayana* which followed in the program reassured the audience of the continuation of the pure, almost flawless tradition of Cambodian palace dancing. Fortunately, on national days or state occasions, when, for instance, the King goes to Angkor to deposit the ashes of some deceased mem-

178

ber of the royal family, the program always adheres strictly to a more sober, less exploratory repertoire.

A few minor dance forms outside the Palace are still to be found in Cambodia today. In any village which can afford a Western style band there is Lamthong, the Rambong of Thailand. In fact, the best dancers of this in Bangkok and in Saigon, the capital of Vietnam, are Cambodian girls who have come seeking a better livelihood than they can find in their home country. And among the soldiers of the Army, whenever there is a celebration, Lamthong is the order of the day. Sergeants dance with corporals, officers with the older wives (only a small percentage are allowed to keep their dependents on the post), and amid French cognacs and canapés, the battalion band blares out Cambodian tunes. Folk dances are rarer nowadays than the Lamthong. On religious holidays you may see a pair of youngsters and a drummer wandering over the town miming some hunting dance. One of them carries a bow and arrow; the other may be dressed as a stag or other animal. They dance outside your house until you toss them some money, then they move on.

At marriage times, when music is very important to the celebrations, there are sometimes spontaneous improvised dances. One of the members of the orchestra when he is sufficiently worked up will emit a "trrrrr" sound, put his instrument aside or hand it to someone in the audience, and then rise to dance a little. Without stepping off the tiny grass mat provided for the orchestra, he jerks and sways, flexes his fingers back and forth, raises and lowers his shoulders. He calls some woman from among the crowd of listeners and the two of them dance together and sing improvised love poetry to each other. If the woman is shy or reluctant to dance, she can get out of the invitation by singing and dancing rejective words. One of these I once heard went simply, "I am a woman, it's true. But I don't want to dance. For I am fearful of my husband." She then stepped off the mat. The man can pursue, even when he has been rejected, sometimes with poems no more substantial than "I love you. There is the bull and there is the cow too."

A tentative embryonic drama form is emerging in Cambodia. In the small town of Siemreap, the Theatre Moderne gives nightly performances. The theatre is a small barn with a platform at one end and the audience sits on the floor or benches, or, if you are a foreigner and pay the few extra cents for the best seats, little folding chairs. The children crowd round the edge of the platform and stare just over the level of the lights. The scenes are short. A whistle blows and the painted canvas backdrops roll down, and we are transported to yet another part of the forest, to still another palace.

The theatre's most recent play was about two warring Cambodian kings. The good one wins of course and kills his opponent, but meanwhile the spirit of the bad king takes possession of one of the sons of a village family and tries in this way to take his revenge on his former enemy. Throughout there is a good deal of low comedy. There is a scene of the domineering wife (played by a man wearing very elegant "falsies" which he kept shifting into position, much to the hilarity of the audience) who bullies her husband about not earning enough money. The ghost appears in the form of the son and falls in love with the daughter of the house, his sister. There is an elaborate chase through the forest with the brother continually making advances to his own sister until the parents reach their wits' end, unable to control their son or to calm their daughter's fears. Finally the parents decide that the only thing to do is to go to the king (a traditional Cambodian custom) and ask his advice which they accordingly do. The king falls in love with the daughter and fights the brother over her. So eventually the ghost gets his chance at revenge on the good king, but loses and once again is defeated. The king marries the village maiden.

Something along these same lines is the private theatre of Dap Chuong, probably the most powerful military commander in Cambodia. During the fight for independence, he kept his troops in the jungle and started his theatre then as a morale factor during the lulls in the fighting. Now he is the military commander of the Siemreap area, his old fighting ground, and his troops have grown to more than three thousand in number. He selects the best actors from among them, and together with the six-piece military band and two women singers (the best in all Cambodia), they perform every Sunday to the delight of the entire countryside. Dap Chuong as a political figure is in considerable opposition to the new government, and a vague note of this discontent runs through his plays. Sometimes the plays mock various officials who have arrived on the scene to implement unpopular policies, sometimes political ideas are hinted at, but in the main the plays are like the Theatre Moderne, slapstick, heroic, and diverting for the rather unsophisticated audiences for whom they cater.

Before the French left, one of the last Artistic Advisers in Cambodia was Guy Porée, who created in Pnom-Penh the Theatre Nouveau. It encouraged a type of drama different from the Theatre Moderne, which at the best of times is crude and vulgar, and yet which completely broke away from the heady traditions of the classical dance. He assembled a group of youths from among his servants, their friends, and friends of friends, and taught them briefly the rudiments of amateur acting. Then he would tell them stories from the West—Shakespeare, Racine, Corneille, and modern plays—and let the group do whatever they wished with them. Their performances were usually on a small temporary stage erected in the garden of the Porée house, and for costumes they used bits and pieces of Mme. Porée's Paris gowns and modelled them vaguely on pictures they found in European theatre albums. Their fame increased and they began to go on tour to neighboring villages, using the back of an army truck for a stage.

Most of their pieces were short farcical skits interspersed with dancing, but sometimes they attempted things on a grander scale. Their half-hour version of *The Merchant of Venice* was an especial favorite, because the problem of money lending is familiar to Cambodians who saw Shylock as a Chinese usurer. Occasionally the King himself commanded performances. Since independence, the Theatre Nouveau has apparently disbanded for lack of money, but there is every likelihood that were further interest shown in this new type of amateur drama, the once enthusiastic group could be reassembled without difficulty.

On the whole, the artistic life of Cambodia is entirely dominated by the classical dancers of the Palace. To all intents and purposes, there is no other theatrical outlet for the people of any genuine significance or standard. At best the people can see these dances only infrequently on public holidays and state occasions, and if they live away from the bigger towns, the probability is that they will never have even this opportunity.

For a brief period under the French there were two or three small classical dance troupes composed of former dancers from the palace who had returned to their homes, and there were one or two drama troupes of the Theatre Moderne type, but the long war dating from the fall of France, continuing through the Japanese Occupation, and including almost nine years of sporadic civil war, froze the possibility of any widespread theatrical activity. The people's minds were elsewhere.

Now that peace has been reestablished, it is possible that Cambodians will turn to these pleasures again, unless, that is, those long intervening years have made them forget. But if the Palace troupe seems insufficient to carry the entire national load of theatrical entertainment, there is consolation in the fact that after all Cambodia is a small country, and the supreme excellence of that one troupe is more than many, many larger countries can claim.

L A O S

The Kingdom of Laos has many qualities in common with Cambodia. It is small, underpopulated, rich, and it won independence from the association of states formerly called French Indo-China at the same time and in the same way. It lies landlocked except for a chain of rivers, surrounded by Cambodia, Thailand, Burma, China and Vietnam. Despite this proximity to foreigners, it remains one of the most isolated, remote, and untouched countries of Southeast Asia.

To arrive in the king's capital at Luang Prabang by airplane from any of the surrounding countries is like being wafted suddenly and unaccountably from reality into fantasy. Everywhere you see ornate pagodas—many-roofed, many-pillared, and plastered with gold leaf which glitters in the warm sun—and pointed stupas in strange, unorthodox tiers and spires quite different from those in other parts of Buddhist Asia. Everywhere you see huddles of saffron-robed Buddhist priests, files of work-elephants wearing clanking anklets of silver around their feet, and lackadaisical, charming, friendly people sitting in the shade, gossiping, drinking sweet syrups or selling scarves and squares of the famous gold-threaded Laotian silks.

As in Cambodia, the King has a private troupe of dancers. But they are modelled on the Thai style, being a somewhat recent acquisition at the Laotian court. A couple of decades back, no one quite remembers when, the King imported a few teachers from Thailand who selected and trained the prettiest of the maidens connected with the Palace, and their pupils now perform in fine Bangkok style the old legends from the *Ramayana* and the better known excerpts from the Buddhist storybooks. The influence of Thailand over the entertainment world of Laos was cordially welcomed from the beginning. The indifferent, passive nature of the Laotians leads them to avoid exertion ("Why make the effort?" is a phrase I heard there more frequently than I have in any other country I know), and it has proved simpler for them to sit quietly and watch the Thais from across the river exert themselves than it has been for them to make their own amusements.

There are, for instance, excellent potential boxers in Laos, but if you ever go to a match it will always be the Thais pitted against other Thais. There is a tradition of shadow-plays with giant, translucent, leather puppets. But if you happen upon one of these rare performances in a village, it will be a Thai troupe, often not even bothering to speak the lines in Laotian. The languages are close enough that a Laotian spectator can follow the general idea without translation and the same stories have been reiterated for generations. Of course, the most popular dance in Laos is the Rambong, called there Lam Vong. For this the Laotians summon their energies and make the effort of performing it themselves.

Dance, music and festivals are popular and by far the greatest activity of the country lies in these directions. Every young girl of good family is expected to dance as a sign of her accomplishment, and dance, together with homemaking and its requirements, constitute the average Laotian woman's total education. These dances are extremely beautiful and may be done individually or as ballets by as many girls as are available. The freshness of the performers, with their hair piled high in a chignon and wrapped in fragrant flowers, their bare shoulders and short, knee-length skirts of fine brocade moving in unison, radiates a special enchantment.

All the dances they perform must contain at some point the four fundamental steps or movements: the salutation, making up, flower taking, and walking. The salutation gesture varies only slightly from its Cambodian or Thai counterpart. The making-up sequence is pure mime. The dancer rubs the flat of her palms in an imaginary powder box, rubs them together and with alternating palms up, palms down, brings her hands to her face and passes them over her cheeks. The flower-taking is also mime. It shows the girl collecting blossoms from a bush and then sewing them together, as if with an actual needle and thread in a slender delicate chain. For the walk, the hands are

184

held at hip level and sway forward and back, palms up and then down alternately as the dancer moves. From the beauty of the execution, the spectator must imagine a princess and her entourage strolling through a garden.

These four basic movements are perhaps best seen in the *Lao Phène* (literally, Laotian suppleness). Here, while the toes mark the steady beat and the dancer's chin bobs gently up and down, the dancer links together the four motions in a progression of charming, decorous movements. The words of the song which accompanies this dance are simple. Roughly paraphrased and divested of the poetic turns of phrase, they run: "We welcome you. Please look at us and admire us. We are well-coiffed and especially made up so as to appear beautiful before your eyes. Here we are, inviting you to look at us."

Another standard item of the Laotian woman's repertoire is the "Twilight Dance." In it a young girl displays the degree of her sensitivity to beauty by enacting her response to a sunset, and while the words simply state the fact—"The sun is setting, the world is beautiful, and I love him"—the dancer pivots on one foot, kneels with one leg raised in the air (to represent profound admiration before an imagined sunset) and sketches in the air with limpid motions of hands and fingers. One of the gestures in which the open-faced hands sweep from shoulder to the knees means, when translated from a single Laotian word, "Look at my body."

The repertoire includes several animal dances, but these draw parallels between animals and lovesick human beings rather than indulge in imitative mime. For the Dove Dance, the song runs, "The male dove has forgotten his lover perched here on a lonely branch . . ." and the gestures express the movements of a young girl rather than those of a bird.

Laotian dancing clings only distantly to its Indian origins. The angularities are softened, the energetic rhythmic pulsations become whispered, and the hand gestures so evanescent and dreamlike that their symbolism transforms into a fleeting, momentary mood. The stories and mythology which originally belonged to India have undergone subtle alterations during the long journey from the homeland to the remote heart of Laos. Everything has a happy ending, and everyone has a good time even in adversity. Life's discords are delightfully harmonized. The result is a pleasing, indelibly Laotian atmosphere. The attenuation of the dances, the fantastic look of the country's pagodas and stupas, the gentle, gentle nature of the Laotians are all of a happy world apart. And away from it, your memories of the country grow faint, your impressions fade into vagueness, and become in fact quite like the unreal qualities which so eminently characterize the dances themselves.

MALAYA

The long peninsula which stretches southward from continental Asia almost to the equator is known as the Straits Settlements or Malaya, but if you say Singapore, the picture of this British colony with its mixed population of Malays, Chinese, Indians and Englishmen, springs to mind perhaps more clearly. The most troubling aspect of this area is the fact that the indigenous population, the Malays, from whom the name Malaya comes, are in a minority, and the majority are the Chinese who are as alien there as the British. Malaya is the product of its peoples, and this carries with it a complex web of contradictory threads and factors.

As a general rule, it can be said that wherever the British have colonized in Asia, theatre has appreciably declined. Equally it is true that the Chinese, whenever they are in numbers, carry their theatre with them and it remains as exclusive and apart from the general life of the country as their other customs and manners. The theatre, which must depend on language before it can be understood, naturally presents obstacles to a foreign spectator; and the Chinese, even in their own country, have no true folk, or even social, dancing to contribute. Added to these outside influences, or lack of them, is the artistically constricting hold of Mohammedanism over the Malays. They have almost no dances, let alone a representational theatre, left at all. A general theatrical aridity spreads deeply over the country, and what little can be found there is foreign.

The Happy World Amusement Park in Singapore illustrates this compactly. Chinese-owned and managed, and consisting of numerous restaurants, night clubs, dance halls, concessions, and games of chance, it also supplies the chief place of entertainment for the island's population of a million or so people. Two of its attractions

187

are a movie house, which shows English and American films, and a permanent regular theatre where South Chinese operas in all their tinsel and spangles, with their ancient history of emperors and generals, perform nightly. The cultural invasion of Thailand is also evident. In the center of the Happy World, an elevated rink, somewhat like a bandstand, provides a place for "Joget Modern," the Malay and Indonesian version of Rambong. To get up on to the dance floor you pass a large sign announcing that no one without an identity card can enter. This is a measure to ensure that no one under eighteen years of age becomes corrupted by the alluring Joget Modern girls too early in life. You then enter a wicket fence and buy tickets for as many dances as you think you would like. As the Western-style band plays its variations and adaptations of the original Siamese tunes, you walk up to any of the unoccupied girls sitting in chairs around the rink, hand her one of your tickets, and start following her hand waves and foot shufflings in the Rambong.

There are amateur plays put on by the English from time to time; and night clubs have dancers imported from Australia, Hong Kong, and even England. Not long ago, Rose Chan, a Singapore strip teaser, took her dance on a tour of Malaya proper, but her performances, though well attended, were greeted with rotten eggs and sometimes even snakes were thrown at her. When the tires of her car were punctured, she finally abandoned her tour.

If you go up country, you may find a few folk dances belonging to the Malays. One of these, native to Malacca, an area not far from Singapore and the first to be colonized—by Hindus, Arabs, Portuguese and the British in continuing succession—is the Donang Sayan, an old Portuguese-style dance performed by two couples hopping and stepping in lively measure to the cheerful half-Arab, half-English music of the band. In the same area there is also the Donak Donay, a fighting dance showing mock hand-to-hand combat between young men.

Further in the interior there is a sporadic guerrilla war going on at present (against the Communists, some say, while others claim it is against bandits left over from the chaos of the last war) and this perhaps curtails the people's wish to dance even more. In the jungles and hills there, you do find the aboriginal ethnic groups who have a few dances once associated with tribal ritual and ceremonies. Although they are rapidly losing the sociological circumstances and environment which produced these dances originally, they still will perform with feathers and flower headdresses for visitors to the jungle forts or safe areas within the battle zones. For celebrations, such as the Queen's Birthday, they come to Singapore and appear there.

Despite the scarcity of dance or drama in Malaya, however, if the chances are exceptionally favorable it is possible to happen upon something of interest. When I was last in Malaya, I heard quite inadvertently that a special dance would take place. A friend merely mentioned to another friend that it *might* take place. The way it came about was this.

It seems that on the Batchok Coast in Kelantan province along the Malaya Peninsula, the fishing catches had been bad for the past several years. The leading men of the villages particularly affected by the terrible times and greatly disturbed by them decided that the reason must be because of the sea jinns. These spirits must be angry, it seemed, because the villagers had not bothered to have a proper *puja* or ceremonies of offerings to propitiate them for ten years. So they were, as a result, preventing the fish from getting into the nets. To make up for this oversight, it was decided that four days and nights would be set aside for the proper devotions.

A huge water buffalo was chosen as the chief sacrificial item. For three days it was paraded up and down the beach (it was estimated that it walked more than twenty-five miles in all), and the priest or *pawang* finally cut its throat and drained away the blood. The meat was parcelled out to the appropriate villagers. On the fourth day, at dawn, the carcass was stuffed with straw and placed in a specially decorated fishing boat and floated out to sea.

During all this religious procedure, there were entertainments—stylized, musical sword fights, a shadow-play with puppets made out of finely scissored pieces of leather depicting myths from India which still pervade Malaya, and several kinds of dancing. These lasted each night from dusk to dawn. Foremost were the *menora* dancers specially imported from Southern Siam for the occasion who were men dressed and made up like women. They wore gold crowns of many tiers, ending in a spire, and tight-fitting costumes. The extraordinary thing about these dancers was they were deep in trance and unconcious of what they were doing. They danced in this state all night long, their torsos sharply slanted to one side, their fingers curling and uncurling in weird patterns, their heads pivoting unnaturally on their necks. At the same time were the *puteri* dancers—actual Malayan women this time, who can dance, it seems, but only do so on rare occasions—moving in a ballet of casual, happy disorder. From time to time during the celebrations, the trance spread and spectators or bystanders having no part in the function would fall mysteriously under some magic spell. Some rushed into the dance circle and joined in with the trained artists. Some plunged wildly into the sea unconscious of the danger of drowning; they had to be fished out by their friends. Nobody minded much. The festivities continued non-stop. When it was all over, de-trancing took place and everyone returned to normal. I am sure the sea jinns were fully pleased—and exhausted. But I suppose it will easily be another ten years, if not more, before Malaya will have another outburst of such dancing.

If you are in search of dance and drama, Malaya is an unrewarding country. For the present, it is of greater interest to students of international politics.

INDONESIA

Dance

No other country in the world, to my mind, is quite as disturbing to travel in, or quite as rewarding, as complex, as romantic as Indonesia. Even calling it a country, which implies a single geographical unit, seems inaccurate. Indonesia is a spray of thousands and thousands of islands (one alone is larger than France), of minor archipelagos within major ones (including the "Thousand Islands" themselves), all straddling the equator almost equidistantly to the North and South and connecting in a desultory way continental Asia with Australia. In the past, it has been variously referred to as Malaysia, the East Indies, the Indian Archipelago, Insulinde, and for three hundred and fifty years—an all-time record for stubborn colonial persistence —Dutch or Netherlands East Indies. Now it is Indonesia or "the islands of the Indies," and as a patriotic local term (somewhat like Columbia to the United States), the Indonesians say Nusantara which means simply and tersely "archipelago."

On these islands live more then eighty million people, speaking about two hundred languages and dialects. Altogether, Indonesia is the largest aggregate of islands united into a single country in the world, the sixth largest nation of any kind, and the largest Muslim country anywhere despite its heavily Hindu atmosphere; if you were to superimpose it on the United States, it would extend from Maine to California. Each area conjures up excitement and adventure in the Western imagination—the Spice Islands, the Wild Man of Borneo, Bali, the prehistoric giant lizards or "dragons" of Komodo, the novels of Joseph Conrad about Celebes or Somerset Maugham about Timor, the orangutans, or forest men, in the jungles of Sumatra, the miniature chickens from Bantam, the island Krakatao that disappeared in the greatest volcanic explosion of modern times. Even the national exports sound highly exotic to our ears: gutta-percha, copra, benzoin, chincona, camphor, dammar, as do the local edibles, sago, cassava bread and jack-fruit, mango, durian, mangosteen and lichees.

The Indonesian, however, sees himself surrounded by less romantic associations. While colonialism at least for all practical purposes is finished in the rest of Asia, the Dutch still hold half of New Guinea which used to be part of the Dutch East Indies, the British still have part of Borneo, and the Portuguese half of Timor.

But however distressing their political problems may seem, from the point of view of dance or music no country could be more thrilling, if the meaning of that word has not been spoiled by indiscriminate use. A scholar, research student, or even an enthusiastic tourist could easily spend a lifetime wandering over the islands observing the incredible number of dances and varieties of music, and still there would remain countless movements and sounds left unexplored. The politically sensitive visitor to Indonesia today may be shocked by the after-effects of the parsimonious isolation in which the Dutch obviously kept their Indies. The searcher after dance, however, finds himself delighted, and a little ashamed at the same time, that because of this forcible obscurity Indonesia's dances have remained relatively untouched. Even now, in a time of tape recorders, movies, cameras, documentaries, and the new self-conscious awareness of dance most Asian nations are feeling, the superlative panorama of Indonesian dance is unexploited and, with the exception of Bali, is a virtually unknown field of study. You can discover, if you look long and carefully, every possible kind of dance from the most rarefied and involuted performances in palaces, to wild, primitive rituals one step removed from headhunting and human sacrifices. But variety and quantity by themselves are not all.

Even by an international standard, which of necessity must be critical and evaluative, Indonesia's dances overwhelm you by their inventiveness and technical proficiency. Rabindranath Tagore, one of the first modern Indians to visit Indonesia, said, in a moment of what must have been bitter acknowledgement for such a patriot, that Lord Siva gave his dance to Indonesia and left India with his ashes. This meant that while India still worships Siva devoutly, the Indonesians have continued since their original period of Hinduization to dance like the god himself, and this has held true in the face of the intervening centuries when Islam conquered and wiped out Siva as a cult from the country. The universality of Indonesian dance is felt even in the West. A few seasons ago a troupe of Balinese dancers succeeded brilliantly before American and European audiences without making a single major concession or adaptation. Miscellaneous Javanese soloists and even small troupes formed from among students and the diplomatic corps abroad have danced in Paris and London to surprising acclaim. I do not know of a single international folk-dance competition held from time to time in Asia and Europe where Indonesia has not taken the honors.

But as with every other phase of life in this complicated country, there are difficulties. The dance is either hard to find or a nuisance to arrange. It is determined by season, occasion and mood. Added to this, there is a disinclination on the part of Indonesians to help strangers. Invitations to the palaces, while they may be granted, are surrounded by more protocol than any other Asian country finds essential. Folk dancers either ask too much money for their dances or refuse to dance because they are not professionals and cannot accept money. Inquiry into dance in this postwar, post-revolutionary, ex-colony is frequently mistaken for intrusion. Indonesians sometimes refer to their dances as "their national soul," and perhaps they guard it too protectively. Even though there is a Jawatan Kebudayaan (Cultural Office) in every city large or small and it can help a little if you are armed with official documents, to seek the dance out is, except for Bali, the exception to all things in Indonesia, often fraught with irritation and frustration. The problems attendant on the outsider should not discourage one. In the end it will turn out to have been worth all the trouble.

The easiest dances to locate are the modern social ones of the cities. While this may seem a curious place to begin a serious approach to dance, travel routes force it on you. The visitor inescapably lands in Jakarta, the capital, the largest and least agreeable city in Indonesia, and it is there that these dances are most in vogue and most tolerated. However, even in Jakarta you can gain some idea that there are other dances elsewhere in the country. When a troupe now and then is on its way back from a tour of some foreign country and passes through Jakarta, they may give a recital—often by invitation only—in the local concert hall (the only one in the city of three and a half million people). There is a school belonging to Mrs. Subarjo, a patron of the arts, which teaches the Javanese court dances of Jogjakarta to a few Jakartans as well as to some daughters of foreign diplomats stationed there. From time to time semi-public recitals of students are announced. President Sukarno holds occasional parties at his palace where distinguished foreigners are entertained with a short program of dances performed by his very young children, or, if the dignitary is important, a group of regional dancers, usually the daughters of the local officials, is flown in especially for the evening. Aside from these, there is little in Jakarta besides modern social dances, and unlike most regions in Indonesia, it has no indigenous dance of its own.

As you walk along Jakarta's flat and level streets, many of which are sliced down the center by wide canals of sluggish brown water, you may be deceived by several remaining signs saying DANSIN-INSTITUT or Dance School. "Dans" in Indonesia means Western-style dancing, and it was, of course, introduced by the Dutch, who built several dance halls for themselves. For a period, it was fashionable for Indo-Europeans, as Eurasians are called by the Dutch, and Westernized Indonesians to go in for ballroom dancing. In a way, coming to Jakarta, or getting an official job in the plodding bureaucracy of the capital, or traveling abroad, were all steps up the ladder of Westernization, and this kind of dancing in which you hold a member of the opposite sex in your arms and glide along together in public places, was an ultimate expression of accepting the colonial way and of turning one's back on native attitudes.

Along with independence came two ancillary factors. One was a corrosive anger against the Dutch, and no ex-colonial power that I know of has ever been so detested by its former subjects, and the other was a prudish morality, which is a combination of inherent Muslim rigidity regarding women and the self-righteousness that often follows in the wake of revolution. Western dancing was an immediate target, and although not many Indonesians ever danced in this way, the government nevertheless inveighed against it. To the people in power it connoted blatant sexuality. Now the dance halls are empty; Dansininstituts have almost no pupils—except to learn the Rambong style of dancing from Thailand via Singapore; and an employee of the government can be fired for dancing in public as quickly as he could be for gross inefficiency. Morality of this sort occupies an almost obsessive place in official thinking in Indonesia today. There is censorship and there are elaborate controls.

To combat the pernicious, undermining influence that Western dancing is supposed to exert, the government not long ago took steps to introduce a substitute for it among students, the Muda-Mudi (young men-young women). Muda-Mudi had its first performance at the University, and President Sukarno sanctioned the occasion by accepting the invitation to attend. The evening started well. Someone spoke on *krisis achlak,* the moral crisis, about which politicians had been worrying for some time. Then, to the accompaniment of phonograph records, a few sample couples began dancing Muda-Mudi as a demonstration of what modern social dancing should be in new independent Indonesia. In it the boy and girl keep a wide distance between them, slowly moving in a misty suggestion of a two-step and cautiously gyrating around the floor while, with their hands steady, they make simplified gestures adapted from the court dancing of the palace at Solo, one of the ancient cultural capitals of Java. The students, undaunted by the presence of the President, were appalled at the spiritless performance and showed their reaction by stomping on the floor and hooting. The party soon ended; and while Muda-Mudi is danced in a few homes as a semi-patriotic gesture and in quiet Solo where it originated, the experiment was a failure.

Distress over Western ballroom dancing in Indonesia seems senseless to the outsider, particularly since the people already have their own modern social dances which serve the same purpose more than adequately. Jakarta has three types of these, Doger, Ronggeng and Joget, named in ascending order of their respectability within the lower and middle classes of Jakarta social groups. The upper classes eschew all three.

Doger is the most vulgar according to the accepted standards, although there is nothing offensive in the dance and its origins are certainly innocuous. It derives from a standard folk dance popular in the neighboring villages where a girl seeks out her sweetheart and dances with him, while the elders look on and approve or disapprove of the couple's skill. The movements are so simple and elementary that they scarcely need to be described. They are roughly along the lines, though less polished and controlled, of Thailand's Rambong.

A clever if incidental use of Doger has been made in a recent film, *After Curfew*, written by Asrul Sani, one of Indonesia's most capable intellectuals, and directed by Usmar Ismail, formerly a playwright and now a film producer. The film actually deals with the problem of adjusting to society after revolution and the settling of old scores incurred during wartime, but there is a long scene in which a Western-style dance party in a rich Jakarta house is contrasted with a Doger being danced around a bonfire in one of the poorer compounds not far away.

Ronggeng, which stands a little higher in the scale of propriety, is, as the derivation of the word indicates, the Indonesian version of the Rambong. Its difference from Doger is largely an economic one. It is practiced by a class of people a little better off financially. Where Doger requires no formalities of accompaniment (a ring of singing, handclapping friends suffices) or costume (you come as you are), or particular aptitude (anyone can join in), Ronggeng needs a small audience, one's Sunday-best, clean clothes, and a lesson or two at the Dansininstitut.

Joget, however, is another matter altogether, and of considerable dance interest. The word comes from the Javanese for "dance," but the dance in its present form owes a considerable debt to Thailand's Rambong and a somewhat lesser one to the rhumba as it is danced in the Philippines. Among the Malay population in Singapore, Joget means Rambong, and in general there is an air of internationalism and reciprocity between countries about the whole dance. Rambong would probably never have been invented in Bangkok had it not been for European influence there, and its success is doubtful in regions where the West had not penetrated to some degree. But since it is in essentials a native dance, the government leaves it pretty much alone.

While it is the most popular and important form of dance in the city, it belongs so intrinsically and almost privately to the ordinary person—the school teacher, the pedicab driver, the office peon—that the foreigner, by the accident of nationality, often is denied any sort of social access to that layer of Jakarta life.

I first came upon Jakarta's Joget in an unexpected way and quite by chance. A friend of mine who was making a broad over-all study of Indonesia once introduced me to a friend of his, and we in turn became friendly. The quarters where my new friend lived with his wife and baby and a relative who visited them for several months each year were typical of Jakarta's crowded slums—jerry-built, one-and-a-half room structures of wood and palm matting walls identical with the hundreds of others in the compound where more than three thousand people jam together to form a single housing unit. Despite the simplicity of their lives, I received endless hospitality from them during my stay in Jakarta, and sat hours in their house drinking the inevitable orange soda, talking, asking questions, and often just watching the compound life.

Not long before I was to leave Indonesia, I felt I had to repay their kindness in some way, and it occurred to me that if I paid for a dance (I would leave the choice to him) to be held outside my friend's house, he would be pleased, his neighbors could share in the enjoyment, and doubtless, since pleasures are expensive in Jakarta, his prestige within the compound would rise. The idea met with favor. "We will have the best dancer in Jakarta," my friend assured me. "We will have a Joget," his wife added. A few days later my friend said that the whole evening would cost the equivalent of ten dollars —"a courtesy gift to the dancer," he explained—and was that all right? He looked doubtful since that amount represented his earnings for a month. He cheered up when I explained that for the best I was willing to pay even more. A few days later my friend called on me. "We'll make it the circumcision of my daughter," he announced without preliminaries and went on to explain that to begin with you have to have a plausible reason in Jakarta for a big "ten dollar" dance, and, secondly, that his daughter was about six which was the proper age to circumcise, according to the custom of the locality, and that this would facilitate matters from officialdom's point of view. People would also not ask bothersome questions about why a foreigner should be holding a dance. A day or two later I received a printed card saying that on such and such a date "Miss Betty" of Jakarta with a special orchestra would be performing at the compound in front of my friend's house on the felicitous occasion of the circumcision of a daughter. When I saw my friend by chance later that day, he told me that he had just secured permission from the headman of the compound as well as from the local police. He had also notified some department of law and order and was now on his way to get the fire department's chop or stamp of approval which would be the last of the red tape.

The night of the dance came, and an orchestra of guitars, tambourines, accordions (called "harmoniums" in Indonesia), violins, double basses, rattling gourds, Javanese drums, and wooden sticks arrived. A microphone was set up outside the house, gas lamps were suspended overhead from a temporary board frame erected especially for the occasion in case of rain, and chairs were put out for us. Others of the compound crowded around absorbed in the preparations. The music began. It was Western jazz of the sort I associate with Berlin of the 1920's. Its sounds were sentimental, spoony and unpercussive, and with the not unpleasant crudeness of being improperly rehearsed. A man sang, reading the words from a little printed booklet of popular songs. Then a woman sang, but she was so shy she stood sideways, not looking at the audience. The orchestra played *Lagu melayu* (songs from Singapore) and then it changed to *gambus* (melodies from Arabia), and each number was announced by name deafeningly over the microphone. By now we had gathered a great crowd, and the heat of the bodies pressing one against the other made the already heavy night air yet more oppressive.

"Miss Betty" (that is the Indonesian word, I am not translating) finally appeared, dramatically late. He turned out to be a young man with long hair, made up and dressed like a woman. He earns his living, it seems, dancing on such programs and is so famous for his Joget and charming appearance throughout the compounds of Jakarta that gruff and normal men even boast of having danced with him. If being able to dance the Joget at all is a social superiority over the Doger and Ronggeng class of person, dancing with "Miss Betty" for an Indonesian is the equivalent of, say, a cotillion at a debutante's ball.

As "Miss Betty" began to flutter his feet and hands keeping his eyes stolidly on the ground in a diffident way, one of the compound men stepped into the ring, picked up a scarf that had been slung over one of the chairs near the orchestra, tied it around his waist—to indicate the festive nature of the dance—and began to follow "Miss Betty's" restless steps. As they shuffled back and forth each waved his hands in arabesques of grace in the air. The dancers never touched each other, never looked at each other, and never smiled. After five or six minutes, this dance was over.

198

Then man after man stepped in and danced—the tough bully of the compound who beats the others up if they do not obey him, the son of the compound's pawn-shop owner, another young man training to be an *ulama* or Muslim priest of the highest mystical power, and others I had not met. I was urged to dance but declined. My friend sat back, chest out, and watched his neighbors enjoy themselves at his party. The dances got more complicated. One step, feet together, another step, feet together again, around the tiny clearing in front of the orchestra. Sometimes the elbows were kept at the hip and the arms twirled around in concentric circles. Occasionally the steps grew more bouncy. At times "Miss Betty" would stretch his knees out and in like an accordion. Some dancers tossed the scarf over their shoulders and let it lie there precariously. Others clamped it in their hands like a ball, and wiped their hands, sweating from nervousness, with it. The audience commented critically whenever "Miss Betty" did a difficult foot kick that his partner could not follow. When a scarf fell off or when an eager dancer would get too close, "Miss Betty" would spring back in a flash of indignation without missing a beat.

The dance went on steadily until midnight—curfew time for the city of Jakarta. No one smiled much that evening, but somehow it was clear that everyone was extremely happy. My friend's wife, as the orchestra and "Miss Betty" were packing up to leave, leaned over to say, "If I were a man, I would love to dance with 'Miss Betty.' He is so good looking." And for an instant I wondered if she were joking. She was not.

The person looking for profundity in dance must leave Jakarta at the earliest possible opportunity. For your first taste of what is genuine Indonesian dance, you need go only as far as Bogor or Bandung, or preferably to Sukabumi, the three main cities of the region known as Sunda. For centuries in the past until the Dutch arrived, Sunda was an independent kingdom which bowed to no other, including the powerful Javanese courts at Jogjakarta and Solo. To this day, a residual pride glows in every Sundanese heart, and they regard their culture as the best in Indonesia.

Sunda is particularly famous for two things: the beauty of its women, which is obvious to any visitor, and the exquisite melancholy of its music, which has almost as much immediate appeal for the visitor. For a few dollars, you can have a private concert of music on the verandah of your hotel room. Although Sundanese gamelans can be as large as the great orchestras of Jogjakarta and Solo, the more characteristically Sundanese music consists merely of three people: one who plays the *kechapi*, a predecessor of the zither but the strings are plucked with the fingers, the *suling* player, a muted, soft-toned flute whose sound fades in and out like etheric waves against the tremulous notes of the *kechapi*, and a singer who pours out love songs in a high, thin, clear voice.

While dance is not a special Sundanese glory, it is still noteworthy. Most of the dances show women in subdued roles and men in defiant moods. Those that have stories come from Hindu mythology or from the Panji cycle—an epic recorded in several versions during the long series of powerful Hindu-Javanese rulers extending from the seventh to fourteenth centuries. Those that have no stories and survive as independent dances are excerpts from these longer dance-dramas, showing princesses of the court at their toilette, promenading, speaking of love, or watching their husbands and lovers go into battle. The movements of these dances are modelled on the great dancing style of the courts in central Java which will be more fully explained in a later section.

The most characteristic of the Sundanese dances is the Tari Topeng or mask dance, the chief item in the Sundanese repertoire at present, and derived from the Panji cycle. It tells the story of a devoted wife who, disguised as a wandering prince (*ksatrya kelana*), goes in search of her husband. She penetrates into hostile country, and disguising herself further with a wildly painted, mustached mask taken from the *topeng* masked dramas (a once popular form of theatre in Java) encounters a demon king and fights with him. The dance is usually performed by three people, because the dance is long and tiring and the styles are so contrasting—two women (one to play the dutiful wife in search of her husband, another to do the masked combat) and a man (who acts the demon role). The full formal Sundanese orchestra for this dance immediately establishes a nervously fast pace. The drummer beats three large drums, stacked one upon the other, in rapid succession with a thick stick. During the battle he shouts "rah, rah, rah" at intervals to incite the performers. The dancers strut back and forth across the stage imperiously. Their hands flap frantically and slap the air, they point at the floor, spin around, shake their heads in violent circles, and extend their legs out in angular, challenging kicks. The woman's long black hair swirls around her; the demon screeches in rage. The tension rises as they begin to strike each other, and the dance abruptly ends.

Just as Sunda offers a special regional heritage of dances, the other provinces of Java, and indeed all the islands, afford a dance repertoire equally rich and equally individual. Of these, of necessity, I am describing only a few of the most representative and most beautiful.

Sumatra claims that it has a different dance for every one of its hundreds of districts and as many dancers as it has unmarried women. Every young girl is taught to dance, and at her marriage as part of the ceremony, she dances for the last time. So popular is Sumatran dance that a number of business firms use pictures of dances from various parts of the island to mark the months on their gift calendars.

To my taste the Gending Sri Vijaya is the most charming of the Sumatran dances. It is performed only at Palembang, the ancient capital of the Hindu empire, Sri Vijaya, in the seventh century; Palembang is nowadays a large sprawling port city of oil refineries and business offices, built along a delta of rivers and tributaries. The dance is the last token of Sri Vijaya's former greatness and graciousness, as floods have washed away the buildings and temples which once marked the mighty kingdom.

Gending Sri Vijaya is a dance of welcome, and traditionally greets any distinguished visitor arriving in the city even today. Bedecked in elaborate headdresses with slivers and spears of gold and draped in thick, multi-colored brocades, seven girls accompanied by two musicians form a square, open at one end, where the guest sits. On each fingertip the dancers wear long arching gold fingernails from which little lozenges and heartshaped trinkets dangle. The girls, representing princesses of the Sri Vijayan palace, move slowly and modestly toward you. They notice birds soaring in the air above, their eyes alight on flowers that are just opening, and finally they kneel before you and make a salute with their two hands palms together, fingers and fingernails curving outwards, in an open "V."

The singer begins his song, which, unlike the dance, is in Western style. It was composed in 1946 by a celebrated patriot and later martyr to the cause of independence, who saw in freedom a return to the greatness of the Sri Vijayan period. While the tune and its accompaniment (piano or accordion) are modern, the words are old. The dancers enact them with their hands in a style vaguely reminiscent of the fluid and simplified Hawaiian gestures. The first line says, "We have heard of your coming from a faraway place . . . We now await your wishes . . . We will prepare anything for you . . . From the lowest to the highest . . ." The words come alive as the movements and motions depict this meaning. The pauses in the music are punctuated with flicks of the hands. The curving gold tips of the fingers flash first one way and then the other, telling of subdued longing and impatience, and the tiny pendants tinkle faintly. Then the dancers rise and retreat with an air of gracious humility, still never daring to look the visitor full in the face.

They pick up a tray of boxes laden with betel nut ingredients and two silver spittoons and glide to a triangular formation before you. The dancers make more obeisances, and approaching you on their knees, place these ceremonial offerings at your feet. You then fold the tender green leaf around the betel nut and chew it, but only the vulgar would spit. The dancers form two small squares and face each other in two groups of four and three. They repeat the gesture of "awaiting your wish," and your formal welcome to Palembang is complete.

The essence of this dance, and of all the others performed by Sumatran girls anywhere on the island, is *gaya* or grace. Grace to the Indonesian means something special however. It is the soft and smooth quality of bodily movement combined with flexibility which is particularly silky and even willowy. This is more important to the dance connoisseur than rhythm and technique which in other parts of the world often take aesthetic priority. There are of course virtuoso dances of immense popularity all over Sumatra, but without *gaya*, Indonesian interest flags.

Two of the virtuoso dances, which despite their tricks and skill depend on *gaya*, are the well-known Candle or Plate Dance (*tari lilin* or *piring*) and the Handkerchief Dance. The Candle Dance is actually something of a national (or should one say insular) dance and although it originated in South Sumatra it is danced everywhere Sumatrans gather together. The girls in curious rhomboidal caps of woven and tasselled cloth enter carrying saucers on which lighted candles have been stuck. On each hand they wear iron thimbles which they click against the saucer in time with the music. The orchestra nowadays is Western-style and obviously reflects the influence of international Singapore which is closer and more important to Sumatra than it is to Java where the political capital of all the islands is. The music is like Malayan film music with the melody clearly predominant over the simple but charming harmonies subtending it.

The dancers assume various fairly rigid and mechanical formations. They stand in a straight line, then break off in pairs and groups of four, they kneel and rise, they crisscross between each other's lines. Then the dance proper starts.

They twist their arms and thrust their hands over and under and behind them, still holding the lighted candles. The flames disappear only to return and resume their bright glowing when the motion stops. The idea of the dance is to pretend to make the flame blow out, but never moving quite so quickly as to do it, or to trick the eye by appearing to hold the plate upside down, or to balance it perilously on the elbow, shoulder, and head during the course of the dance. There is a spiritual interpretation of the dance which scholars sometimes attribute to it. Fire held over the head symbolizes its value to all mankind; held about the wrists, it symbolizes its use in the kitchen; stepping over it symbolizes man's ingenuity in bringing about a balance between himself and the means at his disposal in life. When the dance is over, the performers blow out their candles and silently leave the arena.

The Handkerchief Dance is a little more complicated, and it requires several couples of boys and girls, each holding one end of a large white square of cloth. They do a kind of maypole dance, winding under and over the cloth, turning around and tying it in a series of knots. At the last minute they unscramble it and extricate themselves effortlessly. Sometimes they add a drop-the-handkerchief variation, and without letting their knees touch the floor, pick the handkerchiefs up with their teeth.

In North Sumatra, which centers on Medan, you find a number of dances performed by Bataks, a special racial group who have been converted largely to Christianity, and whose customs generally set them apart from other Sumatrans. Particularly in the Simulungan district, which is the heart of Batak country, you find a number of curious rituals. The most lurid perhaps is a sinister mask dance performed at funerals while the body of the deceased is being washed. One of the gayest is their marriage dance, the Sitalasari. The bride and bridesmaids, holding flowers in one hand, slap their hips and glide across the floor by sliding their heel and toe alternately in a Suzy Q. They flap their hands in the air, showing the flat palm of the hand to the audience, as if they were playing a one-handed "peas pat porridge" game with an invisible partner. Throughout they show their happiness modestly without transgressing the bounds of decorous behavior.

In this, as in all Batak dances, a characteristic gesture predominates. It consists of forming a circle with the thumb and forefinger (the other fingers are held straight), and on the main beat of the phrase springing the circle open. This motion dominates the Artiga ni Sepolin or Full-moon dance performed by pairs of boys and girls. The men keep their hands below their hips, while the women are rhythmically exploding their thumb and forefinger circles at breast level. Occasionally the group holds one hand at the forehead, palm out, like a French soldier's salute, and the other at the waist, palm down, as they sway giddily in unison.

The best of all Batak dances I have seen is the Tading Ma Ham Na Tading, which means sententiously "I am leaving you now." It is a farewell dance performed by all the girls of the village whenever someone leaves his native place. The music is particularly lovely, and the Bataks are famous for the timbre of their voices and the vibrance of their choral singing. The native Batak voice, plus the influence from Singapore, has turned their music now into something quite close to our own crooning—muffled and modulated waves of sound, perhaps a little too tender for most Asian taste in music. The accom-

204

paniment consists of several gongs, softly tapped, some smaller gongs which clink tonelessly, and drums—all held in the hands and played while standing close to the dancers. The traditional words state the village feeling plaintively, "If you leave us now, please come back again . . . You may be far away, but your heart remains in this village . . ." The singer adds that all the village is praying for the traveler's success, and the song ends on a cautionary note, "Do not marry anyone abroad; just come back to us." The final gesture of farewell is literal. The dancers hold one hand across their chest, and wave the other above their head as if saying goodbye to the departing friend and waving away the sorrow of the parting.

Medan, the capital, itself has a number of lively dances. One, the Sri Banang, is a welcome dance formerly accorded all visiting sultans but in these modern days any important visitor may be honored with it. The refrain reiterates the words *dendan meraiyu* which means roughly, "we are here to make our guest happy in our country." Certainly the gentle swaying of the body, like leaves lightly blown in the wind, and the elegant folding and unfurling of the fingers is a delightful introduction to the many pleasures the visitor is to find in Sumatra.

Another popular dance is the Pulau Putri (literally, island of women), which is full of heel kicks and a modified sort of "trucking." The girls even lift up their skirts a little to draw more attention to the quick movements of their feet. The characteristic hand position of this dance is to extend the forefinger and the third finger like an open pair of scissors, and shake it as if scolding or threatening an imaginary offender.

The latest rage in Medan in 1955 is the half-social, half-folk-dance Serampang Duabelas, or Twelve Step, and it is Sumatra's answer to Thailand's Rambong or Jakarta's Joget. When I once asked about this dance, an Indonesian explained it as "now we are modern, this is the way we should dance." The Twelve Step takes place in the center of a group who clap their hands steadily and stand in a square formation. One of the men leaps into the center of this ring and selects his partner. They execute twelve steps at a vertiginously fast rate, and the girl returns to her place. The man then chooses another girl. When he gets tired, someone else takes over this lead role. The dance is something like a fast clog and there is virtually no movement of the hands. For a finale, the Handkerchief Dance is often included, and the boy and his favorite partner tie themselves together.

The dances all over Sumatra are so various that descriptions of them become prolix, but worthy of special mention is a dance from the Lampong district in South Sumatra, in which the men hop about wearing gold hats and holding gilt fans. All the dances should be seen, and all of them, each for a different reason, are delightful.

On the island of Celebes, there are also famous dances in folk style like the Pajaga and Pakarena. In Torajah country, where a special and curious community like the Bataks lives, the dances are unusual. One, the Mabugi, is an after-harvest celebration performed in a wide circle in the fields and accompanied by group chanting. At the end of it, a sort of bacchanalian lovemaking takes place back in communal dormitories of the village.

Another dance, the Maganda, requires a gigantic headdress of silver coins, bulls' horns, and black velvet which is so heavy only men can wear it, and no dance can last more than a few minutes before the performer begins to gasp for breath.

The pleasantest of the Torajah dances is probably the Pagellu. For it the girls stretch out their long slender arms, flutter their fingers, and advance and retreat in slow, measured steps towards the spectators.

The dances of Borneo, or Kalimantan as it is now called, divide into the social ones along the coastal areas which resemble the Medan ones, and the more tribal and ethnological ones in the interior, particularly in the Dyak areas, which correspond to those of the Bataks or Torajahs. Many of these were once associated with cruel and horrifying rituals, and now linger on in a half-remembered, halfhearted way. While as spectacles they afford considerable excitement, with their plumes of feathers, animal skins and blood-curdling screams, their value as dances is greater for the sociologist than for the aesthetician.

Every island of Indonesia has its social, folk and ceremonial expression in dance forms. It would be hopeless to enumerate the variety or describe it in words, a medium so remote from the visual experience and stimulation of an actual performance. In Sumba, they dance like horses with bangs hanging over their eyes like the fringe of a pony's mane; around their shins they tie the tawny hairs of a horse's tail. In Flores they have war dances. On Nias Island, in a continuity which dates from the Stone Age, they still worship and propitiate stone as the most important element of civilization—for tools, for utensils, for pillows, and even money; aged women dance on great, round stones. Bali of course, because of its particular importance, requires a special section.

The most important dances of Indonesia, however, with the possible exception of Bali, are to be found at the *kratons* or palaces of Jogjakarta and Solo in Central Java, one ruled by a Sultan, the other by a Susunan. The courtly performances there extend back through more than a thousand years of uninterrupted calm, placidly outlasting the conversions of the Muslims and the invasions of the Dutch; they are still little changed after revolution and the confusion independence has brought. These dances represent a civilization, almost rarefied in its attenuated cultivation and languid nobility. For sheer refinement, for elegance and perfection, and for one of the deepest aesthetic experiences the human being can evoke, I feel these dancers and musicians to be unique.

The accompanying music is the gamelan. As many as two dozen musicians are needed to play the hundred or so gongs, agongs, bongs, bonangs, and reyongs—all finely tuned and tempered metal instruments shaped like discs, cylinders, xylophone keys, or huge, bulbous, hollow bowls and set in intricately carved, lacquered frames. Their sounds range in tone from thin tinkles to deep, booming reverberations. The feathery harmonies and unpercussive chords throb and vibrate in after-resonances and rippling overtones. There are also drummers to handle the half dozen drums, various singers who intone the delicate melodies and recite the speeches of the plot. Two others beat wooden sticks and blocks of resonant wood, without which Indonesian and most Asian music for that matter, would lose one of its most identifying characteristics and the orchestras their conductors. They snap and crack in metronomic precision and lend a core of brittleness to the otherwise plangent texture of the gamelan. The extraordinary beauty of these Indonesian sounds is not altogether unfamiliar in the West. It was one of these Javanese orchestras at the Exposition Coloniale of 1896 in Paris which inspired Claude Debussy to divide his octave into six divisions of the whole-tone scale and to imitate its new concept of sonority and timbre.

Essentially, the dancing and music at Jogjakarta and Solo are the same. The subtleties which differentiate them may escape the foreigner, but they cause rabid partisanship among scholars. If you talk about preferring Solo, you are on the whole more recondite than if you like the Jogjakarta style which became more widely known during the War of Independence when Sukarno's capital was there.

The repertoire of the palace dancers at both courts is inexhaustible. I have never seen the same program twice, and I am certain that between them with sufficient notification and time for preparation, they could stage all the main episodes of the *Ramayana* and *Mahabharata*, as well as the whole of the Panji cycle and several miscellaneous scenes from other purely Javanese legends and mythology. Such tremendous programs would of course require several months.

Because of their impracticality from the point of view of the spectator's patience, most dances are performed in fragments or sections. These divide themselves roughly into four categories: abstract dances (the promenades, the princesses' toilette, and the like), love scenes, scenes of adventure (in which supernatural events or transformations take place), and battles. The latter two classifications require no explanation because their content is self-evident, and their treatment is already familiar to us from the other countries of Asia concerned with the *Ramayana* and *Mahabharata* type of scene. The abstract portions are generally called *serimpi*, and the word is now so current that any dance performed by women, either solo or in groups of even numbers, which imitates the smooth stateliness and mellifluous gestures of the palace dancers, is called *tari* (dance) *serimpi*.

One of the most exquisite of the love dances is the *Asmaradana* or "love fulfillment" from the *Mahabharata*. Here Arjuna, the god-hero as popular in Indonesia as in India, proposes to Sembodro. He explains first his mortification in "asking" for her hand—he who has never asked anything of anyone before—but his loneliness compels him. The princess Sembodro refuses, and this, too, is a new experience for Arjuna who has never before been denied anything. Finally, the love-duet closes with Sembodro's promise that if he wins the forthcoming battle, she, too, will accede to him. During the dance Sembodro flexes her long-nailed fingers in curling arabesques, kicks her batik train which trails between her heels behind her, and arches her neck gracefully. Arjuna matches her gestures with bold and brave steps, bending his legs in pliés and extending his leg outwards to form a right angle with his torso. His virile actions sharpen the unchanging steadfastness of his princess's mind and heart.

Some of the love dances are of rejection. Two examples are from Solo and Jogjakarta respectively. The first is the resistance of a woman to the advances of a demon. The woman is dressed in full *serimpi* costume of the court, bare-shouldered and with her brown-and-cream colored batik patterned in characteristic Solo style with ascending circles and curves shaped like the letters "s" and "o." On her head she wears the thin perforated gold headdress that wreathes the forehead and extends to a wide curl in back. Tucked in the back of her tightly wound breast cloth is a quiver of arrows. The demon's face is painted red with black-and-white striations around his eyes. His thick mustache and woolly wig of black hair partly hides his face. His chest is bare, and he wears long, loose-fitting trousers of red, green and white stripes. He growls and rushes around the woman, pointing his fingers, clawing the air in simulated anger. Meanwhile the woman circles the stage, unbelievably slowly and intently, never raising her glance, and always managing to escape the thrusts and parries of the demon without changing her languorous pace. From time to time she raises her hands as if to draw an arrow, but soon her hands sinuously return to their place at her hips where they are held in a position which perhaps can best be described as the way old-fashioned women were taught to hold their tea cups. This is all there is to the dance and it ends without any other action being introduced.

The other example, from Jogjakarta, shows an ugly man preparing to meet a beautiful princess. He grooms himself elaborately. He shows his anticipation. He meets her but she remains indifferent, her heart being elsewhere, and the love remains unrequited. It is clear that after his elaborate, hopeful preparations, she has spurned him. And here again the action is so tenuous it is almost as if nothing has happened. The basic posture for women is one of utter repose. The feet are held together at the heel. The great toe rises and falls to mark the rhythm: in the rarefied atmosphere of the Javanese courts, the jangle of bells is considered coarse and anklets are used only for monkeys and animal roles played by men. The hips arch back slightly, the torso leans forward, the hands stay at hip level breaking slightly at the elbow when not gesticulating, and the face tilts downwards with the eyes half closed and staring fixedly at the floor.

Most "business" or filling-in of incidental action involves the long streamers which hang from the sash to below the knees. The woman manipulates them so that they float forward or back. When her hand runs the length of the streamer, holding it lightly between the thumb and forefinger, her arm rises almost to shoulder level. From there the streamer is released and it flutters back to her side. With each step, the pleats of the batik come forward, and this necessitates a quick whip of the heel to push the long hem back between the feet where it is supposed to trail.

Male dancers are, of course, more active. They are always virile, flexing their muscles, extending one leg, trembling in heroics and passionate anger, balancing on their opponent's knees if he is a man, and posing in profile like the angular puppets of the shadow plays, whose paper-thin bodies are always slapped sidewise against the screen to show the hands, legs and face all at the same time.

The court dances sometimes seem to us almost formless, like inconsequential moments chosen at random from among more significant happenings. To a Western way of thinking, they may appear to lack progression or to put it in terms of photography, it is as if something extraneous is in focus at the center of the picture while the main object is off to one side. In contradistinction to the rigidity of the beginning-middle-end formula on which we have been nurtured artistically, this Javanese type of dance composition stirs in the spectator a sense of timelessness, a feeling of static and indeterminate suspension.

Aesthetically, the palace dances of Java concern themselves with the passive and the active, and the contrast between the two states is the seed of the drama within them. Juxtaposition of the two opposite kinds of movement impels the dance and gives it its form. The majority of the repertoire most frequently performed centers on women, the result probably of pleasing the sultans. Men often appear merely as catalysts or for their contrast as a background to set off the extreme *gaya* of the woman. And whereas the Westerner gives his attention to action, the Javanese is more pleased by inaction. Each dance is full of pauses, silences, motions arrested in space, meditative poses, and passages of immobility. Each mood and flavor or *rasa* of Indian stagecraft is filtered through this veil of languor and tranquility.

Nothing could be further removed from the tenets and theories of Western art than Javanese court dancing. Nothing presents quite so different a dimension in art or opens more undreamt-of vistas. Basically, it is an extension of Indian aesthetics, but it has pursued over the centuries a tangential direction. It has taken those aspects which suited the interiorized, ultra-refined tastes of the Javanese. Those very qualities may make the Javanese difficult and perplexing in one's daily contacts with him, but in their dances when you see the Javanese nature at its most remote and withdrawn, you can only be grateful for its art. There, this special atmosphere is sublimated and what is bland and inexpressive in Javanese life is converted on the stage into magical theatre. In retrospect, when the dance is recalled within your mind, its differences from your own familiar aesthetics quickly resolve by acceptance and the incongruities between the East and the West as well as the static tempi telescope inside your brain. Curiously enough, even in remembering, the secret enchantment operates all over again and you are affected anew by the magnificence of the dance.

The plethora of dance in Indonesia can be overwhelming for the outsider, and since he has to limit his dance tour of the islands, one fairly satisfactory way to do so is to concentrate on finding dances of the Penchak or Silat variety. These are fighting dances and can be regarded either as sport—every young man of sound body studies them—or as dance in one of its purest forms, that of varied movements executed rhythmically and gracefully to the accompaniment of music.

For all practical purposes Penchak and Silat are two words for the same thing. The perfectionist, however, separates them, with Silat tending more to the physical culture side and Penchak more to the art side. Both words are current all over Indonesia, and you will have no trouble making yourself understood that you want to see dances of stylized combat by using either word. Penchak actually is a Javanese word which means "evasion" or "warding off," and Silat is a word that conveys the idea of "quickness of action." Both mean in Western terms the art of self-defense plus the element of dance, and by their derivations you can infer the somewhat negative aspect of effectiveness against aggression from a presumably superior power. There is a parallel between Penchak and Japanese Judo (literally, the way of weakness) or Jujitsu (literally, the skill of weakness), although artistically they have no demonstrable connection.

Fighting as a general concept in Asia is the conversion of failure into success, of a disadvantage into a gain, and subterfuge and stratagem have fullest play. This differs somehow from the idea of physical culture in the West which, it seems, is designed to make you stronger than your opponent and to enable you to overpower him through main strength. In Asia, the emphasis is on deftness, intuition, and anticipation. When the dance element appears, it removes the force of an actual combat and elevates the spectacle into a valid art form.

There is a popular theory in Indonesia that Penchak is "continental" and originated in China. There are of course resemblances between the slow-motion shadow boxing of China and Penchak or Silat. But wherever the origin, Indonesia has so thoroughly incorporated and adapted it that it is primarily of Indonesia one thinks when the dance-art of fighting is discussed. In every city you will find clubs and societies assiduously cultivating their local form of Penchak. In one town of Sumatra there are two: the Revolutionary Young Man's Art and Charity Society and the Victorious Religion and Rhythm Club. In addition, there is the IPSI (Ikatan Penchak Silat Indonesia) organized in 1947 which is an inter-island society for the sole purpose of perpetuating this art, with branches in even the remotest areas.

There is no doubt about the hold the art has on Indonesians in general. A recent movie titled *Silat* is the story of a boy's physical and spiritual education at the hands of his Silat teacher with many episodes of the art. The government has recently made a documentary film of Penchak. Now, too, one year's instruction for both girls and boys is compulsory in schools as a substitute for Dutch-style calisthenics. Almost everyone does Penchak. One example out of many proving this happened when I got off the boat at a tiny port town in Sumatra on my first visit there. An aged coolie picked up my bags, asked inquisitively why I had come there. I answered half in truth "to see Penchak." He immediately dropped my bags, his eyes started to glow with special Penchak intensity, and did a few dance steps for me. Then he smiled and waved his hand at the other coolies and said proudly, "Everyone here has seen *my* Penchak."

Every district of Indonesia has its own form of Penchak and the differences between them are as startling as the varieties of folk dancing. The range is astonishing.

In the Jakarta area you have Nampon, an organization which specializes in hypnotic Silat. There, an expert is hypnotized and performs his intricate movements with mysterious, superhuman ability. As a climax to the program, still in trance, and while horns blow and the drums clatter he accepts challenges from any one who wishes to test his artificially induced invincibility. In the interior of North Sumatra, Tumbuklado Penchak, also a trance dance, is performed with one boy combatting two girls, all armed with short curved daggers. In this, even if one of the performers is accidentally stabbed, blood does not flow and no injury is sustained.

In Sunda, a Penchak master, after the standard series of movements, takes a sword and plunging it full strength inside his mouth until the point shows through his cheek muscle almost puncturing it, he tumbles and does a routine of one-hand springs and back flips. Another of his feats is to squeeze the sword tightly between his biceps and chest muscles and then slowly draw it out without cutting himself.

In Bali, where one of the gentlest races of people live, Penchak becomes a quiet exhibition of elegant body control, and the semi-nude bodies of the performers pose and glisten like pictures in a Western-style physical culture magazine.

Penchak everywhere is surrounded by convention and formality. No expert would ever consider beginning an exhibition without first praying. No pupil, once a performance starts, may leave the room or change his seat. When two opponents face each other, they must

213

salute each other respectfully before and after each bout. Penchak usually is performed barehanded at first, and then in rapid succession they take up a variety of weapons and clubs, krisses, curved daggers, long swords, sticks, jagged knives, spears, tridents that jangle with every thrust, and as an ultimate in pyrotechnics, unequal weapons are pitted against each other—a long javelin, for instance, will be held by one man while his opponent will brandish a tiny stiletto. In Sumatra women sometimes fight against men in Penchak matches. Because of training in this art, it is claimed in other parts of Indonesia that Sumatran women are more progressive and talkative than those elsewhere. Penchak thrives in certain areas of Sumatra where there is still a preponderantly matriarchal system, but whether there is actually a relationship between these two facts would be hard to ascertain.

Of all the many kinds of Penchak and Silat in Indonesia, none is more marvellous, and frightening than the special kind found in Bukitinggi, the capital of the Minangkabao area in Central Sumatra. It is interesting to note that no other district of Indonesia has produced as many political figures, ranging from the Vice-President to the head of the most powerful party in the government, and all of them, of course, know how to do Penchak. Of the many performers the city boasts, none is more brilliant than Etek Sutan (a minor princely title) Koli Mudo, who can be found at the Pemerentahan Koto near Bukitinggi itself. Mudo brings to this highly evolved science of combat the sensitivity of the practicing professional artist. His Penchak is along broad, expansive lines with the body articulated from head to toe. In his performance, along with a selection of his prize pupils (a performance comprises around a dozen men), the dance-fight progresses by indirection, the bodies tense in anticipation. Every gesture is controlled, focused, and governed by invisible rules that mysteriously link the two opponents as clearly as a rehearsed *pas de deux* connects the movements in ballet of its two performers. There is only perfect physical coordination and the mental adjustment, improvised and spontaneous, between one mind and body and that of the other. His troupe moves rhythmically and gracefully in what to my way of thinking is the most civilized form of fighting in the world. No hold is pressed, no kick carries through

214

to a hurt, there is no blood, unless there is an accident, and this is almost impossible if the performers are truly expert.

Mudo, above all other Penchak practitioners in Indonesia, makes explicit the aesthetic value of danger within an art form. Penchak is in deadly earnest, and the slightest slip could mean serious harm to one or the other opponent. In the West, we are inclined to associate the quality of danger with either the circus or sports. In Penchak, perhaps because of its steady rhythm and its grandiose gestures, the atmosphere of dance which surrounds it, or perhaps because of the music which usually accompanies it, it is so manifestly art instead of exercise that the aesthetic horizon of dance extends yet again into a new world.

Mudo's Penchak is performed in the rigidly traditional manner of the Bukitinggi area. The clothes of black cheesecloth bordered with silver thread resemble Chinese pyjamas. The crotch of the trousers, however, hangs down to the knees and the wide waist is bunched together and fastened with a belt. On the long sleeves of the jacket, chevrons of silver thread denote the performer's rank. A tightly wound turban of sober blue or brown batik keeps the long hair of the performers from tumbling down over their eyes, and when, in a sudden scurry of activity or during a swift locking of hands and feet, it flies off, you are sometimes surprised to see a shock of gray hair and discover that the young-looking performer you have been admiring is in reality an elderly gentleman. Many of the performers have fierce mustaches that curl at the ends, and on the forefinger of their right hand some of them wear a large agate set in silver as a symbol of strength.

Before Mudo and his men perform, each one walks up to you, noisily slaps the loose fold of cloth at the lowslung crotch (it sounds as if the material is being ripped), brings his knees together, and kneels extending his open palms and clasping your hands in his. He then touches the floor with both hands, brings them to his forehead. He says "minta maaf" (I beg your pardon) which asks forgiveness in advance in case he makes a mistake or is clumsy. Then the group forms a circle and Randai begins. Randai consists of walking slowly, counterclockwise, pausing at intervals, slapping the cloth between the crotch, posing, standing on one foot like a stork for a long time (this prepares the sense of balance which will be necessary in the succeeding Penchak), then executing a subtle turn or leap. Sometimes the group pivoting on one foot twist and turn as if corkscrewing themselves down to the ground and then unwind and rise back up to a standing position. The leader shouts *"ap ap"* to direct and control these practice movements. They finally clap their hands three times, make an obeisance (hands together in front of the face) towards Mudo, and the individual matches start.

Mudo nods to one of the men sitting around him, who then goes to the center of the circle. Penchak begins with the eyes, and suddenly, when the performer is ready, his eyes change focus, his look tenses, he stares into space and makes a series of gyrations, kicks, parries and thrusts all in slow motion.

Mudo nods again and an opponent enters the circle and the fight-dance moves into full swing. Their feet slap against the floor. One spins around the waist of the other. One or other of the fighters is thrown lightly to the ground. He smacks the palm of his hand to break the fall and to give the movement emphasis. Another pair is sent into the circle by a glance from Mudo, this time with daggers of sharp steel. Each lunges at the other. The feet kick at the dagger. Often one of the opponents bites the weapon to wrest it away. The two bodies roll over, without ever losing the rhythm or making a careless accidental gesture. They circle the dance area with excited caution. Their eyes never leave their opponent's, as if they were reading each other's innermost thoughts. They attack with lightning lunges, arcs of arms and legs blur, and the two bodies disentangle again only to re-engage themselves with this wicked skill. A dagger flies spinning out of the area, sometimes narrowly missing a spectator. Mudo stops each sortie with a word, and no pair is allowed to dance-fight for more than a few minutes.

"The passions must cool. The longer you fight the more the spirit rises. If the heart becomes hard, then the dance becomes a fight," Mudo explains. At the end of each performance the players kneel and clasp each other's hands, and again present themselves before you.

I asked Mudo once to show me the most difficult movement in Penchak. He looked at me in alarm, and answered, "To show you that I would have to kill a man. Killing is the most difficult thing."

216

We compromised, and he explained the technique of how to kill. The movement is called "breaking the body" and for it, you must seize the opponent's throat from behind, snap one of his arms backwards, and crack his spine with your knee. The whole process takes one second, is completely rhythmical, and is fatal.

A performance concludes formally with a repetition of the Randai, which now is even more supple and poised. The bodies of the group, being thoroughly flexed, are under perfect control, but you feel the air charged with danger and the electricity of unfulfilled agitation. On a regular occasion—not when you have simply ordered a private exposition of Penchak, that is to say—when a village has arranged a full-scale performance for itself, after the second Randai the Penchak group turns into a troupe of actors and begins a play. (The word for "theatre" in Sumatra is Randai in contrast with *tonil*, the Dutch word used in Java.) These plays are always on an historical theme set in the days when Sumatran empires were strong and before the nation was humbled by the Dutch. All the roles are taken by men and the hero is a stock character—a master of Penchak, a handsome, free-spending, bold and fearless man who spends his time gambling at cockfights and occasionally returns home to his adoring, doting, and wise mother.

Drama

In a country where dance occupies so paramount a place, it is perhaps natural for drama to have a lesser place. *Randai* is only a special folk drama; and *tonil* refers to the drama forms introduced by the West. But another word, *sandiwara* from the Malay language or *ludrug* in Javanese, connotes the kind of musical comedy theatre popular in the larger cities of Indonesia. *Sandiwara* is traditionally put on whenever there is a birth, a circumcision, or a wedding—providing the family is rich enough—and the troupe performs on an improvised stage before the happy house for the benefit of the neighbors and anyone who happens to be nearby.

These regular, professional Sandiwara troupes play historical plays, slapstick comedies, and a few social or domestic plays. In the historicals, kingdoms rise and fall, thrones are vied for, heroes wear powerful amulets and capture mysterious talismans. The "good-prince-gets-the-throne" formula is repeated in Indonesian theatre as often as the "boy-meets-girl" cliché is in ours. In the comedies, disguise and exposure figure importantly. One favorite theme is for a stranger to come to a village and pretend to be an important man with considerable influence and secret connections with the government. He makes passes at the pretty ladies, promising them special favors, is rebuffed, and finally is exposed as the charlatan that he is. Since Independence, a number of political themes and discussions of social issues have also found their way into the theatre. In the largest cities, like Medan or Jakarta, a few plays have had some success on themes even as remote as the national hero of the Philippines, José Rizal. In the socials, the plots are a little more imaginative. Sometimes the sorrows of a stepdaughter are depicted. The wicked stepmother is cruel. She does not feed her child, beats her, and forces her to wear castoff rags. Finally the mother is mysteriously attacked by calamitous ailments in which she develops nervous tics (much laughter here) and discovers in the end that despite all the stepdaughter truly loves her (many tears here), even more than the members of her own family.

There are three or four regular Sandiwara theatre houses and repertory troupes who perform nightly in Indonesia. In Jakarta there is one, and it is the only theatre in the whole city. It is called, rather oddly, "Miss Tjih Tjih" (*tjih tjih* means breast and Miss means Miss just as it does in English). There the plays alternate between Sandiwara and a more traditional form of theatre called Wayang Wong (or human puppet). Wayang Wong, as its name suggests, derives from the shadow plays or Wayang Kulit (*kulit* means leather) which were introduced to Indonesia along with other aspects of Hindu culture during the great period of Hinduization.

To follow the connection, I must first explain the shadow play generally and one of its further derivatives. A shadow play starts at midnight and lasts until daylight. The puppeteer stretches a large white sheet across a stage like a screen. Behind him he lights huge torches and presses against the screen translucent, paper-thin puppets made of perforated and pounded water buffalo leather with feet and arms moved by long bamboo slivers worked from underneath. The audience sees only the dark shadows, sometimes faintly colored by the paint on the leather, through the sheet. A *dalang* or narrator declaims the stories of ancient India, the *Ramayana* and *Brata Yudha* (*Mahabharata*) which are still listened to and watched after a thousand years with rapt attention. Wayang Wong is an imitation by human actors of the movements and stories of these shadows. It is a classical theatre, and the actors, dressed in the costumes of the Javanese courts, move in a stylized manner through the action and dialogue. Because of its more recent appearance in theatrical history, its themes are not confined to the *Ramayana* and *Brata Yudha* alone. Many typically Javanese legends are included in the repertoire.

A secondary development in the Indonesian theatre rising out of the Wayang Wong is Wayang Golek. These show actual puppets, shaped like dolls, manipulated by a puppeteer who sticks them in a banana tree trunk lying before him like a thin stage, and moves their arms by bamboo slivers as in Wayang Kulit. They imitate human beings imitating the shadow puppets.

The concept of Wayang in all its forms is altogether an interesting one. It exemplifies in its characters and stories all the courtly virtues which are still deeply admired all over Indonesia. As Boyd Compton, the most brilliant scholar of Indonesia the West has produced in recent times, says, "courage, loyalty, deference, and refinement, the chief virtues, have never been more palatably presented for popular imitation than in the rousing, brave and complicated stories of the Wayang. The spectator is kept in high excitement or laughter for hours on end as he absorbs the moral lessons which are the final reason for the Wayang's existence." In all Wayangs the struggle is essentially between good and evil, but in characteristic Javanese style, these become more a question of "refined" and "coarse," refined or *alus* being the supreme desideratum.

In the Sunda area of Java the Wayang puppet performances are at their best and extremely popular. In the interior the shadow plays and puppets are virtually the only theatrical entertainment known to the farmer and peasant. A boxful of leather and wooden figures is cheaper than a troupe of live actors who have to be fed and clothed and given salaries. Wayang Kulit and Golek offer an economic competition to live theatre which undoubtedly has been to its detriment.

The live forms of theatre, Sandiwara, Tonil and even Randai, with the exception of Wayang Wong possibly, are, on the whole and despite a few individual actors of merit, rather slipshod and crudely performed. They are disappointing to anyone who is looking for theatre rather than dance. There is an atmosphere about them almost of talentlessness which contrasts incongruously with Indonesia's splendid dances. Perhaps this is due to the tendency towards inexpressiveness on the part of Indonesians generally and the Javanese in particular. But England, to draw an example from the West, another inexpressive country in its way, has managed to produce superb theatre. It may be that the difficulty lies in the fact that drama essentially depends on the communication of ideas and the artificial transposition of real life into the arbitrary limits of a stage, and these are unsuited to Indonesian mentality. Perhaps it is in some way due to the influence of Mohammedanism and its block about literal representation. Perhaps it is simply because the genius of Indonesia lies exclusively in dance. There is a popular song current at the moment in Indonesia, and its refrain tells about hopes for the motherland, "Let her be full of song, full of dance," but there is not a word about theatre. This curious disparity between theatre and dance illustrates the profound difference between the two techniques. In Asia, where this distinction is never very clear, it is all the more surprising to find a national gift for grace and sensitivity to body movement isolated and separate from a sense of natural, lifelike movement on the stage. It may be that it is unreasonable to expect a country, even an Asian one, to excel in both.

Some years ago, there was a modern theatre movement. Today there is none. There is instead a new film industry, small and formative, which is being assisted by the government. One picture out of every four shown in any theatre must be Indonesian-made; and there is an embargo on films from Singapore in Malay, the *lingua franca* of Indonesia. Nearly everyone who was once interested in the modern theatre is now a producer, a scenario writer, a film star or connected with the movies in some way.

Modern theatre even in retrospect started well enough, and it is hard to explain what happened to destroy it. The first drama troupe which was neither Wayang Wong nor Sandiwara was started about fifty years ago by an Indo-European who called it Stambul. His troupe performed extravaganzas like the *Arabian Nights*, with a Western orchestra, many songs, and the declamation exaggerated into a sort of caricature of the grand, heroic Shakespearean style.

Out of this came the modern theatre movement which began in 1925 with Miss Ribut (*ribut* means "noise") and her husband, an Indonesian of Chinese descent. They acted original plays rather than translations, spoke rather than sang, and became very popular because they created something of a people's art. This was quickly followed by Dardenella, a troupe organized by a Russian called A. Piedro; they put on the *Thief of Bagdad, Don Q, The Three Musketeers, The Mark of Zorro,* and other stories of the same general nature. In 1933 a literary group, called *Pujungga Baru* or New Poets, became part of this new theatre movement. It was entirely Indonesian in inspiration and membership. They acted original Indonesian plays, restaged historical ones of the Wayang Wong genre, used modern techniques, and brought old stories up to date in adapting them for the stage. Their chief supporters were students and intellectuals.

During World War II, with the increase of national consciousness and under the encouragement of the Japanese, the theatre movement progressed. Several young writers and artists who wanted an Indonesian theatre with authentic background and talent banded together and called their new attempt Maya (the Sanskrit word for "illusion"). At the center of the movement was the brilliant writer Usmar Ismail, now one of Indonesia's leading film directors and producers, Mochtar Lubis and Rosihan Anwar, both excellent writers and at present editors of Jakarta's most prominent papers and literary journals. The group received assistance from the Japanese authorities, who hoped to use the theatre as a propaganda weapon in their favor throughout Java. Maya extended itself and spread to the other cities of the country.

For the first time plays dealing with everyday life and acted in ordinary street clothes were performed, and their programs reached into the villages where the people saw their first theatre of any kind other than shadows or puppets. Maya continued after the war, and the group managed to put on a few plays, still of course purely on an amateur basis. One was *Api* (Fire) written by Usmar Ismail. It tells the story of a selfish man who uses his Western education and knowledge to invent a destructive weapon of war. This finally destroys him during a laboratory experiment. Woven into the plot are family tensions coming from the man's spiteful cruelty to his wife because she is of higher social standing than he, from the contempt his own daughter feels for him, and from the meanness of his son who can only inspire pity, even from his own fiancée. The last play put on by Maya was *Insan Kamil* (The Perfect Human) by El Hakim, the pseudonym of Dr. Abu Hanifah, the Indonesian delegate to the United Nations. Its story tells of the dilemma an intellectual finds himself in when he tries to find the perfect woman to be his wife.

The group also intended to put on a sexless version of *Tobacco Road*, translated by Mochtar Lubis, which would have been the first American play ever presented in Indonesia. It was thought that the play would be successful because the problems of the farmer class, drought and poverty are the same in that region of America and in Indonesia as a whole. But in 1950 the movement collapsed because of the activity forced on all intellectuals by Independence, and the concentration of talent represented by Maya was dispersed in every direction.

There is no modern theatre today. Very rarely a movie star will perform a play written by a movie hack for one night as a charity gesture to raise funds for some good cause. Two plays of this sort which I have seen dealt with the problem of home life and morality —the wife is really good despite the suspicions of her family. But even these performances, to fill them out, have long entr'actes of movie-style dancing from modern India.

Usmar Ismail founded in 1955 the Indonesian National Theatre Academy in Jakarta. As a result modern theatre may start again in Indonesia, but it seems abundantly clear that at present the need or inclination for it is remote, even among the intellectuals who once spearheaded the movement. For the present, the outsider has the pleasant satisfaction that comes from the greatness of Indonesia's dances.

Bali

On a world map the island of Bali is invisible. Even on a map of Indonesia it is scarcely more than a tiny speck off the East coast of

Java. You need a specific chart of the Lesser Sundas, as that brief spray of islands that links Indonesia with Australia is called, to see that Bali is ninety by fifty miles in area and looks rather like a chicken without its head. To the million and a half Balinese who live on the island, and for most of the thousands and thousands of tourists who visit it annually, Bali despite its minuscule size and absurd shape casts an enchantment so alluring that it is difficult to write about it without being fulsome.

Whether you date yourself from Madeline Carroll on the beach at Bali, or from Bali H'ai, "your own special island," or from John Coast's troupe who appeared with such success a few years ago in America and Europe, the romantic associations of the island are explicit. Almost all the excitement that the words "tropical" or "South Sea Island" conjure up seems concentrated there. It has luminous coral reefs, yellow and sandy beaches, symmetrically terraced rice-fields, coconut tree fronds that glisten in the rain and tremble in the breeze, and, of course, the ubiquitous ever-burgeoning banana tree. Even as you land in Bali you see still stuck up on the walls of the airport or shipping office the old fading Dutch posters advertising Bali as *sfeer en bekoring*, "a world of magic and enchantment." A more apt description would be hard to find. The people are brown-skinned, extravagantly handsome, and unaffectedly friendly. They are sturdy, so much so in fact that for centuries they made the choicest slaves in Indonesia, and occasional plundering slave hunts were, until the Dutch attack in 1908, the only forays ever made against the island.

Spiritually, Bali represents the furtherest extension of the Hindu empire, and it now is the only Hindu country in the world outside India. Islam in the sixteenth century stopped its eastward spread at Java, separated from Bali by only a mile of water. Commercially, Bali has been favored by the absence in an otherwise exceptionally endowed island of gold and silver, spices and precious stones—the lures for past exploiters. Artistically, Asia's highly developed music and dancing and its underlying aesthetic theories reach their boundary at Bali, at their highest peak of attainment. Further east, in the Halmaheras and New Guinea, the arts become aboriginal in character and inevitably of a lesser order.

Almost every Balinese village has a complex artistic organization, and nearly every individual Balinese belongs to a *suka* or society of some sort which may be for dancing, flute-playing, shadow-play performing, or simply for virgin boys and virgin girls whose only group activity is some special dance. Altogether, the island of Bali offers even the most casual visitor an astonishing assortment of pleasures and adventures in art—paintings of fantastically delicate craftsmanship, woodcarvings of painstaking skill, dances, both solo and ballet, dramas lasting all night long, all of amazing beauty and perfection, and, of course, concerts of orchestral music on a grand scale. There are probably, at a rough, unprovable estimate, more music societies in Bali proportionately than there are fraternities and sororities in America. And usually the music they produce impresses the tourist as much as the dances. The conglomeration of metallophones, xylophones, celestes, gongs, flutes, and drums tinkle and reverberate, chime and clang, with such musical discipline that even the thoroughly Western ear responds to their pulsating harmonies.

Bali is unique in Asian art primarily, I feel, because it is a genuinely creative country. The originality so prized in the West is not a characteristic of Asia in general, whose greatness obviously lies elsewhere. The principal concern of art in Asia is with tradition or the inheritance from the past and its legacy to the future. An Asian artist uninfluenced by the West is fundamentally more interested in perfecting a single gesture transmitted to him by a long line of hereditary teachers than in discovering a new one, while his counterpart in the West can scarcely wait to escape the conservatory and spread his own wings according to the dictates of his own conscience. Most artists in Asia, regardless of the degree of their attainment, continue with their teachers until death. I have seen grown men of artistic stature take instruction with the same awestruck humility a pupil in the West has at his first lessons. As a general observation, I think it is fair to say about Asia as a whole that in recent times wherever new forms have been evolved, where creative ideas have been originated and inventions realized to any extent, they have either been firmly rooted extensions of the past or liberal imports from the West. This does not minimize the value of the new things awakened Asia is now doing. On the other hand, it is arguable that far too much importance is placed in Europe and America on being creative and making novelty an end in itself. These aims are, of course, eminently suitable to us, and out of them have come the most prideful elements of our civilization, but the application of such aesthetic criteria to Asia leads only to misjudgment and a failure in appreciation.

Delighting in Bali for precisely these qualities we cherish in the West does not imply that Bali has lost tradition and builds its dance arts out of a brand-new, untrammeled, individual mind. Nothing in Bali is wholly alien to its past or to ancient India, and the country is deeply Asian in a way that other areas where colonization has been more thorough and painful can never recapture. But antiquity in itself is more meaningless to the Balinese than it is even to us in the West who have less of it and therefore prize it more. The quality that sets Bali apart from its Asian neighbors is its attitude to its great and respected traditions. Tradition to the Balinese is a fluid technique or formula, not a rigid acceptance of rules. Contradictory as it may seem, this allows an enormous creativity and output without a violation of already determined artistic principle. Perhaps this attitude can be compared with ballet, which is as close to being classic as any dance we have. It still remains classical and traditional in one sense despite the innovations which carry it out of all the confines originally defining it. But the conclusion one draws at this point is as odious as the comparison itself.

There is, fortunately, between cultures no question as to better or worse. There is only difference between ways of life. To carp at, say, traditionless American dance or to deplore the minimal awareness of the Greek classics in our modern drama is as senseless for the Asian as it is for the foreigner to be frustrated by the lack of cultural erosion in contemporary Asia. I cannot seriously regret the disparity in art between being unusual and being familiar. But I still suspect that the happy combination of the two which Bali offers is supreme. Doubtless it is precisely the Western-like, almost un-Asian creativity and originality which Bali exhibits in dance that makes the island so completely acceptable to the Western visitor.

Bali's changefulness is constant, and the rapidity with which dance forms completely alter themselves is astonishing. Book references to Balinese dancing, except where they deal with basic principles and aesthetic theory, age more rapidly than any others in Asia on similar subjects. Already Beryl de Zoete and Walter Spies' *Dance and Drama in Bali* is outmoded. When it appeared twenty years ago it was a signal event. Now it has become historical, and much, if not all, of its contemporaneous pertinence is lost. In the fourteen years since I first knew Bali, I myself have seen dances appear and fade away, dance fashions transform, and the island undergo substantial reversals in taste.

A case in point is the Janger, possibly the most photographed dance in the world. In it girls with flower-spiked headdresses like a bishop's mitre sit in a square across from an equal number of young men, all of whom chant antiphonally and gesticulate from their seated positions. When I was first in Bali, before World War II, Janger was lingering on in a last gasp of popularity, although it had been created only as recently as 1920 after a troupe of Stambul players from Java had performed in Singaraja and set a fashion with the Russian head-bands they used in one of their numbers. During the Revolution, when I was again there, this dance had almost vanished. In the North a few troupes performed it with the men wearing football sweaters, another fashion borrowed from the outside; in the South its anthropological and remote connections with mating ceremonies had come to the fore and people infused with the *suka* spirit joined Janger societies as an advertisement of their eligibility for marriage. In 1955, when I was last in Bali, the dance had disappeared except for an inferior troupe that appears at the Bali Hotel in Den Pasar when sufficient tourists ask specially for it, and for the Pliatan troupe which prepared a truncated version for its American and European tour.

This artistic restlessness is to a great extent the result of what the Balinese call their sense of *mud* (pronounced just as in English) and meaning "boredom." This produces in the people a high degree of faddism and is of course the genesis of their creativity. Because they bore easily, they periodically seek out new amusements with an almost obsessive eagerness. Sometimes this takes the form of the creation of new dances, sometimes the rearrangement of old ones.

A clear and popular example was Sampih the male star of the Dancers of Bali troupe who was mysteriously murdered by his compatriots after his return from America. He set a fashion that a number of dancers are still following. He used the Kebyar as the main section of any story-dance—one in which he falls asleep and dreams of a group of beautiful maidens, or in which some girls are bathing and he steals their clothes (all these fragmentary stories come from Hindu mythology, and the Balinese name the gods in pronunciations as close as they can to their originals).

The most recent example (1955) of faddism is the current craze of the Joget or "flirt dance," in essence a very old form of dance in Bali, but in its present form, as presented by mature, sexually active girls, it is identified by the added word "Bumbum." The Bumbum part of it refers not only to the new variant it now has, but specifically to one of the instruments recently reintroduced into the Joget's all-bamboo orchestra (other orchestras of Bali are all-metal). It consists of two large bamboo stalks which are struck against the ground and emit a hollow, resonant "boom boom." But the most sensational innovation in the orchestra is the row of fifteen or twenty percussionists who each beat two short sticks of split bamboo in brittle, crackling synchronization with the sputtering rhythms of the dance. For this there is no special identifying word.

The principle of Joget dancing, old or new, is that a girl wearing a gold headdress speared with two sprigs of temple flowers and with a large stick of burning incense smoking from it performs a solo of a brilliant, disciplined caliber. She then flits around the arena, flirting and choosing various men to partner her. The man who joins her in the ring may dance professionally, following her every step, or lead her in intricate steps from other dances, even classic ones, or he may be comic, erotic, and even mime whatever he thinks of to confuse or delight the girl.

It is in a way Bali's ballroom dance, although infinitely more intricate and complicated than what we mean by that term. As the current mania of the island, Joget Bumbum monopolizes Bali nights, and everywhere you go you find it being danced almost to the exclusion of other dances. But I dare say that by the time the next book on Bali is written, all this will sound like ancient history.

The story of Joget Bumbum's first rise to popularity goes back to 1951 and is typical of the unpredictable nature and origins of Balinese fads. It seems that about that time one of the rich rajas of the North had been deserted by his favorite wife, and the only consolation for his loneliness was this provoking and suggestive flirt dance which had just been created as an experiment. Although it distracted him from his grief, it did not quite succeed fully. He finally went amok and killed a large number of people before he at last managed to commit suicide. For about a year until the proper astrological date for his cremation came around, his body was carefully preserved.

Meanwhile this dramatic story spread like wildfire over all Bali. And Joget Bumbum seemed to epitomize that exciting moment in Balinese history. When cremation time arrived, because the deceased had been so rich, and because he was so well-connected and inbred (he was related by blood or marriage with almost every other raja and *chokorda* [minor prince] of rank, each of whom had to contribute money for their relative's funeral), it turned out to be the splashiest, most splendid affair ever held on the island. All of Bali converged on the North, and everyone started calling for Joget Bumbums during these festive celebrations.

It is said that a number of fortunes were lost (even by the cautious Chinese who control most of the island's commerce) simply from hiring girl after girl to dance night after night. Dozens of divorces took place, and the only grounds needed were and still are: "My husband spends all his time and money at the Joget." The worst part of all was that fights started over each performance. The girls danced in earnest, and when they tapped you with their fan to dance with them, it was meaningful and arousing. If you were chosen, you were ecstatic. If your rival was accorded the honor, you were crushed. If the girl dismissed you from the ring by another tap of the fan, you were humiliated. One man stabbed a Joget to death before the horrified eyes of a full audience when she failed to seek him out. There were even scandals of boys marrying Joget girls expecting them to stop the profession as soon as they were married. Sometimes the girls would refuse, partly because of the money (a Joget costs between five and fifteen dollars an evening, which means a lot in Bali) and partly because they were spoiled by the enthusiasm of the crowd and simply could not turn away from the excitement of the dance ring. Every scandal added to Joget Bumbum's fame, and it soon became Bali's most titillating and dangerous dance.

Another more important example of Bali's changing dance styles concerns the curious interplay between men's and women's dances. In accord with Asian principles of aesthetics, Bali has had for a long

228

time the tradition of young boys dancing like girls. This predilection is, contrary to the assumption a Westerner immediately makes, more to prevent vice than encourage it, and to give dance a higher, more sexless and moral tone than it has when women dance. Partly, too, the lesser place of women in Asian society and the greater restrictions on what they can and cannot do conduced to greater public participation of men than women except, of course, in the courts and palaces, but in Bali where dance is entirely a public and religious function and therefore belongs to all the people, the tastes of individual rajas and princes determine nothing. Religiously too, I imagine that young boys were considered purer than young girls, since they were potential priests and holy men. Unlike women who at best could only be nuns, their presence in the temples as dancers was more suitable to the gods.

The chaste quality of Balinese dancing undoubtedly came as a surprise to foreign audiences when they saw the Dancers of Bali troupe, and the reviews all remarked on the surprising youth of its artists. In principle, and certainly in all classical dances of Bali, only girls who have not yet menstruated are technically fit for dancing. Formerly there were even more restrictions on the selection of dancers: they could not be from the classes who work with leather, or slaughter animals, nor could they dance if they had a scar on any part of their bodies. Even today, as soon as a girl marries, and she is nubile whenever she first menstruates, she stops dancing. Bali, however, being a reasonable country, makes exceptions. There are, besides, dances only for old women like the Mendet, and if a girl is exceptionally good, she can dance for as long as she wishes. Moreover, Joget Bumbum has been a serious blow to dance conventions.

Joget originally was a dance performed by a young boy dressed as a girl, and it was because of the absence of sexual titillation in two men dancing together that it was originally tolerated. The new fashion for mature girls ("girls with breasts," as the Balinese put it) to dance in Joget is very recent and it still shocks the older people. But there is something indescribably repugnant to the Balinese about a woman who has borne children dancing in public. Bali rather shares an attitude which Hollywood used to have which resulted in actresses' ages being kept secret, their marriages being hidden, and if there were children, in hiding the fact. In general, the most rigid application of the rules of immaturity regarding dancers applies now only to trance dancers.

The whole question of eroticism in Asia is a complex one, and it is impossible not to refer to it repeatedly as its various aspects arise. To digress a little, Hindu culture has to the Western eye immense areas of unmitigated and abandoned sexuality—in its mass of *mithuna* temple carvings such as the magnificent sculptures of Konarak and Khajurao, in its ancient and sacred texts such as the *Kamasutra*, and in its dances where *devadasi*, who can even be prostitutes, perform as an integral part of religious worship. But very little of this openness has traveled abroad. For instance, in the ancient architectural ruins of Southeast Asia, there is not a single piece of erotic sculpture that I know of, although the styles and workmanship are identical with their Indian progenitors. Whatever prurience you find in the liturgical writings of India is diluted, if not excised, in their transference to other areas overseas. But certain elements of the dance outside India imply a potential "immorality," and the Westerner is apt to be deceived by his first impressions. In the Kebyar, for example, a male sitting dance performed in the center of the Balinese orchestra, the dancer kisses the drummer, who is of course a man. (The Balinese kiss is a *chyum* nose rubbing.) But this stems from aesthetic rather than homosexual considerations. Asians delight in artistic interchanges—boys dancing as girls, women as men, immature girls flirting like prostitutes; and the Kebyar kiss to a Balinese conveys a notion of surprise or unusualness like a trick ending. It rises emotionally from a sense of respect for the drummer, who is the leader of the orchestra, and if you force a Balinese to search his mind for an artistic justification or meaning, he will almost invariably explain that the dancer is showing his rapture over the orchestra's excellence. If you suggest to an Asian that women playing women and men playing men would be better, he is amazed. Obviously, you have missed the point and are trying to thrust eroticism where it is not.

Other parts of Asia extend this concept even further. Nothing so delights an audience as when a young child plays a heroic part and fight-dances formidably against an adult opponent. In Manipur children appear with adults, although all the roles represent fully grown people. In Kabuki very old men sometimes in their seventies continue to dance as young maidens. I remember clearly my surprise when I first read a criticism in a Japanese paper before the War that a certain actor in his forties was not old enough to dance the particularly difficult role of a certain nineteen-year-old girl, meaning, of course, that he had not yet acquired the artistic stature to do this complicated physical and psychological feat.

By fifteen or twenty years ago the custom of boys playing girls in dance had virtually disappeared from Bali. I once saw a boy Joget (called Gandrung in those days), but the dance had that air of clumsiness which forecasts the demise of any dance in Bali. Now men never appear as women and it would be considered ludicrous for them to do so—so rapidly has Balinese taste changed and so fully has Western civilization intruded in the Joget at least. Balinese taste for interchange has, however, remained. The fashion has instead swung almost perversely in the opposite direction.

Today Bali is full of girls doing men's dances, and the most brilliant exponent of this sort of dance is Bali's brightest star of the moment. The most popular dancer of Bali is Dharmi, and she, while being a very good-looking young woman and happily married, dances like a man. To say this is a Balinese compliment, just as it is flattering to tell Ida Bagus Oka of Blangsinga, the most spectacular Kebyar dancer on the island at present, that he is as beautiful as a woman. Dharmi's success began with her dancing the Kebyar, with her hair tucked up high, hidden behind her gold head-band, and dressed in the short, knee-length gold and purple skirt Kebyar men wear. This costume is pretty daring for a Balinese woman, who may with impunity reveal her breasts but is indecorous if she shows her ankles. Dharmi, being a skilled and admired dancer, could do just what she pleased, and this has started several vogues and spearheaded a spate of imitators. More girls now dance the Kebyar than men, and I suppose that this is a sign that this dance too is on its way out. After all, it has been in existence now for about thirty years, and it is probably time for another dance to take its place before the Balinese grow really bored.

To us who are old-fashioned, and a little proprietary as far as Bali is concerned, Dharmi is not as marvellous as, say, Champlung was in the old days, or the Joget of Bunkasa (who stopped dancing as soon

231

as she reached maturity), or the famous Mario and his pupil Gusti Raka. But there is no question that Dharmi is a coruscating artist and one of the most creative dancers Bali has yet produced. She has a wide repertoire ranging from the traditional Legong through the woman's Kebyar to a number of completely original compositions concocted between her and her teacher. One of these is a duet, Ratih Metu, in which the Sun (Dharmi plays this male role) and the Moon are represented. The theme of the dance is that the clouds are always separating the two, but they finally break through and meet—there is a kiss—and the dance ends on an ecstatic note.

Another of her dances is a solo, Maung Nuring, which simply represents a Prime Minister following behind his Raja (who does not appear on the stage), and it is one of the most absorbing theatrical experiences I have known. The dance structurally consists of the progression in a straight line from the back of the stage to the footlights, or in Balinese terms, from one end of the pounded dirt arena to the other where the orchestra sits. For the twenty-minute duration of the dance, Dharmi magnetizes the audience by formidably intense concentration. She charges the air with a constant succession of tensions, only lightened and enhanced by infinitesimal moments of relaxation. While the gamelan orchestra thunders out its shuddering polyphony, Dharmi brings into play all the basic characteristics of Balinese dancing. Her eyes draw into focus, they dilate and open wide, or they squint and peer off over the orchestra into impenetrable distance. Her eyeballs dart with lightning speed to either side or quiver up and down in their sockets. One eyebrow rapidly arches. Her hips undulate in a circular spiral. Her fingers flutter like shivering leaves. Sometimes they open and close like the pleating of a fan. Her mouth forms the bold half-smile of Bali which means everything from seductiveness to contempt. The head clicks on the stem of the neck from side to side. The torso remains always on that Balinese, off-center, asymmetrical bias. The knees splay wide apart, and to add excitement, occasionally one knee trembles up and down. The toes turn up in a curl. The arms always extend out level from the shoulder with the elbows broken and the palms open towards the spectators. Throughout there are the static pauses, where the posture is held and the body rises and falls so imperceptibly it is like secret breathing.

At the beginning of each section she makes the gesture of "opening the curtain" (a stylization of the salute found everywhere in Asia). The hands, palms showing, are before the face, and as the fingers quiver, they separate to follow a diagonal line opening out to reveal the face, only stopping when the full formal posture of Balinese dance is reached. The hands twist and turn, they place invisible flowers in the hair, or pause shuddering like a hummingbird's wings at the forehead as if temporarily plunged in thought or doubt. The walk, and the dance is scarcely more than this, progresses jerkily. It starts and stops. The faithful Prime Minister imagines danger, tenses, and subsides when he dismisses it as imagined. The alertness and watchfulness carry the Raja safely through the promenade, and this completes the dance. In effect, it is sheer virtuosity threaded to the slenderest of themes. Nothing happens, but by the end you are emotionally exhausted.

Changefulness and faddism in Balinese dance has its effect on the old-established dances in many ways. As new dances appear, old ones fall into decline. Dances have even completely disappeared. Wayang Wong, in which the whole of the *Ramayana* was dance-acted by vast casts, is now a memory. Gambuh has not been seen for a decade. But some, however, have remained and are still performed with only slight variations. New Legongs have started in several places, and the traditional one at Saba has been revived because they have found two girls in the village identical in looks and ability. Mas has a new ballet somewhat along the lines of the old Gabor ballet of Ubud. Penchak still thrives in its gentle Balinese way. Rejang is still performed at Batuan with all the women and girl children of the village participating. Baris continues in Den Pasar, in the bigger villages and at cremations. Kechak, or the Monkey Dance, where fifty men chant and shake their fingers in weird patterns like a voodoo rite around a flaming torch and provide an accompaniment to an enactment of a passage from the *Ramayana*, is still a weekly event at Bona—for tourists. Singapadu occasionally presents the Kris dance, where entranced men plunge daggers into their chests in the daytime—for photographers.

Perhaps only one area of Balinese dance is immune to wholesale change, the Sanghyang or trance dances. These are carefully preserved. Described in words, trance dancing sounds like an anthropological report, but when you are actually present and see all its reality, you soon begin to lose your detachment and the performance becomes a serious, if not sobering, experience. The remoteness of trance and your own way of life dissolves in the face of the intensity of the performers and the credulity of the spectators.

The principle of a trance dance, in general, is that after certain magical incantations are pronounced, libations poured, and mandalas sketched in the air, the dancers—sometimes they have never danced formally before—enter a different state of consciousness. During the course of this they dance, perform feats of strength and endurance, and even undergo mild tortures which normally they are incapable of, and they suffer no physical after-effects. Perhaps it is here in the trance dances that you reach below the surface of Bali in a more deep and telling way.

The most startling dance of the extrasensorial sort I have ever seen is the fire dancing at Kayukapas. It can be arranged for about one hundred and fifty rupiahs (five dollars at the open market rate generally used in Indonesia). You must go first to Kintamani, the hill station high in the pine-covered mountains of North Bali, two hours of good road from Den Pasar, where there is an excellent resthouse. From there you hike for a mile down a hill to the obscure village, Kayukapas. It is customary in this village to keep two girls always ready for these performances as a precautionary measure to ward off evil from the village. As soon as the two regular girls mature, two others are immediately selected to take their place. They are chosen, among other reasons, on the basis of their responsiveness to hypnosis.

As you sit outside in the crisp evening air, these two deeply entranced, auto-hypnotized girls in traditional costumes of gold-painted, leaf-patterned cloth and with a headdress of flowers and blanched palm leaf begin to dance for you. Suddenly without warning, and with their eyes still closed, they leap surefootedly onto the shoulders of two men sitting near an orchestra which uses only bamboo sticks and jew's-harps. The men stand up and start dancing around the arena with the girls still on their shoulders. This is the only place in the world I know of where you have to look up into the sky to see dancing, and when I think about it, I have never before seen two people dancing at the same time with only one pair of feet on the ground. During this skyscraper performance, the girls do back-bends that casually defy all gravitational laws and cling to the men's shoulders with only their toes. The men underneath trot about balancing them. Later, some men build a bright fire of dried coconut shells. When it burns down to glowing, broiling-hot embers, the men toss a can of kerosene on it and in that instant, as the flames leap up, a gamelan orchestra of metallic bars bursts into a tumultuous composition. The girls plunge, still dancing, into the knee-high fire, like moths impelled towards light. They remain in the center of the heat stamping and kicking until the last flicker dies.

Not long ago when an Italian motion picture company was making a documentary film, the village elders made a special double-size fire, throwing on an extra can of kerosene. There was, the headman explained, only a slight additional charge for the fuel. But no matter how high the flames, the feet of the girls never burn, although they sometimes get blackened by smoke. Even more mysteriously their costumes never catch fire.

In the tiny village of Joklegi near Selat where the Swiss painter Theo Meier lives, a trance dance of another sort can be easily arranged. While the older women sit around and sing phrases of incantations like sacred runes used only on these special occasions, two girls lean over a burner of incense. When they are in trance they begin to dance. The girls are supposed to become *apsaras*, called *dedari* in Bali, or the celestial nymphs of ancient Hindu mythology. They follow the words of the short phrases, and whenever the singing stops, the dancers flop down on the ground only to rise again—like marionettes lifted by imperceptible strings—immediately the tune resumes. The words tell the girls that they are flowers dangling from a tree. They then do a backbend, perilously balancing over a bamboo pole, which is lifted by two men and carried around the temple courtyard. They say, "You are birds perched on a tree," and the girls sit casually on the bamboo pole and are hoisted high in the air without falling off. And a somewhat modern variant comes when Balinese cigarettes of clove and dried carnation leaves wrapped in a corn husk are handed to the *dedaris*. The song goes, "The gods give the celestial maidens cigarettes from heaven, lighted by the fires of heaven," and the girls toss them to the singers, who light up, and continue singing other lines. An orchestra of jew's-harps starts playing and the dance grows orgiastic.

A Balinese once explained to me this frantic agitation of the *dedaris*: "Music is alcohol to the *dedaris*." But occasionally the girls protest against all sound except the sad songs of the women and I have seen them slap musicians to prevent them from arousing them. The singers finally say, "Now the *dedaris* are going home," and the trance is concluded. They drink a glass of water with marigold flowers in it and return to normal. The girls may have danced all night, but they are not fatigued, nor do they have any recollection of what they have done. It was, if you are crass enough to ask them, celestial nymphs who came momentarily through them to earth, they say.

The prevalence of dance in Bali, the island of dances whose standard and development are universally high, seems anachronistic in a modern work-a-day world. Certainly, no single country anywhere in the world is as full of wonder and delight and dance. The tourist, I am happy to say, is an important factor. Many of Bali's dancers (excluding the trance dancers) are professionals who earn their living by their art. And because there is so much dance in Bali and so much of it has left the temples and become secular and individual, it is impossible for the island to support it unaided. A new element had to enter, and the tourists have now become a paying audience. What the ticket-buying public is to ballet in the West, the tourist is to Bali, and this role has served its purpose well.

The tourist brings wealth to Bali and he affords livelihood to hundreds and hundreds of dancers all over the island. Of course, the Balinese would dance anyway, and there are hundreds of dances which the tourist never sees or happens upon only by living there and being told about some village which has decided to try its hand at something new or is renovating a traditional dance that has lain forgotten for several decades. But I think it is only fair to say that the best dancers in an international sense of universal standard find their way to the tourist public. It has for some reason become fashionable for people to look with disdain on the performances in the dance pavilion outside the Bali Hotel and to call the dances there "touristy." That is unkind. The tourist who never ventures outside the town of Den Pasar is not being cheated of genuine dance experience in Bali. It is as foolish to deplore those performances as it would be to refuse to see Margot Fonteyn at Sadler's Wells on the ground that you prefer to see her dancing in the woods on a summer afternoon unimpeded by a commercial audience. The tourist comes to Bali because of the dances, but the obverse of the axiom is not true. Dance in Bali is not solely because of tourists.

It is a fact that if you were to create the perfect form of dancing to please a tourist, you would produce something quite close to what the Balinese have achieved. An infinite number of qualities in Balinese dancing make it a delight for Westerners. The dance is easy to understand. Most dances have only the merest thread of a story if they have one at all. Many of them are completely abstract, no more than a joyous filling of space with decorative movement. Indian *mudras* are attenuated into meaninglessness and the fingers never form ideas or represent objects to tax your intellectual faculties. With certain exceptions, there are no words to make you follow what the dancer is doing. And, finally, the pace is always fast. There are no slow dances which sometimes try the patience of Westerners. The dances are always short, quick, and lively. In all, the aesthetic burden on the spectator is lighter in Balinese dancing than in any other dance-form in the world. Less is required of him intellectually than even from ballet, and Balinese movement and sound are more familiar and less disturbing to us than many of the innovations of modern dance schools.

In the immediate attractiveness of Balinese dance it is easy to ignore or never to discover that Bali has also a strong drama form called Arja. This is a fully dramatic form performed in classical costumes of flower headdresses and gold-painted cloths. It lasts the whole night, and its stories always deal with kings (speaking high Balinese or Javanese) and their retainers (speaking ordinary Balinese, so that everything is understandable) and with some past event of Balinese royal history, which is enthralling. The sing-song of the declamation (it always starts high and sinks low into almost a moan at the end of the phrase), the fragmentary nature of the stories spun out for hours, and the constant talking in various kinds of Balinese are not as attractive to a tourist as the dances. But to a Balinese, Arja is a part of their life and the people flock to it as we do to Broadway or the West End. The Westerner must, I suppose, bide his time until the Balinese create another theatrical form before he is diverted from the island's dancing which captivates him so completely.

Why Bali produces so many dances, such remarkable ones, and why almost every Balinese can dance with exceptional skill are the first questions which every visitor to Bali must ask himself. If there is an answer, I suppose it is found somewhere in the existence and interplay of three factors: religion, work, and the social structure.

Balinese dancing is profoundly religious in origin and it functions primarily out of religious expression either conscious or unconscious, either devoutly believed or simply accepted and indulged. Work and work-habits are responsible for the instrument of Balinese dancing, a peculiarly articulated body, and prepare a Balinese for formal dance training. The social organization, geared to the group rather than to the individual, accounts for the highly developed degree of concerted performance. These factors in all their ramifications and interworkings determine the special quality of Balinese dance, and perhaps offer a key to its magic.

Life in Bali appears as a continuous stream of religious reminders —daily offerings, temple processions and holy days. Even the national sport, cockfighting, is recognized as a blood offering to the gods. Every house, no matter how poor, has its own shrine. The very poor whose only shelter may be a palm leaf shed have at least a tree toward which they direct their religious impulses. Each community of village size has at least three temples owned and maintained communally. A well-off Balinese has even more temples to claim his devotions. Balinese women divide their time equally between husband, child, home, and religion. Each day the woman makes temple offerings of flowers, food and incense. (The incense of the poor is often no more than a smoking coconut husk.) Twice daily she places tiny trays of delicately woven palm leaves containing food and flowers about her house. Both the forces of good, the higher spirits, and the forces of evil, the lower spirits, must be appeased.

A Balinese is kept in a state of semi-poverty not by indolence but by religious obligations. The system of offerings is a tremendous drain on financial resources. Marigolds, which have the appropriate color for the gods, must be bought if they are not immediately available in quantity. The fine strips of thin palm leaves which are to be woven into various designs for different offerings, as well as incense and even coconut husks, must all be purchased or diverted from more utilitarian uses. I suppose no one has estimated the extent of food wastage on an average day represented by all the food abandoned to the gods all over Bali. As it is, stray dogs, pigs, geese and chickens benefit. There is one exception: huge, elaborate temple offerings of fancy food on festival days. The women transport these to the temple, leave them, but after the gods have eaten the essence, they bring them back for the family.

The wealthy and higher castes have to pay for temple construction. The religious life of the Balinese is to them a matter of perpetual, continuous concern and their temples must be rebuilt whenever they become old. The life of a temple is in theory about twenty-five years. Every six months each household temple must also be purified. The Balinese live in constant readiness for emergency celebrations as when a priest or medium announces gratuitously that a special cleansing ceremony should be held at a certain temple, or in times of epidemics, bad luck, good luck, or when a child reaches three months of age, or if witches or evil spirits are seen or heard in a locality, or if death strikes unexpectedly. At present, for astrological reasons innumerable new temples are being built in a frantic wave of religious work all over Bali.

Some performances are not necessarily religious in theme, but they still need religion to protect them. Where there is an element of danger in the dance or drama, the offerings and prayers increase. An example of this occurred during the War of Independence. After an absence of fifty years the Balinese revived a drama of the Arja type called *Pakang Raras*. One of the women in the village of Badang Tagal vowed that if her husband returned safely from an excursion against the Dutch in Java, she would perform the hero's role herself and of course undertake the exorbitant cost of the performance. Because of the scene where the hero is murdered (oddly enough by being beaten with betel-nut leaves), a great deal of fear is connected with the performance. The Balinese claim that the hero must actually die. So a tremendous number of propitiatory offerings of food and flowers are necessary to ensure the actor's resurrection. And, too, the decline of the famous Kris Dance, which once was performed all over Bali, is due not merely to boredom on the part of the Balinese but to lack of funds for the necessary pre-performance temple offerings. These insure the safety of the performers and warrant that the krisses will not actually stab them.

At the core of all religious activity in Bali are dance and drama and their inseparable accompaniment, music. These arts represent man's highest expression towards the gods, and having been given originally by them to man according to the Hindu theology accepted by the Balinese, man returns them by performing them with pleasure, delight and gratitude. Secular, casual or even profane interest does not negate the primarily spiritual function of dance. What amuses the gods must amuse man, and what was given by them cannot be wrongly used. A dancer must pray before performing even in a dance as erotic as the Joget, and an array of offerings is always placed in the dance arena before the music begins. To the Balinese, dancing and music, by propitiating the bad spirits and incurring favor with the good, weave a magic, protective spell over the island.

Sometimes the relation between art and religion is perfunctory. I have seen temple purification ceremonies—which must include a shadow play—in the daytime. Since sunshine makes the performance impossible, the music plays, the reciter recites, but the puppeteer scarcely makes the effort of moving his puppets, and no one watches the haphazard, token motions. But the gods understand.

Dance is also of practical service to religion. If a community is poor and in need of specific funds for rebuilding a temple, or if the temple's relics are dilapidated and need to be replaced, then a troupe sets out to collect funds. Wherever they are invited they will perform, and the length of a performance depends on the amount of money given. During the large annual festivals of major importance, troupes of strolling players travel all over the island and it is not only good luck to command a performance from them but necessary in case of sickness in a house. But the troupes sometimes travel far afield before all the necessary money is accumulated.

The religion of Bali lends itself naturally to dance and drama possibilities. The pivot point of Bali's religion today is the Rangda-Barong dichotomy, and this affords an infinite number of theatrical and representational opportunities that cannot go undanced, unsung or unacted. The only origin of Rangda acknowledged by scholars is as the Hindu Durga, Siva's wife in her evil aspect. But the concept must have existed in Bali long before Hinduism. In contemporary Bali she appears in a costume of feathers with long wrinkled dugs and wearing a grotesque mask of fangs and bulbous eyes representing a widow. She does all things vile from producing calamities to robbing graves. She eats the dead, and she casts spells over people.

The origin of the Barong is also equivocal. The face of the Barong is like a demon's with protruding eyes and long teeth. But it is benevolent. It appears in Indonesian sculpture generally on gates and doors to prevent evil from entering a temple or house. The body of the Barong may have come from the Chinese, who are known to have been in contact with Bali at least from the sixth century, and who probably brought with them their favorite New Year's dragon. Its fur is usually yellow and suggests the Indian lion. It is always played by two men under a cloth, one working the face-mask and representing the forefeet, the other tagging along as the hind feet.

The religious nature of the Kris Dance lies in the struggle between good and evil. Rangda is the ever-present witch of evil; Barong is the force of good that restores normality. The island balances in a state of equilibrium between good and evil. Rangda is never killed; the Barong never destroyed. Whatever evil appears, the Barong is ready to counteract its influence. No representation of the defeat or death of either is ever allowed for fear of giving offense to the real spirits.

Each village of Bali has its Rangda and Barong masks and equipment carefully stored in the temple godown. Rangda is a very present fear to the average Balinese, and the Barong is the only satisfactory source of comfort. At least half the formal dances of Bali concern themselves with some type of the Rangda-Barong friction. This high proportion is caused partly by the religious purpose of dancing which is to pacify the spirits and partly by the aesthetic sense of the Balinese which instinctively recognizes the theatrical color in witches and bearded animals, and the dramatic interest aroused by the conflict of good and evil.

It must be added, however, that the modern Balinese is not, as might be thought by his religious and dance practices, so superstitious as he appears. The interlocking of religion and dance have made each support the other. No Balinese wants to give up his amusements even if their origin is in superstitions no longer believed. A Balinese once told me that he did not believe in *leyak* (evil spirits that take human form), yet I saw him a few nights later on the edge of a paddy field terrace playing and dancing with all his might in a festivity designed to exorcise a *leyak*. (A man, it seems, the night before had tripped and fallen to his death on the spot.) To him this was only an opportunity to make music and have a good time. The religious aspect concerned him only incidentally.

If religion provides the essential impetus and purport of the dance, then Balinese work-habits and the nature of their daily living provide the basic posture, the basic movements—in short, the mechanics of the dance.

Chokorda Rahi of Sayan, a Balinese prince and a great authority on dancing, once explained to me the reason why foreigners never learn Balinese dancing. "Since they don't work as we do, they can't walk like us. Until you walk like a Balinese, it is useless to try to dance like one." Dance starts from the walk, and it, in turn, from work.

Work in Bali is not a matter for common man alone. Rather it is what all men and women have in common with each other. Princes work side by side with the lower castes. Dancers are no exception either and they work with their fellow-villagers. As soon as a famous professional dancer stops dancing, he returns to all the daily chores of his ordinary life. However, the best dancers because of their fame and publicity all over the island have a chance at making a better marriage than normally. Mario, the great dancer who created the Kebyar, is an exception of this kind. He married a wealthy woman, one above him in station. He now manages her affairs in something close to luxury.

Bali is a rich island by Asian standards but not so rich that the people do not have to extract its benefits. Work in Bali falls into three classifications and they affect almost every able-bodied person on the island: agricultural, transportation, and pastime work. Agricultural work is primarily the plowing, planting, irrigating, hoeing, weeding, nurturing and finally harvesting of the ricefields. The fertile soil which yields as many as four crops a year has to be worked throughout the year with no intervals of rest. There is also the gathering of tree fruits, vegetables and coconuts. A Balinese scales a tree by clinging equally strongly with his feet and hands. The result makes for highly articulated hands and almost prehensile feet and an extremely flexible division between the upper and lower parts of the body.

Although there are cows and horses on Bali, the main burden of transportation falls upon the people. A Balinese must carry his grain from the fields. Every three days is market day, and that means that there are pigs, oil, and cloth to be transported to the market in the hope of gaining a little extra money to afford new clothes, to pay for a semiannual temple purification, or to pay off losses from a disastrous cockfight. In addition, whenever there is a new temple to be constructed, men and women alike join in the sacred chore of transporting the soft sandstone, easy to carve but not durable, the only building stone that Balinese soil produces.

Women transport their goods, often of considerable weight, on their heads. This develops a core of straightness in the back making the spine almost rigid. The hips, like shock absorbers, take on all excess movement in order to keep the line of the back and the load on the head perfectly still. The eyes and their movements become quite independent of motions of the head. A Balinese carrying a load must be able to look to the right and left, lower his eyes to ascertain his footing and raise them to judge the weather or tell the time of day from the sun. A common Balinese greeting is a silent flick of the eyebrows and eyes toward friends who pass on the road. This in dance becomes the rapidly arching eyebrow and the eyeballs flying back and forth in their sockets.

When bending on the ground, it is automatic for the knees to splay wide apart, buttocks pushed backward still keeping the spine and head rigid. Often loads must be held firmly on the head with one or both hands. This, of course, trains the scapulae, and accustoms the Balinese to the strain of dancing for long periods with the arms held up. In the Kebyar the dancer remains seated throughout the thirty-minute performance, but his arms are never allowed to rest or relax.

Balinese men do not carry loads on their heads. They tie them on two ends of a bamboo pole and balance this over one shoulder. The pliant pole springs up and down with each step and the carrier develops a light, bouncing walk which adapts itself well to dance.

243

The torso inclines towards the shoulder burdened with the pole. The arm is held over the pole to steady it. With his loads the Balinese walks along the narrow ridges and pathways separating the segments of ricefields, and up and down the rising and falling terraces of Bali's countryside. He develops articulated feet and a very precise sense of balance.

The pastime type of labor covers a variety of miscellaneous jobs, which primarily require agile use of the hands. Bali is not a country of gadgets and therefore the people must depend on their own finger strength a.1d deftness. Toys to amuse the children have to be made. Thread must be spun and cloth woven. Balinese chain and braid flowers to wear in their hair both as ornaments and as a substitute for perfume. (Often a Balinese will create his own flower, that is, take the stamen from one and carefully insert it in another, and then pare off the edges of the basic flower giving it quite another look.) Most complicated of all are the exquisitely made offerings of hundreds of different shapes and patterns. All of these pastime labors, as well as the finger games characteristic of civilizations who depend on their own resources for amusement, produce an extraordinary degree of fineness and delicacy of fingers and hands. The hand of a Balinese dancer is as trained and obedient as that of a pianist in the West.

In all these work movements, rhythm is stressed. Without specific rhythms, the coordination of endurance, speed and efficiency in work vanishes. At the root of rhythm is breathing. The Balinese breathes in a controlled and steady manner in a special way during the simplest or most difficult chore. If you take a walk with a Balinese you will find that you are taking two irregular breaths to his long and steady one.

Work in Bali develops strong but not hardened bodies. The richness of the island allows for moderation. No laborer overworks or oversteps the aesthetic potential which natural work gives the body. The body is never muscle-bound or stiff from abuse. The rhythmic, easy manner of labor keeps the body lithe. The laborer's diet of rice and vegetables with a minimum of meat perhaps helps this flexibility. Almost any Balinese hand, for instance, can be bent back until the fingernails touch the back of the wrist, or can be compressed into a slender cylinder and pushed through a narrow bangle.

244

Balinese dancing is as much the product of the Balinese scene as its modern-looking, perspectiveless paintings which depict faithfully the look of the island. Out of healthy and active physical movements and work-habits comes the dance. They supply the basic dance requirements of stamina, coordination, and body articulation, but generate inevitably the movements themselves.

One of the things which surprises the Westerner in Asia, and even the Asian himself visiting Bali from other areas, is the enormous complexity of the groups of dancers performing in flawless unison and the orchestra's executing exact harmonies in perfect precision. Although there are assemblies of dancers and musicians in other parts of Asia, nowhere are they as large, as complex, or as orchestral or balletic as in Bali. In fact, an "orchestra" in India or Japan in a classic as opposed to a Western-influenced sense is scarcely more than several instruments duplicating the same melodies or improvising casually a couple of melodies. As beautiful as the music may be elsewhere in Asia, nowhere are the qualities of concerted playing so elaborate and complex as in Bali. Perhaps some of this development is due to the group activity and cooperation that Balinese society forces on its members.

Much of the rhythm and coordination which characterize the movements of the Balinese seems to me to be the result of having always worked together with others as a group. The Balinese is never alone, in work, in play or in his arts. And the Westerner used to doors that lock, reading books in solitude, the long, lonely walk, is apt to find the lack of this solitude in Bali a little oppressive. The Balinese is, of course, first an individual with responsibilities and specific duties of his own, but he belongs to a family and ultimately to his village, and now that nationalism has struck Bali with full force, he belongs to Indonesia as a whole.

Individual labor is sufficient only when fitted together with the additional labors of the full, well-balanced family village and country groups. A badly functioning water drain on one paddyfield not only means damage to one's own rice but to layers and layers of paddyfield further down the terraces. Repair and maintenance of the elaborate irrigation system is therefore the responsibility of an entire group. As rain devastates a ripe crop, rice harvesting must be done quickly and the labor of several people is required immediately—again, a

245

traditionally cooperative endeavor. *Tolong-menolong* or "help and be helped" is a proverb in Indonesia as deeply ingrained in Bali, at least, as the Golden Rule is in the West.

This develops in the Balinese an uncanny sense of who should do what, in household work, on the playing fields, in an orchestra or during a dance. Allocation of duties and responsibilities is carried out silently, without discussion, quibbling or resentment. An individual who thinks in terms of the group instead of himself is assured that sooner or later the work or play will equalize, and he will be helped by the others when he needs it.

In a country composed of a series of village units with no easy transportation between them (a Balinese will always give you the distance to a place in terms of how long it takes to walk there), there is of course a need for a village entertainment. And this explains partly the number of artists on Bali. But because of the exigencies of daily living and the need for work in the fields in order to keep the economy of Bali balanced, a large number of potential artists of a professional caliber remain farmers. A few of these are dancers who have become bored with dancing or music or painting, and simply gone back to farming as their only alternative. Cooperation and division of labor are as necessary in dancing as in work. In the same way that a man will help the group to harvest another man's crop, so will many people be able to replace a dancer or musician at the last moment. The entertainment does not depend on any one individual.

Group activity insures group entertainment. Balinese society is dependent entirely on itself for amusement. Movies can only be found in two towns throughout the whole island. "Canned" or prepared entertainment is unknown, and would be regarded by the average Balinese as a form of social irresponsibility. There seems to be a pattern of vitality in village entertainment and it follows a work-play ratio: the more physically passive and mentally intellectual the work (white-collar labor, desk jobs, and the like), the more passive the entertainment (movies, shows, and radio) and the less it requires participation of the spectator. The more physical the work of the group is, the more energetically, it seems to follow, the people create their own amusements.

The principle in Balinese society of the individual extending to

246

John Coast
Foto Kempen

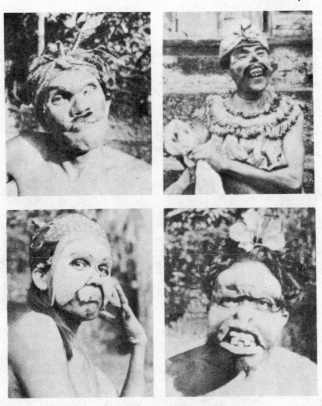

BALI

Stock characters of the dance-dramas

The deformed clown

The stutterer

Another clown

The ugly comedian

Dharmi, Bali's greatest dancer, performing a woman's double Kebyar

Foto Kempen

The daughter of Chokorda Alit rehearsing a Gabor ballet

Marguerite Brown

Marguerite Brown

Two brilliant Pen-
chak performers in
Ubud

Anak Agung Ngurah
in a classic Penchak
pose

Ida Bagus Oka of Blansinga,   Bali's most expert Kebyar performer

A scene from Severino Montano's tragedy, *The Love of Lenor Rivera*

A head-hunting dance of the Ifugaos in Northern Luzon

CHINA

A fighting scene from the classical opera

Puppets of the shadow play

The courtesan Yang Kuei Fei of classical opera

Mei Lan Fang, Santha Rama Rau, Faubion Bowers, and Ts'ao Yü in Shanghai (1949)

A scene from classical opera

Yü Chen Fei as a general on horseback in classical opera

Hsün Hwei Sheng, leading male player of women roles in Peking's operatic theatre

Three scenes from Chiao Ju Ying's "reformed" classical opera *Peach Blossom Fan* where new messages are poured into traditional style and form

William K. H. Fan

the group in order to create a larger, more important unit is transferred to the music and dance in the guise of the aesthetic principle,
simplicity multiplied into complexity. The principle works equally
well in reverse. The complex can be broken down into the simple.
The movements of a group dance can be performed as a solo or
duet when required, with no alteration to the movement or spirit of
the dance.

An example of another sort, in the orchestra, concerns the playing
of the two large gongs which punctuate the beat at wide rhythmic
intervals. They can easily be played by one man, but generally two
men divide the job between themselves, simply so that more of the
village can occupy itself with the means of entertainment. Some of
the instruments are so simple that village children perform on them,
and often when a Balinese tires of playing he will even offer his
mallet to a sightseer. There is even one instrument in the Balinese
orchestra which is performed on by more than one player simultaneously, *reyong* or *trompomg*, a long rectangle with fourteen nodular,
brass pots tuned to two octaves of the Balinese scale. The number
of notes any one player deals with is the three or four immediately
before him.

The orchestras of Bali are the sum total of individual instruments,
individually played, and is contrapuntally melodic. Each player plays
one melody at a time. In the larger more resonant instruments the
melody is a simple phrase, slow and short and repeated again and
again like a round. The smaller and higher pitched instruments like
the quartet of genders play in unison melodies of subtle and swift
complexity. The combination of all these melodies produces a polyphony and massive layers of sound. The chief melodic theme determines the name of the composition.

The difficulty of Balinese music lies in the intricate variations on
this main theme played by the genders and in the rhythmic com-
plexities introduced by the drummer, the leader of the orchestra. The
beat is always a basic 4/4, but the syncopations and added beats, the
creative, improvised expression of the individual drummer, are exceedingly complicated. The *reyong* provides the pulsation, the inner
core of the orchestra's percussive and chordal life.

When you first live in a Balinese village you think that the people
dance so much that they could not possibly have time to work. As

you see more of their lives, you find that work on the land requires so much attention that it is amazing that they still have the energy to dance at night. Because of the unity of the spiritual, physical and social life of the island, almost everyone works and almost everyone dances. Dance movements develop naturally from their work motions, and there is no contradiction between them. Artists and laborers are one, and each contributes equally to the welfare and happiness of the community. Livelihood and entertainment are in the end the same. A Balinese works in order to live. He dances in order to complete his life and make it fuller. And the foreigner today can have all the pleasure of this accomplishment without the hardship or work that has gone to create it.

PHILIPPINES

Dance

The Philippine Islands, while being an integral part of Southeast Asia and sharing with its neighbors similar problems and pleasures, still comes as a surprise to the traveler. Like other parts of Asia, it is a country of incredibly beautiful scenery with all the kaleidoscope of tropics, hill resorts, and contrasting modern cities. Manila is a major capital with enough appurtenances of convenience to make it a simulacrum of an American city—air-conditioning, delicious food, dance-halls, universities, and a moderate mixture of progressiveness, business acumen and indifference. The southern islands, from "fair Zamboanga" to Malay pirate hideouts with their tree-dwellers and pygmies, are no less vividly exotic than the pagans of the north to whom headhunting is only yesterday's reality. Touches of this combination of romanticism and modernity are found everywhere in the rest of Asia, and are not unique to the Philippines. However, the Philippines have several curious aspects which set them apart. Foremost of these is the pattern colonialism took in the islands.

The Philippines were the only area of Asia ever ruled by Spain, and later it became the only country there that ever belonged to America. The four hundred years of Spanish domination, started by Magellan in the sixteenth century, were peculiarly intense. The entire country except for the Muslim south and pagan north was converted to Christianity and the Philippines today remains the only Christian country in Asia. The Spanish policy of proselytizing instigated by the Viceroy of Mexico, who was directly responsible to the Spanish throne for the administration of the islands, took the form of burning heathen books, banning native dance and drama, and suppressing almost everything except an artificially inspired Catholic life. Whatever civilization the Filipinos might have had was largely destroyed by the Spanish. There lies over the Philippines a dance and drama aridity somewhat similar to what one finds in the Muslim countries of the Near East. Christianity and Mohammedanism share a missionary zealotry which injures the local culture.

There was, however, much later a good deal of encouragement given to the arts by a few missionaries, and of course the aesthetic instincts of the people generally are still apparent. The artistic vacuity of the Philippines today troubles the intellectual almost as much as his pressing political problems, and it troubles him like a guilty conscience. But because of it, more is actually being done about art than in many other basically more fortunate countries.

America took the country over from the Spanish about fifty years ago and began one of the shortest colonizations in history, but in its way it was as intensive as the Spanish. A popular catchphrase in Manila describes Filipino history roughly as "four hundred years in a convent; fifty in Hollywood." It is true Filipino jazz bands are as snappy as ours, the men wear sports shirts as loud as anything in Florida, and milk bars, comic strips, soda fountains are all accepted as part of Manila life. There resides today an affection for America and a closeness and frankness between the two peoples which, sadly enough, is absent from Asia's former colonies elsewhere. (Perhaps the friendly relation between India and England is another exception.) Of course, America was the only Western power that has ever ruled an Asian country smaller and less rich than itself. America also promised and eventually gave the Philippines independence, while in the rest of Asia freedom from the West came only after pressures ranging all the way from passive resistance to bloodshed. And these two factors explain perhaps the pleasant relations.

Culturally, the Philippines is a mixture of its indigenous elements and its colonizations. Dance and drama there primarily divide into four types: Spanish, residual Filipino, Igorot or proto-historic, and the Muslim, and these exist, in order, in the large cities, the main villages, in the mountainous North, and in the voluptuous, almost lurid, southern islands.

Of the four, Spanish-influenced dances are the least interesting to any outsider who already knows Europe or America. At any Manila dance hall you will see Filipinos performing rhumbas, tangoes, mambos and paso dobles, accompanied by electric guitars or banjos, and double basses beaten like a drum. They perform these with extraordinary grace. Were you to see two Filipinos on a ballroom floor in New York, for instance, you might easily mistake them for exhibition performers. This demonstrates that aptitude, in this instance in a Western form, which marks the Asian sense of dance. In most provinces of the Philippines the local folk dance is Spanish in name as well as movement—Polkabal, Mananguete, Surtido, Los Bailes de Ayer.

In Laguna, for instance, the Pandango Malaguena is a charming version of its original prototype, the Fandango of Malaga. The women dress in the puffed sleeves and the shoulder-framing wide collar of old Spain; the men wear the *barong tagalog* shirt made of diaphanous pineapple fibre, with ruffles and frills running down the front and around the cuffs. Both are shod in comfortable house slippers. The couples form a square and amid much hand-clapping and kiss-throwing at their partners, they skip in and out of the dance's regular, symmetrical, four square formations.

Another is the Subli from Batangas province, where the couples dance with bandanas and large panama hats. The women kneel for a time and snap their fingers in the air while their partners dance around them. Sometimes they dance with hats on, sometimes the partners take hold of the hats and crisscross in and out, over and under, until they have to untangle themselves from the twisted knot of arms and hands and hats they make. These same movements are again repeated with large bandanas, like the Handkerchief Dance of Sumatra.

On the islands of Cebu and Iloilo where some of the most conservative Filipino families live in the decaying elegance of Spanish aristocracy, formal balls are still occasionally held. For these, crinolined ladies and tuxedoed escorts, each with heirloom jewelry of diamond tiaras or pearl studs, perform the opening dance, a stately quadrille called Rigadon d'Honor. The chief and most repeated item of such an evening is the Maria Clara described usually as a "drawing-room dance." It was of such immense popularity towards the end of the Spanish times that it became something of a national dance and despite a measure of decline, it is still seen in the homes of the older families, in the larger villages, and on the stage whenever historical plays are enacted. The Maria Clara has its characteristic costume all in light blues and starched whites—long frilly sleeves, wide collars, and fans for the ladies; velvet jackets and tight fitting trousers for the men. The Maria Clara is essentially a minuet, full of bows and curtsies, gentle claspings of the hands high overhead, occasionally interspersed with a few lively steps of a polka.

In general, the influence of Spain over the Philippines seems extraordinary to the foreigner. It is everywhere, in dances, in daily life and manners, and in language. Converts were made to take Christian names, and the Manila telephone directory now reads like that of a Madrid suburb. Spaniards living in the Philippines like to point out that during the time of Spanish colonization when very few people went to school, there were a number of literary Filipinos who wrote Spanish better than most Spaniards; however, during American rule, while everyone went to school, this ability was, and is, a rare exception. Many Filipinos are still brought up entirely in Spanish, and even those who speak English or Tagalog or one of the regional languages, find their speech permeated with Spanish words and phrases. When a dance program is arranged by the government for visiting American dignitaries, the occasion is invariably called "Fiesta Filipina." And if you want to see folk dancing even in the remotest provinces, you must ask for "cañao" (from the Spanish for singing) which means any festival with dances.

But despite this domination, one at least of the Spanish dances in the Philippines has a note of protest against the colonizers. It is called Palo-Palo, and to the lonely accompaniment of a single violin it shows a row of Spanish soldiers, with stiff, high, military hats, blue sashes and wearing shoes, fighting against barefoot natives, scantily clothed, and wearing bright red and orange bandanas wrapped around their head. The soldiers are armed with swords, the natives with gaily decorated wooden sticks. The two sides move in stilted, high-stepping hops and jumps, and from time to time their weapons clatter against each other in stylizations of mock combat. Neither side wins, to judge from the dance.

The only two dances that I have seen which obviously were being danced in the Philippines before the advent of Spanish colonization, and which therefore can be called residual Filipino folk dances, are the Binusan Candle dance and the famous Tinikling. For the first, the dancer, accompanied by a strumming guitar (playing Spanish tunes) and an audience of clapping admirers (the rhythm of

252

the dance sounds beats one and two while three and four are silent rests), begins to dance in a series of virtuoso feats with lighted candles set in glass tumblers. He or she balances the candles on the head, rolls on the floor without losing a beat or letting the candle go out, wriggles arms and hands still clutching the candles, and writhes, twists and turns with increasing speed.

The Tinikling is another dance of the trick genre, and its popularity is such that it comes close to being a national pastime. Here four people form a cross with four long bamboo poles. In time with the music's simple 4/4 beat, they bring the poles together and separate them with regularity. At the center of the cross, on every third beat, a little open square appears. The dance consists of hopping on one foot in and out of this square without getting caught and executing various turns and variations. If you miss a beat, you get your ankle crushed in the pinching shutter of the cross center or if you miss your aim, you crash down on one of the poles and trip. An expert doing this dance makes it look simple, but if you ever get lured into trying it, expect to be exhausted after the first few jumps. You will be lucky, too, to end up without a limp the next morning. Nobody really knows the origin of this dance (you find it in several places in Asia), but one authority in the Philippines interprets it as a folk re-enactment of the greedy little rice bird who furtively peeks at the baited rice traps the farmers set as each harvest time nears. Both the Candle and the Tinikling dances are essentially more amusing to do oneself, like square dancing, for instance, than to look at from a spectator's point of view. Basically they require skills which are more athletic than artistic.

A movement has recently begun, largely inspired by Leonor Orosa-Goquingco, a ballet-trained dancer, to incorporate those folk-dance elements belonging to the Philippines proper (that is the non-Igorot and the non-Muslim areas) into a national school of dance. For one of her creations she took the Tinikling and added a thread of a story to give the dance continuity and variety. For others she has adapted purely Western techniques to Filipino situations and stories. But dance, even in these palatable rearrangements, is not the best of Filipino qualities. In Manila there is however a certain taste for ballet, as was proved by the successful tour of Danilova, Slavenska and Franklin. But if dance is to figure at all in this era of resurgent

253

nationalism which is affecting all Asia as well as the Philippines, doubtless its new form will be along the lines of present-day innovators like Miss Goquingco. But at the moment, in Manila at least, if you ask to see dancing, you will be directed to the Winter Garden Room of the Manila Hotel.

Among the Igorots or the aboriginal inhabitants who still survive in the mountains of northern Luzon, dancing continues as a part of tribal life. Most dancing is occasioned by weddings and by the conferring of tribal titles; it occurs before battle or headhunts, at deaths, burials, and at harvest or planting times. There is also dancing which the Igorots call "general welfare." This takes place when a visitor or official brings a pig for the village and everyone celebrates. Since liquor flows freely in this part of the world, the people will also start dancing simply for a few bottles of the local rum, and this too is classified as "general welfare."

Headhunting has been discouraged since American times—except for a brief interlude during the Japanese occupation—and the Igorots now use in their dances belonging to these occasions the nut of a tree fern which substitutes for a real head. One tribe, the Ifugaos, use a special head of carved wood. The headhunting dance is now performed whenever a person dies from violence—a fall, an accident, lightning striking; the urges of the people in these directions are vicariously satisfied by this. Dancing is also considered a kind of medicine, and if all other remedies fail, a dance is always sure to cure the sick and ailing.

The formula for all dance in the Luzon hill area is similar, although the most colorful dances are found in the Kalinga area. Both men and women dance at the same time. They always move in a circle clockwise and direct the dance toward the center of the ring. The accompaniment consists of songs and gongs—round discs of bronze, the larger ones being called "male" and the smaller ones "female," and some of the older ones have a quantity of gold and silver alloyed with the metal to improve the tone. The rhythm for each type of dance varies rather more than the actual gestures do. Sometimes the arms extend out like airplane wings and the hands pat the air. The women rarely lift their feet but clutch the ground with their toes and wriggle along the circle. The men hop a good deal, and sometimes slap their feet against the ground with a loud smack for emphasis. Both men and women saw the air with their hands in regular, back and forward motions. Sometimes they hold the flat palms near the hips, sometimes they rub the back of their index fingers against their hips as if poking at the ground behind them. The dancers themselves add a kind of percussion to the throbbing of the gongs. They breathe heavily, sigh and heave or pant, and these sound effects substitute for a drum. The climax of the Vengeance Dance comes when the dancers emit several long sustained hushes, like "shh, shh, shh." This means, I am told, "Keep quiet, for we have succeeded and taken our revenge."

Although the Spanish had little or no effect on the Igorots (they were apparently too fierce to be converted), the Japanese and the Americans did. One of the dances done in Bontoc, the capital of the Mountain Province, performed in a circle with the men in the center and the women hovering in another circle around them, is accompanied by a song which lists the people's grievances against the Japanese soldiers. But the dance itself is non-pictorial and simply serves as a succession of movements to keep in time with the rhythm. Another of the Bontoc dances is the Bontoc Bogé, derived, surprisingly enough, from the Boogey Woogie. The men dance more directly towards the women—an innovation in this part of the world. They occasionally cross hands and the woman turns around under the man's arms, and from time to time they walk slowly side by side for a few steps. At the end the couples shake hands. For most dances the people are fairly naked—a thin loin cloth and tiny basket hat with feathers from the red hornbill for the men, and a short, woven skirt and blouse for the women. Nowadays, some men like to dance with souvenirs of World War II—a khaki shirt or a G.I. helmet liner. The best dancers, it appears, are ex-soldiers of the Constabulary or the guerrillas. They were kept in practice by performing so much for the Americans with whom they were stationed after the reoccupation of the Philippines.

The most important dancing in the Philippines, both artistically and visually, is found among the Muslims or Moros (from the word Moor introduced by the Spanish) in the South. This is a curious phenomenon, because in the Arab world in Asia and elsewhere, for example, in Northern India where Mohammedanism has been so widespread, dance has declined. The exception to this is of course

Indonesia, but there the fundamentally Hindu undercurrents explain the prevalence of dance. Perhaps, too, it is Indonesia's proximity to the Southern Philippines and its cultural expansion (there is a large migration of Indonesians from the Celebes to the richer areas of Mindanao) over the Southern Philippines which account for this. Or it may be because the Philippines is part of this outermost reach of Islam. The remoteness of these islands naturally produces an emasculated, less rigid, form of religion, and dance obviously has not met with such antipathy and intolerance. There is no question that a journey through the Muslim areas of the Southern Philippines is one of the most dramatic experiences the dance traveler can have. And these Muslim areas have more dance variety and quantity than all the other areas of the Philippines put together.

In the heart of Mindanao Island is the tiny town of Dansalan, the capital of Lanau province and one of the most beautiful hill stations in the world. You climb the road from the sea and in a few hours you are there, nestled in a green valley, surrounded by pastel-shaded hills and alongside a vast, clear-blue lake. You are in a world completely removed from other parts of the Philippines. The people look darker and less European. The costumes are brighter, the head-bands decorated usually with an oleander flower are tied in a curious knot at the back, the sarongs of the women which reach to their armpits are held up by their clamping one elbow tightly to their ribs. Hospitality, music and dance are the special prides of the area.

Dansalan is perhaps the only place in the world where it is a pleasure to be an official guest and have the local authorities decide for you what you should do and see. In order to see the best the area offers in the shortest space of time, it is wise to arrange for the Government Tourist Bureau in Manila to alert Dansalan to your arrival and to have some music and dancing ready for you. There have not been many visitors to Dansalan, and a foreigner is something of an event for the whole town. My wife and I arrived there one day after having asked a friend of ours, a junior officer in the Army who knew the mayor of Dansalan only slightly, to send a wire ahead to say that we were en route elsewhere, but that we were interested in dance, had only a few hours to spend and could he arrange something for us. This request was purely private, and there could have been no mistaking us for anything but unimportant dance-curious tourists.

As we drove into the town, the mayor's office and the house where the dancers were waiting (both on the main street) were decorated with signs saying "Welcome to Mr. and Mrs. Bowers," and immediately hordes of curious villagers surrounded our car. The sounds of music filled the air. Everyone greeted us warmly ("Have you eaten? Are you not staying tonight?") and we were finally led into the house.

There, four girls, lightly powdered and with flowers in their hair, were seated in front of a long row of agongs—round, brass pots with a knob on top. The girls were hammering the agongs with sticks decorated by paper frills. The instrument is called Kulingtan, and is to the Muslims on Mindanao what I imagine the ukelele is to a Hawaiian. Each of the girls played only two of the agongs, and each performed a different rhythm from the other so that a staccato melody rippled up and down with breathtaking precision. Near them, two handsome boys of the town were holding gongs and pounding them with tiny mallets. On the floor another girl was playing a cymbal, the handle of which was ornamented with flowers, and near her a man played a goblet-shaped drum. The orchestra sputtered flashes of rhythmic changes and shuddering, fragmentary melodies.

One of the town dignitaries seated in the chair beside me asked if I found the music "romantic." I was far too interested to think of romance, but answered yes. He added that the Muslims of this area make love while they play this music, and went on to explain that only unmarried people are usually permitted to perform on the Kulingtan, otherwise everyone may fall in love and there would be divorces. To prove the power of this music, he pointed out that last week a boy had stabbed his rival who played the big gong while his sweetheart performed on the Kulingtan. The music ended.

A chair was placed in front of us and next to it, a tall, cameoed spittoon of silver. Then a man about fifty years old sat down. He wore a red plaid sarong over his loose fitting trousers, a white shirt with blue collar and cuffs, a bouquet of yellow flowers embroidered over the breast pocket, and on his head a wine-colored velvet cap. His name, I learned, was Macabangkit which means "destroyer of the

257

world," and was befitting his eminence as a great singer and dancer.

He began to hum in a low, throaty voice, and then as the melody rose, his head shook, his neck muscles distended and the sound came out like the dulcet cooing of a pair of turtle doves. Then he sang, "Our visitors deserve hospitality and praise," and expatiated on this sentiment for a while. Again the melody began to soar, establishing a strange scale of intervals and microtones I have never heard before anywhere in Asia. From time to time, he would pause on one of the notes and trill, as if impressing the tonality on our ears. "Before me sits our beloved pair from the United States," and then with a tap on the spittoon he opened out his fan—about fourteen inches in length, with several dozen, closely placed stays of red pine and covered with blue paper on which white birds had been painted. He held the fan over his chin, and waved it in a wide circle before his face ("this shows graciousness," the mayor explained). Then picking up a thin bamboo sliver with his other hand, he began beating on the spittoon in time to his song. "America appears to us as a reflection in a mirror. It teaches righteousness and democracy, and it is the greatest country on earth. Everybody knows that . . . The mayor is host to our visitors, and even if their visit may not be repeated, we most specially rejoice today for them . . ."

During the song, the fan was constantly kept in motion in a kind of a self-accompanied, one-hand dance. It spun in the air, curled around his fingers, and dipped towards the earth. Sometimes he would rise out of his seat to follow the swan-like archings of his fan and turn bright red from the strain of a long melismatic phrase. During the brief pause he would spit into the spittoon. "I am so happy," the song continued, "because I am singing, and if I kept this song inside my heart, it would surely burst," and he would dilate on these words. He began to tap his bare foot on the floor as the rhythm now steadied itself. As his head wobbled, the melody quivered. "Like resplendent wraiths they came from the sky [actually we had arrived by car] and they came here to the country we love the most. We want them to like our country, which is so beautiful, so invigorating with its cool climate . . . Our powers have increased by the Bowers' [no pun was intended] and the Mayor deserves his official position." The audience roared with laughter and shouted out their approval as he began mentioning people in the audience directly.

The singer then took up another fan, painted with flowers, and began to move them both. "Our mayor cannot be excelled. Moreover, he is related by blood and by marriage to all the distinguished people of all Lanau province . . . Yet everything he does is with the fullest cooperation of all . . ." The fans moved simultaneously, describing the curving mountain, the level surface of the lake, and like a bird in flight it soared and fluttered in the air.

Then the regular song-dances began. A young man sang a few. His name was Mamasaranao or "man of Lanau." One song was about a man who loved a girl so much he did not know what to do. Another was a war song about Bantogan, the warrior-hero of Lanau, who sang and danced with two fans, "just like this," before he went into battle. The words went, "he fought everywhere, all over the island, and everywhere in each city, he had a lover." The singer peered through the spokes of the fans, framed his face with them, and then rising to dance out a valiant exploit, he flicked them slowly so that they drooped forward, then held them out before him with the pattern in full view, and finally plunged them to his feet. Meanwhile, during the dance portions, the appreciative audience shouted, "Do it harder" or "Don't stop now."

One of the town's dancing girls then performed. She was dressed in a white-and-gold skirt and a transparent blouse of pineapple fibre, and her hair was tied in a knot on the side of her head. Her body was covered with jewelry all made from gold coins—bracelets, a necklace, buttons for her blouse, earrings and a brooch stuck on one shoulder. She sang and danced (there is no separation between the two arts) standing up, and she danced alone. Two people never dance at the same time, nor do men and women ever perform together. She postured with her two fans, and walked with a casual, hip-swinging abandon that delighted all of us. When she sang, she gesticulated. "We are happy that our honored visitors have come from faraway land (she could not pronounce "America" and the Mayor apologized to me), and concluded her song and dance with "Who would not agree that it is romantic to be entertained with a beautiful song?" She was too shy to dance anymore, and I inferred that the rest of her repertoire was of a more seductive and private sort.

The performance over, the Mayor walked us back to our car. "Do you like our Kulingtan? Did you like the dance?" I tried to explain how impressed I had been with this graceful and refreshing coupling of the arts and the charm and skill of the improvisation. The Mayor smiled and said, "Sometimes Christian brothers think what we do is noisy or immoral, but how much we love our arts." He waved his hand at what by then must have been the entire population of Dansalan clustering around to hear the music and have a look at the dancing. "Look at this crowd, they have only to hear the sound and they will come any distance."

We got into the car, and suddenly he looked grave, and as an afterthought asked, "Tell me, what about this darkening situation of the world today?" After the enchantment of such music and dance I had quite forgotten politics or that there could be anything in the world ever to ruffle the charm of Dansalan. We waved goodbye.

Even more impressive, if that is possible, both as country and as a dance area are the Sulu islands, the southern and westernmost extremities of the Philippines, and another stronghold of Muslim culture. The Sulus are an archipelago of hundreds of South Sea islands, rocks, reefs, and sand banks, some of which, although inhabited, appear only at low tide. And the islands' commodities range from pearls, for which the area is famous throughout the world, to turtle eggs, which look like ping pong balls and taste like gritty duck eggs, and birds' nests for Chinese soup, one of the islands' chief exports.

The largest of these islands as well as the capital is Jolo (pronounced with a gutteral "j" as in Spanish, and with the accent on the last syllable). And it is as romantic and as paradisical as Bali or Manipur. You find there a wide variety of people—sea gypsies who live only on the water in tiny boats they moor to the stilts on which most Jolo houses are built, courageous bandits who are descendants of the original "Malay Pirates," and the special Suwa-suwa dancing boys who are eunuchs.

The dancing of the islands is of a marvellously high standard, especially on Jolo and further south on Sitankai, probably because that island belongs exclusively to a professional class of prostitutes and young men, whose lives are dedicated to it. These young men, most of them children of prostitutes, are castrated. They grow taller than average and their flesh puffs out with the years. Nearly all I have seen have frizzy hair, but whether this is because of their emascula-

tion or the marcelling iron, I do not know. They are quite feminine
in their manner. While they are looked down on by respectable society, they are still called upon to dance at weddings and household
celebrations, and the outsider can with impunity have them dance
on the verandah of the town's one hotel without risk of embarrassment.

Suwa-suwa dancing boys work together with a prostitute or dancing girl (who may be his mother) and a dance program usually begins with the Sangbai. Sangbai is a rhymed and metrical chant to
introduce the main dancer. In Jolo city which considers itself "international," the Sangbai is chanted very rapidly in three languages—
the local Jolo dialect, Tagalog (the *lingua franca* of the Philippines),
and English. One of the English ones I have heard—while it does
not rhyme the way the others do nor even scan for that matter—does
give an idea of what Sangbai rhythms and meaning are like:

> Darling, darling
> Is my darling.
> Gentlemen, how do you do.
> This lady is from Jolo
> So nice you can
> Kiss her every Sunday
> She is so attractive
> When you touch her
> She will love you
> Sweetheart
> Answer yes or no
> Do you love her true?
> My darling.

Meanwhile the xylophone of bamboo, the *bula* (a homemade
violin played like a small cello), gongs and drums sound the music,
and the dancer quivers her or his fingers, slides the head sharply to
one side or the other on the stem of the neck, cracks the elbow
double-jointedly, pulsates up and down from a stationary position or
walks energetically around in a circle.

There are four basic dances in Jolo, and the word for any dance
is Joget. The linguistic relationship of this word to dance in Southeast Asia does not, however, imply any sort of choreographic similarity. Suwa-Suwa literally means singing but it refers to dancing as
well. It is used if you specifically mean a prostitute or catamite type

of troupe. Joget applies primarily to two eunuchs dancing together, usually singing at the same time.

Kasi Kasi Joget is a love dance where the boys follow each other around a circle, passing their upraised palms in front of their face, bending their knees, and moving their long, curved fingers with the rapidity of butterfly wings.

Joget Bula Bula, a dance of prosperity, is danced with a pair of castanets in each hand which click as they snap them together in rapid tempo, and the movements are similar.

Joget Ivan Jangai, a dance of long life and peace, is performed with special silver claws which curve backwards exaggerating each finger movement. These long nails symbolize longevity for some reason and the motions of the dance differ very little from those of the others.

Perhaps the most amusing of all the Jogets and certainly the most popular is simply called Ma Dalin Ma Dalin or My Darling, My Darling, and was invented about twenty years ago while the Americans were in Jolo. There is no accompaniment for this dance, only the constant snap of the open heel sandals which the boys cleverly manipulate with their toes to snap against the floor. Against this steady percussion, the boys sing to each other a short couplet, and wiggle their fingers in teasing or erotic gestures. The words suffer badly in translation. One goes: "How nice you are; I can hardly express my love for you." Another is: "A bird in the tree can hardly compare with your beauty." Another more seductive one says: "Come to an island; I will comfort you there." But in the language of Jolo they are immensely charming and full of double meanings. The movements of the hands look like sleight-of-hand tricks.

One type of the Ma Dalin Ma Dalin Joget is the Kinjing Kinjing, a sort of poking dance. As one of the pair turns his head up and down, to the left and right, around and around, the other pokes with his long pointed finger always just missing his partner's nose and yet making a pretty pattern of movement with the other. Shortly after Ma Dalin Ma Dalin was started by the dancing troupes in Jolo, it became a rage and all the men on the island began to dance it. Some entrepreneur built a special dance hall in the center of town, and night after night the boys danced while the women watched. Not long after, though, the building collapsed from the heavy pounding of the sandals on the floor. Since then the dance has returned to its monopoly by the professional dancers.

There are a few other even more fragmentary types of dancing on Jolo, done mostly in the villages such as in Parang on the opposite side of the island. These are non-professional. There is one spear dance in which a man gigs an imaginary fish. There used to be sword dancing, but the performers angered so quickly and killed each other so often that it was banned. Even boxing is forbidden in the schools for the same reason.

There are also short little dances performed by blind singers who gesticulate as they sing. These songs are beautiful, curiously out of tune to our ears, dulcet and subtly impassioned, and the themes are always improvised. A greeting must always be made to the visitor and praises offered to Allah or Awuha as it is pronounced on Jolo; and you can of course ask the singer to improvise on any theme you care to suggest. I once asked for a song about the sea, and the words came out, "The sea is calm, the waves are not moving, wherever we sail it is motionless." But when the singer finally hit upon an idea he continued: "There are times, even when there are no waves, a boat will capsize. All this is through the will of God. The high seas are deep but in spite of the deepness, and for an answer to the desire of the American we will sacrifice and sail out into the high seas." The singer went on and finally running out of inspiration or mood again, he sang, "Would it not have been better to take a picture of the sea? This would show its curiousness best to those who wish to know it." Throughout there were gestures describing the movement of the sea, highlighting a word here and there or languid waves of the hand to indicate thought or perplexity.

Dances of course cannot sound as affecting in words as they appear during a performance. And Joget dances, which are the slenderest enucleations of almost passing thoughts, do not lend themselves well to description of analysis. The movements are fairly varied, the flexibility of the fingers and arms is extraordinary. The angularity of the motions, particularly in the gesture of framing the face with the hands, arms extending out at shoulder level, the elbows and wrists bent at right angles, and the finger curved upwards making a picture frame around the head, is a new and pleasing extension of the concept of dance movement. The chief joy of these dances is in

263

the wonderful sense they give of whiling away one's time amusingly and pleasurably.

Drama

Educated Filipinos find their lack of a theatre tradition disturbing and the absence of a first-class professional theatre in the metropolis of Manila even now frets them. However, a country of more ardent and dedicated theatre amateurs would be hard to imagine. It is not fair to say that there is no theatrical tradition indigenous to the Philippines, but what there is stems from Spanish times. At Easter-time throughout the islands, in cities and villages, the Passion Play is enacted, and this annual event is important to the Filipinos. The Passion Play is always well-attended, even by the less pious, more amusement-loving Filipinos, because during Holy Week movie houses and all other places of entertainment are closed. But Passion Plays, unlike the religious dramas of India, are static and too specialized on a narrow theme either to produce great actors or to stimulate a theatre of wider appeal. These performances stand as an annual event with little bearing on the general or national theatre movement.

The only folk-drama the island produces, and this is of considerable interest to the theatre student, is Moro-Moro. Moro-Moros always have the same theme—the victory of the Christians over the Muslims—and tell this story throughout the islands in an infinite number of variations. The set, if there is one, is simply a tower on one side of the temporary stage to represent a Muslim stronghold and a larger, better tower on the opposite side for the Christians. Christian princesses walk onstage; they are captured and sold by the Muslims. Muslim princesses disguised as men fight Christian heroes. Always there is a theme of love between the chief protagonists, and always there are long battle scenes full of sword-fights, blood and thunder. The poetry of these Moro-Moros is epic and grandiose. Until recently villagers could recite whole plays from memory—often prompting the actors if they forgot their lines—and it was a distinction to be pointed out as the person who plays a particular leading role in a Moro-Moro. There is music—sometimes only a local band borrowed from the nearest military installation, at others sweet and sentimental songs such as Kundiman which has a plaintive note of sadness characterizing all Filipino songs.

Unfortunately, Moro-Moros have almost disappeared from Filipino life. They are never performed in the cities, although during April and May, the fiesta months in the Philippines, there will probably be a number of performances, some of them lasting for three days, in outlying villages. However, the consciousness of their value as a folk tradition and an awareness of their genuine poetic and histrionic contribution to any theatre of the future in the Philippines assures them of a measure of protection by Manila's large body of students and art patrons. Moro-Moros in their present religious forms were started by the Christian missionaries in the seventeenth century and were based on a dramatic form already germane to the islands. Because of this connection with a pre-Christian civilization, they are particularly welcomed by Filipinos during this period of historical introspection and nationalism.

The only other form of theatre which the Philippines yield is the Zarazuela, or song-plays from Spain, which had a brief vogue during the late nineteenth century and the early twentieth century. Zarazuelas were extremely popular at that time, largely because of their anti-American propaganda. The Filipinos had been promised freedom if they cooperated in overthrowing the Spanish. They fulfilled their side of the pledge, but the Americans remained in occupation of the islands. Through the Zarazuelas this deception was aired, and the revolutionary movement which lasted for a number of years was fanned by the actors and singers who made skillful use of propaganda. In one play they all dressed in various colors, and at the climax they momentarily assumed positions on the stage which produced the Filipino flag of independence. They immediately broke the formation and continued the story. Another was called *Tagalog Tears* and still another *Martyrs of the Country*, both of which contributed to furthering political awareness among the people. Zarazuelas are now rarely performed, although the music of some of them is still sung and remembered.

Remnants of the Zarazuela continue in vaudeville and their chief outlet is the Clover Theatre in Manila, the only legitimate theatre in the whole of the islands. It is here that the famous Katy de la Cruz, now in her fifties, still holds her audiences spellbound with humorous skits and tuneful songs of love and satire. The Clover Theatre, run by a Polish ex-female-impersonator, is air-conditioned, and a ticket costs less than a quarter. Several times a day, every day of the week except Sunday, thick rows of standees at the back as well as capacity houses applaud the long series of songs, variety acts, and brief comedy sketches. Katy de la Cruz's long popularity is exceptional; the average life of a singer is brief in Manila. The rule of the Clover Theatre and the Zarazuelas that preceded it is that as long as the audience claps the artist must give another song. I once heard the most popular singer of Manila, an imitator of Johnny Ray, sing fourteen songs in succession. At that rate, no voice has much of a chance to last in Manila, no matter how well trained.

The Filipino theatre in a modern and contemporary sense received its greatest impetus from the Japanese Occupation. The people were not only cut off from American movies, but were starved for any entertainment to divert them from the hardships of the war years.

A few tentative efforts towards purely modern theatre had been made before. The Ateneo de Manila, a college started by the Jesuits, for many years has not only had a high standard of education and instruction but has emphasized its courses in dramatics. From there nearly everyone connected with the modern theatre today stems. The Ateneo encouraged a respect for theatre and even produced two young playwrights who later became distinguished politicians, Don Claro Recto and Carlos Romulo.

Senator Recto, the most controversial figure in the Philippines and probably their most brilliant intellect, has written two plays, one of which, *Solo Entre les Sombras* (Alone in the Dark) was recently performed by the Dramatic Philippines organization with Emma Benitez Araneta as the heroine in both the Tagalog translation and subsequently in the original Spanish.

Recto wrote the play in 1917, and it won a first prize in Spain, a formidable achievement for anyone writing in a foreign language. It tells the story of two sisters, one rather conventional and married, the other educated in New York and unmarried, who live together in Manila. The unconventional sister has a love affair with her brother-in-law, with the result that when it is discovered, her sister falls ill and dies of grief and shock. The repenting sister leaves the house, and the husband finds himself deserted and "alone in the dark." The success of the recent performance was fostered to a certain extent by a controversy over whether Recto was anti-American in sentiment by making the faithless sister a returnee from New York. But with the public at large, the play was nothing more than a moving tragedy without political overtones, and an extraordinary piece of writing for a twenty-year-old who in the succeeding years has never found time to write another play.

The best of Carlos Romulo's plays, all of which are in English, is *Daughter For Sale*. It tells the story of a father who wants to marry his three daughters to rich men, but contrary to his desires, they end up marrying poor men of their own choice. All live happily ever after. Romulo has written a number of plays, all well-made, light farces, with a tinge of social conscience to spice them and give them purpose.

Manila today blossoms with several theatre groups—all amateur, all successful, all very active and deeply serious about their work, and all of excellent ability. The Dramatic Philippines organization started during Japanese times. Their plays were used either for propaganda to encourage the people or to convey messages to the guerrillas. It became even more active in 1951 and played short skits lampooning politicians and government officials in cabarets and night clubs. An historical play was given at the grand Civic Opera House based on the love story of José Rizal, the great Filipino patriot and his sweetheart Maria Clara (after whom the dance is named). Nearly all Dramatic Philippines plays are done in Tagalog, and for this reason they are referred to as *bakia* which means that they attract the Tagalog-speaking people who wear wooden clogs (*bakia*) which places them as too poor to buy leather shoes. Throughout the performances you hear the scraping of these clogs against the floor of the top gallery.

A Manila theatre at best is noisy. You hear the constant clicking of opening and closing fans which all the women carry. Since many of the actors are drawn from Manila's top social layer, performing as an act of charity, newspaper photographers click their cameras and flash their bulbs without stopping. But these distractions are actually less than at a concert by the Manila Symphony, which is performed almost in its entirety beneath Klieg lights and under the whir of movie cameras.

Perhaps the most unusual aspect of Dramatic Philippines is that it uses the theatre in part as a sounding board for public opinion. One reason why the *bakia* class loves these plays, it has been explained to me, is that on this stage they hear everything they think and that ordinarily they would not say in daily life for fear of controversy.

Severino Montano, the Philippines' most eminent and steadfast theatre personality, is a playwright, actor, director, and organizer. In addition, he has created the Arena Theatre which gives performances in-the-round at the Normal College in Manila. This type of theatre is not only economical and well within the reach of the general public, but it is quite suited to the provinces. In every village of the Philippines there is a circular wooden structure with bleachers (what the bull ring is to Spain) which is used for cockfights, the favorite diversion of Filipinos. Although its acting area is small, it still is adequate, and theatre-in-the-round has an enormous future in the Philippines. Montano's biggest success so far has been *The Love of Leonor Rivera*, a three-act tragedy about the ill-fated love of Rizal and Leonor (Maria Clara). Its brilliant second act concludes with a grand Maria Clara dance and the parting of these two heroic, beloved figures of Filipino history. The latest production of Montano's group was Robinson Jeffers' *Medea*, his first excursion into foreign theatre. To the outsider, perhaps Montano's best play is his one-act comic satire, *The Ladies and the Senator*, which is an almost vicious cartoon of Filipino diplomatic life in Washington.

The Barangay (Community) Theatre Guild was organized by Mr. and Mrs. Avellana during the Japanese Occupation, largely because they were cut off from making films, their primary interest. They started with an adaptation of *Private Lives*, transferred to Filipino life in Manila and Baguio. The Japanese at first censored it for being too Western, but finally approved it on the ground that it showed the decadence of Western life. But the second-act fight, so famous in the West, was excised, because, according to them, no woman should strike a man. Barangay Theatre Guild today makes its money from radio performances, although periodically they perform highly original versions and adaptations of foreign plays. The latest was *Joan of Lorraine*, which was half Maxwell Anderson and half Bernard Shaw.

268

Their audiences, feeling no loyalty to the original authors, approved warmly.

A number of the guiding lights of theatre in Manila today are either American men married to Filipino women or Filipino men married to American women, and the theatre groups that result are a happy mixture. One of these, Rolfe Bayer, a former pupil of Lee Strasberg and Actor's Studio, has created a fine Drama Workshop in the back of his home. There, a miniature theatre, perfectly appointed and artistically decorated, seats fifty people. Jeep lights with beam and dim strengths have been converted to footlights, local Filipino burlap has been made into curtains and backdrops, and ordinary cardboard provides sliding wings. His new group is still in an experimental stage. Their first program not long ago was *Three Studies in Fear,* designed to show the audience the potential power of theatre.

Another similar group is the Philippines National Theatre organized in 1953, the product of Gerard Burke, a man married into the Ocampo family, who was trained at the Abbey Theatre in Dublin. They have presented a variety of plays ranging from *Affairs of State* to Quintero's *Sunny Morning,* and have toured with the *Merchant of Venice.*

Jean Edades, an American of long residence in the Philippines, is the most active figure in university circles not only as an English professor but as one of the Philippines' most enlightened leaders of amateur theatre there. Her students have put on dozens of one-act plays, and she herself has commissioned and solicited dozens more from students of talent wherever she can find them. Perhaps the most brilliant of her discoveries is the young Alberto S. Florentino, who recently won two of the three prizes offered in an island-wide playwriting contest. His winners, both one-act plays, were *The World Is an Apple,* which shows the tragedy of a man who loses his job because he stole an apple for his sick daughter, and *Cadaver,* which presents the theme that the living are crueller than the dead. His hero is a poverty-stricken man who once took shelter from the rain in the tomb of a rich Chinese merchant. Seeing this wealth in death, he then becomes a scavenger and systematically robs graves in order to eke out a livelihood. Finally he dies from an infection contracted from one of the graves he has robbed. Most of the plays that come to Mrs. Edades deal with domestic problems, either complications in marital life or exigencies and pressures coming from the outside and affecting the helpless individual—the impact of the West, for example, being one of these. Many treat the theme of poverty with ghastly, horror-stricken fascination, some of them talk of land reform, education, and the many solutions that lie before the youth of the country who hope to build a new Philippines. Some are good, some are bad; but the chief impression one gains is that there is a voluminous amount of plays being written in the Philippines.

The most profitable theatre organization in the Philippines, the Manila Theatre Guild, is, oddly enough, not Filipino at all but is drawn from the foreign community of Americans and English stationed in Manila. Their corporation dates from 1951 and already their membership is well into the hundreds. A member pays about five dollars a year and pays only half price for tickets. They have even built a large theatre which seats nearly four hundred people in the back of the Army and Navy Club, and they average six shows a year, each of which runs for at least a week. The reason for their success is that they keep abreast of Broadway and perform within a year or so whatever is most successful there—*The Seven Year Itch, Born Yesterday, Dial M for Murder, Glass Menagerie*, and even a show as ambitious as *The King and I*, to cite only a few examples. They manage to use the music and the settings in a reasonable facsimile of the original play and give it a thoroughly professional touch. Manila Theatre Guild is of course an amateur outfit, but they have managed to achieve a theatre discipline and a cooperative group spirit that is admirable. The most dedicated member of the group is Virginia Capotosto who not only directs and organizes but also acts, and her persistent efforts in bringing Broadway to Manila have been rewarded by genuine success.

From the ferment in Manila, the drama has begun to spread to the provinces. The Tagalog-speaking theatre groups, the Arena Theatre, and even student amateurs from the Arellano University all make annual tours of the other islands. The result has been that the local areas are beginning finally to create their own groups hesitantly, diffidently, and amateurishly. One can comment unfavorably on the standard of Filipino theatre as it is at present. It obviously does not compare with Tokyo or China, but one cannot help being impressed by the tremendous yearning Filipinos show toward drama. Out of such a welter of good intentions, a fine Filipino theatre ought to emerge. Manifestly, there is too much talent for theatre in the country to remain submerged, forever content with poor stagecraft and lesser plays.

CHINA

The gigantic country of China contains in an area considerably larger than the whole of Europe about a fourth of the world's population. Despite this overwhelming bulk, there is little diversity. The Chinese are the largest homogeneous civilization in the world. There is less difference in appearance, racially and socially, between a Northern and a Southern Chinese than there is between an Englishman and an Italian. A common means of communication both in writing and literature unites the length and breadth of this vast land mass. An almost perplexing unanimity of thought about religion and social values, or absence of them, and about music and theatre solidifies China's culture and gives it a curious national consistency.

Of all Asians, the Chinese are the most familiar outside their country, so large a body of Chinese lives in commercial capitals all over the world. Wherever the Chinese go, they carry a shadow of the greatness of their country, which makes itself felt in countless places not only in a business sense, but sometimes morally (whether for good or ill is another question) and, unexpectedly enough, even theatrically.

The Chinese are passionately keen about their classical operas, and overseas Chinese, wherever they are in any numbers, soon build their own theatres. A traveler comes across them in places as far away as Southeast Asia or as near as lower Manhattan in New York City. Now that a Communist regime has taken the destiny of China into its hands, freshets of cultural delegations with actors and singers are being sent abroad by the government—to India, to Bulgaria, to Paris —and China itself is beginning to permit visitors from the West beyond the bamboo curtain where we can again see their theatre at first hand. Chinese theatre on the whole, outside as well as inside the country of its origin, seems to be the most available and most easily to be experienced of all Asian arts.

Asia divides itself culturally and in a broad sense between China and India. Up to this point we have been dealing with countries which belong aesthetically more to the Indian sphere of Hinduism, with its ancient tenets of religious significance and artistic dedication, and of dance as a primary art outlet. With China an equally powerful, civilizing force, India's sway over more distant countries thinned out, and China begins to dominate—in Vietnam, Hongkong, Korea, Okinawa and Japan. For a long period in the past there was a fairly steady exchange between these two spheres of influence though border skirmishes, itinerant pilgrims, and diplomacy. Indian Buddhism two millenia ago swept through China and her adjacent territories with almost as much passion as it had in Southeast Asia, and although mutated and degenerate, it is still alive there. The devout priest, Hsuan Tsang, made one tour of India in the seventh century and returned with several hundred Buddhist books and countless stories which formed the basis subsequently of several novels and operas. One of the most famous concerns the antics of a monkey king, who is obviously Hanuman from the *Ramayana*. And the lion stories and their stage presentations also have their remote origins in India.

Inevitably the pulse of Indian art, however faintly, beats through China today. If you want to build a towering structure of similarities based on relationships between the two countries, you can; but with China an enormous aesthetic shift in Asia takes place, and it is with this fact, that is, with the contributions and generic creativity of China, that we are primarily concerned. The greatness of Chinese art does not lie in its derivativeness or in contiguity of aesthetic principles shared with India. Having examined India and the areas over which it exerted its greatest artistic power, we are really only better equipped and more sensitive to observe the distinctness of Chinese civilization. Artistically, the two spheres are differently motivated.

The most salient feature of China to the student who has so far pursued dance and drama in Asia lies in the fact that China produces virtually no dance at all. It is almost an axiomatic generality that the Indian area is dance-conscious, while the Chinese area is more theatre-conscious. There are a few folk dances of sorts, a stilt dance in Swatow, a butterfly chase from Fukien, a lotus flower procession from Shensi, and a piggy-back dance from Hunan, but these are rare exceptions. This absence of dance has been something of an embarrassment to the Communists, who like to use folk dance as a means of fostering national spirit and to publicize their people as happy and cheerful. The best the Chinese could do was to import Yangko, a simple little skipping dance, from Sinkiang or Turkestan, China's outermost province on the borders of Russia. It is this alien dance which is now taught to Communist youth who use it to greet important visitors from foreign countries on arrival at the airport in China's capital cities. Clearly corroborating the contention that dance is not a part of China's life is a book published by the Communists in 1954 called the *Folk Arts of New China*. The only dances it mentions are those of China's most distant borders—Tibet, Korea, Mongolia—and among China's most removed and atypical peoples—the Uighurs, the Yis, Lis, and Yaos.

Instead of dance, however, China has both classic and modern theatre flourishing to a degree of popularity and grandeur throughout the country that has few equals in Asia. The classic theatre of the Chinese is more correctly called "opera," although some scholars object to that term because it excludes speeches and talking. Perhaps "musical tragedy with comic interludes" is the cumbersome but most accurate phrase. Chinese actors are primarily singers; the dialogue is punctuated with arias and recitatives. This in itself is not alien to the Indian concept of theatre art as *sangita* or the triangle of dance, drama and music fused into one whole. But where India has cultivated dance and music to the detriment of drama as such, China has developed the drama and music elements to a point virtually excluding dance. This fact, together with the existence of a full-fledged modern theatre, makes China's theatre and the Chinese approach to it closer to the West in one way. Chinese opera is technically nearer to, say, Italian opera than Indian theatre is to European drama.

The reason for the shift of emphasis from dance to drama is—this comes suddenly and with a shock of surprise as you move from India and Indianized areas to China—clearly religious. China, to begin with, is the least devout country of Asia, and I think as a generalization this too allies it somewhat with the Western world. China's gods are not dancers. The fragments of the Hindu pantheon that filtered through, and even the romance of Buddha, were turned, largely because of the overwhelming domination of Confucius, away from mysticism and toward moral values and problems of right and wrong. These were, it followed, determined not by gods but by human beings. The theatre trailed along and its interest evolved from legend to actual events, from religious mythology to actual, recorded, national history, from faith to morality, from the vague and mysterious will of god to arbitrary human judgment and decision. There are of course exceptions. Gods, spirits and supernatural happenings occur in Chinese opera, but the principle of this transition from heaven to earth, from god to man remains and in itself contains the genesis and operative force of drama over dance. Because of it and the attitudes they represent, a theatre divorced from all but the merest suggestion of dance movement and a modern theatre which eschews even incidental music have grown and developed.

When the civil war ended in a Communist victory, those of us who knew China and were interested in its theatre were worried. Many people feared that the new government would ride roughshod over theatre much in the same way that they were crushing the other symbols of old China. And there is no doubt that even by American democratic standards a good part of the classic theatre is offensively feudal and grossly reactionary. Much of it concerns concubines; scenes of cruelty, deceit, violence and revolt are usual; and solipsistic plays extolling emperors and empresses provide a good part of the subject-matter.

Fortunately, the present rulers of China proved unexpectedly lenient. There are, at the time of writing, certain governmental strictures on theatre and a number of compulsory changes are being made. But this degree of interference is scarcely new in China. Confucius himself once ordered the immediate execution of an entire troup of actors who performed a play not in accordance with his moral principles. And in the space of five years, as recently as 1935, forty plays were banned outright from the operatic repertoire. At best the atmosphere of any Communist country seems less desirable for the artist as we think of him than our own, but Chinese opera on the whole is being protected and even coddled at the present time.

Part of this may be political expediency. Opera is the main, and in

275

many areas the only, entertainment outlet for the people, and Chinese devotion to it is a formidable factor in the national life of the country. Unlike ballet in the Tsarist days, it is not an aristocrat's pastime. Any pedicab driver can sing an aria from one of the famous operas. The names of the greatest singers are household words in the most far-off provinces. And, internationally speaking, it is obviously China's greatest contribution to the world of the theatre. The government has little choice but to foster it. But more important, I think, is the simple truth that even the Chinese Communists, like the others, enjoy their theatre.

A friend of mine tells a story which illustrates this point. Mei Lan Fang, the greatest of the operatic singer-actors, was scheduled to perform for a week in Shanghai at the time it rather suddenly and unexpectedly fell to the Communists. When word spread that the city was taken, most prominent citizens were afraid to use their already bought tickets for fear of being seen at so classic a Chinese form as opera. To complicate matters further, Mei Lan Fang has always been a political enigma. He had grown a beard during the Sino-Japanese War which made it impossible for him to perform when Japanese officials asked him to. He also had declined several invitations from Chiang Kai-shek as well, and it was tacitly assumed that he too, like most of China's intellectuals during that period, was leftist by default. But he had been to America in 1924—he had an immense success there—and there was little doubt in talking to him that his sympathies were close to the American way of life. Certainly, he had never expressed himself as being in favor of the Communists and clearly opposed the new operas on suitable themes which the Communists were trying to encourage. Besides, most of his plays, whose stories were based on two and three thousand years of history, were hardly appropriate in a new and Communist China. That night Mei Lan Fang sang for the first time in his life to a nearly empty house. However, a day or two after, Mao Tse Tung himself arrived in Shanghai and while matters of administration waited, he and his top ranking leaders sat in the theatre applauding. Mei Lan Fang still performs as frequently as ever and before huge audiences.

On the whole the Chinese Communists, despite a flurry or two in the beginning, have shown themselves kindly towards the theatre. They even celebrated the two thousandth anniversary of Aristophanes, although this was as much for his being a "great fighter for Peace and Democracy" as it was for his place in the world as a dramatist. In 1954 fifty-three state dramatic troupes toured the country, and over fourteen hundred performances were given at factories, construction sites and villages. The Communists claim that three hundred fifty thousand people are engaged in various kinds of stage performances with their direct approval. These are of course mostly propaganda troupes. But because of the happy tolerance of Chinese opera, corroborated so far by reports from inside the country, by testimony of visitors returning to the outside world, and by the first-hand evidence of government-sponsored cultural troupes performing abroad, we can deal with the subject almost as if there had not been the intervening years of war tension and strain and the problems of the China mainland being cut off from the West by mutual political antagonisms.

Chinese classical theatre or opera is at its best in Peking, and it is from there that the art in its present form has spread. The word for China's opera varies from province to province, but *ching hsi* or "the theatre of the capital (Peking)" is the most current expression with the widest usage. It conveys the idea not only of opera as a whole in China, but in its purest form as it is seen in Peking. All other operas in China, and all its theatre, except for the modern, derive directly from it. For this reason our interest lies chiefly there.

More has been written in Western languages about Chinese opera than about all other Oriental theatres combined, but these records pale beside the mountainous bulk of literature the Chinese themselves have on their own theatre. From documents of the past, it is possible to reconstruct the entire history of Chinese theatre from its remotest origins to the present time in a way which is impossible anywhere else in Asia. There is a striking contrast between India and China in this respect. India which abounds with durable granite temples and steles of stone inscriptions has comparatively few writings describing its antiquity. China, on the other hand, which has almost no really old stone sculptures aside from a few rare caves, few historically important temples and buildings other than wooden ones (none of which has survived more than a hundred or so years of fires and floods), teems with manuscripts, scrolls, archives, libraries and written history dating from most ancient times. This too has a connection with the separation between dance and drama. Dance is a transitory, unrecordable art that vanishes the instant the dancer stops. Only its theory or the spectator's impression can be recorded. Drama, on the other hand, is essentially a written art, and while its actors disappear and their styles with them, the framework endures.

Out of the mass of material concerning theatre the first references which have a direct connection with the opera as it is performed to-day date from the T'ang Dynasty of the eighth to tenth centuries. One of the Emperors of that time established a college of dramatics, and to this day actors are sometimes referred to as "people of the Pear Garden," an allusion to the original name of this place of instruction. Theatre was a profitable venture from the beginning, but it was during the Yüan dynasty in the fourteenth century when invading Mongols from the North captured the capital (they were soon absorbed by the Chinese and eventually become indistinguishable from their former subjects) that the opera reached its height. Many of its best texts were composed then. One reason for this was that the Mongols, in taking over the administration of China, deprived large numbers of the scholarly and educated class in Peking of their occupation as government officials. This enforced leisure led them to the theatre, and many of them began to write plays for their own amusement. Out of these came the only masterpieces in China's theatre history, and they are the only works of drama that are still studied in universities as literature and regarded as having other than mere theatrical or representational merit. While technically there is as much difference between Chinese opera of the Yüan dynasty and to-day as there is between Elizabethan theatre and Drury Lane, the operatic formula clearly established then is still followed.

The actual crystallization of Chinese opera, as we see it now, dates from the nineteenth century during the rule of the Manchus. The Manchus, like the Mongols, were another racial fragment of what we think of as Chinese, and they too were absorbed as soon as they established their conquest of Peking. In the beginning, to insure a strict measure of control over the capital, the Manchu emperor decreed that no courtier could go farther than sixty miles from the capital. This was a boon to theatre, and both public and private dramatic entertainments mushroomed. Many of the princely palaces at Peking

278

had their own troupes, and nobles patronized the artists generously. The late Empress Dowager, the last of China's hereditary rulers, whose reign extended well into this century, was passionately keen about opera, and even acted privately before her friends and courtiers. She constructed a special triple-deck stage with pulleys and ropes to haul actors from one level to another, depending on whether the action was taking place in heaven, hell or on earth, and this building still stands in the Summer Palace in Peking. The property and wardrobe rooms are now sealed and no longer used, but the theatre house has been turned into a national monument under the protection of the government.

Theatre is never entirely free from the political vicissitudes which sometimes surround it, and during the dark days of China in this century when the country suffered in rapid succession the end of an Imperial dynasty, several revolutions, a questionable measure of foreign interference, Chiang Kai-shek's anomalous rule, and now the Communists, only the genius of the actor-singer, Dr. Mei Lan Fang, the great performer of female roles, has been able to give a degree of tranquility to the art. China has been extremely fortunate in having him at this juncture of its theatrical history.

Mei Lan Fang is known to Europe and America from his brilliant but brief tour thirty years ago. But it is only in his setting in China and without the concessions a foreign tour entails for any Asian artist performing abroad that his extraordinary attainment can be grasped. The position of the actor in China has never been exalted. Chinese theatrical history is full of stories of handsome men and women of the stage seducing or being seduced by ardent theatre fans. Imperial households have even been thrown into chaos by passionate relationships between actresses and emperors or actors and empresses. Because of the dangerous and immoral associations, for centuries the statute remained on Chinese legal code books classifying actors for purposes of jurisprudence with "prostitutes, barbers, and bath attendants." Even their children were debarred from official or respectable employment "unto the third generation." Scurrility has always been associated with theatre in China, and the Emperor Chien Lung in the eighteenth century barred women from the stage entirely in an effort to rescue it from some of its depravity. It was not until 1924

279

that women began to reappear as actresses, and in the beginning they performed with all-woman troupes, taking all male roles including those of bearded generals.

Mei Lan Fang, almost single-handed, has acquired for theatre a respectability which it had never known even during its periods of Imperial patronage and noble association. Through his talent and erudition he has achieved this miracle. Mei Lan Fang, born in 1894 of a long line of actors, made his debut at eleven in a woman's role. He was one of the first actors to be educated, and his title of "doctor" academically corresponds to his other title, the theatrical one, "Foremost of the Pear Garden." He was the first to apply the principles of general scholarship to the stage, and the result has been a series of plays in which he variously revived forgotten masterpieces, created and composed new music, and completely rescued at least one entire form of opera from extinction. This was *kun ch'ü*, more quiet and refined than *ching hsi*; it corresponds vaguely in Western terms to what lyric opera is in relation to grand opera. He used his education to restore historical accuracy to the stage, to improve old costumes, to discover new gestures, arias, and devices which, while complying with the rigidity of the past, brought freshness to the art. Of course, coupled with Mei Lan Fang's intellectual abilities was a phenomenal assortment of physical gifts—extraordinary beauty, a perfect body, and a voice, whose falsetto soprano is of such mellow clarity ("like a pear," according to Chinese) that even now, in his sixties, it still has the power to affect and move even the uninitiated foreign listener to whom Chinese music above all other music in Asia is apt to be disagreeable.

It is also due to Mei Lan Fang that what little dance there is in Chinese opera today was reconstructed and reinserted by him. His movements are in our eyes closer to mime than to what we think of as dance in a pure sense. He has reinstated somewhat the era of the past when the three arts of *sangita* were more equal. He continued the standard works of the Chinese operatic repertoire, but roles which he either revived or created became so popular that overnight they were performed by his imitators all over the country. His heroines—Yang Kuei Fei, Kuei Ying, Shang Yuan, The Heavenly Maiden who scatters flowers—have now become even more famous because of him than for their place in actual history or literature. There are many actors of great distinction in China, some of whose special eminence depends on Mei Lan Fang's own innovations, but even among them no word of criticism of him is ever voiced. Few actors in the history of world theatre have ever commanded such warm affection and adulation from his countrymen. The gentle, kindly doctor seems above reproach or resentment or jealousy.

There can also be little doubt that the immunity the opera is enjoying under the Communists is in large part due to Mei Lan Fang's unassailable position as an artist. The Communists, as might be expected, are opposed to the tradition of female impersonators on the ground of absurdity and obscenity, and in all the operas they approve and advance, women take women's roles. Kuo Mo Jo, one of the Vice-Presidents of the People's Republic of China and a great playwright of the modern theatre, a few years ago attacked a classical opera being performed in Shanghai. This was interpreted as the beginning of a move to ban Chinese opera. He chose as his target a play which tells the story of a villain who deceives the Emperor by saying that the Empress has given birth to a cat, and substitutes one for the actual baby. This, according to Kuo Mo Jo, was too foolish a plot for a people who must now be concerned with the reconstruction of a modern and progressive country. He further asserted that the techniques of Chinese opera were outrageous, again on the ground of irrationality. He stated that when an actor sings an aria that is supposed to be sad, it is still the same tune that a happy song can be sung to, that it is still sung at the top of the voice and against the same orchestral din that equally accompanies a battle, a rape or a disastrous fire or earthquake. The protagonists for Chinese opera replied that through the actor the opera becomes reasonable and the art becomes logical, and if the singer weeps in his heart, the audience will feel sorrow. And they had only to cite Mei Lan Fang to prove their point. Chinese demand for their opera was too great to oppose, and the matter has now been dropped. The government is even filming ten movies in color of Mei Lan Fang's greatest roles.

One opera of Mei Lan Fang's was recorded before the Communist regime in 16 mm film (1400 feet in length) and is available in Hong Kong, and, I believe, through Cinema 16 in New York. Called *Sung Ssu Heng* or "A Wedding in the Dream," it shows Mei Lan Fang at the height of his powers. It tells the Sung Dynasty story of a tragic

281

husband and wife. The couple during a period of internecine strife in China are captured by the enemy and although of noble birth, they are taken away as slaves. The wife exhorts her husband so urgently to escape, he begins to suspect her of treachery. He informs the lord in whose bondage they now are, and thus learning of her intention the lord beats her and sells her to a neighboring lord as a concubine. Meanwhile, the husband and wife have exchanged souvenirs; she has taken one of his slippers, and he one of her earrings. Thus, in the event they meet again after a long interval, their true identity can be established by matching the two objects which they will guard with their lives. The husband is of course distressed at his unwitting betrayal of his faithful wife and the cruel anguish he has caused. After their separation he finally escapes, returns to his proper country, and rises to be governor of the province. The lord who buys the wife turns out to be a kindly old man, and eventually allows her to go in search of her husband. She finds him, they compare their proofs of identity, and she dies in her husband's arms from consumption which she has contracted during her long search for her husband.

Chinese theatre, and there are dozens of theatres in every city of size in China, has a special atmosphere about it. Performances start early in the evening and last until well after midnight. The star makes his entrance for the first time late at night, around eleven o'clock, after the lesser actors have all performed and the audience is warmed and receptive.

Going to the theatre is also something of a family occasion. Mothers bring their children; businessmen bring their mistresses, and people from all walks of life including the poorest attend as many performances as they can afford. The majority of the audience is usually composed of petty merchants and shopkeepers, and the connection of theatre and commerce has always been close.

At one point in China's history, theatre was used to propitiate the god of money. Guilds of merchants were formed and paid for special performances to keep their particular god in good humor and smiling with favor on all their enterprises.

During the show, which consists of several plays and interludes of choice scenes from the masterpieces, members of the audience chat companionably with their friends or nibble on pumpkin seeds. Tea is brought by attendants constantly. In the old days tickets were not sold, you simply paid generously for your tea. Steaming hot towels are brought at intervals, if you ask for them, for you to wipe your face and keep fresh throughout the evening. There are no intermissions and the orchestra which sits in full view on the right of the stage does not stop playing until the entire performance is over for the evening. Silence from the audience is achieved only at climactic moments when the stars perform particularly difficult passages. Such moments of quiet are soon interrupted with a torrent of shouts from the spectators of *hao, hao* ("good, good" or "bravo"). Stage discipline as we think of it in the West is unknown, and intense attentiveness or concentration is applied only to leading actors and particular bits of the play. Actors frequently spit, blow their noses, drink tea, and readjust their headdresses, when not actually occupying the center of the stage. And with utter disregard for the actors' dialogue, the lead musician will tune his penetrating *er hu* (a two-stringed violin) several minutes prior to an aria. Children wander over the stage or peer out from the wings, and stage attendants with cigarettes dangling from their mouths set up blackboard notices reading "Is Mr. so-and-so in the audience?" or walk about preparing tables and chairs for the next play before the preceding one is finished, sometimes in the midst of a tragic death scene. While all this seems distracting to the foreigner used to an almost hospital-like hush in his theatre, and only Mei Lan Fang of all the actors insists on such Western-style discipline, there is a conviviality and relaxation about a performance which makes it natural and quickly acceptable even for the outsider.

The Chinese theatre by any standard is bare. You enter it to find the curved apron stage which extends well into the audience, covered with only a square rug of a gaudy pattern. Off to one side is a little box for the orchestra to sit in. There is no curtain, neither are there sets or changes of scene. Plays are performed against a multicolored backdrop which is owned personally by the star actor of the troupe. The brilliance of these backdrops increases according to the wealth of the actor, and Mei Lan Fang has about six of them, each more elaborate than the last. Stage properties are sparingly used, and consist exclusively of a simple table and some ordinary straight-backed chairs. They serve multiple purposes—as thrones, garden benches, towers (if the actor stands on them), impenetrable barriers (if a heroine in distress stands behind them), or surmountable obstacles (if a military hero jumps over them in an acrobatic tumble). A curtain suspended in front of two chairs symbolizes a bed (an actor "sits" in bed even when he dies). A castle wall, however, is represented more or less realistically by a piece of blue cloth held up by stage attendants with bricks painted on it in white. Wine pots and cups, brooms, oars (if a boat is to be indicated) are actually handled on the stage; but more stable properties such as doors, thresholds, and stairs are suggested in pantomime. An actor is always careful to pretend to open a door and he takes a high step whenever he is supposed to enter a room. Not to do these bits of business would be a solecism.

All entrances are made left stage, and all exits right stage through two doorways, which are the only means of access to the stage. During a fighting scene, the man who exits first is considered defeated, at least for that particular encounter—he may return through the entrance doorway for yet another bout. The horse figures prominently in plays and is symbolized by a riding crop. If the actor enters, whip in hand, this is sufficient for us to know that he is on horseback. One magnificent scene of pantomime occurs repeatedly in several plays. A footman pretends to hold a skittish horse while his master mounts. The two actors synchronize their miming—one actor holding and the other riding the non-existent mount which theoretically shies and cavorts around the stage. Another frequent scene is when a weary general (his degree of rank is told by the number of flags which stick out from his shoulders) forces himself again and again into the battle fray. At last his horse buckles under him represented by the actor flinging himself into the air and coming down to the floor in a split. He exhorts his horse and strains and pulls at him. Gradually with enormous muscular control he rises from the split to his full height, but the horse can go no further and collapses again.

Other conventions are also highly stylized. A ghost is recognizable by bits of straw hanging from his ears. Death or a swoon is portrayed by the actor crossing both eyes and falling backwards into the arms of a waiting stage attendant. Wind is shown by a man careening across the stage with a small black flag in his hand. Billowy clouds crudely painted on boards are waved at the audience to show the outdoors or summertime. A ricksha or chariot is created by two yellow silk flags on which wheels have been painted, carried by the actor himself. He climbs between them and whirls them while he pretends to ride off the stage. Fire, however, is used realistically—from gunpowder explosions to show the burning of a village to small funeral pyres of glowing, smoking incense. The foreigner finds himself taxed to understand the sometimes esoteric symbolism of the stage. The Chinese, on the other hand, feel that the detailed realism of Western drama atrophies the imagination and therefore impairs the spectator's highest aesthetic responses.

Altogether Chinese opera is classical theatre in a most formal sense. Through the centuries of its growth and popularity it has, of course, accumulated an enormous number of conventions, customs, rules and regulations. And it is within the rigid framework of these that each actor must work. It is only from accepting and recognizing the formula of this theatre that the spectator is able to appreciate and judge an actor.

All Chinese opera divides itself, not into tragedy and comedy as in the West but into military (*wu*) and civil (*wen*) plays. The total repertoire at present consists of well over five hundred different plays and scenes. Military plays are heroic, full of loyal generals, glorious emperors, wise government officials, all of whom struggle against traitorous, opposing forces. Civil plays concern themselves with domestic joy or sorrow, filial piety, faithful wives, and the effect of ghosts and spirits on the lives of ordinary people. Nearly all plots are drawn from historical events or incidents out of classical novels. The stories and their characters are familiar to the audience from childhood, and in a way it would be comparable with our theatre, were it dominated by Bruce, Canute, William Tell, George Washington, and the like.

Plot outlines are fairly uniform. For a military play, there is good versus evil, they fight usually after some strategem (climax), evil is killed (denouement). For a civil play, A abuses or deceives B, as a result B suffers (climax), C appears and resolves the misunderstanding or wrong (denouement). Revenge figures prominently as the clearest example of the moral necessity for righting wrongs. All Chinese plays are full of a high consciousness of virtue, although the heroine is often a seductress who causes a considerable amount of damage to the social structure of respectable families. The operas dwell on sorrow and any evening in the theatre always means at some point tears.

If a play ends happily, the audience has about the same feeling of surprise that an American audience has when a true-to-form Hollywood film ends tragically.

Although not too many of the plays stand up to full translation, the isolated scenes as vehicles for actors, however, are magnificent—the concubine parting from her lover who does a sword dance in farewell, the junior wife who gets drunk while her husband spends the night away from her, the general who tricks his opponents into abandoning the battle by leaving his city's gates wide open, the fickle widow who goes to her husband's grave to pray and flirts en route with a government official, the scholar who stays all night in the rain outside a pavillion to avoid in feudal fashion speaking to a virtuous woman (he is rewarded by passing his examinations), and the picking up of a jade wristlet, or the rowing of a ferry boat, across a river. These moments are all masterpieces of theatre.

In essence, Chinese opera is a virtuosic display of the actor's ability. But the actor has only a prescribed set of characters or role-types which he can personify. The stylization that controls each of these is rigid and opera would lose its special flavor if a particular set of mannerisms were not followed. An example to prove this is seen in the modern operas where women occasionally appear. They still act in precisely the manner of the traditional male actors. The system of role-types which has evolved substitutes for characterization or the representation of unique individuals on the stage is a subject I shall say more about later.

Role types are divided into male (*sheng*) and female (*tan*). The male is subdivided broadly into military heroes, handsome young men (usually a scholar), old, or comic people. The female comprises the *hwa dan* (literally, "flower"), *ching yi* (literally, "subdued dress"), comic maidservants, and old women such as mothers-in-law. Although technically Chinese opera is a man's field of endeavor, the female roles are its chief items of interest. While there are many celebrated players of men's roles, who are particularly famous for gymnastics, as generals, or for their melodiously tender renderings of scholar roles, it is difficult for them to draw a full house. The greatest and the most popular stars are all players of women's roles. As the Chinese would say, they have the most lavish backdrops.

Of all the women's roles in Chinese opera none is more enchanting than that of the "flower." She is vivacious, voluptuous, usually immoral, and a wholly attractive girl, concubine, second wife, or widow. While on stage she paces restlessly, her left hand presses against her waist, while with her right hand she waves a white handkerchief-like scarf. Her eyes constantly flash, and she never leaves the stage without stopping abruptly and casting a lascivious, broad smile directly at her audience as if there were a secret understanding between them. The "flower" dresses gaudily with headdresses of diamantes and sequins and artificial flowers. Swaying strips of cloth sometimes hang like streamers down the front and back, and these too drip with sparkling bits of tinsel. Her make-up of flour-white has, besides lipstick and mascara, two bright triangles of red serving the double purpose of eye shadow and rouge. The red extends from the nose, over the cheeks, and covers the eyelids to the eyebrows. This gives a flush to the face and is considered by the Chinese (and I agree with them) extremely alluring. The younger and more salacious the "flower," the deeper the red color. Around her head under her headdress, the "flower" wears an agonizing band of cloth which tightens the flesh of the face and draws the eyes up into an almond-size slant.

Hsün Hwei Sheng, one of the best "flowers" of Peking, is the only actor to dispense with this head-band. His unorthodoxy extends also to his mouth, which he paints into a cupid's bow instead of the traditional, tiny, little pout the Chinese call "the small cherry."

All players of female parts speak and sing in a falsetto except players of old women roles who use their natural masculine voices. The "flower's" intonation is, however, special, almost like a shrill whine which rises and falls with each phrase. She lingers on the "*er*" sound (the indeterminate "uh" with a Middle Western "r" tagged on) whenever it occurs in a word, which gives a sharp, almost grating brilliance to the diction. The hissing sibilants and throaty gutturals, especially in the Pekinese pronunciation, all make the declamation brittle and crisp.

The basic position of the woman's hand, and with the "flower" it amounts to a mannerism, is to form a circle with the thumb and middle-finger, then the tip of the fourth (the "no-name" finger in Chinese) rests on the middle joint of the third, and finally the fifth or little finger in turn touches the joint of the fourth. In holding this position, the index finger points straight out. There is no meaning to

287

this gesture nor are there any *mudras* anywhere in Chinese acting. Movements in general are made mimetically and depict action either gracefully or literally.

The most erotic part, however, of the "flower's" appearance in Chinese opinion are her tiny feet or "golden lilies." These are miniature shoes of wood hardly more than three inches long and an inch and a half high, gaudily painted in varying designs of flowers. These are attached to the bottom of a boot into which the actor slips his pointed foot (he is in effect standing on his toes) and laces it securely around the shins. The long, bell-bottom trousers Chinese women wear covers this apparatus and all that the audience sees are the delicate shoes presumably encasing an exiguous bound foot. The only giveaway is that the knee breaks rather high up the leg, and the "flower" is always apt to be the tallest person on the stage. These stilts produce a characteristic walk. While the neck is held rigid, the arms swing from side to side like a pendulum in front of her and the "flower" teeters as if on high spike heels. Sometimes in a military play a woman is called upon to assume the disguise of a man and she fights like an Amazon with her opponent doing cartwheels and whirls and balancing on one leg without losing her equilibrium despite her unsteady, artificial shoes.

Since all Chinese operas are laid in some period of past history, the feet of the women must appear to be bound. This custom, although no longer practiced in China, is sometimes explained to be a kind of guarantee that a woman could not run away from her husband or family. Actually, however, a more reasonable explanation seems to be that small feet are a sign of beauty. In Japan, for instance, where the feet of women were never bound, an actor playing the role of a woman still wears sandals half the size of his actual foot. The long, flowing kimono hides all but the toes of the foot, but when he removes the footwear at a gateway or before stepping into a house, the audience sees from the sandals remaining behind how dainty a foot the woman must have. The Chinese have always found the tiny feet of its women sexually arousing. In Chinese literature a passionate scene frequently contains a reference to the lover's touching or pinching his sweetheart's foot. And in the play *Going to the Grave*, the "flower's" prurience is climaxed when she sticks her foot straight out and waves it to entice a man.

The "subdued dress" women or *ching yi* are faithful wives, dutiful daughters, or any other long-suffering and truly good women. In these roles attention is focused on the long and beautiful arias and the sober, restrained and graceful movement of the long white sleeves. Mei Lan Fang excels here as well as in the mischievous "flower" roles, and in this ability to execute two such contrasting types he is again virtually unique in China. The other female role types are self-explanatory and in any case have so small a place in the theatre that they are little more than supernumeraries.

Of male roles the most striking visually are the "painted faces," *ching* or *hwa lien*. Characters who appear with their faces painted in these startling ways may be either terribly brave or terribly evil. Oily paints are used for good men, but a villain's must be powdered and lustreless because his face is not allowed to shine. White is for wickedness, red for loyalty, green and blue for demons and ruffians, black for uprightness, and purple for brigands. In general, though not always, the amount of white in the make-up determines the degree of villainy. Short black lines over the white base also indicate villainy except when they are used at the edge of the eyes to look like decorative crow's feet. These characters usually wear beards of red or black or white, which in general imply rank, importance, and excessive virility.

These make-ups are often grotesque and extremely strange to a spectator accustomed to the natural look of a human being on the stage. In all, there are around two hundred fifty different designs, and each belongs to a specific standard role. An average Chinese can name the role simply by seeing the make-up. Many of these masklike face designs, unlike those of Kathakali in India with which there may be some historical connection, do not follow the contours of the face. Artificial eyes may be painted above or below the natural ones. Fangs may be drawn on the chin. Some of them are no more than swirling spirals which start at one cheek and extend over the whole face blotting out all heights and depths or lights and shadows cast by the features. Others are graphic drawings of swords and objects.

The character Pao Kung, for instance, who judges all souls in the next world, has his face painted solid black and on his forehead appears a large, yellow, full moon. Another role representing a leopard which has taken a human form shows gold spots like coins on the cheeks, vaguely reminiscent of a leopard's spots. To accompany the grandeur of these extraordinary countenances, the actor wears high, thick-soled shoes, broad padded shoulders, and heavy silk brocaded robes symbolic of armor and military trappings. The actors sing and speak in a gruff and ferocious way, and their hyperbolic acting is full of bombastic, expansive gestures. In the special hierarchy of Chinese role types they rank lower than the "flowers" and "scholars" and are therefore paid less, which fact perhaps accounts for the steadily decreasing number of genuinely great specialists in "painted face" roles in recent times.

Scholar roles are gentlemanly, their actions quiet and reserved, and they sing more than any other males in the Chinese stage. They are always handsome, with white make-up, accentuated by a pale touch of red around their eyes. They also smear a finger-thick line of red on their forehead—something like an Indian caste mark—from the hair line to the bridge of the nose as an additional mark of beauty. Their hats are especially identifying with wide ovals of starched cloth sticking out behind them that flap like enormous ears when they shake their heads. Although their actions are virile, they speak and sing in a high semi-falsetto, and are rarely called upon to fight or engage in strenuous movements. They are often poor; always eager to rise in Government service, they undergo gruelling examinations, and are often victims of abuse at the hands of wicked, corrupt officials.

Every opera has several interludes of clowning. The clowns wear no make-up except for a patch of white across their eyes and bridge of the nose which looks like a pair of spread butterfly wings. The clowns, as elsewhere in Asian theatre, speak colloquially in ordinary language without poetry, allusions, or the archaic phraseology which characterizes the verbiage of the main actors. The clowning is riotously funny, even slapstick, and often ribald.

I believe Chinese opera is one of the most perfect forms of theatre anywhere in the world. It is an evolved art of a complex kind with a style governed by conventions and fixed aesthetic dictates. The actor must look the part, he must know the minutest shadings and meaning and gestural nuance, he must be an acrobat (this is to a certain extent due to the Empress Dowager, who especially liked to see her heroes stripped down to the waist engaging in feats of agility, juggling, tumbling and brute strength), he must sing and act, and he must not only observe the rigid technique but add a personal magic to each role. The Chinese artist is always appearing before an audience who has seen the same role performed hundreds of times by dozens of different actors. His spectators know not only the lines and tunes of the opera but its minutest conventions. And this places a peculiar burden on him.

The actor starts early in childhood learning the intricacies of his craft. Actor-fathers teach their sons as soon as a child shows aptitude for the stage. In Peking alone there are half a dozen schools where children are trained. They first spread their wings at special performances in early evening before the main show with tickets at half-rates. Specialization in the role types the actor is to pursue for the rest of his life begins immediately the child enters into training. In the West a role in a play is usually written so as to adhere to a true picture and at the same time to depict the human being on so deep an inner level that a majority of people can find something of themselves in the portrayal. In Chinese opera a role type presents a total of all the aspects which suit a character. When a man is bad, he stops at nothing; when he is virtuous, little that is admirable is omitted. The result is a concentrated essence or dramatic exteriorization which leaves little room for human processes or psychological motivations.

To the Chinese, theatre is either a model of ideals or the nadir of infamy. He finds it all the more affecting because it lacks the relevant human correlations we find so necessary. The emotions engendered are the same—tears, laughter, pathos; the sympathy and repugnance are the same; but the Chinese in their theatre are reacting to a different set of aesthetic stimuli. They are responding to a distillation of humanity and not to humanity itself. Aesthetically, it is a purer theatre than our own; humanly, it is a lesser one. Aside from its archaic morality, it contributes little to life or society; but artistically no one can quarrel with its deep satisfactions.

Anyone who has ever had an Asian ask him to explain why Bach and Beethoven, for example, are considered great, will realize how difficult it is to communicate the beauty of music. Chinese music which runs through the opera has, according to Western ears, almost everything against it. It is loud, noisy, banging, and more unkind adjectives have been applied to it by foreigners than almost any other expression of Asian life I know. Every instrument is strange—gongs, wooden clappers, cymbals, rattles, reed organs, raucous horns, shrill flutes, thudding drums and the penetrating, shrieking, two-stringed violin or *er-hu*. The melodies are confined to about thirty scales or modes, and sound repetitious to the untrained ear. The orchestra plays non-stop and at a fortissimo which is only relieved during special, rare moments or when the play belongs to the quieter *kun ch'u* category. A considerable number of arias are recorded, such as "Going to Visit the Grave," "The King Parting from his Favorite Lady Yü," the songs from "The Four Scholars," "The Fisherman's Revenge" and "The Pah Cha Temple," and nearly all of Mei Lan Fang's repertoire can be heard. The only thing for the appreciative student to do is to listen to them over and over again until order begins to emerge from the seeming chaotic confusion. If you make this initial effort, eventually the extraordinary charm of Chinese music will convince you that here is a bearable and rewarding use of sound.

Even before the Communists took over, several important artists, such as Chiao Ju Ying and Yang Yu Ch'ien propounded what they called "Reformed" Chinese opera. In these the music was softened, inconsistencies in the plots and characters reduced and made more realistic, and the stories infused with social significance. The Communists, while letting the old operas continue, are encouraging Reformed operas with as much energy as commensurate with the unbending traditional tastes of the people and popularity. Some of this is only a matter of reviving old operas which were formerly banned like *The Unfrocking of the Emperor*. But some of them are entirely new compositions with only a technical connection with the classical opera form. One of these new operas, *The White-Haired Girl*, was something of a sensation in China and even won the Stalin Prize for opera in 1951. It tells the story of a beautiful peasant girl who is forced to marry the rich tax-collecting landlord of the estate. He rapes her, her father commits suicide and she flees, her hair turning white from suffering. The peasants revolt finally, the girl is liberated, and everyone rejoices at the end of feudal tyranny.

An adjunct of the opera also fostered by the Communists is the shadow play or *ying hsi*. At one time shadow plays were a vital part of China's entertainment world, but little by little they faded in popularity. When I was last in Peking there was only one troupe left.

The puppeteer worked as a rickshaw coolie by day and occasionally performed at night at private houses for a rare engagement. The Communists have now subsidized this man, and a crop of young puppeteers is being trained to carry this simplified form of opera into areas where there is no regular theatre. The history of the shadow play goes back to the first century before Christ when the Emperor Wu Ti was shown a shadow of his favorite concubine on the anniversary of her death, and was told it was her spirit. When the deception was discovered, the Taoist priest who had perpetrated the fraud was beheaded; but the possibilities of the shadow as a form of dramatic entertainment were subsequently exploited. Colored leather puppets are held behind a lighted screen of transparent cloth, and the figures are moved as the puppeteer himself sings all the arias and recites all the speeches. Gradually the shadow plays took over the repertoire of the operas and became the "poor man's opera." The poor could see exactly what was being performed in the theatres by human artists without paying as much.

Another art which is of great interest to the student of theatre is T'ai Chi Ch'uan or gymnastic exercises. These quasi-dance movements are widely practiced throughout China. They are designed as exercises to strengthen the body, to extend one's control over it, and to cure it of certain ailments. In looks they resemble a slow-motion kind of shadow boxing, although many of the movements have an originality and novelty that elevate them far beyond mere calisthenics. Sophia Delza now in New York has studied this art and, together with selected extracts from the more active operas, has devised several programs of considerable beauty. In her hands the movements come as close to dance as anything actually found in China, except, of course, for Mei Lan Fang's mimetic scenes from the operas.

Modern Theatre

Contrary to the untraveled Westerner's preconception that the Chinese are inscrutable and expressionless, even the casual tourist cannot fail to notice the theatrical nature of the people and the daily dramas enacted on the streets of China. A pedicab driver will put on a real scene before his customer in the hope of more money. The streets often resound with people shouting or weeping out their sometimes real, sometimes pretended sorrows. That these performances usually improve according to the number of passersby who gather around, shows, if nothing else, a flair for the public that is a testimony to dramatic instinct.

On a higher level, the Chinese, unlike many other Asian nations, have a marked ability to charm and persuade, to present their problems and wishes effectively—a quality which amounts almost to a national characteristic. It is conventionally considered dangerous to generalize about a country, but all the same any traveler is certain to absorb countless small impressions that together make up a picture, however imprecise, of a nation's general character. In the same way that one is justified in generalizing about the Japanese, say, as being naturally artistic with their hands, you will find, I think, that the Chinese are a nation of actors. The enormous number of theatres all over China substantiates this. Shanghai's counterpart of New York's Coney Island, "The Great World," for instance, instead of being filled with amusement concessions consists almost entirely of theatre and forms of live talent entertainment. For something like two and a half cents, a person can spend a long evening moving through the large two-storey wooden structure of auditorium after auditorium seeing various types of theatre—opera in Shanghai-style, opera in Peking-style, parodies of operas performed by all-male or all-female casts, modern plays, vaudeville, jugglers, boxing matches, and a movie hall.

Part of the Chinese feeling for drama can be traced to their extraordinary lack of inhibitions. From the beginning, children are indulged. They play as late as they like, sleep and get washed as little or as much as they please. A Chinese in general grows up in an atmosphere of release, where restrictive manners and suppressive religious measures are, for the most part, absent from society. I have found that while there are a number of quiet Chinese in my acquaintance, a shy Chinese is a rarity. The bold environment into which every Chinese is born contributes somehow to a sense of security, and this shows particularly in being able to play-act without self-consciousness or fear of ridicule. This attitude has been a problem to politicians, and Chiang Kai-shek once in an effort to reform the Chinese character started a "New Life Movement" which among other things tried to inculcate a "sense of shame." The daily drama of China's cities was not affected while I was there, and even now under the Communists, according to reports, the street scenes, the little children's theatre movements, and the public and private actors have not as yet become plain and uninspired.

Like every other country of Asia, drama with music (as in China) or with dance (as in India) has been so deeply ingrained in the aesthetic consciousness that the idea of an unembellished theatre of ordinary speaking and acting was late in developing. In Chinese, the words for modern theatre generally used are "new theatre" and "speaking theatre" (*hwa ju*), but "Western" or "foreign" theatre would be equally appropriate because the history of this theatre is also the history in large part of Western influence.

The beginning of modern theatre in China goes back to 1907 when *La Dame aux Camellias* and *Uncle Tom's Cabin* were translated and adapted for the Chinese stage. Interest in this strange form of talking drama grew steadily but one of the first obstacles was language. Literature up to this time was almost entirely confined to the formal written language whose antiquity made it unintelligible to any but scholars. When read aloud, in all its special vocabulary and periphrasis, it was scarcely understandable even to them. The problem of these early dramas from the West at first concerned the near impossibility of translating them into so archaic a mould.

The vernacular, spoken language of the people called *pai hwa* was considered vulgar and unsuitable for any form of art, and the universities and government circles maintained this artificial barrier between the language of the people and the spoken word. A number of intellectuals worked to get the authorities to recognize *pai hwa* as a legitimate means of public or official expression, but not until 1919 when students all over China agitated so violently as to constitute what is now called the "Literary Revolution" was the point won. The vernacular was finally adopted for all literary and stage purposes. Only with this recognition of colloquialism could modern drama progress in earnest. The use of the language of everyday life now permitted a series of meaningful translations from the West. The native drama was, of course, modelled on these. With the language difficulty behind them, they felt free to adopt wholesale from the West an approach of complete realism, Western techniques of staging, modern dress (either of the West or of the local Chinese), and the exact, literal representation of actual human beings. Theatre houses with curtains, lights, and the usual Western equipment were built in the major cities. When companies went on tour, however, they accommodated their plays to the old-fashioned stages.

As in the question of language reform, the students were among the first pioneers in these new techniques. The students of Nankai University in Tiensin performed a translation of Ibsen's *Enemy of the People* and called it *The Stupid Doctor* in order to pass the censorship of the day which felt its theme too radical. Later, another group of students in Peking found a message of emancipation for women in *Lady Windermere's Fan* and produced it with great success. Shaw and Galsworthy soon after were translated and acted more for their messages than for their art.

Finally, Chinese playwrights began to appear. Ting Hsi Ling, a physicist by profession, was the first. He wrote one-act plays with problems in the style of Ibsen. Hung Sheng and T'ien Han are regarded as China's first professional dramatists. Their plays were anti-Confucian in that they deplored the old codes of moral behavior, and they steadily advocated the abolition of the family system, the right of youth to choose their partners in marriage, and freedom for women. These themes seem almost commonplace to us in the West, but they dominated the theatre as thoroughly as the problems themselves dominated the minds of the people who were seeking out fredom from the past. A play like Ibsen's *Doll's House*, for instance, which is already old-fashioned in the West, is still an exciting favorite among Chinese.

In the early thirties the modern theatre movement found itself in difficulties. The political and literary revolutions which had set all China in ferment and filled it with hope had soured. Intellectuals and idealists were forced into opposing political factions. Theatrically, there were painful reverses. The language itself posed problems. The language of the stage was found to be more than merely talking out loud as you might in your own home. Writers were confronted with the task of creating legitimate beauty and expressing new ideas in a medium which had been until then confined to the trivialities of commonplace life. The artist was suddenly without heritage or tradition to look back to for help. The wilderness of dialects and regionalisms which was opened up by the acceptance of the spoken rather than written languages seemed to prohibit a centralized theatre or a focused drama movement. The slowness of the Chinese to embrace a new attitude toward theatre proved an additional difficulty. Nothing seemed able to compete with the established opera. Most important was the fact that China's economic helplessness precluded the luxury of a live modern theatre with dramatists and actors earning their living by it.

From a theatrical point of view the War with Japan intervened opportunely. The feelings of the people were aroused and anti-Japanese propaganda inspired ready-made audiences and more than willing playwrights. The mass evacuation of the government, troops and even intellectuals to Chungking made the city a natural center for original and creative work in the arts as well as in the administration of the Resistance. Amusements of the local variety were, of course, unsuitable for the sophisticated evacuees from Peking, Shanghai, Nanking and Hankow, and new plays had to be written to match their sentiments and keep them entertained in their new home. Many plays appeared during those War years and the first of them was *The Gold Rush*, dealing with brokers who profited by the War through unpatriotic speculation, which unexpectedly ran for what was, up to then, a record-breaking fifty-four nights.

Outside the wartime capital of Chungking, a people's theatre arose. Twenty troupes regularly toured the inland provinces performing "street plays" or "living newspapers" (*hwo pao ju*). The Communists in the North were quick, too, to exploit this type of simple theatre as a means of stirring war sentiment. Hu Shao Hsuen, a Kuomintang playwright, produced the first of these propaganda plays, and called it chauvinistically *To Be A Soldier*.

By 1941 there were more than a hundred in the repertoire, the most famous of which was *Lay Down Your Whip*. This playlet centers on an actor dressed as an ordinary strolling magician such as you frequently see on the streets of any city in China. He stops at some street corner and begins a series of sleight-of-hand tricks. An accomplice, a young girl, helps him. After a sufficiently large audience has gathered, she begins to make mistakes and the magician finally whips her. A member of the audience (a plant, of course) rushes to her rescue crying "Lay down your whip!" and then makes several rousing speeches in favor of the motherland. The implication is that the wicked magician and the conquering Japanese are alike and the poor innocent girl is China. Whenever *Lay Down Your Whip* was played it fanned the fury of the Chinese and served as an important morale factor. Many of the "street plays" were also published in pamphlet form as literature. The government was pleased with the new theatre, as were the people themselves, and there were even drama troupes attached to most regiments on either the Kuomingtang or Communist side.

By the time the War ended, modern theatre had reached a high peak of production and a class of genuinely professional actors and playwrights developed.

There were at least half a dozen major playwrights who after long experimentation had evolved their own clear styles and forms. T'ien Han, one of the earliest of the pioneers, had finally completed his political and artistic development starting from simple plays of social reform and ending with colossi of Marxism. His most extended masterpiece is a 21-act tragedy of political import called *Ballad of the Fair Women*. It embodies what he calls "synthetic propaganda" in which slides and motion pictures are used in conjunction with the drama proper. The separation between audience and performer is minimized, and didacticism is interspersed with scenes of lively action. He is now the Chairman of the Union of Stage Artists under the Communists and doyen of modern Chinese playwrights.

On the other side of the political fence was Hung Sheng who became recognized for his moulding of the new language and Li Chien Wu whose moralistic farces brought laughter into an otherwise politically stormy period. Kuo Mo Jo, a poet, historian and playwright, acquired a wide reputation from his historical tragedies which he usually laid as far back as the third century B.C. At first critics attacked his plays for the wide disparity between their modern language and their archaic setting. The Kuomintang government deplored the plays for their unflattering analogy between the past and the then present. Immediately after the war he visited the USSR and later went into voluntary exile in Hongkong, only to return as Vice-President of the People's Republic when the Communists took over power. Also in Hongkong, under similar circumstances, was Hsia Yen, one of China's most able playwrights. His plays in the simplest possible language deal with the emotional troubles of the intelligentsia and the smugness of the common citizen. Like Chekhov, his plays have little climax, but they have power and are moving by their directness, sincerity and sound craftsmanship.

In my opinion the greatest of all the playwrights China has produced in modern theatre is Ts'ao Yü. Born in 1905, Ts'ao Yü first began his theatrical career in his teens by acting the part of Nora in *A Doll's House*, (women were still not permitted on the stage at the time). For a while he divided his time between acting and playwriting, but soon it became clear that his greatest talent lay in literature. Between the years of 1934 and 1937 he produced a trilogy of gigantic proportions which brought unprecedented popularity to modern theatre: *Thunderstorm* (nine editions), *Sunrise* (twenty-two editions), and *Wilderness* (twelve editions). These figures, which do not indicate the hundreds and hundreds of performances the plays have been given and their continuing popularity, indicate the immense success of this brilliant playwright; so far in China's modern theatre no one has exceeded him.

Thunderstorm, the most grimly tragic of the three, sets out against the background of a coal mine strike seven characters who are unknowingly involved in varying degrees of incestuous relations. The last act sees two of the characters electrocuted by a wire blown down by a thunderstorm, another commits suicide, and two go insane. The underlying theme is the uncontrollability of tragedy and man's helplessness against fate.

Sunrise also contains rather complex sexual relations which add a darkly emotional interest to a struggle between a scoundrelly speculator and some honest workers. The heroine has already taken a dose of sleeping tablets when her lover arrives. Unaware of her dying state, he tells her that the sun has risen, and spring has come; he exhorts her to join him in fighting against the injustices of life. Mao Tse Tung sent a special congratulatory message to Ts'ao Yü in Chungking after seeing its first performance and it was performed with great success in the Communist as well as Kuomintang areas.

Wilderness tells of a man frustrated in love who takes a revenge that reaches beyond the perpetrator and his unyielding lover to the children of both their families. In an agony of impotent rage he commits several murders and alone in the wilderness finally kills himself.

From this outburst of pessimism and tragedy, Ts'ao Yü progressed steadily towards hopefulness and a belief in a new order of life which would replace the corruptions of the past. *Peking Man,* another of his plays, tells of an anthropologist's research on the skull of the "Peking Man." He is presented as ultra-civilized against the background of the old-fashioned family with which he is temporarily staying in Peking. The skull becomes a symbol of the indestructible life force of man as opposed to the vicious superstructure of civilization. *The Clan* depicts four generations under the same roof, their clashes, the disintegration of the old and the triumph of the new. *Bridge,* his last play before the collapse of the Kuomintang, was concerned with the importance of industry in a modern China.

Ts'ao Yü also produced the best play of the War, *Metamorphosis.* The leading character, Dr. Ting, soon became a household word and her service in curing wounded soldiers represented China's spiritual unity in the face of Japanese aggression. Like all modern theatre writers Ts'ao Yü came in for political repercussions. The Communists attacked the play for presenting a noble character whose existence would be impossible, they said, under a government so bad as the one in Chungking. The Kuomintang had objections too. Before the play was performed, the Commissioner of Education ordered that some propaganda lines for their side be inserted. When the play was performed privately for Chiang Kai-shek, he asked that in future performances, in order that there be no confusion about the play politically, a Kuomintang flag should be placed on the hospital wall and the color of the stomach band (worn by the Chinese to prevent chills and colds) which a wounded peasant soldier gives Dr. Ting in repayment for her kindness, be changed from red, the usual color, to white.

In 1946 Ts'ao Yü was invited by the State Department for a year's visit in America, along with Lao Shaw, the novelist. After his return, Ts'ao Yü gave up the theatre temporarily and turned his attention to making films. He abandoned this too, and then embarked on a long silence, the "silence of despair" as he termed it, into which the political turbulence of China during the years immediately before the expulsion of the Kuomintang plunged almost every creative writer. Now, under the Communists, Ts'ao Yü is working, but another success of the sort he wrote earlier has yet to emerge (1955).

In 1948 an encyclical survey of fifteen hundred plays and novels of modern China was prepared by a group of Jesuits in Peking in response to the literary dilemma confronting the Chinese artists and their public. The introduction to the book has the following remarkable passage which I think should be quoted at some length.

> Modern Chinese writers . . . are atheistic, materialistic, positivistic, rationalistic, nihilistic, agnostic, sadist, a skeptical, freethinking, unhallowed crowd . . . Nearly all the younger writers were either intimidated or brought over to their (Communist) camp and became members of their rank and file. And as for the writers of longer experience and greater distinction, they were either intimidated into subscribing to the Communist tenets or, with an apologetic attitude towards them, were allowed to maintain a precarious independence, so that there was no one left with the courage to make an open stand against them. Thus the whole literary movement in China became a monopoly of the Communists. It now becomes clear that the writers and the works mentioned in the following pages will form nothing but a review of leftist literature.

I do not think this was written in a fit of passion, but even taking into consideration the perhaps prejudiced point of view of the Jesuits, it seems to amount to a condemnation of an entire nation's modern literature. It is of course true that a leftist tinge colored all of China's intellectuals long before the Communist victory, and this fact is a little puzzling to the outsider and disinterested observer. The proportion of modern playwrights who either opposed the Chiang Kai-shek regime or who were leftist or even actually Communist was staggering. Certainly it indicates the sickness that lay at the root of China's political situation before Communism. Modern theatre as a whole in China was born of revolution. Even the basis of the language and its right in literature was established by revolt. Inevitably, art of any kind came to be to the Chinese a weapon, an instrument of achieving social aims and political ends, or in other words, most Chinese felt the plight of their country to be so desperate that all efforts, artistic or otherwise, had to be channeled towards bettering the social structure. The plays China imported from the

West from Ibsen to Galsworthy contributed to this. Under the Communists this state of affairs is hardly likely to change. And while good art of course can belong politically either to the right or left, the incessant pressures China's playwrights have been and certainly now are being subjected to, may mean that a genuinely good, untrammeled modern theatre cannot continue, and that the brilliant beginning a Ts'ao Yü, for instance, has made will come to nothing. There is always the opera to fall back on or perhaps even the ardently Communist type of drama will turn out to be sufficient entertainment for the people. China's sense of theatre ought to be indestructible, as the phenomenal rise of the modern theatre shows, and fine plays logically should continue to be written. But then again there is the possibility that China will shift from her classical operas directly into the movies and ultimately do without a live modern drama altogether.

Part of China moved from the ox-cart to the airplane directly without the intermediate phase of railway trains ever appearing. It is possible, too, that China will avoid the conventional industrial revolution by going straight from an agrarian civilization into an atomic one. Perhaps there is a parallel with the theatre to be drawn from all this.

VIETNAM

Few countries were ever designated more accurately than the group of states that used to be known as French Indo-China—Cambodia and Laos representing the Indianized components, Vietnam as it is now called (the old provinces of Annam, Cochin-China and Tonking), the Chinese side. Over both there is still the thin layer of Western influence provided by the French who brought this odd amalgam together under a semblance of European rule and unifying influence. Perhaps the only thing this old terminology overlooked was the people themselves and their national aspirations. The recent independence of these separate parts of French Indo-China has restored a measure of political individuality to them, and the historic, cultural alignment with India on the one hand and China on the other has become clear once again on an international level, despite the split into Communist and non-Communist halves which has subdivided Vietnam.

The people of Vietnam are known ethnologically as *viet*, a Chinese word. From the ninth century, when the southernmost provinces of China were not yet integrated, the Chinese called all people of the South *bach viet* or "hundred viets," and even though they were racially very close to them, this was something of a pejorative because all the people north, east, or west and especially south of China were automatically thought to be inferior. Of all the "hundred viets," the ones in Vietnam were the most fierce in resisting China's inexorable march of expansion and absorption. In the ninth century, China annexed the area by force and called it, to remind the people of their subjugation, *Annam* or the "Pacified Southern Country." From this period onwards until the French arrived, the history of Vietnam was largely the story of Chinese mercilessness to the Viets and their struggle against it. From time to time, they threw off their shackles and immediately changed their name—sometimes it was "Nam Viet" (literally, South Viets), sometimes "Dai Viet" (The Great Viets), and for one brief arrogant period, the all-inclusive designation "Dai Nam" (the Great South). These periods of Vietnamese rule never lasted very long and the Chinese kept reconquering the country and reapplying the old humiliating word "Annam." Curiously enough, the new name Vietnam, which means roughly "The Land of the Southern Viets," is accepted as the legitimate name of the country by all Vietnamese today—those in the Communist North as well as in the South—and it now connotes freedom from both ancient Chinese rule and from the more recent enemy, the French.

The Vietnamese people look Chinese in physique and appearance. Their language is a tonal, derivative dialect that see-saws up and down their special scale. Nearly all the local customs are Chinese from kowtowing in formal society to burial rites. Until a few decades ago, when the French romanized the language by giving it the alphabet and diacritical marks used in Europe and America, their only writing was Chinese ideographs. They have borrowed from the Chinese with little or no modification Confucian morality, ancestor worship, a mysterious, implacable code of behavior, and even their basic eating habits—bowls of polished white rice with condiments of mustard and soy sauce served in dragon dishes of blue and white china. Their theatre as well, with its cymbaled music and historical stories of emperors, generals, filial children and dutiful wives, is altogether Chinese, except for language. However, Chinese theatricals performed in Chinese, at least in the Saigon area, the capital, for instance, are more popular than local ones, partly because the overseas Chinese outnumber the Vietnamese there.

The beginning of Vietnamese theatre goes back to the thirteenth century when a Chinese actor was found to be among the troops of the Chinese Army then invading Vietnam in another of its periodic conquests. He was captured and in exchange for his life agreed to train a troupe in the art and secrets of Chinese opera. This theatre was known as *Hat Boi*, the classical theatre of Vietnam, and still today is performed occasionally, undoubtedly in a greatly modified

304

version, under the subtitle "sino-vietnamese theatre." It differs in no degree, other than that of excellence, from Chinese opera.

The plots chiefly concern the period of Chinese history known as The Three Kingdoms dating from about the time of the third century A.D. The headdresses of red, fluffy puffballs and costumes of sparkling diamants and sequins are identical. The long white sleeves which cover the hands are waved around to punctuate the actor's gestures. The "great painted faces" have similarly terrifying make-ups to indicate goodness, wickedness, bravery, or silliness. Symbolism is preserved in that a chair is a mountain, a whip a horse, and a branch a forest. And even the Chinese poetic meters of phrases of five feet for sorrow and seven feet for gladness, are imitated despite the considerable amount of linguistic forcing necessary to make Vietnamese accents and tones fit the foreign framework.

Hat Boi has declined over the centuries. It is usually spoken of wistfully as an almost forgotten part of Vietnam's cultural heritage. It recently had a flurry of attention paid it when Doan Quan Tan, one of Vietnam's most distinguished scholars and former national librarian of ministerial rank, revived the greatest masterpiece in the Hat Boi repertoire and adapted it so as to reach the general public of non-initiates. To ensure that its proper merit received the widest and most sympathetic attention, he preceded each performance with an explanatory, exegetic lecture. The particular Hat Boi he chose was called *The Path of Hue-Dung* or "An Example of Confucian Wisdom," a Sino-Vietnamese musical tragedy in four acts. It is laid in the time of the Three Kingdoms, and in its womanless cast deals with the theme of friendship between men (in this case four devoted blood brothers who are officials of the Court and generals of the Army) as a higher attainment of the human being than even noble and self-sacrificing love between a man and a woman. Around a traitorous general who has usurped the throne stirs the intrigue and treachery so characteristic of Chinese opera, and his ultimate overthrow comes about through oblique and subtle strategy, forbearing obedience to the high principles of manly conduct, and a rhadamanthine sense of true right and ultimate wrong on the part of the four friends.

About fifty years ago a reformed type of Hat Boi arose called Cai

Luong and it is now the most popular theatre in Vietnam. In form it is based entirely on Chinese opera but it is a Vietnamese renovation and freshening of the form. The themes while still preserving the ancient appearance of Chinese pomp are given a social tinge which reflects some of the problems of modern Vietnamese life— the freedom of the individual in opposition to the family system, the control of the Mandarin, and domestic relationships between husband and wife within the home.

The music which interrupts the action at each important moment, however, does not consist of the traditional melodies but versions of old French and American songs. A four-piece band plays between the acts. Cai Luong is scarcely more than a kind of Vietnamese operetta and comes at times even close to being vaudeville. During a performance stage hands experiment with lighting, and the favorite effect seems to be drenching the stage in red whenever a revelation (such as a mother recognizing her long lost child) is made. The chief job of the playwrights attached to the few Cai Luong troupes performing in Saigon and the larger cities is to invent new plots and to fit new lyrics to the now established main tunes.

There has been an attempt to have a theatre without music or songs and dependent entirely on acting, words and humor. This is known as Kich. Its plays up to 1955 have been light comedies, and curiously enough, their chief area of interest has been among youth movements and boy scouts where children sit around a campfire, dependent entirely on their own resources for amusement, and invent their own Kich. During the fight against the French, a children's theatre of this sort was used partly to entertain the troops and partly to convey secret messages between the lines. The influence of the French on Kich is apparent and there are a few writers who see it at some future date as a serious form of expression with genuine contact with the people of Vietnam.

Vietnam, as I write, is a country in distress and its theatre reflects this as clearly as do its politics. The handful of intellectuals in the country write articles from time to time deploring their plight. One recently wrote that the Vietnamese were "awakening from a long sleep" and that at present there is only "intensity without content, exaltation without object, a sort of empty ecstasy." Another in speaking of the low standard of literature sighs that Vietnam is "quite sufficiently troubled and confused." Still another bemoans the fact that "the government takes little interest in problems of culture and art, because it is concerned above all else with propaganda." And he adds, "it is precisely art and culture which propose the best of all propagandas." But the true problem of Vietnam is to find its art and culture. At present what little there is, is of poor quality.

Meanwhile Vietnam, crushed first by a war against a colonial power, then torn ideologically into two opposing camps with both sides pretty much pawns of outside influence, lies culturally prostrate. The grand and imposing Theatre Nationale in the heart of Saigon and one of the largest buildings in the country, is today a symbol of the country's theatrical stalemate. It was built originally for troupes of French actors visiting the Colony to play the latest successes from Paris, but for most of the nine long years of the recent war in Indo-China it lay idle. For a while it was used for political rallies and civic speeches. Now it is filled to overflowing with refugees from the Communist North. It seems hardly likely that in the forseeable future it will ever be used for theatre from any country, Chinese or the West or even from Vietnam itself.

12

HONGKONG

Hongkong is an island off the South Coast of China, and together with Kowloon, a slice of the continent itself, comprises what the British there call "the Colony." The accession of this territory was the outcome of the notorious Opium Wars of the nineteenth century in which historians claim that England and America wanted so much of China and China wanted so little of them that selling opium was the only way to balance this unwilling trade. Hongkong has a considerable number of charms in its well-ordered, sensible way of life. Unfortunately, theatre is not the chief among them.

Although an integral part of China proper geographically, culturally and historically, Hongkong is like a foreign, neighboring country. It is also a kind of reservoir to absorb the excess population from the mainland. Many of these are seeking political asylum. When I was first there in 1949, Hongkong was like a vast Communist camp of leaders and intellectuals waiting to return triumphant. In 1955 it was rather like a secondary Formosa, full of merchants and anti-communist partisans who had fled for their lives and were living in despair. Most of the population, despite the influxes of political refugees, are from Kwantung, the richest province of South China, and particularly from the capital city, Canton. The theatre of Hongkong consequently is Cantonese.

Cantonese opera, called *kosing* (literally, "great theatre"), is basically the same as opera in Peking. And an artist like Mei Lan Fang plays in South China and Hongkong to audiences as large as those in the North who actually understand his words. Just as the Cantonese language is a dialect (it has, for instance, as many as five tones in its sing-song lilt while Pekinese has only three), so is the theatre there related to but different from its parent form. Hongkong, with its

308

strong influence of the West, is a clear illustration of the degeneration Chinese opera undergoes when it is so far removed from its home and apex of perfection. In essence, the form is the same—historical plays of emperors, generals, big painted faces and vivacious maidservants, actors' eyes that roll to the right or left in synchronization with the crash of the large cymbals, clanging music, arias, recitatives, and comic interludes. But a number of novelties have permeated the art and removed it considerably from its original, characteristically Chinese atmosphere. These changes have extended from Hongkong back to China itself, at least as far as Canton.

If you ask a Chinese the difference between the two forms of opera, he will say without hesitation that it lies chiefly in the music and the scenery. Music for Cantonese opera, and especially as it is seen in Hongkong, is called "yellow music" meaning that it is mock-classical and bears the same relationship to the art that the "yellow press" has to respectable journalism. It does pay a measure of homage to the classics, but it injects a note of sentimentality and softness into each aria, and often the tunes are even danceable in a Westernized ballroom way. The orchestra consists of mandolins, violins, and saxophones, and out of the exotic assembly of instruments in classical orchestra, only the wooden clappers and the cymbals remain. Every month or so, brand new music is composed (the themes can still be those of the older standard operas) to meet the jaded tastes of the modernized Chinese of Hongkong and Canton. This perpetual churning out of songs is, on the whole, about as trying and relentless for song writers there as it is for composers in Hollywood.

As for scenery and properties, the whole concept is alien to classical Chinese opera. The responsibility for these two parts of stage-craft resides, according to Chinese aesthetic theory, entirely with the actor and within the poetry of his lines. If an actor is worthy of his career he need only point for you to see a mountain or a lake, a spirit or a disaster. To depict actually and realistically the background in which the character is supposed to be moving can only enervate the artist's capabilities. To the classicist, scenery and literal properties throw the actor's miming off balance and stultify the fast-moving pace which imagined changes of scene give. However, in Hongkong, backdrops fly up and down—often in the middle of a scene—showing everything from castle walls, to temples, to palaces. Potted plants fill the stage if it is a garden; heavy moon doors, if it is a house, provide ingress and egress for actors who leap and spring through them. Thrones of cushions, exteriors and interiors of every grade of Chinese house imaginable add, strangely enough, only to the unreality of this Chinese stage. Because, the Chinese say, you tire of actual sets more quickly than of those your imagination conceives, each new play requires new sets to keep abreast of the exacting tastes of the people. To add to all this modernity, most singers stay near a microphone, and electric fans whirl over the performers on stage as much as they do over the audience in the hall proper. The spectators instead of cracking pumpkin seeds with their teeth and sipping tea as they do in Peking or Hankow theatres chew gum throughout the performance, and there is a spittoon at the end of each row of seats along the aisles.

In Hongkong women play women's roles exclusively and most of the actresses divide their time between the opera and the movies. The leading star of Hongkong and Canton today is the beautiful Fong Yim Fun, and if anyone saves Cantonese theatre from complete vulgarity, it is she. She is, of course, extremely attractive physically in that groomed and manicured way of Hongkong which appeals equally to Chinese and foreigners. Her singing voice, the chief source of her immense popularity, is of a crystal clarity and almost rivals Mei Lan Fang's radiant falsetto. Added to her good-looks Fong Yim Fun also has acting ability of a serious sort, and without apparent effort can make audiences laugh or cry.

Her fairly regular appearances are always at the Po Hing Theatre near the Peninsula Hotel in Kowloon, the best and most expensive of Hongkong theatres (a good ticket costs around two U. S. dollars). She plays only a few of the classical items in the operatic repertoire, so it is hard to judge her on any sort of comparative basis with her male models on the mainland of China. The constant newness and freshness she brings to the opera, however, is extremely interesting. Her costumes are extravagant, and to compete with the distracting scenery, every actor of her troupe wears an enormous number of sparkling sequins to keep the show glittering even in its dullest moments. The serving girls, for instance, who stand around her on stage as a silent, inactive sort of chorus, drip with diamond-like headbands and robes, bracelets and earrings. Fong Yim Fun spares no device

310

to increase her allure. Her sideburns—those little wisps of hair that traditionally are supposed to peek suggestively out from under the headband—are painted all the way down to her chin. Her palms are rouged with the same brightness and blush as her cheeks and eyelids. If she is playing the role of a Manchu Princess who is required to take a bath, she takes off her silk stockings and a few outer garments, and gives the same feeling to orthodox Chinese that a real strip tease does to an American.

But Fong Yim Fun still conveys, despite the blinding meretriciousness of her setting, a real sense of theatre. Sometimes she puts this to a test. In 1955 she starred in the first opera ever set in comparatively recent times and costumed in modern—again comparatively—clothes. The story was of a young girl who runs away from her home, she meets a man, falls in love and marries him, and it turns out he is the man her parents had chosen for her from the beginning. The first scene shows a London-style street lamp, a public telephone booth, and Fong Yim Fun in a grey travelling suit—something quite like what Queen Mary might have worn a generation ago—long-sleeved, high-necked, buttoned down the front, and the skirt reaching to the floor. In her hands she carries two Gladstone bags to indicate her intention to run away. The play was of course a success like all the others in the repertoire of Fong Yim Fun.

The only classical artist of Peking Opera of any note in Hongkong at present is Yü Chen Fei. He is a distinguished performer of *kun-ch'ü* (the quiet and formal operatic type revived by Mei Lan Fang a number of years ago), a scholar of good family, and a refugee from the Communists. He makes only occasional appearances and despite his fifty years of age still specializes in the delicate roles of youthful scholars. Formerly, he often played opposite Mei Lan Fang but now he acts with his wife whom he trained in Hongkong, for lack of other experienced personnel. Sometimes he also pairs himself with Wang Hsi Hua, another amateur actress whose real fame was as "Miss Shanghai" during Kuomintang days. Whatever comfort his political exile may give him, artistically there is little for Yü Chen Fei in Hongkong. His style of performance requires a taste for pure, undiluted Chinese opera, and this appreciation is more than Hongkong can give. The Cantonese like to understand what they are seeing, and not only is Yü Chen Fei's speech far removed from them, but his remote and austere *kun ch'ü* is insufficient to win a really wide public. The competition of the fashionable Miss Fong is formidable. And there is as well the problem of whom to act with. Any opera requires around twenty people to compose a troupe. While no Cantonese would say that Yü Chen Fei was not an artist of the first caliber, few of them care to pay to see his rare and infrequent performances.

Cantonese opera at best has serious defects for anyone expecting more than the most superficial of entertainments. Part of the reason for this is the already familiar story of Westernization and the colonial effect on art. Part is simply the taste of Southern Chinese for the vulgar in theatre. Meanwhile this form will have to remain the only theatrical fare of the native of Hongkong, the Cantonese, the refugee and the theatre-hungry visitor as well.

13

OKINAWA

One of the connecting links between China and Japan is Okinawa, the largest island in the scattered Ryukyu archipelago that hugs the coast of the Asiatic continent and extends from Formosa to Kyushu, Japan's southernmost island. For centuries in the past, Okinawa belonged to China and paid regular tribute to Chinese emperors. For a while, when the Japanese first began exerting their influence, Okinawa also began to acknowledge military rule of Japan and both countries exacted equal due at the same time. Finally, during the last century, Japan annexed all the islands of the area including Okinawa, and remained there in power until her defeat in World War II. Now, America has taken over the island making it a permanent military base, and today, if you visit it, you can live for weeks without realizing that you are not in, say, the Presidio at San Francisco. Only your servants, (and everyone on this vast Army post has servants) remind you, if you notice them, that you are in a foreign country.

Otherwise the wide paved roads, the suburban, concrete houses, the chicken-in-the-basket inns, the bars, movie houses, PXs and barber shops, and even the corner bookstore, swathe you in a little America and the provincial way of American life. Even the little flavor of native life the Americans stationed here can have is filtered through America. The restaurant called The Teahouse of the August Moon, named after the book and the Broadway play is run by an American. There you can have a sampling of local food, pork spare rib soup, crumbled bean sprouts and pig fat, raw fish, and on special order, snake soup, and afterwards, Okinawa geishas will dance for you and even with you in one of their several folk-dances. For most of the people living in Okinawa, this is their only contact with Okinawan life on any other than a business level.

313

Underneath the artificially transplanted American surface the old Okinawa world lies uneasily. Many of the people are eager to leave their island home and get safely away from the stockpiles of atomic bombs, the ammunition dumps and foreign life which is engulfing whatever is left of their culture. Others hope to make the best of it and count on the good sense of their new rulers. Some have turned to religion. But most, in an effort to divert their minds from the tragic possibilities of another war and another destruction of their island home, have turned to pleasure and their traditional pastimes of dance.

Okinawa is a curious blend of China and Japan, and while Japan's rule of the island was the more determining and the more recent, while the people speak Japanese and feel Japan as their mother country (the American authorities call this by the ugly word "reversionism" and discourage it), there are residues of China's ancient connections with the island. A dancer, for instance, wears a flag stuck in his *obi* belt of brocade to indicate that he is a warrior or a general. For some dances, women wear their hair in a high knot on the top of their head and pierced with a slender, silver, stiletto-like hairpin in the style of the T'ang dynasty figurines of terracotta. There is a curious head-shaking gesture in several dances which recalls the "big painted faces" of Chinese opera rather than their counterparts in Japan. But on the whole Okinawa is culturally closer to Japan than China.

It was in fact the Japanese who were responsible for establishing Okinawan dances and preserving them in the high state of development which they are still enjoying. They did this by introducing the custom of geisha and semi-private restaurants (inaccurately called "teahouses" in the West) where of an evening one can dine, while away the time with beautiful girls, see dancing and escape both the drudgery of the office and the tensions of the home. This institution is of considerable significance to the art of the country (*geisha* means literally art person), and the habit of using dance, even in this small-scale, intimate way, creates a body of professional, money-making entertainers. It affords them a profitable livelihood and results in maintaining their art on a substantial and realistic basis. Before the geisha system was introduced to Okinawa, undoubtedly the Chinese had exported a number of their sing-song girls, but the system is different. Sing-song girls are "talkers" rather than performers (the literal meaning of the word for them in Chinese is "book woman"), and they neither sing nor dance. Their function is a social rather than artistic one.

Not all Okinawa is derivative, however. It is true that during most of its history, it, together with Korea, served as a channel of communication between China and Japan, and through them the great determining factors of Chinese civilization reached Japan and affected its people with Buddhism, theatre, a script, literature and Confucian morality. But along the way Okinawa contributed to Japan's culture one important thing, the samisen or three-stringed, guitar-like instrument which completely dominates Japanese music and dancing even today. Originally, this instrument was the Okinawan *jahisen* (literally, snake hide and strings) and it, with its mottled, black-and-white scaly resonator, still accompanies all dances on Okinawa. The Japanese changed its name to samisen, or three flavored strings, increased its resonance by using a stronger skin to cover its sounding box, and introduced plectrums of ivory to extract the maximum tone and color. But it is of Okinawa a samisen player in Japan thinks when he lifts his instrument to play.

Any evening, if you walk along the back streets of Naha, the capital, and away from the Americanized districts, you will hear coming from a number of houses the sound of a pounding drum, sharp, plucked twangs of strings, and the steady, thin tones of a high-pitched voice. These are usually restaurants and a geisha dance will most certainly be in progress.

The most elegant of them in Naha is the Shoka ("Flower of the Pine") and in it you will find the Okinawan atmosphere at its most charming. You slide the gateway door to one side instead of opening it in the Western way; you call out that you are there; the master or mistress of the house comes out and welcomes you; you take off your shoes and step up in your stocking feet on to smooth, polished, spotlessly clean floorboards. Then you put on velvety house slippers and glide along the corridor until you come to the straw-matted room where you will eat. Immediately a flutter of geisha will appear out of nowhere to sit beside you, pour your wine and chat with you. During

315

your repast, or after, the partitioning doors of blue with silver cranes painted on them will be removed and the next room opens before you. This is where the dancing will take place.

So far, except for the rather guttural accents of the geisha and the special flavor of the tasty food, the procedure has been patterned after the Japanese. But when the dancing actually begins, you are in an Okinawan world and despite its overtones of Japanese fashion and Chinese mode, it is individual and peculiarly characteristic. An experience with dance on Okinawa is one which you cannot quite duplicate anywhere else in the world.

Usually the first dance, particularly if it is a felicitous occasion or a special celebration, will be one of the oldest dances in Okinawa and one which goes back 400 years—the *Rojin No Odori* or "old man's dance," more technically called the *Kajiyade fu bushi*. Every dancer learns this but its special excellence is shown when Shimabuka Koyu, the greatest dancer on Okinawa and the island's leading teacher, performs it. Wearing a white beard, and with his face made even older by streaks of black lines to serve as wrinkles, he carries a cane to assist the illusion of great age. He dresses in a blue kimono girded with a brocade obi, and on his head he wears a strange pie-shaped gold brocade hat. In his other hand, he holds a gold fan which he opens as he begins to move slowly and with taut control. He poses first in one direction, then in the other, softly bending the fan and cane to follow his delicate gestures. The words of the song are brief: "How splendid this day is for us. With what can we compare it. It is as if a budding flower had first encountered the dew." The movements vaguely outline the words, but the quiet restraint that underlies each motion of the hands and feet or the body, is more to convey the mood of auspiciousness and beatific serenity.

After changing his costume to a simple kimono with a flag to identify him as a warrior and wearing silver rings that dangle from the third, fourth and fifth fingers of each hand for ornaments, he dances again. This time it has a dramatic element derived from an ancient play of Chinese origin. The warrior is disguised. His helmet is camouflaged with flowers. He seeks out his enemy furtively. He finds him and the second section begins. Taking a lion's mask in his hand, he moves it in a series of realistic motions depicting the animal's

316

antics. He works its wooden mouth to clatter open and shut. Gradually the enemy before whom the dance is supposed to be enacted relaxes his guard. The third section consists of the warrior, without his hat or his lion's hand mask, stealthily creeping up and striking the air to symbolize that he has killed his enemy (the actual stabbing is not shown as that would be unsuitable and indecorous for dance). Then he performs a dance of victory, full of hops and leaps, and flag waving.

After a series of dances performed by men (all are short lasting only a few minutes), the geishas begin one by one to dance. Each of their dances is identified by the object they dance with—fans, branches of flowers, huge, floppy hats shaped like inverted lotuses in full bloom, bamboo sticks, or wax paper umbrellas; sometimes they merely clap with their bare hands. Perhaps the most beautiful piece in their repertoire is the melancholy solo called Kashi Kaki. For it the geisha, wearing a headdress of silver and gold paper flowers and an elaborately embroidered kimono with one sleeve hanging at the waist to reveal the equally beautiful and decorative undergarment, carries two small squares of light wood, for carding and combing thread in the traditional way. She pivots and sways, and slowly twirls these squares of wood and somberly moves across the straw mat floor. The words of the song sadly tell us of love-sickness:

> Shackling loom, thin and good thread
> Seven and twenty times over and over
> I'll weave him cloth fine and soft
> Like wings of a dragonfly.

> Shackling threads, and a heavy loom
> Weaving, weaving cloth
> His image appears clearer
> With each shackling sound.

> At the loom, weaving, weaving
> I cannot speak my love
> Only the sound over and over
> Hardens my love-sweet sickness.

> Now I've woven enough
> Shackled enough
> I'll return home where
> Perhaps he waits for me.

The most popular dance with the Okinawans frequenting their restaurants seems to be the Chizia Bushi, or as the Okinawans who have learned a little English describe it, the "Okinawan Home Sweet Home." It is danced by a girl in the century-old national costume of deep blue kimono patterned with large, white jagged crosses. Her head is bare except for the high coiffure and the silver hairpin. She postures and walks, punctuating each phrase with willowy gestures. She sinks to her knees only to rise again and form more patterns with her quiet, reposeful hands and fingers. The words tell of her travels away from home and her longing to return to her parents.

> Going on a journey
> Sleeping on a beach
> My pillow of grass
> Makes me think of home.
>
> Waking from my sleep
> My ears pricked by grass
> It is midnight and
> My sadness returns.
>
> Only one shining moon above
> The seas divide us even more
> Are they looking up too
> At this same moon?
>
> As sure as I plant flowers here
> As sure as I plant bamboo there
> I will see my home again.

Nearly all Okinawan dances have the same form. There is always a slow introduction, followed by a section of faster movement, then an interlude of slow dance again, and finally a swift conclusion. All entrances and exits are made on the diagonal, and to advance or retreat in a straight line directly towards your audience is considered ungraceful. The words are suggestive and evocative rather than literal, and the gestures are indicative rather than fully expressive. The idea of the dance is to attract by controlled grace, and to convey the deepest of sentiments through a mask of understatement.

The few theatres on Okinawa are largely taken up by recitals of this standard repertoire of dances which you see to perfection in restaurants like Shoka. Every young girl of good family, whose parents can afford it, learns to dance, although she may never appear anywhere except at a public recital on graduation from her dance school or within the confines of her own home. Perhaps the Okinawan wife, unlike the Japanese one, hopes to compete with the geisha by entertaining her husband at home.

Occasionally plays are staged in the theatre but these are only dramatic dances. The actor-dancer appears and explains who he is and what he is going to do. Then the other characters of the play follow, and they enact exactly what they first explain. The spectator's chief interest therefore lies in the execution of movement rather than in plot or staging. Most of the plays today are extremely fragmentary. They may be only the thin story of a man flirting with a vendor in the market or a man who attempts to make love to a woman other than his wife. But virtue always triumphs and always the man is chastised by the woman. Most plays end on a comic, farcical note. The only note of tragedy appears in the dances where sadness, loneliness, or love-sickness prevail.

Islands, particularly those in the Pacific, seem to have a special leaning toward dance to the neglect of drama. Okinawa, too, is full of folk dances—for planting and harvesting rice and for festival days. Its classic dances, or those done primarily by the geishas, occupy an extraordinarily important place in the lives of the Okinawans. They reserve their most tender emotions, their most serious feelings for them, and it is there in the dance and nowhere else that a foreigner can have free access to such an intimacy.

JAPAN

Japan's dances and dramas as they are seen today contain 1300 years of continuous uninterrupted history. This prodigious feat of conservation, theatrically speaking, makes Japan an extraordinary and unique country. In the West, it is true that we still see once in a while a tragedy of Aeschylus or a comedy of Aristophanes written three thousand years ago, but such performances represent only the loosest kind of guesswork about the original presentations, for in reality we do not know what costumes or props were required, exactly how they were staged, or even what Greek music sounded like. Even when we see Shakespeare, we are witnessing only an old text performed as modern theatre. The acting techniques and conventions of the past are for all practical purposes exhausted in the West and audience-reaction has changed so radically that it would be foolhardy, even were it possible, to try to revive them. With the temper of our countries as it is today, I think even a serious attempt to cast young boys as actresses or to reconstruct the original, anachronistic costumes would be absurd.

In all of Asia, where generally tradition is sanctified and change eschewed, Japan stands as the only country whose theatre in its entirety has never suffered an eclipse nor undergone any drastic re-vivification or renovation. Japan appears to the student as a vast theatrical museum. It is as fully documented as the Chinese in records, but the examples are still living in actual practice. Both its dance and drama are intact, obedient to their original conceptions, and all their traditions of hereditary acting families, conventionalized stagecraft, and archaic costumes have been preserved.

Many adjunctive and ancillary qualities concerning Japan's various theatre forms add to this lustrous initial truth. For instance, one of the most impressive aspects about Japan's theatres is that they are profit-making and actively supported by a ticket-buying public. Whenever this happy circumstance prevails in any country, theatre becomes genuinely professional. Statistically speaking, there are something like 4,000 theatres in Japan and one producing company alone, Shochiku Producing Co., Inc., paid the highest amount of income taxes last year of any business or commercial enterprise in the country. Nearly all actors and dancers in Japan regardless of their particular domain of specialization or type of theatre possess an ability easily demonstrable before international audiences of critical repute. Many of their vehicles compare as literature with the best works of any country Asian or Western, and translations proving this can be found in every major language of the civilized world. In addition to the force of tradition which dominates Japanese theatre, there has also been a potent urge towards creativity.

The kinds of theatre they have produced over the centuries, while indebted in part to India and China (in much the same way our theatre in the West relates to Greece and Rome) are nonetheless original (like ours) and unique in their final Japanese forms. A considerable amount of inventiveness surrounds the theatre as well. Independently of the outside world, nearly three hundred years ago, at a time when Shakespeare plays were being performed in relatively primitive theatres, the Japanese constructed a revolving stage, freely used such devices as trap doors through which actors rise and sink through the stage floor, and lighting techniques which bathe the actors in sunlight or shadow, and even such special effects as long candlesticks which project out to the actor's face to serve as a spotlight or pin spot. Japan, too, alone among the theatres of the world has been able to maintain on a major scale that original synthesis of the arts which subtends the Asian theory of drama. There is as much dance as there is drama and for both there is music, and none of these has ever suffered the troubled fluctuations felt in the histories of other countries.

Japan is also the only country of Asia that has a professional body of full-fledged critics. The function of the critic normally in Asia is absorbed by the scholars who speak usually in private. And the few critics that do exist have to earn their living from other work. But in Japan it is different. Every newspaper has a staff of regularly paid

321

special critics for the classical theatres, another set for the modern plays; critical articles by guest reviewers cram the pages of the country's several theatrical magazines and intellectual periodicals. This existence of critics and the craft of regular criticism is another by-product of good, first-class, professional theatre.

Contrary to one's expectation, the contemporaneous existence of ancient and classical theatres side by side has not impeded Japan's thriving, energetic, modern theatre. The boards of the larger cities carry not only works of the classics but new plays by present-day playwrights and adroit translations of the latest plays from the West played with a verisimilitude that make our Chu Chin Chows, Cho Cho Sans and Mikados, in comparison, absurd. In this way the modern theatre of Japan has an internationality and breadth about it that outstrips theatre anywhere else. The Japanese see productions of *Death of a Salesman* or *Streetcar Named Desire* patterned almost imitatively on New York. But they also turn an introspective searchlight on themselves when they deal with themes closer to their own life and society. The Japanese playwright and actor handle foreigners on the stage with a subtlety and fairness that make even translations from Western plays natural on a Japanese stage. There are of course quibbles with Japan's theatre to be made. The classic theatre is not uniformly excellent. Few modern plays are as good as the better Broadway productions. But taken as a whole, Japanese theatre in scope and vitality and in its greatest moments of classical theatre is, in my opinion, unequalled anywhere in the world.

It is almost unnecessary to itemize the specific types of classical Japanese theatre for the Western reader, because there have been so many and such excellent translations and descriptions of it made over the last few years. The fourteenth-fifteenth century form, No, has been familiar for some time in Ezra Pound's and Arthur Waley's translations, in reports and travelogues. In 1954, for the first time in Japan's history a special composite troupe of the greatest No actors appeared with immense success at the International Theatre Festival in Italy.

News of Kabuki, an entirely different genre belonging to the seventeenth century, reached Europe in the 1920's when a troupe of actors were invited to Russia. The results of this visit were various. On the one hand, Kabuki staging devices new to the West were tried out in the theatres of Russia, Germany, and France. On the other hand, one of the Kabuki actors turned Communist, and later, with Russian techniques, had a considerable influence on Japanese modern theatre. Kabuki as a name became further known when a somewhat spurious troupe of dancers and musicians called Azuma appeared in America and Europe. The Bunraku puppet theatre has been for decades a special preserve of Paul Claudel. The French, therefore, through his writings have long been familiar with its marvels. A young American, Donald Keene, the brilliant Japanese scholar, has more recently introduced a number of puppet plays through his books to the English-speaking world. Even Bugaku, the austere dances of the seventh century, with their strange orchestral accompaniment of Gagaku zealously protected by the successive emperors of Japan, was seen by large numbers of Americans and Europeans who were members of the Occupation and who attended the two or three outdoor performances given during the early postwar years. Even the Western movie-going public has seen at least a fragment of Bugaku in the recent Japanese film *Gate of Hell*.

But there are many more kinds of theatre in Japan which are less widely known. The reasons for this are fairly obvious; few of these forms would stand up as literature in translation or would be impressive divorced from their actual presentation on the stages of Japan. However, most of them command large audiences and are commercially successful. One such form acts as a kind of bridge between the classic and the modern theatre. Shimpa is a hybrid of Kabuki and modern theatre begun in the late nineteenth century, a slightly old-fashioned, half-exaggerated, half-naturalistic theatre. Several dramatists write exclusively in this medium and some of Japan's most glittering stars appear in it. Yaeko Mizutani, the best of them, who appears sometimes as a geisha, sometimes as a beautiful but neglected wife in the various stories of the Meiji Era, is so beautiful as a woman and so expert as an actress that she manages to disguise the structural weakness of the plots and the indeterminate quality of the Shimpa form. To the Japanese who regard theatre art as the difference (not the closeness as we do in the West) between real life and the stage, she is certainly an example of purest art. In actuality, she is a rather ordinary wrinkled woman in her fifties, unconscious to a point of carelessness about her personal appearance. But on stage, transformed by the thick makeup of Shimpa and the radiance of her acting, she is an Utamaro print come to life. An added distinction is that she is often the only woman on the stage; all the other female roles are played, as they are in Kabuki, by male actors. That the mixture of the two is neither strange nor particularly discernible is a solid tribute to Yaeko Mizutani's technique (she competes with actors who have been trained to act since childhood) and at the same time is a proof of the aesthetic validity of Kabuki tradition which has evolved a type of stage woman so thoroughgoing as not to be made odd by the presence of a real woman.

Another more flashy form is represented by Takarazuka, the all-girl musical comedy troupe created about thirty years ago, which has its headquarters in a town called Takarazuka. This is halfway between Kobe and Osaka and the town is dedicated solely to show-business. At the center of town an enormous theatre almost as large as the Roxy Music Hall gives a constantly changing, steady stream of operettas, skits and arrangements of classical theatre twelve times a week all the year round to its special "theatre tourists" who travel there only to see one of these splendid performances. Before and after the show, the ticket holder can wander through Takarazuka visiting the zoo, the botanical gardens, or "insect house." Most of the Takarazuka fans, however, peer through the gates and fences around the long rows of barracks like a military camp where the hundreds of Takarazuka actresses, singers and dancers live. Although Takarazuka is primarily a bobby-soxers theatre, where the stars' adolescent fans mob backstage doors, beg for autographed photographs, and shriek and swoon during performances, it has by now become an established institution all over Japan with special Takarazuka theatres in the main cities. The biggest of these, the Ernie Pyle theatre, is in Tokyo and was taken over by the Americans after the war for their performances and only returned to Takarazuka this year. These theatres are movie houses most of the year except when the girls of one of the various sub-troupes called "Star," "Moon," "Snow" and "Flower" come on their annual tour and give their audiences a chance to see them without the expense of a trip to Takarazuka.

In Tokyo there are a number of theatres in Asakusa, a flamboyant, rather lower class section of the city, where the shows include everything from snake swallowing acts to erotic plays acted in straight, modern theatre style. Most of the stage performances in Asakusa are sexy—girlie-shows, strip-teases, burlesques, and exhibitions—and they flourish on a scale of lavishness and technical excellence that makes Minsky's or Kearney's pale by comparison.

For our purposes, however, the main focus of attention must be on the masterpieces of the classic repertoire of Japan's theatre.

Much has happened in Japanese theatre during its incredibly long history. In the fifteen years I have known it, I have seen some of those changes at first hand, and while many are for the better and some for the worse, the core of theatrical vitality has remained adamantly fixed and persistent. The Japanese, who adopt fashions almost as zestfully and even more cleverly than the Balinese, have still maintained all their theatre arts in a way no other country has managed. As each new form emerged, the others simply moved over to make room. Little was lost; much, obviously, was gained.

The clearest example of Japan's acquisitive genius in the arts is to be found in Bugaku. Foreigners in Japan can be luckier here, at least in one respect, than the Japanese themselves. Occasionally, under the guise of being "visiting dignitaries" and therefore entitled to special State privileges, they may be invited to see Bugaku and hear Gagaku, the oldest regularly performed dances and orchestral music extant today in the world. Such a performance, if the cautious Imperial Household accords an invitation, will probably take place in the Music Building, one of the three or four tall, two-storied, concrete buildings deep within the outer walls and past the double moat of the Imperial Palace. There the visitor will sit with a handful of other persons, either guests like himself or members of the Emperor's staff, sprinkled thinly through the large auditorium. Far outnumbering the actual total of spectators, the orchestra of perhaps twenty-five musicians performs its pieces with a concentration and finish that in the West we associate more usually with huge public concerts and recitals.

The extraordinary occasion of hearing Gagaku (pronounced nga-nga-koo and meaning literally "graceful, authorized music") begins with a series of reverberating thuds on the orchestra's giant drum. In appearance alone this drum or *taiko* shows the antiquity and far-off connection of the dancing soon to begin. The heavily carved, wooden, oval-shaped frame represents the sacred flames which encompass the Hindu God Siva. This halo of fire is supposed to have begun with the original drum rhythms with which he created the world. The thick hide which covers the drum itself is painted in red and black with two interlocking "S" shapes, familiar in ancient Chinese religion and philosophy as the yin and yang symbols of duality. As the windows and skylights shudder with the drum's sound, the musicians and dancers, dressed in costumes whose styles of long silk sleeves, baggy pants that tie at the ankle, and soft felt-soled shoes have been traditionally repeated for the last thousand years, take their places at the far end of the hall. On their heads they wear the thin transparent, black gauze hats with curling flaps at the sides and back which announce their official rank as Regular Musicians and Dancers of the Imperial Court, hereditary posts handed down from father to son.

Several kinds of flutes, both long and short flutes, flageolets, gongs, and small drums constitute the bulk of the orchestra. But three additional instruments add their special flavor to the ensemble, and give Gagaku a unique and inimitable timbre and sonority. These are the *koto*, which is a 13-stringed dulcimer played with the fingers on which metal or horn plectrums are attached like finger nails, the *biwa*, or four-stringed lute, and most unusual of all and unlike any Western instrument the *sho*, a miniature hand-held pipe organ of seventeen slender bamboo pipes and reeds. These three instruments give the orchestra its harmonic substance. The Sho, for instance, plays solid chords of ten notes and while the performer blows continuously in or out through the mouthpiece he alters the inner tones as the music requires. The various melodic passages of the "dulcimer" and the "lute" add contrapuntal background passages as well to the tonal lines. But they are so intricate and considered so refined they are omitted whenever Gagaku accompanies dancing. The theory behind this practice is that only coarser music belongs with the less subtle sister art of dance and that the athletic motions of dance destroy the gossamer-spun melodies of the strings.

Then the dances begin. As the dancers move they extend their arms stiffly and symmetrically with the fingers held taut. They bend their legs in deep pliés. Sometimes they wear huge frightening masks with gaping maws. Meanwhile the dissonances and weird melodies of the music collide and the pulsing beats of fives and nines or fours and twelves, punctuated by the drums, vibrate delicately and uncertainly in the Westerner's ears. Somehow the antiquity of the dance and music is immediately evident. In fact, the entire performance is so remote from one's previous artistic experience either in Asia or the West that after such a program it comes as no surprise to learn that Bugaku and Gagaku first appeared in Japan thirteen hundred years ago, not long after the fall of the Roman Empire and considerably before England, for instance, was very civilized, and nearly a millenium before the violin and the piano, for another instance, were used in the West. Already this magical dancing and music was weaving its spell over the Japanese court. Some dances are attributed to certain emperors themselves, and their fanciful and charming titles such as Dragons Basking in the Sun, The Polo Game, were given and danced by them. By the twelfth and thirteenth centuries, the Japanese taste for this dance and music spread to the Shogun's court. (These were the military rulers who actually controlled the country while the emperors lived in elegant retirement which gave them leisure to continue their protective practice of these fragile arts.) They quickly took up the Imperial fashion. One of them, Minamoto no Toshie, is known to have insisted on dancing Bugaku with his sword and spear to a martial piece of music known as Bairo (from Vairocana, an Indian deity of war) before engaging in any combat with the enemy.

At the turn of the twentieth century, at the time of the great period of Japan's Westernization, the only concession the Imperial Court musicians made to the new era was to take up a European counterpart of Gagaku, the classical little symphonies of Hadyn and Mozart. Now the court musicians divide their three rehearsals a week more or less equally between this Western music and Gagaku, the accompaniment for Bugaku.

Although today's foreign visitor may have an opportunity to attend one of these Bugaku and Gagaku performances, the average Japanese —even if he spends his life within walking distance of the Imperial Palace—is never very likely to. On rare occasions an invitation performance might be seen at a public shrine. Sometimes an approximation of the music will be played at weddings or at other ceremonies connected with shrines and ancient Japan. Also at the Kabuki theatre, if the play calls for an Emperor to appear, a reasonable facsimile by Bugaku will be performed. But real Bugaku ever since its first importation from India, through Tibet and from China through Korea, has been kept out of reach of the people. It has remained the pursuit of princes and the exclusive preserve of the Imperial family and the nobles of the court. Originally, Bugaku came to Japan along with Buddhism from China and the world beyond. But while Buddhism and the Chinese classics gradually sifted down to the people, Bugaku and Gagaku did not. They remained guarded by their high ranking patrons and this exclusiveness continues even now.

To Westerners, whose traditions and customs are so different from the Japanese, the artistic snobbishness surrounding Bugaku may seem at first to be decidedly selfish. But the problem of preserving the past even for the West has only recently been solved in the field of the lively arts with the discovery of several means of recording sound and movement. Phonograph records, tape recorders, and motion picture films now insure the permanent availability of at least part of our cultural heritage without the cumbersome and often faulty method of transposing dance movements and music to writing.

Japan during the past thirteen centuries has been concerned with maintaining its ancient arts and practices accurately and in a state of relative purity. The only way that Bugaku could be perpetuated in all its luxury of gorgeous costumes and elaborate instruments was by maintaining families of hereditary dancers and musicians within the confines of the Imperial family, the most stable and continuous element of Japanese society. But perhaps another aspect is even more significant. Bugaku never had to be popular. The keeping of the art away from the people meant that it never felt the pressures of the times nor was it ever submitted to contemporary tastes. What would have happened had it not been confined so exclusively to court circles can be surmised by looking for it in the countries of its origin.

Here is the most astonishing aspect of this ancient dance and music. In India and China where it fell from royal pleasure it has long been lost and forgotten. Melodies which in Japan's Gagaku today have Sanskrit names are now unheard in India. Masks which once were common in the Indian Bugaku are now unknown there and can be found today only in Japan. Some of the instruments of the orchestra which were borrowed straight from China of the pre-T'ang era can now be seen there only in old cave temple sculptures. This dance and music is remembered now in India and China only in their moulding, lichened stone sculptures and brittle perishing documents of the past. As faithfully as it is probably possible in this "changing unstable world" as the Buddhists call it, the Court of Japan has kept this art in its pure and pristine magnificence. For this musicological feat alone, the world owes Japan a tremendous debt of gratitude.

No is now about five hundred years old and the second oldest form of theatre in Japan. It like Bugaku owes its miraculous state of preservation to the aristocracy. Still today an appreciation and understanding of No among Japanese is a mark of breeding. No other theatre demands so much from a spectator, and unlike Kabuki, which has a spontaneous appeal, it requires a certain adjustment and intellectual preparation. It is slow, unbearably so for the Westerner who is used to a certain raciness in theatre. Its language is incomprehensible even to persons who have a working knowledge of modern Japanese. The Japanese themselves usually follow the written text at a performance in order to understand the play better, much in the same way that people follow a libretto or score at the opera in the West.

The texts of No, as is already well-known in the West, are superb. There is perhaps no other literature of the theatre which is so extensive (there are around 300 plays altogether) and at the same time so uniformly excellent.

Visually No's miming is so symbolic, so pared down to its aesthetic quintessence that it presents a problem. A kimono lying on the stage will represent a sick person, a stab at a sedge-hat means the consummation of a revenge, a lift of the mask is a smile, a downward glance indicates tears, and the lifting of the hand weeping. The moaning and punctuating shrieks of the drummer and the accompanying singers is, unfortunately, apt to sound like caterwauling to the untutored outsider experiencing No for the first time. The only advice I can give is to bear with these initial obstacles and impressions until No which is so vastly alien to one's previous sense of the theatre gradually becomes familiar. It requires time and a little

329

patience to learn the basic essentials of the art. But once this is achieved, and it is a small price to pay, there is no doubt that No has many of the greatest moments of drama in the world today.

Merit in the theatre is hard to prove by words, and anyone who has not seen No must simply accept on faith the profound aesthetic reward it presents. Out of the quiet repose of No rises an exaltation. Once the spectator becomes geared to No's rhythms, each lift of the hand, each movement of the tightly stockinged foot, the opening and closing of a fan, the twirling of a long, rustling sleeve, assume immense meanings. Your mind rages with emotions, but they have been aroused almost imperceptibly. You leave the theatre sensitive to the fact that an entire new set of feelings within the human soul has been exercised. You find yourself in a realm of concentrated reality doubly distilled by the very economy of its theatrical means.

Postwar Japan saw an unprecedented wave of enthusiasm for No among Japanese as well as foreigners, and as yet there have been no signs of this abating. Today there are eighty-eight No theatres—more than at any period in history. The new Kanze Kaikan, built last year in Tokyo and making the sixth in that city alone, is perhaps the most perfect. A No theatre is really a house within a house. The polished stage is a platform fully covered with a curving temple roof. Around this on three sides sits the audience, and stage, roof and spectators' seats are again roofed over by the auditorium proper. A passageway off to one side and railing runs from the stage across the back wall of the theatre to the dressing rooms. The audience is separated from the stage itself by a wide space of garden made of gravel and growing pine trees and plants. The design of a No theatre is so particular that it is suitable only for No; and the construction of such a theatre house means that no other type of play or show can ever be performed there. But perhaps even more indicative of No's popularity today than the existence of so many of those exclusive places is the fact that No troupes of actors have begun to tour. Some parts of Japan have for the first time now been able to see the country's greatest No actors.

There are two reasons, I think, for the phenomenal re-emergence of No after its five hundred years of tranquility. The Japanese during the bitter years of defeat in War began to rely more and more on their own cultural values. In many ways the best of Japan's heritage,

No soothed somehow the hurt of failure and restored in part the shattered national pride. Added to this, a new custom has risen which makes No more palatable to the average person than ever before in its history—the Shimai programs. Every No has at its climax an important dance called Shimai. Previously the mood has been brought to a white-heat of intensity by the story of the play, by the rich poetry of the words, and by the steady succession of the actors' action. Suddenly a moment arrives when the spectator's excitement seems unable to increase and the drama turns into dance. If you isolate these Shimai and perform a series of them as excerpts from the fuller No plays, you have a complete program. This makes No accessible even to a layman, and from here those that want to can go on to more serious study. The expert disdains such programs as we might a gala night of scenes from operas or a recital of the first movements of several sonatas. But as an introduction to No, whose subtleties can only be realized after considerable effort, nothing serves the purpose better.

One other aspect of No breaks the intense concentration a performance requires. Kyogen, which are farcical interludes or playlets, intervene between the more ponderous and grave No plays. They have recently come in for a particularly enlightening analysis by Donald Keene who has translated nearly all the texts into English.

Kabuki, of all theatres in the world, is probably the most immediately appealing, and its ability to dazzle seems foolproof even among those who most resist exoticism of any kind. To begin with, the milieu of Kabuki is overwhelming. The Kabuki Za in Tokyo, where the best actors perform all the year round, is the largest legitimate theatre anywhere. It seats 2599 people and its enormously wide stage stretches for ninety-one feet across the auditorium. Running through the audience and connecting the stage with the back of the theatre house is the famous *hanamichi* forty-five feet in length which functions as an auxiliary acting area on which important movements of the plays are performed literally in the midst of the spectators. If you attend a performance on opening day (the programs change usually on the first of every month) you will find the tickets sold at a reduced price since the first three days of each play are in the nature of dress rehearsals. On the first day, only the most ardent connoisseurs are present and their vociferous shouts of approval which ring out through the hall guide you exactly as to who the famous actors are, which are the finest bits of acting, and what are the best loved scenes. Their delight in this theatre, even if it seems strange to you, is contagious and their thrill communicates itself to you.

The settings of Kabuki are perhaps the most complicated and elaborate anywhere in Asia or the West. Sometimes the stage becomes a house, a lake and a forest all at the same time. Some sets are huge boats that extend the entire length of the stage. Others are three-story palaces in which a counterpoint of action takes place on all three levels. Others are bare with only the pinetree backdrop of Nō to set off the wide, expansive gestures of Kabuki. The costumes which follow with absolute authenticity each period of Japan's history are gorgeously splendid. Layers and layers of richly embroidered hand-painted kimonos encase the actor. Court ladies, for instance, wear twelve multi-colored kimonos one on top of the other. Courtesans and supermen wear high stilts which raise them several inches off the ground. A dancer will sometimes change her costume as many as nine times in the course of one dance. And maidens will change within a space of a few minutes into the costumes and make-up of ferocious demons with long manes, striped faces, and fantastic costumes of gold and silver. In summer time, when the plays are supposed to match the season the costume will be simple—open down the front of the bare chest and pulled up high to expose the thighs —but the pattern will be beautiful and the silk or cotton material of the finest weave. But these are all exterior considerations.

The genius of Kabuki lives in its actors and their manifold skills— of stylization, of imitating puppets or animals, of realism, and of course, since Kabuki is a synthesis of the arts of dance and drama and music, of dancing, of playing musical instruments and of singing. And most actors, as a special favor to their fans, can draw a creditable picture or compose an exquisite poem.

While the Kabuki Za provides the most spectacular setting, there are Kabuki theatres in other major cities of Japan, each with its special atmosphere. Perhaps the Misono Za in Nagoya is the most correct of these, and though small, Kabuki played there acquires a bright and shining lustre close to what it must have had two and

332

three centuries ago when spanking new theatre houses were being built and fresh plays and first performances were a more usual occurrence.

Kabuki as an art started in the early seventeenth century about the same time as Shakespeare, and there are parallels between England's Elizabethan period and Japan's Genroku period when Kabuki arose. It was a period of exuberance, of national happiness. Despite the weighty hand of nobles and warriors over the social structure in general, the common man was irrepressible, and he found expression in the theatre, in its poetry, in its dazzling actors, and in the riotous comedies and the enveloping tragedies of its master playwrights. There are something like three hundred Kabuki plays, classified as historical (dramas of dense seriousness dealing with war, murder, revenge, events in palaces and courts), domestic (plays of the common man in love and out, happy or troubled by his fate and the circumstances of his life), and dance-drama (stories of spirits, ghosts, courtesans, commoners and persons of rank dancing out stories of their lives and moods). Many of these have been written by men of literature and live as poetry and paragons of theatre construction. The plays of Chikamatsu Monzaemon or the more modern work of Kawatake Mokuami fall into this category. Others are hack-written plays which are scarcely more than improvisations of a show-off actor and endure because of a single moment of good theatre—a superman challenging a noble warrior, a prince and a princess falling in love at first sight and exchanging fans while the stage glows with fireflies, a fight at night near a graveyard.

The repertoire increased steadily until the beginning of the twentieth century, and Kabuki as it stands today is a mass of revisions and redactions of old plays, new plays, and faithful repetitions of traditional plays guarded by individual acting families. Some of the actors are direct descendants of the first Kabuki actors, and after they achieve genuine theatrical distinction, even take their names. To identify these, the actor appends a "generation number" after his name and by this you can tell how many great actors before him have borne this ancestral name. The next Uzaemon, for instance, will be the 17th, and the present Kanzaburo is the 18th.

Kabuki, like Chinese opera, classifies its characters according to role-types, but being an older, more evolved theatre, the subdivisions

333

are more detailed and the number and scope of roles are greater. Some of these are the strong-minded woman, the beautiful but weak hero, the warrior with the divided mind of doubtful loyalty, the courtesan of elegance and dignity, the geisha of vulgarity, and there are something like a half-dozen villains who range from being thoroughly wicked to being unwillingly so, from those who are treacherous in high places to those who are vicious as an unpleasant next door neighbor.

The secret of watching Kabuki is relaxation. The theatre will affect you whether you want it to or not, but your cooperation or anticipation is not necessary to this experience. The attentive concentration we are prepared to give our theatre in the West is apt to deter you from appreciating Kabuki. Kabuki is long, the stage line sags at intervals so that its intensity can rise higher and more strikingly. Many of the plays of fantasy are intended merely to divert you casually and to keep the spectacle of staging varied and colorful. The foreigner must choose his play carefully, and until he is accustomed to the rich conventions and the wealth of panoramic display, it is best to see in that day only the one play. Since Kabuki runs from morning to night, there are arrangements at every theatre for you to buy a ticket for only the play, the act or even single scene which is of particular interest to you. If you see only those parts of Kabuki which are most intense or appealing, and if you let the power of the drama carry you from a state of repose into genuine feeling and response, the marvel of Kabuki at its best will be more clearly marked, and your basis for a full and wise understanding of Kabuki made. In this way you will join the ranks of so many foreigners who find in Kabuki the deepest, most absorbing experience in their theatrical lives.

One of the most significant lessons of Kabuki is the flowering that old age brings to the stage. Kabuki actors normally make their debut at five and continue to act until they are decrepit and can scarcely move. By the time they reach so exalted an age that Westerners would think they have lost their usefulness on the stage, their purest acting only begins.

In 1954, Kichiemon appeared as Kumagai, the warrior general who sacrifices his own son instead of one of the enemy and who then renounces bushido (the way of the warrior) to become a priest. The role is a great one in a solid masterpiece of the Kabuki repertoire.

Kichiemon, nearly seventy, already seriously ill and unable to walk except very slowly and cautiously, still suffused this final role with a special Kabuki magic. Compared with the many times I have seen his other performances of the role, it was of course the least active and unenergetic. But he suffused the stage with a glow and tension I had never seen before. His voice was all the better for the inactivity of his body. His lines, for which he had always been famous, were projected with such clarity that even someone not familiar with the text could understand their import. But most of all, each meaning was so charged with feeling that actor and interpretation, stage and real tragedy become one. In the most famous scene of the play, for instance, when Kumagai, recounting a battle, casually picks up his sword and brushes it with his fan (dusting the enemy warrior he supposedly lifts from the ground), Kichiemon demonstrated in a single gesture a whole vocabulary of stage terms—ease, conviction, mastery, focus, and meaning in movement.

Another such magnificently impressive performance remembered by Japanese and foreigners alike was Baigyoku's last appearance at the age of seventy-three as Tamate-Gozen, a nineteen-year-old girl. It was only at this exalted age with decades of experience behind him that his technique was consummate enough to permit such an extraordinary stage deception.

To reach this peak of mastery on the stage the Kabuki actor from the time of his debut at five has not only already spent a childhood playing with make-up and properties in the backstage greenroom of his father, but has learned besides that his personal life and position in society will be as carefully guarded by traditions and rules as the Kabuki stage itself. For years he will receive the most stringent kind of training under the direction of the senior members of his acting family. Here he must accept the laws of complete obedience to his instructor, a thorough grounding in classical forms, and so great a concentration on the Kabuki stage that as Kichiemon once told me, "The stage becomes the reality, and the rest of the world a dream."

The Japanese consider that you cannot judge a Kabuki actor until he is forty. By this time he has established the role-types to which he is most suited, he knows his own particular excellences on stage, and at last reaches the period in which he can become a creative actor within the ancient rules. This has led to different schools of acting, different styles, and the establishment even of certain mannerisms as a tradition, and altogether permits an actor more individuality than you think indicated by his rigorous training. Kikugoro, for instance, whose voice was his weakest point, developed an almost trick pronunciation of words so as to make them carry further in the huge Kabuki auditoriums. Even now junior actors of his family imitate this although their own voices need no such aid. Kichiemon, whose Moritsuna was the fullest interpretation that that play has had, imbued each sentence with so much meaning, required so much time to convey emotional subtlety to his audiences, that the first section of the play was usually cut to keep within the time limit, and this will certainly set a fashion among young actors who will try to match his intensity.

With the tragic death of Nakamura Kichiemon in 1954 a whole era of grand Kabuki came to an end. Coming at this particular juncture in Kabuki history, his death had an artistically disturbing significance that it might otherwise not have had. For several years before, Kichiemon was alone. The titans of Kabuki, Koshiro VII, Kikugoro VI, Baigyoku, Sojuro, Enjaku, and Uzaemon XIV had disappeared one by one with frightening acceleration. Only he of all the flamboyant, spectacular senior actors lingered. He was the last of the great Kabuki actors of our generation and the end of a long line of traditional actors in the grand manner. His final performances illustrated perhaps better than any the culminative power of the aging Kabuki actor. Fortunately, however, his last years were filled with testimonies of his greatness.

Two years before Kichiemon's death, the Commission for the Protection of Cultural Properties in the Ministry of Education undertook to film in sound a complete on-stage performance of another of the pinnacles of Kabuki theatre, *Moritsuna's Camp*. The story is of the tragic fortunes of war in which two brothers are on opposite sides and the sacrifices each makes. Happily those interested can see this unique record of Kichiemon's great acting.

The occasion of the filming was also unprecedented for another reason. At that time, the Emperor of Japan entered a Kabuki theatre for the first time in history and saw his first play. By this, Kabuki and Kichiemon were both given Imperial sanction, and it was the only time that this people's theatre, unlike Bugaku and No, was ever touched formally or officially by any member of the aristocracy or nobility. After the performance the enthusiastic Emperor (who was so unaccustomed to theatre etiquette that he applauded with his arms stretched out as if clapping before a Shinto shrine to invoke the gods) awarded Kichiemon a high court rank. This was again elevated posthumously immediately after his death. Kichiemon was also a member of the coveted Art Academy, and the government declared him a "human national treasure." Through him Kabuki which for three hundred fifty years had depended for support entirely on popular opinion and the loyalty of the general public gained final respect.

But with his death that tradition is severed and the fate of present-day Kabuki lies entirely in the hands of five junior actors—Ebizo, Utaemon, Koshiro, Baiko and Shoroku—sometimes called the Great Five. Two decades separated Kichiemon from these younger actors, but those twenty years were crucial. Acting styles in any country change with the years but they can be sustained as long as a master through his special genius can hold the audience loyal to the past. The younger actors inevitably, without a doyen to keep them in check, will evolve their own idioms and mannerisms, and a new mode of Kabuki must emerge. Already entirely new flavors are emanating from the stage. Fortunately for Kabuki, these five actors have brilliance and intelligence and another spectacular flowering of Kabuki can be again expected, as has always happened in the past, when they reach maturity. But for the moment, while we wait for that fulfillment, the Kabuki lover is pausing—remembering the great Kichiemon and looking forward eagerly to the future.

Two events have occurred in Kabuki recently, which have surprised those of us who are old-fashioned and who have followed Kabuki for many years. One is the appearance behind the scene of a young critic Takechi Tetsuji, the bellwether of Osaka Kabuki today, and the other is the vigorous growth of "New Kabuki" or the "New Historical" form of the Kabuki type play at the hands of two new playwrights, Hojo Hideji and Funahashi Seiichi.

To understand the story of Takechi Tetsuji and Osaka Kabuki we must go back a little. For years until 1948, Kabuki in Osaka was sustained solely by the consummate mastery of a single actor, Baigyoku, (who at the age of seventy-three was still performing the roles of young women with unbelievable grace and delicacy). By his appearances alone the vast Kabuki Za in Osaka, almost as large as the one in Tokyo, was kept filled. When he died, Kabuki in Osaka, for lack of a "Great Five" to carry on, fell into a state of collapse. There simply were not enough actors, and of those that remained, even Ganjiro, the senior actor of Osaka, was frankly insufficient to attract sizeable audiences to the theatre. In one frantic effort to save Kabuki in Osaka, Shochiku Producing Co. transferred a number of the lesser actors from Tokyo on a permanent basis. But this was only stopgap assistance. Osaka's need was for stars comparable to Ebizo, Utaemon, Koshiro, Baiko or Shoroku (their indelible association with Tokyo Kabuki by heredity and acting styles made them unavailable except for an annual guest tour).

At this point Takechi Tetsuji, the bright son of extremely wealthy parents in Osaka, an ardent No scholar, and an original and inventive critic of Kabuki, came to the forefront. He was known first by his occasional articles in various journals and magazines of Japan (there are dozens of these devoted exclusively to the theatre). He attracted a somewhat grudging attention by his iconoclastic, explosive, and very prejudiced opinions. For instance, he made a point of attacking Kichiemon and his talented actor son-in-law, Koshiro. His dogged vituperation of them was close to being scandalous. Then he achieved respect by a series of innovations in No. He adapted a modern play and produced it in No style to the accompaniment of Western musical instruments. He directed a Kyogen in which he used a Takarazuka star, Yorozu Mineko, as the heroine in the midst of classical Kyogen actors. These experiments were fantastically successful with all levels of the public, and Yorozu won a cultural prize from the government for her distinguished performance.

The desuetude of Osaka Kabuki together with Takechi's gifts as a director led him to undertake the training of two young actors both *onnagata* or players of female roles. One was Senjaku, the son of Ganjiro himself; the other was one of the new imports from Tokyo, Tsurunosuke, the son of Azuma Tokuho, who has appeared in a program of dances in New York.

Takechi Tetsuji set about his responsibility toward them with admirable earnestness. He held rehearsals in his home, he saw the actors constantly, he corrected the minutest points of their performances, he taught them new roles, he returned to original texts, he imbued their acting with a sense of scholarship on one hand and a modern realism on the other. All in all, he advanced these two actors far beyond their years and subjected them to a discipline which the father-son relationship on which Kabuki had been based, had not bothered with to such an intensive degree. He turned these actors into theoreticians and experimenters rather than practitioners and technicians which Kabuki actors normally are until their age gives them liberties and lets their personal genius shine through the outward formality and rigidity of Kabuki tradition.

In a short time both actors became famous. Part of this was a competition which arose in the audience's mind between the two actors. People came to see how each was progressing and which was better. Tsurunosuke finally lost in 1955 and while he still has a small following of admirers, he has become merely another Kabuki actor in Osaka. Senjaku, however, has electrified Japan with his new quality of acting. Particularly successful are his interpretations of Chikamatsu Monzaemon's original texts of the seventeenth century with all their eroticism (the period was less strait-laced than the present) and their humanistic emotionalism (which the intervening years of Kabuki tradition hardened into something bordering on artificiality). Senjaku also brings to the tradition of playing women's roles a youth, amazing personal beauty, and a realistic femininity (entirely absent from him, of course, in private life) which Kabuki until now has lacked. If he is supposed to bathe on stage, he actually removes his kimono and bares his shoulders and arms, a practice unheard of in pure Kabuki. His critics say he has copied the geishas too closely for Kabuki, but his protagonists claim that only this injection of naturalism will save the *onnagata* tradition at all.

At any rate, ignoring the querulousness of the scholars, the Ministry of Education awarded Senjaku a special prize this year for his portrayal of O-Hatsu in *The Lovers' Double Suicide at Sonezaki*. The scene where O-Hatsu bares her foot and extends it over the edge of the verandah so that her lover who is hiding from his enemies under the flooring can grasp it and caress it in a mute pledge of eternal love, has already become one of the new Kabuki's classic moments of theatre. It is possible that Senjaku is nothing more than a vogue, that he has simply become chic in the eyes of modern theatre-goers. The lightness and over-realism he injects into Kabuki cannot seduce audiences away from the maturer, more classic impersonations of either Utaemon or Baiko. But for the time being at least the theatre is revelling in Senjaku's fresh approach and the audiences are responding as if a new star has actually appeared on Kabuki's horizon.

The place of New Kabuki and New Historical Plays is rather more problematical. Already Kabuki texts, because of their age, have become increasingly difficult for the average Japanese to understand. It is true that the "Great Five" of Ebizo, Utaemon, Koshiro, Baiko and Shoroku as actors and despite their youth are familiar the length and breadth of Japan. (In Japanese restaurants, where the waitresses are talkative and feel that part of their work is to entertain as well as serve, you can easily have long discussions of a technical nature as to which is the best and why.) But their plays present certain obscurities. Kabuki like No is in the midst of an avalanche of enthusiasm. Whole families and groups of office workers, who before made Kabuki only an occasional event, are now regularly attending this theatre but their taste is affecting the stage. The contact between spectator and theatre has always been the secret of Kabuki's long and sustained dominance over the Japanese. Whenever this special attunement is lost or begins to fail, there is a dark period and Kabuki suffers both commercially and in prestige. Perhaps "New Kabuki" is the reflection of the postwar generation before whom it now appears. Perhaps it is no more than a temporary concession. But it seems likely that Kabuki after three hundred fifty years is inevitably yielding to the changing times.

The two most important playwrights leading the vanguard of "New Kabuki" and answering the new requirements of Japan's new audiences are Hojo Hideji and Funahashi Seiichi. Both write in simple modern style, but their plays in subject-matter and acting styles are, at least on the surface, classical. Their plots derive from ancient literature or history, such as the *Tales of Genji*, and even from actual events within the Kabuki world itself such as the Ejima Ikushima scandal of the eighteenth century where a beautiful Kabuki actor eloped with a lady of noble birth, and these themes suit the Kabuki stage well. The Kabuki actors who perform the plays are already immersed in the stylizations and mannerisms of their traditions and have no difficulty in giving the stories the atmosphere historical and

340

antiquated subject-matter requires. The peculiar techniques of pure Kabuki are dispensed with—the actors do not cross their eyes at climaxes, they do not dance or imitate puppets, no side singers declaim the action while the actors pantomime, and the make-up for each character is authentic rather than fanciful.

In mood these plays resemble the film *Rashomon* and the same type of criticism is leveled at both. Many people feel that both fail either in contributing to a modern theatre or in improving the theatre of the past. The main complaint is one of aesthetic incongruity. To the Japanese it is odd to see something that belongs to a thousand years ago in which everyday modern Japanese comes from the characters' lips. This is a vulgarism to many Japanese. But whatever the opposition, or the nostalgic regret at the rise of this neither-Kabuki-nor-modern theatre, its success compels the most serious if reluctant attention.

Hojo Hideji has the distinction of being the highest paid playwright in Japan's theatre history, and Funahashi Seiichi, almost as wealthy, can fill a house with scarcely more effort than adapting line for line one of his countless novels. Hojo is perhaps the better playwright in that he blends in a subtle way the actor's gifts (he writes only for specific actors he particularly likes) and the role he chooses for him. The actor has to act less hard, while the characters from history become more lifelike and human. He disregards the formalities of custom and tradition which Kabuki or No have preserved so carefully. To him as to Funahashi the conventions of the past, instead of being accepted, are used only for their effect. The theatre becomes illusionless, and the personages of the past act with their foibles and weaknesses which link them in an unhallowed, unsanctified way with any human anywhere in the world. Women make advances to men when they feel like it. Men who take second wives suffer from domestic confusions and the problem becomes one of inflicting pain and loneliness.

Funahashi while being less subtle but more flagrantly ebullient is perhaps closer to Kabuki than Hojo is. He lays a stage in which the lustre and rodomontade of Japan's past spreads before you like a series of extravagant color prints. His lines too are bold—"What else is there in this world except two bodies becoming one with each other?"

341

is one that impressed his audiences—and his characters move majestically with Kabukiesque archaisms and conventions as their words illumine the action with frank, startlingly modern, clarity.

Some of Funahashi's new historical plays extend the Kabuki boundaries so far that they must be performed by a mélange of Kabuki and Shimpa actors. And some of the Kabuki actors have the astonishing experience of acting for the first time in their lives with an actual woman on the stage. The most famous of such plays is *The Story of the Black Ships* in which the brilliant Shimpa actress Yaeko Mizutani starred with Kabuki actors, one of whom in fact played the role of an American. The play deals with a favorite theme in Japan, that of Townsend Harris, the American Consul at Yokohama at the end of the nineteenth century, and his Japanese mistress, O-Kichi. For the American spectator, the play was extraordinarily sympathetic. Harris was charged with the task of securing a treaty of commerce between America and Japan. An influential group of samurai wanted to keep Japan in isolation from the outside world at all costs. They hoped to do this by persuading O-Kichi, a beautiful geisha, to become Harris's mistress. She was supposed to distract him from his purpose as well as spy for the samurai.

Two scenes from this play were particularly impressive and raised the enthusiasm of audiences for New Historical plays. One is when O-Kichi under immense pressure from the samurai, knowing that her relations with her own lover were rapidly deteriorating under the stress, slowly getting drunk in her room alone, resolves at last to become a *rashamen*, the term of opprobrium for the mistress of a foreigner. The other is when Harris, who is shown throughout the play with warmth and kindliness as a just and equitable and completely moral man, launches on a long, perceptive, and controversial analysis of the Japanese character. Theatre of this calibre, while it is neither Kabuki nor modern theatre nor even Shimpa, has certainly found its place among the theatre-loving audiences of Japan.

Takechi Tetsuji and his Senjaku, Hojo and Funahashi all with their fantastic popularity are, I believe, ultimately sounding the death knell of Kabuki. The loss of Kichiemon underscores the broad changes being inflicted on Kabuki. But Kabuki from its beginning has been accumulative. Now it is an amalgam of many flavors, the compound of many explorations, and the fusion of many aesthetic

Yoshiki Yamamoto

Two poses from the old man's dance, Kajiyade-Fu-Bushi, of longevity

The carding dance of the lonely lover

A gesture of embracing one's absent lover in thought

Yoshiki Yamamoto

Yoshiki Yamamoto

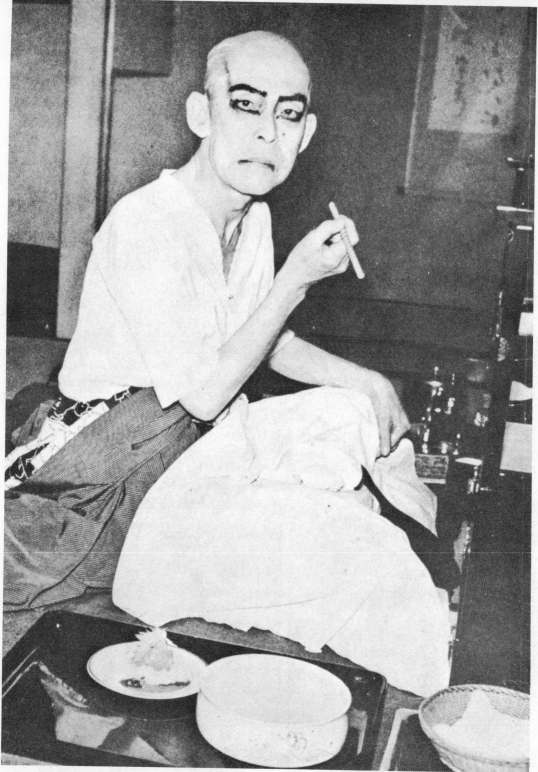

JAPAN The late Nakamura Kichiemon in his dressing room at the Kabuki Za

Geishas of Kyoto performing during the annual Cherry Festival a scene from classical Kabuki (above) and a bright geisha dance adapted for the stage (below)

The puppet theatre of Osaka

The great Shimpa actress Mizutani Yaeko as O-Kichi, Townsend Harris's mistress

Koshiro and Utaemon, two of the most brilliant young Kabuki actors of today in the suicide scene of *Toribeyama*

Koshiro as he kills his lover in *Toribeyama*, a Kabuki play adapted from the puppet theatre

Eliot Elisofon

A Bugaku masked dance of great antiquity originally performed in India

Utaemon, leading Kabuki player of female roles, waiting
under stage to rise up supernaturally before the audience

Chekhov's *Ivanov* performed by Actor's Theatre, Japan's leading modern theatre troupe

Mizutani Yaeko and Ichikawa Ennosuke as Townsend Harris and his mistress in a "new" Kabuki play

Two scenes from *Summertime, Nude Studio Ballyhoo* at
the Nichigeki Music Hall of Tokyo

creeds picked up from many periods of history, highlighted by the fancy of its actors and audience. Today is hardly more than another moment of that long history. Certainly, as long as Japan has the "Great Five," no theatre can ask more assurance of a sound future in whatever direction it may lie.

The Bunraku puppet theatre has had its headquarters for centuries in Osaka. It dates from the Kabuki period and the two arts have a brotherly relationship so intimate that plays are exchanged between them and styles copied and studied reciprocally. A Kabuki actor will take elocution lessons from the chanters who recite off to one side while the puppets enact their words, and a puppeteer will watch a Kabuki actor in order to make the dolls' movements more lifelike. Scholarship in the one means automatically knowledge of the other. The puppet theatre of Japan, despite the connotations the Western words "puppet" and "doll" convey, is an adult theatre in a very serious sense. The puppets are nearly life-size, even their eyes, eyebrows and fingers are separately articulated (it takes three men to operate one puppet), they are manipulated against elaborate scenery, and accompanied by singers and musicians who perform *gidayu* or *joruri* which is considered the most difficult and dramatic music in Japan. Both the men who sing and those who work the puppets begin their training in childhood, and by forty or fifty they attain an extraordinary standard of artistry.

One singer, the aged Yamashiro no Shojo, was awarded an Imperial title and is generally recognized as the greatest singer in the country. A puppeteer, Yoshida Bungoro, now nearly ninety and blind and deaf, still is acknowledged as a master of manipulating his puppets to represent young girls and beautiful ladylike heroines. (In Bunraku a puppeteer specializes in male or in female puppets, and few attempt the techniques of both.) He still performs regularly each month. One of his most famous roles in which the heroine has been blinded by weeping about her lost lover and spends her time wandering over the countryside looking for him (he can, of course, restore her sight) earning her keep as a blind musician, shows an almost eerie relationship between manipulator and puppet. The doll's eyes are shut in simulated blindness, her wooden hands grope nervously, and

Bungoro stands behind her in full view, showing a withered, sightless face.

Bunraku is the only classic art of Japan which is actually in some difficulty today. There has been, ever since Kabuki with its live actors first swept Japan and began to dominate the theatrical scene (as it still does), a gentle but unrelenting decline in the popularity of the puppets. Since 1920 Shochiku has virtually subsidized Bunraku by using some of its excess profits from Kabuki to make up the annual deficit. In 1926 the remaining Bunraku theatre was destroyed by fire and a new, even smaller one was built. The War with its curtailment of all theatres further separated the people from all but their most lively entertainment and assisted the collapse.

Bunraku's most recent trouble arose a year or so ago when the single remaining troupe of puppet manipulators and singers split into two factions—the Chinami Kai headed by the great Yamashiro and Bungoro and the Mitsuwa Kai of the gifted young puppeteer Monjuro. The schism grew out of the eagerness of young workers in this theatre for more freedom and greater opportunities to perform the favorite roles which Bungoro and the other doyens have monopolized. A series of labor union troubles and strikes affected Bunraku, whose organisation is different from Kabuki and the other theatre forms of Japan. In 1954 the plight of Bunraku became so grave that the month-long performance of *Chushingura* (the classic perennial which enacts the story of the forty-seven *ronin* who avenged their lord's death), which is usually guaranteed to attract large audiences whenever it is scheduled, had to be cut short (it stopped on the twentieth) because of the poor attendance.

Those Japanese who were aware of the irreplaceability of the art and keenly distressed by its hastening disappearance, agitated to save it. Various steps have been taken. Shochiku has constructed at a cost of 200,000,000 yen a new Bunraku theatre in the heart of the gayest, gaudiest entertainment district of Osaka. The theory behind this, in characteristic Japanese fashion, is that people will attend the theatre as much to see the theatrehouse as the show. (This is certainly one reason why the new Kanze Kaikan No theatre is so packed with spectators.) The government not long ago exempted Bunraku from all taxation, which makes it now the cheapest good theatre-form in Japan. There is every indication that within a year or two the government will completely subsidize Bunraku under the aegis of the Commission for the Protection of Cultural Properties. Already the first step has been taken by the designation of Bungoro as a "National Treasure" or a "Human Cultural Property."

However, there is one faint ray of brightness concerning Bunraku. Momentarily in Tokyo it is fashionable, and whether or not this taste for it is ephemeral or something more substantial, for the time being Bunraku has begun playing there for two months annually instead of its usual one month of touring. It seems ironic that now after centuries, Bunraku must look so far from its home for popularity and recognition, and if the trend continues, Bunraku may move to Tokyo altogether. Meanwhile, despite the fact that the texts and methods of performing of these Bunraku plays are exceedingly complicated and extremely subtle, the visitor to Japan will be wise to make a special trip to Osaka merely to see them. And, besides, there is a huge Kabuki theatre in the center of town, and you are only forty-five minutes from Takarazuka as well.

Through each classic theatre of Japan including the puppets courses the art of dance. Every No (except for the Kyogen interludes) has long dance sections and climaxes, and to our modern eyes the entire performance appears like a dance of an elaborately dramatic and poetic character. Kabuki falls even more clearly into this pattern. One-third of its repertoire is straight dance; one-third dense tragedy of a grandiose, historical kind; and the remainder consists of romantic and domestic pieces. But all Kabuki has an overlay of dance.

It may emerge in a *monogatari* where the actor suddenly begins to recount the details of a past event and he dance-acts the happenings with a fan, a sword, a piece of cloth. At other moments the stage transforms itself into a puppet theatre and the central characters, by virtue of the aesthetic irrationality of Kabuki which makes all things possible, begin dancing like dolls with jerky, irregular movements. Or, again, a heroic actor may dance-act his entrance and exit instead of getting on and off the stage more unemphatically. Or you can see it in a *sawari* where a woman soliloquizes on her fate or about her sweetheart and strings out her gestures and posturings in a long succession of movements that glide one into the other, more like a

345

dancer than an actor in the conventional sense. Sometimes, the central character if he is a ruler or noble will simply ask his attendants to dance for him "to divert his mind," and a sequence of pure dance begins. In some plays the hero will take a dancing lesson before the audience. And in one play a doll maker creates an image which comes to life and the two characters begin to dance together.

This manoeuvring of plot to make an excuse for dance is also used to include other adjunctive arts of the theatre, especially music. Music in some form accompanies all Kabuki. If the actor is supposed to be a blind singer, for instance, he will also have to sing to add verisimilitude to his impersonation. And he has to accompany himself on the samisen. In one Kabuki play about a certain courtesan, Akoya, a favorite role of Utaemon's, the act consists largely of his playing successively on the samisen, the koto, and the kokyu, the three traditional instruments of Japan which a lady of elegance several hundred years ago was supposed to master.

The theatrical resources of Japan taken as a whole are infinite. The classical theatre instead of destroying the dance urges of the country as they have in China have only absorbed them. And music and dance instead of swallowing drama, as they have in India and Indonesia, are suspended in a balanced equilibrium. In addition to all this Japan still has folk dances of various sorts—Harvest dances, Lion dances (from China), Cock dances, Horse dances, the Great Catch Fish dance, and the famous Bon dances performed at the end of summer when the whole countryside celebrates their equivalent of All Soul's Day by dancing late into the night. Each of these dances can be seen professionally and appropriately in season in the dozen or so music halls and vaudeville shows of downtown Tokyo. The Nichigeki theatre, for instance, runs an hour-long show between its movies three times a day, in which the most divergent tastes of the audience are satisfied by these and other kinds of Japanese and foreign dances. There is too in Japan a wide demand for Western ballet. In Tokyo, several private ballet schools have turned out two more or less full-time troupes. One of these was able to bring Nora Kaye to Japan last year and for two months, using her as a star, the ensemble performed items as difficult as *Swan Lake* (in its entirety), *Lilac Garden*, and *The Fire Bird*. The public responded with incredible enthusiasm and Nora Kaye received a welcome even warmer than that shown Pavlova when she danced for a week thirty years ago in Japan. All tickets were bought up by the day of the opening, several repeat performances were demanded and given, and Japan's appreciative bobbysoxers and students deserted Takarazuka momentarily to mob the backstage dressing-rooms of Western ballet.

Out of all this dance ferment in Japan, it is the ubiquitous geisha dances which are by far the most widespread and familiar. You may see them on a grand scale in the springtime in either the Miyako Odori (called by foreigners the "Cherry Dance") of Kyoto or the Azuma Dance of Tokyo. For these, the best geishas in town pool their talents and take over one of the larger theatres and perform for two weeks all day long on a public professional basis. Because the demands of the large stage are different from the miniature drawing rooms where they usually dance, they borrow several of the dance interludes of Kabuki and perform them with their special and delightful geisha nuances. Occasionally, a geisha teacher will present all his pupils and ex-pupils of merit in a long recital at some public theatre. But normally you will see the geishas dance in the private rooms of restaurants where you can call them at your pleasure to perform for you alone.

The art of the geisha dance is in control, in almost not moving, in sustaining inner tension with a modicum of outward display, and in reducing dance to its aesthetic essentials so that the blinking of an eye or a flick of the finger appears emphatic. In geisha dances as in Takarazuka and, in reverse, as in Kabuki, girls soon specialize in dances of either men or women. For the men's dances, they will dance-act brief scenes of drunken warriors, or to cite another example, a battle scene where an archer simply draws his bow and hits his mark. For women's dances, the repertoire is literally inexhaustible. The theme, however, is always love.

The conventional picture which the Westerner is apt to have of Oriental dance—exotic and erotic girls draped in transparent silks and shaking their hips—is just about the one thing which is impossible to find. The GI's in Japan were the first large-scale victims of this myth. They had all heard of "geisha girls," but they were in for a disappointment when they went to the straw-matted houses, sat in the private rooms, and while a lonely samisen twanged watched the geisha dressed in several layers of heavy, full-length kimonos perform her stylized, innerly directed, and underplayed dances.

The songs which the geisha enact in slow almost motionless gestures and with, at first sight, intangible suggestions of movement may be about love (and to a Japanese passionately stimulating), but to the outsider they remain just as remote and truncated as their translations—"I am a nightingale; thou art the plum tree. I nestle in your branches . . ." Many of the songs are sad, and deal either with tragic, unrequited love or the pain of separation and the impossibility of joining the beloved. Any traveler who sees O-Han-san, for instance, an Osaka geisha who now owns a luxurious restaurant with a stage of its own in Tokyo and who ranks unequivocally as the greatest woman dancer of Japan, in one of her unprovocative, almost mystically focused dances is more apt to shed tears than to be erotically titillated. For people expecting strip-tease dances, Asia on the whole has little to offer. Most dancers would rather forfeit their fee than expose their knees, and there is no Asian dance that I have seen where as much of the human body is exposed as it is by the ballet's *tutu*.

Beginning with Shimpa in the nineteenth century, dance was separated from all subsequent types of theatre, and this applied particularly to the modern theatre. To the outsider, it is almost contradictory that in dance-conscious Japan, where each theatre-form is a synthesis of the other arts, there is still place for a totally danceless theatre, but the fact remains that modern theatre is a force in the life of present-day Japanese despite its revolt against the classics and its rejection of dance and music as aids to the art of entertainment and an extremely important part of Japan's vast theatrical development.

Modern Theatre

To the Japanese, however sanctified their classic theatres are, and however much they enjoy or rediscover them intellectually, they have begun after so many centuries to wear a little thin. An increasing number of the public is turning to modern theatre or *shingeki* (literally, new theatre) as a closer, more contemporary expression of their minds and thoughts. For this group of people and for anyone else looking towards the future of Japan's theatre instead of its great past, the last few years have been of special importance.

In 1953 the modern theatre movement became exactly thirty years old. However short this may seem in matter of time to us, it means far more to the Japanese. It proves that modern theatre is enduring and that it has survived against heavy odds. During the various celebrations of special commemorative performances, of new theatre openings, memorial banquets and countless congratulatory articles and messages in newspapers and magazines of all types, uppermost in Japanese thought were two realizations: modern theatre had at last reached a status of popularity comparable with the classics, an achievement always before thought impossible, and also politically for the first time modern theatre had definitely turned away from its leftist and Communist beginnings and was flowering uninhibited by any consideration other than that of good theatre.

The history of the modern theatre movement in Japan is reckoned from the 17th of June, 1924, when a small barn-like hall called the Tsukiji Little Theatre quietly appeared in downtown Tokyo. The idea behind the founding of this theatre was complicated. It was partly to be for propaganda and protest against the government and at the same time it was for art. The hope was that it would mould public opinion and only incidentally reflect it. Because Japan, ever since Commodore Perry opened her doors to the Western world, had been undergoing a series of major changes in her social structure, and because she had rapidly modernized herself along Western lines and emerged as a world power, it seemed obviously contradictory to the Little Theatre people that theatrical fare should remain the same as it had for so many centuries before. The Little Theatre, planning to adjust to the demands of the new situation, modelled itself after the West with naturalistic acting, lifelike situations, and realistic atmosphere, all of which contrasted strikingly with traditional Japanese theatres and even with the semi-modern Shimpa. One story goes that the first time a murder was performed in modern-day dress a spectator rushed to the stage to prevent it.

Before the Little Theatre, however, Japan had not been entirely ignorant of Western theatre. As early as 1896 most of Shakespeare had been translated, and not long after so was Ibsen. In 1902 a wayward troupe of pseudo-Kabuki actors had even gone as far as Europe, and they returned to Japan as authorities on Western theatre. In Tokyo they billed their version of Hamlet as "the greatest drama of Europe," and made him come on-stage riding a bicycle along the *hanamichi* passageway through the audience. But by the time the Little Theatre appeared on the scene, the modern theatre movement's chief contact was with Soviet Russia. The revolutionary ideologies that that country represented were welcomed and embraced by nearly all the founders and guiding lights of the movement. They saw in their government a tsarist-like iniquity and in Japanese society a corruption and superstition comparable to that of pre-revolutionary Russia.

Two events illustrate this ideological and practical intimacy between the theatres of the two countries. A few years before the inception of the Little Theatre, Count Hijikata Yoshi went to study at the Moscow Art Theatre. He returned to Japan without his title (he renounced it with much publicity) and with an unchallengeable position as Japan's ablest director along Western lines and its most knowing showman of a truly modern style. He automatically assumed his place as leader of the Little Theatre and was its most Sovietized, propagandizing, and effective personality. The other signal connection with the USSR occurred a little later in 1928 when the troupe of Kabuki actors returned from their visit there. One of the actors, Ichikawa Chojuro, was so impressed with such Soviet experiments of theatre as community living that he broke with Kabuki and created his own troupe which he called the Progressive Theatre (Zenshin Za). It divided its repertoire between Kabuki and modern plays. He built barracks on his family property for the actors he rallied around himself and they all lived there together, tilling the soil in between study classes and rehearsals.

Within ten years after the start of the Little Theatre, the leftist atmosphere permeating Japan's modern theatre became too much for the government. After a prefatory period of banning plays, censoring lines, and having the police attend all performances sitting in specially constructed boxes, the government closed down the Little Theatre. Hijikata went into exile to Russia. The Progressive Theatre began performing classical Kabuki again.

By the time the Pacific War began, all the people ever involved with modern theatre were suspect. Senda Koreya, for instance, now Japan's most distinguished actor-director, was placed in domiciliary confinement. Even Funahashi Seiichi, today Japan's moneymaking and conservative playwright, who as a high school student had been brought up on the Little Theatre productions, remained unheard and unperformed until Japan's defeat. Other modern theatre actors were for the most part unemployed.

When the Occupation of Japan began, Hijikata returned home and the others re-emerged. Not long afterwards Ichikawa Chojuro and his Progressive Theatre openly became an official organ of the Communist Party. The theatre once again seemed to be even more allied than ever with Russia. The first plays to be performed on the modern theatre boards were Simeonov's *Under the Chestnut Trees of Prague*, Gorki's *Lower Depths*. Dostoevsky's *Crime and Punishment*, Chekhov's *Cherry Orchard*, and Tolstoi's *Resurrection*.

To the outsider, this, together with the left wing exuberant flurry of excitement that postwar May Days, red flags, and labor unionism first brought, looked like a complete capitulation to the Soviet side. "Why," Americans used to ask the Japanese, "are no American or British plays being put on?" But the answer was simple. While the Russians gave the Japanese all the scripts they wanted, free of charge and with no reservation of rights, the Americans were bogged down with royalty payments, copyright restrictions and ideological embarrassments. In connection with SCAP handling of Japan's theatrical situation, there were a number of rather famous scandals. At one time Arthur Miller's *All My Sons* was urged on the Japanese, only to be hastily withdrawn when the officials on later reflection judged it unsuitable for a defeated Japan. Even Gilbert and Sullivan's innocuous *Mikado* was once the center of a behind-the-scenes tornado of confusion. Certain Occupation officials had persuaded the Japanese to perform it in the hope, incredibly enough, that it would be a step towards breaking down the myth of emperor-worship. But on the day of the final rehearsal, other officials, this time the British, fearing that it would reflect from a Japanese point of view on England's royal family, or worse, be seen for what it originally was, a satire on British politics, forced the Americans into re-persuading the Japanese—this time to abandon the project and refund the immense amount of money taken in on the advance sale of tickets. In ways like these, even the Occupation unconsciously played into the strong hands of the leftwing elements of the Japanese theatre. The curious part of all this is that during this time modern theatre was never popular. Its productions, while recognized sometimes for their artistic merit and sometimes for their skillfully contrived message, were never well-attended nor ever very profit-making.

Unexpectedly, within the last few years, and after the vicissitudes of these beginnings, modern theatre at last began to emerge as a theatre of genuinely artistic intention and merit. More extraordinary was its immense popular success. Statisticians, watching this phenomenon with something akin to disbelief, provided some convincing figures. Here in Tokyo alone, close to twenty troupes were operating. There had been a maximum of three before the War. Each had a staff averaging around fifteen persons and several of the larger ones managed to support full-time some fifty members. About fifteen theatres and stages were permanently available to them. And now almost any good run for a play reaches about twenty thousand people (three thousand before the War would have been maximum), and "hits" are seen by fifty thousand.

An example of this was the big success in 1954 of the Japanese translation of Arthur Miller's *Death of a Salesman*. The way it came into success is perhaps typical of this unexpected favor which greets modern theatre these days. *Salesman,* or "Seruzuman" as it is familiarly pronounced here, started as a production of the People's Art Theatre (Mingei Za), one of the many troupes that sprouted up out of nowhere after the War (now it is one of the largest). The director, Sugawara Takeshi, a postwar luminary, made his reputation first with *The Voice of the Turtle* and shortly after with *The Moon is Blue.* Like his other mild successes, "Seruzuman" started modestly at a small theatre away from the center of town or what we would call "off-Broadway," but from opening day onwards for a month it played to packed houses. The clamor to see it was such that for the following month the whole production had to move to the chic Imperial Theatre with its seating capacity of 1,400 persons and its central location directly opposite the Imperial Palace. There it continued with tickets selling at the equivalent of a dollar and a quarter (top price for most modern theatre productions is normally seventy-five cents).

Nor did the run end there. Afterwards, troupe, sets and all went on tour and played to noisy applause in Kyoto, Nagoya and Okayama.

When *Salesman* was put on in Tokyo a number of foreigners expressed doubt about the wisdom of the choice. Some felt it did not reflect the best aspects of America (it could be construed by the Japanese as an unfavorable commentary on the American way of life) and others felt that the problem was too foreign for Japanese to understand. The overall reaction of the Japanese, however, according to the reviews and to after-theatre talk, was that no Japanese left the theatre dry-eyed, and that the most frequently heard comments always went something like "all families are the same . . . so ambitious for their children . . ." Certainly no wave of anti-Americanism swept over the city.

Ivanov, Chekhov's first play, put on to commemorate the fiftieth death anniversary of the playwright, is another case in point. From any normal Western point of view, the play with its vague theme of pre-Freudian and therefore inexplicable self-hate and misery would be too remote from Japanese thought patterns. But it was not, and played before enraptured audiences. Just as foreigners living in Japan and still carrying their Occupation sensitivities are often wrong in their estimation of the Japanese, so is the Japanese way of looking at Western plays different from ours. Sometimes it is unfortunate. An actor, because he lacks an intimate knowledge of Western manners, may make mistakes. He will keep a cigarette holder locked in his teeth or leave a glass of sherry sipped but almost full lying about the stage or wear a false nose that is just a little too large. Or if for a foreign role he does not dye his hair (auburn is the only color black Asian hair can be converted to), he wears a wig which sometimes seems unfortunate in Western eyes. And certainly he sees the plays in his own terms—family quarrels are more moving than, say, indecision, or perhaps eroticism will be taken as the theme when the point lies elsewhere. In *Ivanov* the biggest laugh of the evening came, surprisingly enough, when talk about suicide is referred to as being "too Schopenhauer." But however different Japanese and Western eyes may be from each other, a common denominator of understanding certainly binds the two, as the popularity of this type of modern theatre in Japan shows.

Along with modern theatre's success has come honor. The wealthy

Mainichi Daily newspaper and various private and official cultural groups have started giving prizes and awards to modern theatre. The Ministry of Education similarly, through its annual Arts Festival, has since 1948 encouraged all theatrical performers by offering substantial cash grants for particular excellences. Today modern theatre actors, playwrights, and directors have become eligible for this official recognition. Formerly only artists of time-hallowed classics like No and Kabuki were feted. The first of these Ministry awards to modern theatre went to an actress in 1949, Tamura Akiko, an original member of the Little Theatre, for her performance in *I Remember Mama*. Another award was given to one troupe as a whole, the Actor's Theatre, simply for excellence and brilliant progress over the year. A final indication of the change in modern theatre came when the Ministry of Education gave its annual award in 1955 to Senda Koreya (only a few years earlier he had been prevented from performing any plays because of leftism and government interference) for directing *The Angel*, a domestic tragedy based on Christian morality written by one of Japan's women playwrights, Tanaka Sumie.

Of all the signs of affluence the modern theatre has shown these past few years, perhaps none has been more welcome than the completion of the quarter-of-a-million dollar Actor's Theatre. It represents the first fully-equipped, especially designed theatre to be dedicated exclusively to modern plays since the Little Theatre's brief existence thirty-two years ago. Architecturally it is one of Tokyo's most modern buildings and looks rather like a strange sort of airplane hangar. Inside, the sound-proofed walls of plain wooden planks form a three-quarter circle around the four hundred seats of the ground floor and the balcony.

Since the opening in April of 1954 until the time of writing, each play has been so popular that auxiliary folding chairs have been lined along each aisle to accommodate the overflow of spectators. The stage, together with the wings and backstage, occupies more actual floor space than the total audience area and all the facilities and equipment have been handled with originality. To cite only one instance of this, microphones have been built in at strategic intervals clear from the proscenium arch, over the ceiling, and back to the rear of the auditorium. This permits a new realism in sound effects which was used in the Actor's Theatre's production of *Red Lamp* by

Mafune Yutaka, a play drawn from the playwright's personal experience in Manchuria before the War, which treated the emotional struggle of Japanese intellectuals against the gradual domination of China by the militarists. (The "red lamp," incidentally, symbolizes the danger of war coming to Japan, not Communism.) One scene depicts an air raid. On stage while the actors seek shelter, cower and cringe, these microphones relay a screeching drone and the sound of machine guns sputtering to simulate an air attack overhead. As the sound seemed to come up from behind and disappear in the distance in front a number of people in the audience would momentarily duck before they remembered they were in the theatre.

Modern theatre despite its similarity with Western theatre still works according to special Japanese laws of its own, and to a foreigner brought up on Broadway, many of its practices are confusing. For instance, if *Gammer Gurton's Needle* were to be performed in Japan, it would be classified as "modern" theatre, and no one would think twice about the inconsistency. It is sufficient for a play to be from the West or Western in style for it to be "new theatre."

From this point of view the popular musical comedies of Tokyo form part of the modern theatre movement too. Sometimes they are taken directly from the West, such as *Student Prince* or *Lilac Time*. Sometimes they are quaintly Japanese. A recent success at the Imperial Theatre was the *Comedy of Miss Butterfly*, and its story hinges on Butterfly *not* committing suicide, Pinkerton *not* abandoning her, and Kate has to adjust unwillingly to the situation after all. Often only an idea will be borrowed. I have seen a *Wish You Were Here* swimming pool at the Nichigeki, and a chorus of strip-teasers playing on a row of xylophones in the nude at the Nichigeki Shogekijo.

But modern theatre is a serious matter and even if it sometimes concerns itself with the West and even if, simply put, it is a new style of theatre imported at times wholesale from the West, there has still been a reorganization, and certain elements of the classic Japanese system have been incorporated to respond to Japanese requirements. The revolving stage is one example, and it is still used before the audience's eyes to speed up scene changes.

Another carryover from the past is the troupe system. And this is perhaps the most characteristically Japanese aspect of modern theatre and the element the most remote from anything we have in the

West. Actors, directors, playwrights, business managers, producers, down even to prompters, bringers of tea and servants, are members of a troupe. Such troupes, a little like a family and partly like a business company, provide steady work of practicing, rehearsing, studying and performing, all on a regular salary basis the year round. A playwright belonging to such a troupe knows that all his plays will actually be staged and he knows intimately the actors who will perform in them. There is always room for a succession of plays here, as another of the traditional customs still continued is for all theatres to change their program each month. Even in the case of a "hit," the run is not likely to exceed two months, regardless of its popularity although it may be revived at a later date. All troupes are expected to perform each month of the year.

If you try to explain the American system to a Japanese brought up on the troupe system, your first difficulties come when you mention the long periods of unemployment for the not-so-successful actors and the inhumanly long periods of repeating exactly the same role for the successful ones. Both alternatives frighten the troupe-protected Japanese actor, who even through the leanest and most poorly attended years was able to keep up at least a semblance of steady and varied work. Such a system inevitably stems from a country where production costs are less than they are in Europe or America, and also where labor unions exert a less powerful control over their personnel. A modern theatre play can be set up adequately for the equivalent of only a few thousand dollars. And it would be possible to ignore the added costs that theatre unions inescapably impose on the basic outlay for any production. In some instances, members of reputable and professional troupes have managed a whole show by themselves from selling tickets to painting the scenery without running into opposition with the various unions concerned.

In the early days of modern theatre the troupe system lent a political cohesiveness to the movement, making it a moral force as well as a practical one. Now it stays on because it is the most economic way of running modern theatre in Japan. But the artistic protection that the troupe system afforded the modern theatre from the beginning has been of inestimable value. Modern actors can now start a career in their middle age and be assured of work (in the classical theatres, roles are always hereditary and actors have to be trained from childhood by their parents). Directors have begun to appear as forces in the whole Japanese theatre world (in the classical theatres actors are so thoroughly trained and used to the plays they put on that there is no need of direction).

Perhaps the most significant factor of all to come out of the troupe system and its effect on modern theatre is the new Japanese playwright. In the classical theatre a playwright was scarcely more than a property man. He revised old plays according to the star's instructions and on opening day he was dressed in black (to be invisible) and hid behind the actors on stage, prompting them when they forgot the hack lines he had ground out for them the night before. Because of the modern theatre's troupe system, creative playwrights and men of literature have been given a steady livelihood and security through their period of experimenting and finding themselves. The result has been that genuine talent is appearing, and for the first time since the West's influence was brought to bear on Japan, the preponderance of translations from Europe and America is gradually being supplanted by original scripts coming from indigenous Japanese writers.

The most important of these new playwrights are the brilliant young Kinoshita Junji and Mishima Yukio. Still in their early thirties, they have become a hope for the future of Japanese letters and leaders of an enormous, adoring following. Examples of their work translated into English can be found in Donald Keene's excellent *Anthology of Japanese Literature* published by Grove Press.

Kinoshita Junji's greatest success so far has been *Yuzuru* or *Twilight of the Crane*. There was a special magic about this play that captured the imagination of virtually everyone who saw it. The story in simple words sounds colorless. It is a sentimental, very Japanese folk tale matching loosely the European fairy tale of the goose that laid the golden egg. The story goes that a crane takes human form and marries a man. One day to amuse her husband she gives him some cloth which she has secretly woven from the soft down of her feathers. He is delighted with it, and recognizes as well its marketable possibilities. Not realizing that she is sacrificing part of her life blood with each feather, he persuades her to produce more and more so that they can become rich. Finally, as she gives him her last piece of cloth she dies, and because of greed, the husband finds himself bereft of both money and her wifely love. This play so captured the Japanese that it has been revived a number of times and besides has been made into an opera, ballet, a radio version, and even adapted as a Nō play.

While a certain number of Kinoshita Junji's most famous works treat folk stories in a contemporary manner and elevate them to the level of sophisticated literature, he also writes more conventional and ordinary dramas. The plot of one of these tells of what happened when city people were evacuated during the War to the country and the effect of their contact with the people of the provinces. Another well-known play of his is historical. In it several factions within a small town come to the mayor to pour out their woes and reactions to the lightning-fast, bewildering changes taking place in Japan—the Japan of the Meiji Restoration. In general, all his plays are adult, thoughtful, affectionate and human expressions of what mature Japanese are feeling and thinking about at the present time.

Mishima Yukio has had an extraordinary series of successes not only in the theatre but also with his novels. Perhaps his two best known plays are the *Sunflower in Darkness* (Yoru no Himawari) and *Young Man Back to Life* (Wakodo Yo Yomigaere) recently mounted with superb finish and polish by the Actor's Theatre. All of Mishima's plays are comedies that grapple only indirectly with problems. One of them describes the end of the War, another a schoolboy crush, but in each of them the people are lifelike and intelligent, and above all amusing. Everything Mishima touches has lightness and civilization, and I think most Japanese see themselves in his plays as they would most like to be—charming, entertaining, unburdened, wise, and with problems that are either easily solved or ignorable.

Of all Japan's modern playwrights only Mishima has created sophisticated characters of the upper classes who manage to please without being affected and to move without being overwhelmed by the gloom of inevitable tragedy or outside circumstances. A quality that his audiences find particularly pleasing is the special and unconventional twist that Mishima gives to conventional situations. A favorite situation in Japanese theatre is when a boy and a girl are caught in a thunderstorm and compelled to take shelter in a cave. The conventional development of this moment is that the rain makes the boy and girl very romantic, that they fall in love, but finally discretion prevails. In Mishima's treatment, however, the boy falls asleep, the girl takes off her clothes to dry them. The boy wakes up, and the girl, far from being coy, makes him take off his clothes too.

Mishima also produced an amusing inversion of the familiar prince-disguised-as-a-beggar theme. A herring vendor, who pushes his cart up and down the street calling out his wares, disguises himself as a nobleman to woo a girl of high rank. She, however, rejects him because she is in love with the voice of the herring vendor whose voice she hears each day from her window. Another theme popular in modern theatre is the return of the soldier from the horrors of war to the comfort and love of his sweetheart. In a Mishima play, the soldier returns only to find his dream girl disillusioning and a soured note permeates the scene. Perhaps most startling of all was Mishima's adaptation of the only No play which has a happy ending. Of course, he turned it into a tragedy.

Looking at Kinoshita Junji, Mishima Yukio and the many other playwrights who are being so surprisingly successful and original today, it also becomes evident that the Communism which accompanied the early days and the founding of Japan's modern theatre movement has become unimportant. Within the past few years the biggest productions and most widely hailed ones have been *Salesman*, Tennessee William's *Streetcar Named Desire* (it so entranced the Japanese that one ballet troupe performed it), *Man of Flame*, a free adaption by Miyoshi Juro of the life of Van Gogh, along with *Twilight of the Crane, Sunflower*, and *Young Man*. A number of purely Japanese plays, also popular, have dealt with themes as varied as what happens in the life of an ordinary middle-class woman to comedies of manners with divorce as the center of attention.

There is little bias in any of these that smacks of politics or propaganda. When you talk directly with the persons who are now dominating the modern theatre movement, the red tinge of Communism seems to have left them. Not, as it has with some Americans because of disillusionment in Russia, but rather as if leftism were a stage in the development of modern theatre which has now outlasted its original purpose. It is an incontrovertible fact that with the sloughing off of leftism, modern theatre became popular. If there is a logical sequence between these two facts, it would indicate that leftism was not what the Japanese wanted in their theatre.

Whether this is so or not, there is, I think, still another reason.

359

Somehow the climate for Communism has left Japan's modern theatre today. Modern theatre is no longer martyrized by persecution or bans. No longer are there only one or two Moscow-trained artists to steer the movement and arbitrate on plays and staging. Now there is a wide audience of people of all colors of opinion, and they are seeking entertainment. The personnel connected with modern theatre are making money. They no longer live in garrets or cellars. They dress respectably and eat decently. Now that they have grown older and become senior, they even rank in some instances with great artists of the classical stage. Today, they can be heard properly and accepted for what apparently they have always wanted to be—practicing artists of a legitimate stage.

For the first time during its thirty-two years of history, the theatre is healthy in every way—technically, financially and intellectually. And if this steady increase in maturity and artistic perfection continues, modern theatre may be headed for heights as great as Japan's magnificent classical past. Talking with Senda Koreya, I almost became convinced of this. To prove his point, he said, "Historically it is now Japan's turn. In the sixteenth century England had Shakespeare. The seventeenth century saw France's greatest dramas. The eighteenth century was German and the nineteenth Russian. The twentieth century," and he believes the logic follows naturally, "belongs to Japan's modern theatre of tomorrow."

Certainly if Asia is to be the arena of the next flowering of world theatre, Japan seems to me to be the most likely country.

In writing a book of this sort, which is essentially a journalistic report on what dance and drama in Asia is like today, where it is found, and how to understand it from a practical and theatre point of view, I have relied chiefly on direct experience and conversations with scholars and dancers and actors. In the sixteen years that I have studied dance and drama in Asia, I have of course come across several books which have been of great help to me. Certain of those have been of particular value.

INDIA: The most brilliant Sanskrit scholar of India, Dr. V. Raghavan, head of the Sanskrit Department at the University of Madras, has written innumerable pamphlets and brochures on aspects of Indian dance and drama which are absolutely essential for anyone wishing to pursue the subject more deeply. Fortunately, these are in English, and can be had by writing to the University of Madras. *The Religion of the Hindus* published in New York by the Ronald Press contains a number of translations and commentaries on Hinduism which are most helpful for a full understanding of the stories and meanings of dances in India.

The Indian Stage in five volumes by Hemendra Nath Das Gupta, published by the Metropolitan Printing and Publishing House Ltd., 56 Dharamtala Street, Calcutta, is an interesting and complete account of the Bengali stage. *The Bengali Drama* by Guha Thakurta, also published in India, is one of the best books on theatre in India.

Beryl de Zoete's *The Other Mind*, a Study of Dance in South India, published in England, is of interest, as is Kay Ambrose's *Classical Dance and Costume of India*, also published in England. There are a large number of books on Indian Dance published in India itself of varying degrees of importance to the student of this subject.

CEYLON: Dr. E. R. Sarathchandra of the University of Ceylon has written an authoritative and definitive book, *The Sinhalese Folk-Play*, which is by far the best work on the subject. There are, of course, a number of books in German on witchcraft and demonology which cast interesting sidelights on devil-dancing in Ceylon.

BURMA: The only book I know of about Burmese theatre is the excellent little volume *Burmese Drama* by Dr. Maung Htin Aung, published by the Oxford University Press. It is indispensable for any visitor to Burma.

THAILAND: The most thorough book on Thailand's dance and drama is *Classical Siamese Theatre* by Dhanit Yupho, published by Hatha Dhip Company, 1326/1 New Road, Bangkok. I saw this originally in manuscript and found it most helpful and informative. In printed form, it has copious and excellent illustrations. Mr. Yupho is publishing another book, *The Preliminary Course of Training in Siamese Theatrical Art*, which should be a valuable addition to the growing literature on Thai dance and drama. There is also a fine and lucid pamphlet called *Siamese Music in Theory and Practice* by Phra Chen Duriyanga published by the Department of Fine Arts, Bangkok, with examples in Western notation of Siamese music.

INDONESIA: The Ministry of Information in Jakarta has published an interesting and lengthy article by Armijn Pané, one of Java's most distinguished writers called *The Production of Play-Films in Indonesia*, which traces the development of theatre informatively. Bali of course has a number of books filled with copious references to dance. Covarrubias's *Island of Bali* has now become a classic. Colin McPhee in *House of Bali* writes exquisitely of the effect Balinese music and dance had on him. John Coast's *Dancers of Bali* is an enlightening review of his experiences in training and arranging for the brilliant tour of the Balinese dancers a few seasons ago. Beryl de Zoete's and Walter Spies' *Dance and Drama in Bali* is unique—beautifully illustrated with the finest photographs I have ever seen and with an illuminating text; it is a valuable addition for anyone's library. It has fortunately been reprinted recently by Faber and Faber in London. Boyd Compton of the Institute of Current Affairs has written with deep insight on various aspects of Indonesia's arts.

PHILIPPINES: There are several books of a miscellaneous order which help to give a picture of dance and drama in the Philippines: *Philippine National Dances* by Francisco Reyes Tolentino published by Silver Burdett Co., New York; *Short Plays of the Philippines* edited by Jean Edades, printed by Benipayo Press, Manila; *3 One Act Plays* by Severino Montano, M. Colcol and Co., Publishers, Manila; and an article, "Filipino Drama of the Past and Present," by Jean Edades in The Theatre Annual 1947, P.O. Box 935, Grand Central Station, New York 17. Nick Joaquin, the most brilliant writer of the Philippines, has a magnificent article, "Popcorn and Gaslight," on theatre published in The *Philippines Quarterly*, September 1953.

CHINA: Unfortunately, most of the books on Chinese theatre are old and unavailable, but some of them, particularly the beautiful and learned book by L. C. Arlington, *The Chinese Drama*, published by Kelly and Walsh Ltd., in Shanghai in 1930, can be procured from bookstores specializing in rare books. Others are: *Mei Lan Fang*, Commercial Press Ltd., Shanghai; *The Chinese Drama*, R. F. Johnston, Kelly and Walsh Ltd., Shanghai, Hongkong, Singapore; *1500 Modern Chinese Novels and Plays*, Jos. Schyns, Catholic University Press, Peking; and more recently, under the Communists, *Folk Arts of New China*, Foreign Language Press, Peking and *The White Haired Girl*, Foreign Language Press, Peking.

JAPAN: The literature on Japan in English is enormous and increases continually. Arthur Waley has translated magnificently all the No plays and the extraordinary document *Kadensho* by Zeami which outines the aesthetic theory of No. Donald Keene, published by Grove Press in New York, has written a series of books that contain translations and revealing explanations of No and Bunraku dramas which are essential even to a lay reader. Earle Ernst of the University of Hawaii has a remarkably good book, *Kabuki Theatre*, published by the Oxford University Press, 1956. Charles Tuttle Co., 28 South Main Street, Rutland, Vermont, handles a number of extremely useful books: *Highlights of Japanese Theatre* by Earle Ernst and Francis Haar, a series of summaries of all the important Kabuki Plays compiled by Mr. and Mrs. Aubrey Halford, as well as *Japanese Theatre Pictorial* published by UNESCO. Iwanami Shoten in Tokyo publishes a remarkable series of picture books on all forms of Japanese theatre. A. S. Scott of the University of Hong Kong has made several illustrated translations of Kabuki plays published by the Hokuseido Press in Tokyo, and his *Kabuki Theatre*, published by Allen and Unwin, London, appeared in 1955. The Japan Tourist Bureau, Tokyo, issues several splendid volumes devoted to various theatre forms in Japan. *An Outline History of the Japanese Dance* by Makoto Sugiyama and published by the Kokusai Bunka Shinkokai is fine, and *Japanese Noh Drama*, a book of translations and illustrations published in 1955 by the Nippon Gakujutsu Shinkokai, Tokyo, is expert and scholarly.

Many countries of Asia have no literature on the subject of dance and drama at all. I think it is safe to say that the majority of books about Asian theatre as a whole are out of print, and in general there has been surprisingly little material. There are also several articles of mine which have appeared in the *New Yorker, The Saturday Review* and *Holiday*, and a number of articles by my wife, Santha Rama Rau, which have appeared in *Holiday*, all of which touch to some extent on dance or drama. Judging from the enormous awakening of interest in the subject that Europe and America are now showing, the list will eventually increase. Meanwhile, the student must for the most part content himself with the few available books and articles, or, best of all, with exploratory research directly in the field.

INDEX

Abbreviations in parentheses following titles of Asiatic dances, dance forms, plays, etc., indicate country or region of origin.

DANCE

A Books for Libraries Collection

Ashihara, Eiryo. **The Japanese Dance.** 1964

Bowers, Faubion. **Theatre in the East.** 1956

Brinson, Peter. **Background to European Ballet.** 1966

Causley, Marguerite. **An Introduction to Benesh Movement Notation.** 1967

Devi, Ragini. **Dances of India.** 1962

Duggan, Ann Schley, Jeanette Schlottmann and Abbie Rutledge. **The Teaching of Folk Dance.** Volume 1. 1948

————. **Folk Dances of Scandinavia.** Volume 2. 1948

————. **Folk Dances of European Countries.** Volume 3. 1948

————. **Folk Dances of the British Isles.** Volume 4. 1948

————. **Folk Dances of the United States and Mexico.** Volume 5. 1948

Duncan, Irma. **Duncan Dancer.** 1966

Dunham, Katherine. **A Touch of Innocence.** 1959

Emery, Lynne Fauley. **Black Dance in the United States from 1619 to 1970.** 1972

Fletcher, Ifan Kyrle, Selma Jeanne Cohen and Roger Lonsdale. **Famed for Dance.** 1960

Gautier, Théophile. **The Romantic Ballet as Seen by Théophile Gautier.** 1932

Genthe, Arnold. **Isadora Duncan.** 1929

Hall, J. Tillman. **Dance! A Complete Guide to Social, Folk, & Square Dancing.** 1963

Jackman, James L., ed. **Fifteenth Century Basse Dances.** 1964

Joukowsky, Anatol M. **The Teaching of Ethnic Dance.** 1965

Kahn, Albert Eugene. **Days with Ulanova.** 1962

Karsavina, Tamara. **Theatre Street.** 1950

Lawson, Joan. **European Folk Dance.** 1953

Martin, John. **The Dance.** 1946

Sheets-Johnstone, Maxine. **The Phenomenology of Dance.** 1966